THE EROSION OF
TRIBAL POWER

THE EROSION OF TRIBAL POWER

THE SUPREME COURT'S SILENT REVOLUTION

DEWI IOAN BALL

UNIVERSITY OF OKLAHOMA PRESS : NORMAN

To Helen, Joshua, and Matthew

and

in memory of Gwendoline Ball

Library of Congress Cataloging-in-Publication Data

Names: Ball, Dewi Ioan, author.
Title: The erosion of tribal power : the Supreme Court's silent revolution / Dewi Ioan Ball.
Description: Norman, Oklahoma : University of Oklahoma Press, 2016. | Includes bibliographical references and index.
Identifiers: LCCN 2016020389 | ISBN 978-0-8061-5565-4 (hardcover : alk. paper)
Subjects: LCSH: Indian reservations—United States. | Land use—Law and legislation—United States. | Tribal government—United States. | Indians of North America—Legal status, laws, etc. | Land tenure—Law and legislation—United States. | United States. Supreme Court. | Federal-Indian trust relationship. | Self-determination, National—United States. | Indians of North America—Government relations.
Classification: LCC KIE2055 .B35 2017 | DDC 342.7308/72—dc23
LC record available at https://lccn.loc.gov/2016020389

1 2 3 4 5 6 7 8 9 10

Contents

Acknowledgments

The long and eventful path to this book has taken fifteen years. It all began in 2001 whilst I was swimming in the sea at Three Cliffs Bay, Swansea, Wales, and looking up at the picturesque cliffs. In that cold sea I decided to accept the Thomas and Elizabeth Williams Scholarship from the City and County of Swansea and to study for a PhD at the University of Wales, Swansea.

Fifteen years later, I look back upon that decision with happiness and think about the wonderful memories and opportunities as well as the kindness of individuals, the joy of friends, and the love of family on that long and eventful path.

The support of my loving wife, Helen Ball, has been immeasurable and I thank her for her unending support and patience and her love. To my wonderful boys, Joshua Ball and Matthew Ball, I thank you both for making my life a world surrounded by love, smiles, and happiness.

To my mother, Morwen Ball, I thank you for your love and dedication, and to my father, Dr. John Ball, I thank you for your support and guidance. To my sister, Angharad Ball, I thank you for your strength and kindness.

I have become indebted to many institutions and numerous individuals over the past fifteen years. Thank you to my three dedicated PhD tutors in the American Studies Department, Swansea University—Michael McDonnell, David Bewley-Taylor, and Joy Porter—and to the excellent staff at the Manuscript Division of the Library of Congress in Washington, D.C. Thank you to Matthew L. M. Fletcher, who supported an initial draft of an article from the PhD dissertation and whose belief in the project instilled a personal confidence in me along this long path. Thank you to Blake A. Watson for giving me wonderful advice and encouragement in the latter stages of this monograph. Thank you to Bruce E. Johansen for wonderful direction, for sharing important work, and for making this monograph a stronger piece of work. The University of Oklahoma Press staff have been magnificent. Thank you to Alessandra Jacobi Tamulevich, senior acquisitions editor, who offered invaluable advice and guidance from as early as 2007. Thank you to

Thomas Krause, assistant acquisitions editor, who has been a superstar and a consummate professional. Thank you to Steven B. Baker, managing editor, for his excellent guidance, patience, and constant support. Thank you to John Thomas, freelance copy editor, for his heroics in shaping the end product and for his dedication to this project. Thank you to John Jacob, archivist and special collections law librarian at the Washington and Lee University School of Law, for being such a wonderful person and sending me numerous case files from the archives of Justice Lewis F. Powell in such a short time.

The foundations of this work were laid in 2005 with a research trip to the archives in Washington, D.C. It was possible only because of family. I would like to thank Richard and Barbara Ball (now with five children, Rachel, Megan, Jocelyn, Alexander, and Hannah), family members who reside in Maryland, U.S.A., for looking after me and for making sure I was up at 6:00 every morning for my long bus ride downtown to do research at the Library of Congress.

THE EROSION OF
TRIBAL POWER

Introduction

For years I read, reread, and wrote on my copies of the U.S. Supreme Court opinions in federal Indian law. Week after week, I tried to categorize the cases and form links between disparate arguments and principles. For me, walking through federal Indian law was an interesting and complex adventure filled with divergent issues and real people, and at the center were the opinions of the Supreme Court, which affected the lives of individuals, communities, and Native nations. However, the words that filled the Supreme Court's opinions were to me always just that—words on printed pages. They needed more background and context, and in October 2005 I embarked on a trip to the National Archives in Washington, D.C., to find out why the Court's justices had chosen these words and ideas.

At 6 A.M. on a dark and muggy Monday morning, I took the bus downtown and over an hour later saw the grand old walls of the U.S. Congress, the White House, and the Supreme Court. The bus stopped and on my right were the archives. A little while later I was sitting at a brown desk, probably used by thousands of energetic researchers before me, with a number of brown boxes placed on a silver trolley. Within these boxes were personal notes and correspondence about the opinions that I had read over many years more than 3,000 miles away in Wales. All of these documents that I was going to read had been seen and, on many occasions, written on by the Supreme Court justices. Suddenly it felt as though I was within the corridors of the high court, privy to secret deliberations and votes carried out by numerous justices many decades before. It was 2005, but as I read the thousands of pages of documents, I was living in the Supreme Court in the last half of the twentieth century.

The foundation of this book is a close analysis of the workings of the Supreme Court and an examination, from the justices' viewpoint, of the changes the Court's decisions made in federal Indian case law from 1959 to 2001. I also examine a small number of cases decided between 2001 and 2015 to show that the trend of these changes continues to the present day. To achieve this book's goals, chapters contain exhaustive chronological analyses of key cases in civil, criminal, and taxation law to show how the justices have reinterpreted federal Indian law over time. Rather than try to decipher the meaning and principles of the opinions from a position outside the Supreme Court, this work situates itself within the Court's offices and corridors.

Federal Indian law is an important topic within the field of Native American studies; the opinions from the highest court of the land directly affect people and the everyday activities and authority of Native American tribes.[1] The Supreme Court's opinions are the dominant law of the land and take precedence over state and tribal law. For many years, the Court's actions have eroded tribal civil, criminal, and taxation authority over nonmembers on the reservations and gradually allowed increasing levels of state law to apply within the reservations.[2]

In the following pages, I present evidence to suggest that between 1959 and 2001 the actions of the Supreme Court precipitated the erosion of the Indian sovereignty doctrine. This doctrine had been based on the presumption that tribes had inherent sovereignty over the lands and people on the reservation unless Congress acted to alter the attributes of that sovereignty by legislation or by treaty. I show that from 1959 onward an identifiable and gradual trend based on a tangible set of principles developed within the mindset of the Supreme Court justices away from the Indian sovereignty doctrine.

The actions of the justices during what I have termed the "silent revolution" have never been thoroughly challenged by Congress, even in the political era described as that of tribal self-determination, within which Congress purportedly supported all positive outcomes for Native America. My study of case law up until the cases of *Nevada v. Hicks* (2001) and *Atkinson Trading Co. v. Shirley* (2001)—in which the justices, for the first time, presented clear and public views about their negative views of the Indian sovereignty doctrine and the power of states' rights on reservations—allows me to examine the unprecedented legal response of Native America to defend tribal sovereignty. That Native American response caused a small ripple of hope in Congress during 2002 and 2003, when a bill to reaffirm inherent tribal sovereignty was introduced, but in 2005 Congress all but reaffirmed the Court's silent revolution. Native America responded once again and within eight years had helped form two important pieces of federal legislation that focused on the justice system in Indian country: the Tribal Law and Order Act of 2010 and the Violence Against Women Reauthorization Act of 2013. One act challenged aspects of the silent revolution, but whether this means that Congress is returning to an active role against the Court's continued assault on tribal sovereignty remains to be seen.

Although the Court has eroded the fundamental attributes of tribal criminal, civil, and taxation power over nonmembers on the reservations, tribal sovereignty over tribal members was not dismantled by the justices and has held firm. This core of tribal sovereignty is the root upon which many tribes have built successful economies and preserved tribal cultures. Within the political arena there has been affirmation of tribal political strength and the recognition of the resurgence of Native America. Tribal sovereignty over tribal members has been an essential tool supported by the federal executive, legislature, and, for the most part, judiciary.

My research relies on archival records and a large body of important books and articles in Native American history and federal Indian law. Specifically, the ideas in this book build on the scholarly literature to show that more focus needs to be paid in Native American studies to the opinions of the Supreme Court from 1959 to the present day as well as to their effects on the lives of Native Americans and the tribes. Only a small body of work within the writings on federal Indian law and Native American history examines the real effects of Supreme Court case law.[3] My work builds upon this literature to address the practical and everyday effects of Supreme Court taxation, civil, and criminal case law on Native American tribes and tribal authority within the reservations.

Many legal books give detailed and useful accounts of Supreme Court case law and the effects of the case law on the law itself,[4] while others argue about the inconsistency of the opinions themselves, which have been based on a random set of principles and have created doctrinal uncertainty.[5] Many books view the movement of the Court away from the sovereignty doctrine as an aberration in principle; some portray the actions of the Court as designed to protect the tribes;[6] others examine the idea of racism as a principle used by the Supreme Court over time to divest tribal sovereignty.[7] Numerous legal articles discuss the movement of the Court away from the sovereignty doctrine. Although some assess this movement in terms of trends and theories,[8] others see it as devoid of theory, principle, or trend,[9] which has caused uncertainty in the law itself.[10] I argue, instead, that the thinking of the Supreme Court justices had and has a clear focus and direction; unfortunately for Native America, it is the antithesis of the Indian sovereignty doctrine and the inherent sovereignty of the tribes.

Research I conducted on the private papers of seven Supreme Court justices—Harry A. Blackmun, Thurgood Marshall, William J. Brennan, William O. Douglas, Hugo Lafayette Black, and Chief Justice Earl Warren, held within the Library of Congress, Washington, D.C., and Lewis F. Powell Jr., held within the Washington and Lee University School of Law—makes this monograph an original work. In addition, I use Supreme Court opinions and oral arguments contained within the Library of the United States Supreme Court in Washington, D.C., to provide original materials in support of this work. For the first time in Native American studies, the Harry A. Blackmun papers, William J. Brennan papers, and Lewis F. Powell Jr. papers are used to inform the debate regarding the erosion of the Indian sovereignty doctrine by the Supreme Court.[11]

With any written work, there is always a decision to be made about focus, and with this in mind I use what I consider the key attributes of tribal power to narrow the numerous legal subject areas and inherent complexity contained within the discipline of federal Indian law. Such areas include, but are not limited to: civil law, criminal law, labor law, taxation law, water rights, labor rights, treaty rights, land rights, and issues of religion. The attributes of tribal power I have in mind are civil, criminal, and taxation jurisdictions in which the tribes once had inherent authority over nonmembers on the reservations and, by virtue of their territorial authority, were able to prevent the application of state law on the reservations. These attributes of tribal power were made clear by Chief Justice John Marshall's judgment in *Worcester v. Georgia* (1832) and for more than a century have remained vitally important to the tribes.

My subtitle's reference to a "silent revolution" is intended to characterize the cultural and ideological changes that took place within the workings of the Supreme Court from 1959 to 2001. Unfortunately, this revolution has continued to the present day. The "silence" refers not only to the gradual movement of the Court away from the idea of inherent tribal sovereignty but also to the Court's deliberation away from public scrutiny. It was only after analysis of the private papers of the justices that I sensed a sweeping ideological change. From 1959 to 2001, the Court turned the Indian sovereignty doctrine on its head—a "revolution" in Supreme Court dealings with Indian sovereignty issues. Equally, the incursion of state law onto tribal reservations can also be interpreted as a revolution.[12] In sum, the Supreme Court allowed unprecedented amounts of state law onto the reservations and fundamentally eroded key attributes of tribal power over reservation nonmembers.

The position of the tribe within the framework of the U.S. Constitution, which recognizes only the federal government and the fifty states, has never been properly resolved. The idea of inherent tribal sovereignty has existed for centuries and is reflected in the hundreds of treaties conducted between Native American tribes and both the United States and European nations. Furthermore, in *Worcester v. Georgia* the inherent sovereignty of the tribes on the reservations was recognized by Chief Justice Marshall. The Marshall trilogy, a set of Supreme Court cases from 1823 to 1832, had delineated the boundaries of federal, state, and tribal powers on the reservation, but from 1832 to 1959 these boundaries were blurred. Although tribal sovereignty had been recognized by the Supreme Court in 1959, it began to weaken its own reliance on inherent tribal sovereignty and the Indian sovereignty doctrine. Rather than continue to recognize tribal sovereignty as an independent source of power, from 1959 on the Court judged cases on the basis of federal versus state authority, thereby incorporating tribal authority within the parameters of federal power. This change of direction is central to an understanding of the emerging power struggle after 1959 involving federal, state, and tribal authority.

I encountered two main difficulties during the research phase of this project: the unavailability of the private papers of Chief Justice Warren Burger and Chief Justice William H. Rehnquist, which are closed to researchers; and the limited availability of information from specific tribal governments, museums, and other organizations about the effects of Supreme Court case law on Native American tribes and tribal authority. Notwithstanding these setbacks, I have since acquired more information and I am grateful to those who have contacted me.

Chapter 1 provides a broad historical examination of the development of federal Indian law and the Indian sovereignty doctrine, as well as the changing powers of the tribes, from the nineteenth century to 1959. Despite the limitations placed on tribal authority by the Court up until 1959, the tribes had retained inherent sovereignty over nonmembers on the reservation and, generally, the authority to prohibit state law from entering the reservation. Chapter 2 presents the foundations of the silent revolution and the principles that underpinned it. It traces through specific case law the formation, from 1959 to 1973, of a new principle that states had authority on the reservation unless revoked by Congress, eroding the principles of the Native sovereignty doctrine established by Chief Justice Marshall. Chapter 3 traces the development of the silent revolution between 1973 and 2001 and the principles that drove it, referred to in this work as the "integrationist trend," and shows the gradual erosion of the Indian sovereignty doctrine and the key attributes of tribal power. This chapter also discusses the small number of civil and taxation federal Indian law cases that were before the Court between 2001 and 2015. Chapter 4 examines the Native American legal response to the watershed *Hicks* and *Atkinson* cases, from 2001 to 2015, and identifies signs that show that the erosion of the sovereignty doctrine and of key attributes of tribal power have leaked into Congress. In 2013, Congress passed the Violence Against Women Reauthorization Act and partially overruled *Oliphant v. Suquamish Indian Tribe*—a case indicative of the silent revolution. The set of circumstances that led to that legislation was, however, unique, and offers little justification for thinking that Congress will further undermine Supreme Court case law in this area in the near future. Chapter 5 discusses the practical effects of civil, criminal, and taxation case law of the Supreme Court on the authority of specific tribes on their reservations. Chapter 6 examines the importance of tribal sovereignty over tribal members in the political and economic resurgence of many Native American tribes during the silent revolution.

Though it is easy to sit in the twenty-first century and trace the unfortunate direction taken by the Supreme Court justices in federal Indian law, one cannot forget, be generally silent about, or ignore the impact that this federal institution has had on Native Americans, particularly over the past few decades. As well, this research identifies signs that suggest a proliferation of the erosion in Congress to the present day.

❖ 1

The Tribes, Federal Indian Law, and the Indian Sovereignty Doctrine from the Nineteenth Century to 1959

This chapter examines the development of federal Indian law and the Indian sovereignty doctrine by the U.S. Supreme Court from the early nineteenth century to 1959. Beginning with a trio of cases commonly known as the Marshall trilogy, I trace the origins of the sovereignty doctrine in federal Indian law and its application throughout the divergent policy eras—Indian removal, assimilation and allotment, the Indian New Deal, and termination—adopted by the U.S. Congress and president toward Native America.

The Marshall Trilogy

During the early nineteenth century the Supreme Court laid the foundations of federal Indian law and in doing so outlined the powers of the tribe and the Indian sovereignty doctrine within American and constitutional law.[1] Federal Indian law is Supreme Court case law involving Native Americans, and it began with three judgments handed down by Chief Justice John Marshall during the 1820s and 1830s.[2] The three cases, which came to be known as the Marshall trilogy—*Johnson v. McIntosh* (1823), *Cherokee Nation v. Georgia* (1831), and *Worcester v. Georgia* (1832)—placed limitations on certain aspects of inherent tribal sovereignty, outlined the nature of the Indian sovereignty doctrine, and set out the legal relationship between the federal government, the states of the Union, and the tribes.[3]

Interestingly, the justices in *Cherokee Nation v. Georgia* and *Worcester v. Georgia* were divided over the relevance of tribal sovereignty over reservation lands and people upon those lands.[4] The fundamental principle of the sovereignty doctrine was that the tribes retained authority over reservation lands and the people on those lands until Congress explicitly acted to reverse that authority. From 1832, the sovereignty doctrine was a tool to protect the interests and rights of Native America in case law before the Supreme Court. The bulwark of Native American rights was *Worcester v. Georgia* (1832). Under the rationale of *Worcester*, the tribes were separate and held independent sovereignty from the states, with inherent sovereignty over the lands and people on the reservation. These powers were dependent only on the plenary power of the United States.[5]

Long before the Marshall trilogy, the legal status of all Native American tribes was one of independence from the United States.[6] Tribes were outside the control of the U.S. Constitution and considered by the federal government, including the Supreme Court, to be extraconstitutional.[7] The three Marshall cases symbolized the end of the external sovereign powers of the tribes, except for one powerful tool, the right of tribes to conduct treaties with the U.S. government. Such treaty making lasted until 1871, when the U.S. Senate unilaterally ended it. Federal legislation introduced by the Senate explained: "Hereafter no Indian nation or tribe within the territory of the United States shall be acknowledged or recognized as an independent nation, tribe, or power with whom the United States may contract by treaty: *Provided, further,* That nothing herein contained shall be construed to invalidate or impair the obligation of any treaty heretofore lawfully made and ratified with any such Indian nation or tribe."[8]

The dichotomy between the Marshall trilogy, which ended the external sovereignty of the tribes to interact with nations such as France or Great Britain, and the continuation of Native American treaty-making powers up until 1871 remains one of the unexplainable contradictions in the history of American law and politics. In addition, the question still remains to this day: where did Marshall and Congress expressly obtain the authority to unilaterally extinguish essential aspects of Native American sovereignty, and was it legal?[9]

Johnson v. McIntosh (1823)

The first case of the Marshall trilogy was *Johnson v. McIntosh* (1823).[10] In this case, the Supreme Court had to determine whether Native American tribes or the United States had the right to grant land title to prospective buyers. Nonmembers had purchased lands from the Illinois Indians in 1773 and the Piankeshaw Indians in 1775 and subsequently moved onto those lands. Then, in 1818, William McIntosh bought the same lands, which had passed from the control of the Virginia Colony in 1784, from the U.S. government. In a unanimous opinion, the Supreme Court held that the land rights of the federal government were superior to those of any Native American tribe. Therefore, the nonmembers who had bought lands from the tribes lost land title to a counterclaim made by other nonmembers over forty years later. Overall, the judgment of Chief Justice Marshall generally limited the external sovereignty of the tribes, extinguished Indian land title (ownership of the lands), and ruled that tribes could sell lands only to the federal government.[11] Marshall had to balance the interests of the United States with tribal rights. "Marshall was caught between two competing interests: the desire not to disturb previously settled expectations about land title and the desire not to dishonor the many treaties and proclamations protecting Indian property rights, and by implication, tribal sovereignty."[12]

The chief justice ruled that the United States had superior rights based on the doctrine of discovery, a two-hundred-year-old European convention that allowed a European nation the right to trade and acquire lands from natives; the right of discovery by one European nation prohibited any other European nation from trading with the same natives. Marshall did not apply the conventions of the doctrine of discovery in its original form but instead applied it literally, such that the discovery of lands dispossessed the Indian tribes of their land title and automatically vested ownership in the discovering nation. Marshall's opinion confirmed the limitations on the inherent sovereignty of the tribes:

> The rights of the original inhabitants were, in no instance, entirely disregarded; but were necessarily, to a considerable extent, impaired. They were admitted to be the rightful occupants of the soil, with a legal as well as just claim to retain possession of it, and to use it according to their own discretion; but their rights to complete sovereignty, as independent nations, were necessarily diminished, and their power to dispose of the soil at their own will, to whomsoever they pleased, was denied by the original fundamental principle, that discovery gave exclusive title to those who made it.[13]

Thus, the Supreme Court circumscribed the inherent sovereignty of the tribes in their relations with other sovereign nations and limited tribal sovereignty over lands in favor of a title based on occupancy. This occupancy continued until it was purchased or conquered by another sovereign power, for example, the United States. The "tribes lost their status as complete sovereigns and, in particular, their ability to engage in external relations with any sovereign other than the European discovering country."[14] The Court considered the tribes to be the occupants but not the owners of the lands that made up North America: "The absolute ultimate title has been considered as acquired by discovery, subject only to the Indian title of occupancy, which title the discoverers possessed the exclusive right of acquiring."[15]

Despite the limitations imposed on the tribes by the *McIntosh* opinion, it was a halfway-house decision. As Joseph C. Burke explains, Marshall did not fully extinguish Native American land title, nor did he give the Native Americans undisputed title to the lands.[16] Ultimately, the limitation placed on Native America was justified by the superior Christian rights of the United States:

> On the discovery of this immense continent, the great nations of Europe were eager to appropriate to themselves so much of it as they could respectively acquire. Its vast extent offered an ample field to the ambition and enterprise of all; and the character and religion of its inhabitants afforded an apology for considering them as a people over whom the superior genius of Europe might claim an ascendancy. The potentates of the old world found no difficulty in convincing themselves that they made ample compensation to the inhabitants of the new, by bestowing on them civilization and Christianity, in exchange for unlimited independence.[17]

Christianity was one of the fundamental reasons, if not the principal justification, for the acquisition of Indian lands by the United States.[18]

Cherokee Nation v. Georgia (1831)

Only eight years after the watershed case of *Johnson v. McIntosh* came the second case of the Marshall trilogy. In *Cherokee Nation v. Georgia* (1831), the Supreme Court justices were deeply divided over the status of the Cherokee Nation.[19] Chief Justice Marshall delivered the opinion of the Court, Justices William Johnson and Henry Baldwin wrote separate opinions, and Justice Smith Thompson, joined by Justice Joseph Story, wrote a dissent.

In this case, the Cherokee Nation sought an injunction to prevent the Georgia legislature from passing acts that limited Cherokee sovereignty. In a bill presented to the Supreme Court, the Cherokees claimed they were a foreign state under the Constitution and argued that their sovereignty was confirmed in the many treaties ratified by Congress: "This bill is brought by the Cherokee nation, praying an injunction to restrain the state of Georgia from the execution of certain laws of that state, which, as is alleged, go directly to annihilate the Cherokees as a political society, and to seize, for the use of

Georgia, the lands of the nation which have been assured to them by the United States in solemn treaties repeatedly made and still in force."[20]

Initially, the Marshall opinion interpreted the Cherokees to be sovereign, with all of the attributes of a distinct and independent state:

> So much of the argument as was intended to prove the character of the Cherokees as a state, as a distinct political society, separated from others, capable of managing its own affairs and governing itself, has, in the opinion of a majority of the judges, been completely successful. They have been uniformly treated as a state from the settlement of our country. The numerous treaties made with them by the United States recognize them as a people capable of maintaining the relations of peace and war, of being responsible in their political character for any violation of their engagements, or for any aggression committed on the citizens of the United States by any individual of their community. Laws have been enacted in the spirit of these treaties. The acts of our government plainly recognize the Cherokee nation as a state, and the courts are bound by those acts.[21]

However, despite such a ringing endorsement of Cherokee sovereignty and its manifestation in treaties, the chief justice declared that the Cherokees and all Native American tribes were not foreign nations under the Constitution. In reaffirming his *McIntosh* judgment of 1823, Marshall declared that the tribes were under the general authority of the United States:

> Though the Indians are acknowledged to have an unquestionable, and, heretofore, unquestioned right to the lands they occupy, until that right shall be extinguished by a voluntary cession to our government; yet it may well be doubted whether those tribes which reside within the acknowledged boundaries of the United States can, with strict accuracy, be denominated foreign nations. They may, more correctly, perhaps, be denominated domestic dependent nations. They occupy a territory to which we assert a title independent of their will, which must take effect in point of possession when their right of possession ceases. Meanwhile they are in a state of pupilage. Their relation to the United States resembles that of a ward to his guardian.[22]

Native Americans were considered "domestic dependent nations" because they were within the boundaries of the sovereign nation-state of the United

States. Robert Porter argues that Chief Justice Marshall made sure that America took legal control over the tribes, noting that he "was able to cement American hegemony over them in such a way as to ensure that this became the foundational principle of new American Indian subjugation jurisprudence."[23] Porter views federal Indian law as a process of exploitation that severely limited the rights of the tribes. In contrast to Porter, Burke believes that the 1831 Marshall opinion was ingenious, fitting in with the climate of the time. The Supreme Court was weak, the political pressure to grant foreign status to the Cherokees was too dangerous, and morally Marshall could not allow the state of Georgia to repress Cherokee rights when in fact the laws of the United States took precedence over Native American sovereignty and interests.[24]

Marshall explained that the United States had the right to control the external relations of the tribes because numerous treaties held that the tribes were "completely under the sovereignty and dominion of the United States"[25] and the protection of the U.S. government. This reading of the treaties by Marshall did not, however, take account of the fact that the word "protection" was introduced into treaties with European nations long before, meaning that European nations did not lose any attributes of sovereignty. The protection of a stronger state over a weaker state should have resulted in an alliance where the weaker state did not surrender its sovereignty. Interestingly, this point was eloquently made by Justice Thompson in his dissent (see below).

In a separate opinion, Justice William Johnson argued that the Cherokees were not a state because they were "a people so low in the grade of organized society" with no sovereignty over any territory. Furthermore, the Cherokees were not a foreign state because the Constitution described Indian tribes as "an anomaly unknown to the books that treat of States, and which the law of nations would regard as nothing more than wandering hordes, held together only by ties of blood and habit, and having neither laws or government beyond what is required in a savage state."[26]

In a second separate opinion, Justice Henry Baldwin argued that foreign states did not surrender their sovereignty and assume protection from another state, as he believed the Cherokees had done in the Treaty of Hopewell of 1785: "There can be no dependence so anti-national, or so utterly subversive of national existence, as transferring to a foreign government the regulation of its trade and the management of all their affairs at their pleasure."[27] Furthermore, he believed that it was impossible for a foreign state to exist within the boundaries of the United States; thus, "Indian sovereignty cannot be roused from its long slumber, and awakened to action by our fiat." Justice Baldwin echoed the views of Justice Johnson when he argued that "the Indians were considered as tribes of fierce savages—a people with whom it was impossible to mix and who could not be governed as a distinct society . . . and nowhere declared to have any national capacity or attributes of sovereignty in their relations to the General or State governments." In sum, he argued that to declare the Cherokees a foreign state would not only divest the state of Georgia of sovereignty but would "reverse every principle on which our Government has acted for fifty-five years and force, by mere judicial power, upon the other departments of this Government and the States of this Union the recognition of the existence of nations and States within the limits of both, possessing dominion and jurisdiction paramount to the Federal and State Constitutions."[28]

Justice Smith Thompson dissented, arguing that the Cherokees constituted a foreign state within the meaning of the Constitution.[29] Thompson was joined in his dissent by Justice Joseph Story.[30] From the outset, Justice Thompson argued that the Cherokee tribe's inherent sovereignty was not divested because of the assumption of U.S. protection:

> We ought, therefore, to reckon in the number of sovereigns those states that have bound themselves to another more powerful, although by an unequal alliance. The conditions of these unequal alliances may be infinitely varied; but whatever they are, provided the inferior ally reserves to itself the sovereignty or the right to govern its own body, it ought to be considered an independent state. Consequently, a weak state, that, in order to provide for its safety, places itself under the protection of a more powerful one without stripping itself of the right of government and sovereignty, does not cease on this account to be placed among the sovereigns who acknowledge no other power.[31]

The Cherokees, Justice Thompson argued, had never lost their rights of self-government and were therefore completely sovereign. They had an "exclusive right to the possession of their lands," and "every invasion of their possessory right is an injury done to the Nation."[32] Treaties, such as the Treaty of Hopewell of 1785 and the Treaty of Holston of 1791, Justice Thompson suggested, were examples where sovereign nations engaged in contractual negotiation over peace and war, cession of territory, and jurisdiction.[33] He noted that Article 8 of the Treaty of Holston declared that "any citizens of the United States, who shall settle upon any of the Cherokee lands, shall forfeit the protection of the United States, and the Cherokees may punish them or not as they shall please."[34]

Although it was unfortunate for the Cherokees that the Thompson interpretation formed part of the dissent in the *Cherokee Nation* case, it added to the foundations of Marshall's *Worcester* opinion in 1832. On the insistence of Marshall, the dissenters (Thompson and Story) in the *Cherokee Nation* case penned their dissents nine days after the case in order to expand the suggestions made in the Marshall opinion regarding the protection of Cherokee property rights against the illegal acts of Georgia.[35]

Worcester v. Georgia (1832)

Only a year after *Cherokee Nation* came *Worcester v. Georgia* (1832), the final and most important case of the Marshall trilogy.[36] Chief Justice Marshall delivered the opinion of the Court and Justice John McLean delivered a concurring opinion.[37] Justice Baldwin dissented, with the same reasoning offered in the *Cherokee Nation* case.[38]

The case involved a nonmember minister, the Reverend Samuel A. Worcester, who was indicted by the Superior Court for the County of Gwinnett, Georgia, for not having a license from the governor of Georgia or other authorized person to be within Cherokee lands. Reverend Worcester argued that he was a citizen of Vermont who had entered the lands of the sovereign Cherokee Nation as a missionary under the authority of the president of the United States. In addition, he argued that the Cherokee Nation was not within the jurisdiction of Georgia, and therefore that the State of Georgia was acting contrary to the Constitution and the treaties signed between the Cherokees and the U.S. government.

Once again, Marshall began this case, as he did in 1831, with a ringing endorsement of the independence and sovereignty of Native American tribes: "America, separated from Europe by a wide ocean, was inhabited by a distinct people, divided into separate nations, independent of each other and of the rest of the world, having institutions of their own, and governing themselves by their own laws."[39]

In contrast to his opinions in *McIntosh* and *Cherokee Nation*, Marshall suggested that the doctrine of discovery did not grant the European nations or the United States automatic claims to Native American land or limit the rights of Native America: "It is difficult to comprehend the proposition, that the inhabitants of either quarter of the globe could have rightful original claims of dominion over the inhabitants of the other, or over the lands they occupied; or that the discovery of either by the other should give the discoverer rights in the country discovered, which annulled the pre-existing rights of its ancient possessors." In addition, the doctrine of discovery, Marshall explained, regulated the rights of Europeans against one another to compete for discovered lands and to purchase them. Importantly, the principle of discovery did not extinguish tribal rights:

> This principle, acknowledged by all Europeans because it was the interest of all to acknowledge it, gave to the nation making the discovery, as its inevitable consequence, the sole right of acquiring the soil and of making settlements on it. It was an exclusive principle which shut out the right of competition among those who had agreed to it, not one which could annul the previous rights of those who had not agreed to it. It regulated the right given by discovery among the European discoverers, but could not affect the rights of those already in possession, either as aboriginal occupants or as occupants by virtue of a discovery made before the memory of man. It gave the exclusive right to purchase, but did not found that right on a denial of the right of the possessor to sell.[40]

In 1832, then, Marshall believed that Native Americans were more than occupants of the land and reversed his interpretation in *McIntosh*, where he believed that discovery gave the European and American nations an inherent right to land title. The very basis of his ruling in *Johnson v. McIntosh* (1823) was ridiculed by Marshall himself in the *Worcester* opinion of 1832: "The extravagant and absurd idea, that the feeble settlements made on the sea coast, or the companies under whom they were made, acquired legitimate power by them to govern the people, or occupy the lands from sea to sea, did not enter the mind of any man."[41] Indeed, it may be argued that Marshall, in principle, overruled the foundations of his earlier decision.[42]

Moreover, the *Worcester* opinion also contradicted the analysis of Native American treaty rights made by Marshall in the *Cherokee Nation* case. In *Worcester*, Marshall held that Native American tribes were sovereign entities capable of entering into treaties on an equal footing with the United States and preserving their sovereign qualities of tribal self-government. The first treaty conducted between the U.S. government and a Native American group was a treaty with the Delaware Indians of 1778.[43] Marshall believed that this treaty was akin to those treaties made between European nations: "This treaty, in its language, and in its provisions, is formed, as near as may be, on the model of treaties between the crowned heads of Europe."[44] Furthermore, Marshall's interpretation regarding the issue of federal protection of Native American tribes had changed from his analysis in 1831. Now, Marshall pointed out that the Cherokee Nation had not surrendered its national character by opting to be protected by the United States:

> This stipulation is found in Indian treaties, generally. It was intro-
> duced into their treaties with Great Britain; and may probably be found
> in those with other European powers. . . . The Indians perceived in this
> protection only what was beneficial to themselves—an engagement to
> punish aggressions on them. It involved, practically, no claim to their
> lands, no dominion over their persons. It merely bound the nation to
> the British crown, as a dependent ally, claiming the protection of a
> powerful friend and neighbor, and receiving the advantages of that
> protection, without involving a surrender of their national character.[45]

The new 1832 interpretation supported the preservation of Cherokee and Native American rights when they were under the protection of a European nation. In addition, the protection of Native American tribes by the United States meant the protection of Native American rights. As Marshall explained, "Protection does not imply the destruction of the protected."[46]

Marshall's *Worcester* opinion relied on two fundamental principles: the recognition of inherent tribal sovereignty, and the recognition that Congress also had the right and authority, or plenary power, to protect the tribes from state law. Marshall clarified these two principles when he discussed the trade and intercourse acts passed by Congress: "All these acts, and especially that of 1802, which is still in force, manifestly consider the several Indian nations as distinct political communities, having territorial boundaries, within which their authority is exclusive, and having a right to all the lands within those boundaries, which is not only acknowledged, but guaranteed by the United States."[47] The *Worcester* judgment openly declared that Native American tribes had inherent sovereignty over their lands and every person on those lands and, therefore, prohibited state jurisdiction over a white citizen inside Cherokee lands.

Nell Jessup Newton has challenged the interpretation that the Marshall opinion relied on tribal sovereignty. Instead, Newton explains that Marshall used congressional power to prohibit state law from the reservation, pointing out that, "although the Court in Worcester recognized that Indian tribes possess inherent sovereignty rights, the decision was really a defense of federal over state power, not a defense of Indian tribal sovereignty—the tribe was not even a party to the suit."[48] Despite Newton's view, it is clear that the *Worcester* opinion relied on the inherent sovereignty of the tribes, because the Supreme Court had recognized Cherokee treaties and Cherokee land rights. It had also confirmed that Congress had the right to bar state law from inside any tribal lands. Tribal authority was answerable only to the federal government and not to any of the states. As Marshall pointed out, the relations between Native America and the United States were regulated "according to the settled principles of our constitution, are committed exclusively to the government of the union."[49] The laws and jurisdiction of the State of Georgia had no force over a nonmember within the boundaries of Cherokee lands. In conclusion, Marshall held that the authority of the State of Georgia within Cherokee lands was repugnant to the treaties, the Constitution, and laws of the United States.[50]

Despite the positive outcome of the *Worcester* case, Marshall did not directly overrule his rulings in *McIntosh* or *Cherokee Nation*, which had confirmed the limitations on the external sovereignty of the tribes. Nevertheless, the Indian sovereignty doctrine established in *Worcester* reaffirmed the inherent sovereignty of the tribes over their own lands and protected them against the application of any kind of state law on the reservations. It also confirmed that the federal government had overarching sovereignty to protect the tribes against state law.[51]

In a concurring opinion, Justice John McLean considered the Cherokees to be a sovereign nation with the rights of self-government and inherent sovereignty: "At no time has the sovereignty of the country been recognized as existing in the Indians, but they have been always admitted to possess many of the attributes of sovereignty." Tribal inherent sovereignty was diminished, though, "where small remnants of tribes remain, surrounded by white population, and who, by their reduced numbers, had lost the power of self-government," and as a result state law extended over them.[52]

The inherent sovereignty of the tribes was echoed in the treaty process and in the manner commerce was enacted by the United States over the tribes. The Constitution placed regulation of commerce with the tribes, McLean stated: "In this respect, they have been placed by the federal authority, with but few exceptions, on the same footing as foreign nations." Cherokee sovereignty negated the outreach of state laws as did the fact that states had "parted" with the powers to regulate tribes, and they "have been expressly and exclusively given to the Federal Government."[53] In sum, for McLean, the laws of the State of Georgia were repugnant to the Constitution.

❖ From 1823 to 1832, then, the Marshall trilogy of cases had limited tribal sovereignty: *McIntosh* limited the external sovereignty of the tribes and the right of the tribes to sell their lands to any number of sovereign nations by declaring that tribal lands had to be sold exclusively to the United States. *Cherokee Nation* also limited the external sovereignty of the tribes and their ability to act in international relations. *Worcester* held that tribal power was dependent on the superior or plenary authority of the United States.

Despite these boundaries imposed on inherent tribal sovereignty, collectively the three cases declared that tribes had inherent sovereignty over reservation lands and people on those lands unless Congress acted to reverse attributes of that sovereignty, and that inherent tribal sovereignty and congressional power prohibited all state law on tribal reservations.

The Indian Sovereignty Doctrine and the Federal Policy of Indian Removal

Soon after the Marshall trilogy, federal policy began to place additional limitations on tribal sovereignty. The *Worcester* ruling and the treaties conducted between the tribes and the government were powerless to prevent the removal of many tribes from east to west of the Mississippi River.[54] The purpose of removal was summed up by the Indian Removal Act of 1830, "an Act to provide for an exchange of lands with the Indians residing in any of the states or territories, and for their removal west of the river Mississippi."[55] The population of the United States was growing, requiring, the federal government believed, more land freed up in the East. As a result of economic, political, and social pressures, many tribes conducted treaties with the United States to cede eastern lands in exchange for lands in the West.

During the period of Indian removal, the Supreme Court applied the principles of *McIntosh,* whereby tribes were seen as occupiers of the land but had no sovereignty; the United States had dominion over these territories. In 1846 the Court decided its first tribal rights case since *Worcester* of 1832. In *United States v. Rogers* (1846), the facts of the case concerned William S. Rogers, who had murdered Jacob Nicholson in Cherokee country.[56] Both were white men but had resided with Cherokees long before the offense and were considered part of the Cherokee Nation. Rogers argued that U.S. courts had no jurisdiction in this matter. Chief Justice Roger B. Taney delivered the opinion of the Supreme Court and ruled that Rogers was to be tried and if found guilty was to be punished under the Act of Congress of 1834.[57]

The primary argument made by Chief Justice Taney was that the crime occurred on American soil because Cherokee land had "been assigned to them by the United States." In direct contradiction to *Worcester,* the tribes were not viewed as the owners of the lands, because the lands were considered to be vacant and unoccupied. Furthermore, an Act of Congress of 1834 extended the laws of the United States over Indian country but contained a provision that negated the implementation of these laws if "crimes [were] committed by one Indian against the person or property of another Indian." In addition, the Treaty of New Echota of 1835 allowed the Cherokees to make laws for the Cherokee people "or such persons as have connected themselves with them . . . [but] such laws shall not be inconsistent with acts of Congress."[58] Taney ruled that Rogers was not considered to be "Indian" within the meaning of the law, and the 1834 Act controlled and explained the words contained in the treaty.

The Indian Sovereignty Doctrine in the Assimilation and Allotment Era

After the relocation of many tribes, around the turn of the century federal government policy shifted from removal toward assimilation and allotment. Two pieces of major legislation were passed by Congress in this period. The Major Crimes Act of 1885 began the movement of federal authority onto the reservations and transferred responsibility for the judgment of serious crimes from tribal authority to Congress. Then, the General Allotment Act of 1887 authorized the division of tribal lands into individually owned lands where the head of the family was allotted 80 acres of agricultural land or 160 acres of grazing land, and half the amount was allotted to a single person over the age of eighteen or an orphan child.[59] The lands were held in trust for twenty-five years, and after the expiration of the trust period the tribal members became subjects of state law.

The 1887 act significantly decreased the tribal land base of Native America, from 138 million acres in 1887 to only 47 million acres in 1934, a reduction of two-thirds.[60] President Theodore Roosevelt believed that the General Allotment Act was designed to eviscerate the tribes and their powers, noting that it was "a mighty pulverizing engine to break up the tribal mass."[61] In 2002, William C. Canby, former judge of the U.S. Court of Appeals for the Ninth Circuit, agreed with the Roosevelt assessment and believed that allotment had been destructive in many ways: "Over the ensuing years there were major movements in Indian law initiated by Congress or the executive branch, including . . . in the 1880's, a policy of allotment designed to break up the tribal landholdings into small individual farms."[62] Influenced by these government policies, the Supreme Court began a gradual accommodation of federal and state jurisdiction on the reservations.[63]

United States v. McBratney (1881) and Draper v. United States (1896)

Four cases during the federal government's policy of allotment weakened *Worcester*. The first case to facilitate the federal policy of allotment and allow state jurisdiction on the reservation was *United States v. McBratney* (1881).[64] In this case, the defendant had murdered Thomas Casey inside the boundaries of the Ute reservation, and the Supreme Court had to decide whether the state had authority to prosecute crimes committed by one white person on another on a reservation. This case was followed by *Draper v. United States* (1896), which considered whether the State of Montana had jurisdiction to prosecute a crime committed by a non-Indian on another non-Indian on the Crow reservation.[65] Because the individuals involved in the *Draper* case were not Native Americans, the Supreme Court ruled that the State of Montana had authority to punish the crime.

Both *McBratney* and *Draper* ruled that states had inherent sovereignty over state citizens who committed crimes against each other on Native American reservations. Although the lands in question were treaty-made reservations and *Worcester* held that tribes had exclusive authority on the reservations, the Court held that the inherent rights of the state took precedence over Native American treaties and *Worcester*, in particular when state citizens were involved.[66] As well, the *McBratney* court had conceded that the Ute reservation was outside the remit of state jurisdiction. This was highlighted in the treaty with the Utes and the original act of Congress that provided temporary government for the Territory of Colorado. Despite these explicit exceptions, the Supreme Court held that Colorado, "without any such exception as had been made in the treaty with the Ute Indians and in the act establishing a territorial government, has acquired criminal jurisdiction over its own citizens and other white persons throughout the whole of the territory within its limits, including the Ute Reservation, and that reservation is no longer within the sole and exclusive jurisdiction of the United States."[67]

The Court determined that the State of Colorado had the right to prosecute crimes committed by nonmembers (state citizens) against nonmembers on tribal reservations, since Congress had not prohibited this action. In doing so, the Court allowed state jurisdiction onto the reservations.

United States v. Kagama (1886)

In the case of *United States v. Kagama* (1886), a Native American man named Kagama had murdered a Native American man named Iyouse on the Hoopa Valley Reservation in California. Another Native American man, Mahawaha, was charged with aiding and abetting the murder.[68] The ruling of *United States v. Kagama*, a case brought after the introduction of the Major Crimes Act of 1885, held that the United States had criminal authority to try the crime of murder committed by one Native American on another. In the view of Sidney L. Harring, *Kagama* was a low point for tribal sovereignty, "the judicial embodiment of Congress's policy of forcing the assimilation of the tribes, recognizing none of their sovereignty, none of their status as domestic nations."[69] In its opinion, the *Kagama* court determined that the federal government had plenary authority over tribes as a result of the opinions in the Marshall trilogy of cases. In his opinion, Justice Samuel F. Miller wrote:

> These Indian tribes are the wards of the nation. They are communities dependent on the United States—dependent largely for their daily food; dependent for their political rights. They owe no allegiance to the States, and receive from them no protection. Because of the local ill feeling, the people of the States where they are found are often their deadliest enemies. From their very weakness and helplessness, so largely due to the course of dealing of the federal government with them, and the treaties in which it has been promised, there arises the duty of protection, and with it the power. This has always been recognized by the executive, and by Congress, and by this Court, whenever the question has arisen.[70]

The phrase "domestic dependent nations" was used by the Supreme Court to allow federal authority to control aspects of tribal affairs, contrary to *Worcester* itself.

Lone Wolf v. Hitchcock (1903)

The authority of the federal government over the tribes was also involved in *Lone Wolf v. Hitchcock* (1903).[71] In this case, Lone Wolf, a Kiowa chief, lived in the Indian Territory created by the Medicine Lodge Treaty of 1867. Article 12 of that treaty itself stipulated that three-fourths of the adult males in each of the Kiowa, Apache, and Comanche tribes had to agree to future changes to the treaty terms. In 1892, Congress passed legislation that altered the reservation and in so doing changed the 1867 treaty and opened two million acres of reservation land to settlement by non-Indians.[72]

In this case, the Supreme Court upheld the sale of tribal land by the federal government despite the presence of the Medicine Lodge Treaty. Once again, the Court ruled that the federal government had plenary power over tribal land interests because of the dependent nation status of the tribes. In his opinion, Justice Edward D. White wrote:

> The contention [that the treaty lands were protected by the Fifth Amendment of the U.S. Constitution] in effect ignores the status of the contracting Indians and the relation of dependency they bore and continue to bear towards the government of the United States. To uphold the claim would be to adjudge that the indirect operation of the treaty was to materially limit and qualify the controlling authority of Congress in respect to the care and protection of the Indians, and to deprive Congress, in a possible emergency, when the necessity might be urgent for a partition and disposal of the tribal lands, of all power to act, if the assent of the Indians could not be obtained.[73]

In addition, Justice White wrote that the United States had the authority to abrogate a treaty unilaterally when circumstances could be justified by the government "in the interest of the country and the Indians themselves" and "consistent with perfect good faith towards the Indians."[74]

The New York Indians (1867) and The Kansas Indians (1867)

Although case law and legislation in this period removed some of the foundational rulings of Chief Justice Marshall, they did not overrule *Worcester* or extinguish the Indian sovereignty doctrine. On many occasions in this period the Supreme Court used *Worcester* and the Indian sovereignty doctrine to prevent the application of state law over tribes on reservations. In *The New*

York Indians (1867) and *The Kansas Indians* (1867), the Court ruled that the states did not have authority to tax tribal members, upholding the rationale of *Worcester.*

The *Kansas Indians* case considered whether the State of Kansas had the right to tax lands held by individuals of the Shawnee, Wea, and Miami tribes.[75] These tribes had ceded their original territories in exchange for lands in Kansas, pursuant to treaties conducted between each tribe and the United States. The Court addressed its opinion to the three tribes involved. With reference to the Shawnees, the Court stated: "If the tribal organization of the Shawnees is preserved intact . . . then they are a 'people distinct from others,' capable of making treaties, separated from the jurisdiction of Kansas, and to be governed exclusively by the government of the Union. . . . If they have outlived many things, they have not outlived the protection afforded by the Constitution, treaties, and laws of Congress."[76]

The Court determined that the Shawnees had inherent sovereignty, which made them independent from the states, and that Congress had plenary power over them. On this assumption, the Court held that the State of Kansas did not have the authority to tax the tribe. In stark contrast to *McBratney,* the *Kansas Indians* court held, "While the general government has a superintending care over their interests, and continues to treat with them as a nation, the State of Kansas is estopped from denying their title to it. She accepted this status when she accepted the act admitting her into the Union." The only means to preclude exclusive tribal government over a reservation was by treaty or the voluntary abandonment of tribal government. Until that point, the Court held, "their property is withdrawn from the operation of State laws." The Court applied the same rationale to the Wea and Miami tribes, noting that the Miamis "are a nation of people, recognized as such by the general government in the making of treaties with them, and the relations always maintained towards them, and cannot, therefore, be taxed by the authorities of Kansas."[77]

The Supreme Court followed the same principles in *The New York Indians* (1867).[78] In this case the State of New York had taxed the Buffalo Creek, Alleghany, and Cattaraugus reservations of the Seneca Nation. The state had introduced legislation to tax the reservations, but the Senecas argued that their rights were protected by treaties. The Court held that state laws were "an unwarrantable interference, inconsistent with the original title of the Indians, and offensive to their tribal relations." The original tribal rights were paramount, and the Court noted that the tribes "are to be regarded as still in their ancient possessions, and are in under their original rights, and entitled to the undisturbed enjoyment of them."[79]

Ex parte Crow Dog (1883) and Talton v. Mayes (1896)

In *Ex parte Crow Dog* (1883), the facts of the case involved a Native American named Kan-gi-Shun-ca (Crow Dog), a member of the Brule Sioux Band of the Sioux Nation, who had murdered Sin-ta-ge-le-Scka (Spotted Tail) on the Great Sioux Reservation. Crow Dog was convicted by the Sioux tribal government and ordered to pay restitution to the victim's family.[80] At the same time, the government of Dakota Territory charged Crow Dog and found him guilty. Crow Dog appealed and argued that the federal court had no jurisdiction and that the United States had no authority over him on the reservation. The opinion of the Supreme Court reversed the conviction of Crow Dog by the First District Court of Dakota and held that the United States did not have criminal authority to prosecute tribal members because the inherent sovereignty of the tribes ousted federal law from the reservation.

In the case of *Talton v. Mayes* (1896), a Cherokee named Bob Talton had murdered another Cherokee on Cherokee Nation lands.[81] Talton was tried, found guilty, and sentenced to death by the Cherokee Nation. Talton appealed to the federal courts and argued that he had been deprived of his liberty without due process of law in violation of the U.S. Constitution and the Cherokee Constitution. The Supreme Court ruled that the murder of one Cherokee by another was not an offense against the United States and that the Fifth Amendment did not apply to the Cherokee Nation. The inherent sovereignty of the tribes, pursuant to the sovereignty doctrine, was upheld in this case: "As the powers of local self-government enjoyed by the Cherokee Nation existed prior to the constitution, they are not operated upon by the fifth amendment . . . and the determination of what was the existing law of the Cherokee Nation . . . was solely a matter within the jurisdiction of the courts of that Nation, and the decision of such a question in itself necessarily involves no infraction of the constitution of the United States."[82]

Morris v. Hitchcock (1904)

In the early twentieth century, the Supreme Court sanctioned the inherent rights of the tribe to tax a state citizen on the reservation. In *Morris v. Hitchcock* (1904), Edwin T. Morris and nine other people, all U.S. citizens, began an equity suit in the Supreme Court against Ethan A. Hitchcock, secretary of the Department of the Interior, and three others.[83] Morris and the others all owned over five hundred cattle and horses, valued at more than fifteen dollars a head. These animals grazed on Chickasaw Nation lands under contracts with members of the Chickasaw Nation. In 1876 the Chickasaw Nation passed legislation to prevent unauthorized intruders into its territory and to raise revenue. The latter involved land rental to state and U.S. citizens for an annual fee, and permits had to be obtained. Similar acts were passed by the Chickasaws in 1898 and 1902.

In his opinion, Justice Edward D. White stated that refusal to pay the tax would lead to the animals being "wrongfully in the territory." This explicit use of tribal sovereignty was upheld, with the Chickasaw Nation allowed to tax nonmembers inside its territory: "It is also undoubted that in treaties entered into with the Chickasaw Nation, the right of that tribe to control the presence within the territory assigned to it of persons who might otherwise be regarded as intruders has been sanctioned. . . . And it is not disputed that, under the authority of these treaties, the Chickasaw Nation has exercised the power to attach conditions to the presence within its borders of persons who might otherwise not be entitled to remain within the tribal territory."[84] The powers of the Indian sovereignty doctrine and the principles of *Worcester* sanctioned the inherent sovereignty of the tribes over nonmembers (state citizens) on the reservations.

✛ During assimilation and allotment, the Indian sovereignty doctrine and the principles of *Worcester* were modified. Some case law weakened the Indian sovereignty doctrine. Such precedents allowed state laws onto the reservations in certain circumstances and more federal government authority to apply and encroach upon tribal members on the reservations. That said, the principles of *Worcester* were never reversed or nullified. On the contrary, the sovereignty doctrine, reliant on the inherent sovereignty of the tribes, continued to exist. In some Court opinions this doctrine protected tribal members from state and federal laws on the reservations and allowed tribes to assume authority over non-Indians.

The Indian Sovereignty Doctrine in the Era of the Indian New Deal

After the Indian sovereignty doctrine survived federal policies of removal and assimilation, it underwent further change in the federal policy period of the Indian New Deal. This period was defined by the Indian Reorganization Act (IRA) of 1934 and *The Handbook of Federal Indian Law*, published in 1941.

The IRA of 1934 formally ended the process of assimilation and allotment and provided tribal funds to rebuild tribal economies. Under this act the tribe was established as a political unit.[85] Many different groups united under the politicized umbrella of the tribe and formed tribal governments, based on the political model of the United States, with tribal constitutions.[86] The IRA did not, however, restore the loss of tribal lands since 1887. The Indian New Deal reinvigorated tribal sovereignty, and the Supreme Court ruled in favor of Native Americans on several occasions during this period.[87]

In 1941, Felix S. Cohen produced the authoritative work on the powers and rights of Native Americans and the tribes within the U.S. legal system. Cohen served in the Solicitor's Office of the Department of the Interior between 1933 and 1948 and as head of the Indian Law Survey.[88] The *Handbook of Federal Indian Law* effectively codified Native American rights within the American legal system and examined the effect of treaties, statutes, and case law on Native America and the constituent tribes. Frickey describes this work as Cohen's "monumental attempt to systematize federal Indian law."[89] The section titled "The Scope of Tribal Self-Government" examined the effect of case law and government policy on *Worcester*. Despite federal policy and Supreme Court case law contrary to the *Worcester* principle, Cohen explained that the principles established by Chief Justice Marshall were those that had been regularly used by the Supreme Court: "John Marshall's analysis of the basis of Indian self-government in the law of nations has been consistently followed by the courts for more than a hundred years. The doctrine set forth in this opinion has been applied to an unfolding series of new problems in scores of cases that have come before the Supreme Court and the interior federal courts." Cohen made clear that the Indian sovereignty doctrine had been consistently used by the Supreme Court from 1832 and that it remained an important factor in defending the rights of tribes against state and federal administrations: "The case in which the doctrine of Indian self-government was first established has a certain prophetic character. Administrative officials for a century afterwards continued to ignore the broad implications of the judicial doctrine of Indian self-government. But again and again, as cases came before the federal courts, administrative officials, state and federal, were forced to reckon with the doctrine of Indian self-government."[90]

In short, the Indian sovereignty doctrine had become an integral part of federal Indian law and the broader American legal and political system. Cohen's work was "an attempt by the Interior Department to reaffirm federal power over Indian tribes in a more conceptually consistent manner."[91] Cohen, in a seminal passage, defined the powers of the tribe:

> The whole course of judicial decision on the nature of tribal powers is marked by adherence to three fundamental principles: (1) An Indian tribe possesses, in the first instance, all the powers of any sovereign state. (2) Conquest renders the tribe subject to the legislative power of the United States and, in substance, terminates the external powers of sovereignty of the tribe, e.g., its power to enter into treaties with foreign nations, but does not by itself affect the internal sovereignty of the tribe, e.g., its power of local self-government. (3) These powers are subject to qualification by treaties and by express legislation of Congress, but, save as thus expressly qualified, full powers of internal sovereignty are vested in the Indian tribes and in their duly constituted organs of government.[92]

The Indian sovereignty doctrine held that tribes had authority, power, and sovereignty, termed inherent sovereignty, over all lands and people on the reservation unless authority was explicitly withdrawn, divested, or annulled by a clear and plain act of Congress or by treaty. In addition, Cohen's definition of tribal powers was a reminder that the tribes had always had inherent sovereignty over lands and people on those lands.

The Indian Sovereignty Doctrine in the Termination Period

The 1934 IRA and Cohen's *Handbook of Federal Indian Law* of 1941 reinvigorated tribal sovereignty and the *Worcester* principle. But during the late 1940s and 1950s America once again began assimilating Native America into American society. During the 1950s, Congress and the Supreme Court had to reconcile the integrationist demands arising from the desegregation of black America and the continued demands for autonomy and separation by Native America. In *Brown v. Board of Education* (1954), the Court declared that the doctrine of "separate but equal," established in *Plessy v. Ferguson* (1896), was not applicable to public school education in America and was contrary to the "equal protection of the laws guaranteed by the Fourteenth Amendment."[93] As a response, the Court met the demands of 1950s black America and decreed that the separation of black and white students in public schools was unconstitutional. The process of integration was a principle pursued by black America and facilitated by the Court in 1954. Yet the *Brown* decision was contrary in principle to the demands of Native America in the 1950s, which wanted the federal government to end the policy of termination and to allow more tribal autonomy.

During the 1950s, the federal policy of termination sought to end the autonomy of tribes and assimilate Native America into mainstream society.[94] Arthur V. Watkins, a strong proponent of termination, believed that the federal government should integrate Native Americans and the tribes into mainstream American culture:

> In view of the historic policy of Congress favoring freedom for the Indians, we may well expect future Congresses to continue to indorse the principle that "as rapidly as possible" we should end the status of Indians as wards of government and grant them all of the rights and prerogatives pertaining to American citizenship. . . . Firm and constant consideration for those of Indian ancestry should lead us all to work diligently and carefully for the full realization of their national citizenship with all other Americans. Following in the footsteps of the Emancipation Proclamation of ninety four years ago, I see the following words emblazoned in letters of fire about the heads of the Indians—THESE PEOPLE SHALL BE FREE![95]

Termination was, then, a policy to undermine the *Worcester* principle and the Indian sovereignty doctrine by bringing the tribes under state law and forcing them to pay state taxes. During termination, some tribes lost reservation lands, tribal businesses, and economic systems. This process assimilated tribes and threatened tribal rights as well as the future survival of the tribes. In 1955, Ruth Muskrat Bronson, Cherokee specialist in Native American affairs and former executive secretary of the National Congress of American Indians, pointed out that if Congress pursued assimilation "the American Indian (like that other living creature associated with him in history, the buffalo) is likely, similarly, to continue to exist only on the American nickel."[96]

The federal policy of termination was an important factor in the Supreme Court case *Tee-Hit-Ton Indians v. United States* (1955), in which the Tee-Hit-Ton Indians, a group that belonged to the Tlingit Tribe of Alaskan Indians, argued that the United States had taken timber belonging to the group near Tongass National Forest in Alaska.[97] The Supreme Court ruled that Congress had never recognized any legal interest of the Tee-Hit-Ton Indians in the land and that without government recognition of ownership there were no rights against taking the timber. In addition, Indian occupancy of lands could be extinguished by Congress without compensation, justified by the doctrine of discovery and *Johnson v. McIntosh* (1823). In sum, the Supreme Court ruled against the Tee-Hit-Ton Indians and held that they had no right of compensation under the Fifth Amendment for tribal lands taken by the U.S. government.[98]

✠ Over more than a century, the development of federal Indian law and the Indian sovereignty doctrine by the U.S. Supreme Court was not smooth. From the establishment of the Indian sovereignty doctrine in *Worcester v. Georgia* (1832) to 1959, the Supreme Court placed limitations on the doctrine itself and thereby directly circumscribed the inherent sovereignty of the tribes. In spite of this gradual degrading, in 1941 the Indian sovereignty doctrine was reaffirmed in Felix S. Cohen's seminal work, *The Handbook of Federal Indian Law*. In a dramatic turnabout beginning in 1959, the Supreme Court contravened the federal government policy of termination and pursued a direction that aided a resurgence of a separate and autonomous Native America. The *Worcester* case, the sovereignty doctrine, and inherent tribal sovereignty had survived 127 years, and in 1959 *Williams v. Lee* "opened the modern era of federal Indian law."[99]

The Foundations of the Silent Revolution, 1959–1973

Central to the assessment of Supreme Court case law between 1959 and 1973 is the way individual justices and the institution of the Court reacted to the power struggle between federal, state, and tribal authorities. In 1959 the Court reinvigorated the Indian sovereignty doctrine and used tribal sovereignty, also referred to as inherent tribal sovereignty or tribal authority, to defeat the application of state authority on the reservations. The Indian sovereignty doctrine was based on the principle that tribes had inherent sovereignty over lands and people on the reservations until Congress acted to reverse attributes of that sovereignty or it was done by treaty.

Beginning in 1959 the Court began moving away from the sovereignty doctrine, instead preferring to use federal authority to assess whether state law should be prohibited on the reservations. The justices' mindsets shifted from an approach based on tribal versus state authority to one based primarily on federal versus state authority with tribal authority tied up in federal interests.[1] In reconciling power struggles between these three levels of government, the Supreme Court weakened the use of the Indian sovereignty doctrine, as shown in this chapter through in-depth examination of eight important Supreme Court cases between 1959 and 1973.

Over a twenty-four-year period the thinking of the Supreme Court justices gradually shifted away from generally excluding state law from the reservations toward allowing the application of state law over tribal members and non-members on the reservations until it was reversed by federal authority.[2] Five Supreme Court cases, *Williams v. Lee* (1959), *Kake v. Egan* (1962), *Metlakatla Indians v. Egan* (1962), *Warren Trading Post v. Tax Commission* (1965), and *Kennerly v. District Court of Montana* (1971), highlight the ideological movement toward allowing state law into the reservations. Then in the sister taxation cases *McClanahan v. Arizona State Tax Comm'n* (1973) and *Mescalero Apache Tribe v. Jones* (1973), along with *Tonasket v. Washington* (1973), the Court summed up this process into a workable idea. This working idea allowed state authority over nonmembers on the reservations and limited tribal sovereignty over nonmembers on the reservations, which thereby fundamentally weakened the Indian sovereignty doctrine that had been established by Chief Justice John Marshall in *Worcester v. Georgia* (1832) and reinvigorated in *Williams v. Lee*.[3]

The Indian sovereignty doctrine gradually gave way to what I term the "integrationist trend," which fit in with the general movement of the Supreme Court toward judging case law on a federal-versus-state basis. The Court gradually brought state law onto the reservations and allowed the states to have more control over nonmembers on the reservations. This process opened up the reservations to state law rather than preserve the autonomy and notion of separateness of the reservations. But this integration did not mean the dissolution of the tribes; instead, it served to limit tribal authority over nonmembers.

The integrationist trend takes its name from two sources. Contained in the Blackmun opinion files of *McClanahan v. Arizona Tax Commission* (1973) is the statement, "The narrowing of Worcester [from 1832] has reflected the growing belief that Indians should, like Negroes be integrated into American society."[4] Justice Potter Stewart supported this position and observed that the "pendulum has swung from Worcester v. Georgia to [the] integration of Indians."[5]

There is no question that the *Williams* opinion revitalized the Indian sovereignty doctrine and the Court's reliance on the territorial sovereignty of the tribes.[6] But the most important aspect of this chapter centers on the argument that the *Williams* case also began the weakening of the Indian sovereignty doctrine and the principles of *Worcester,* a process I identify as the foundations of the silent revolution.[7] Thereafter, cases reviewed in this chapter all played important parts in the movement of the Court away from the sovereignty doctrine and toward the use of federal authority to determine the scope of state power on the reservations.[8]

Supreme Court: The Institution and Legal Processes

The arguments I offer in this book rely on the primary documents of seven justices. Only two contemporary articles have used the private papers of justices to examine federal Indian law.[9] For those less familiar with the mechanics of the Supreme Court, this section offers a brief review of the procedures and legal terms contained in the justices' private papers.[10]

A federal Indian law case is decided when a majority of justices agree on a common position and one of them writes the majority opinion. The other justices either agree completely with the opinion or write a concurrence (opinions that agree with the result reached by the majority opinion but for different reasons) or dissent (disagree with the majority opinion). The origins of a potential case begin on Labor Day, the first Monday in September, when the justices return from the summer recess. Incoming cases arrive at the Supreme Court when a losing party in a case files a petition for certiorari. This is a formal request for the Court to hear a case involving an issue of federal law. Only a small number of petitions are granted review by the Court. The nine justices attend a conference and choose the petitions they feel are in need of review. With four votes in favor of proceeding, the petition is granted review and scheduled for argument.

In the days following oral argument, in which the parties argue their cases and viewpoints before the justices in open court, the justices meet in conference to discuss the cases that were recently argued. The chief justice leads the conference discussion of a case. He reviews the facts of the case, the lower court ruling, and the issues raised by the case in oral argument before stating his position on the case. Thereafter, the discussion moves to the most senior associate justice and proceeds from the more senior justices to the most junior. Each justice casts a nonbinding tentative vote. After two weeks of oral argument, the Court breaks to concentrate on writing opinions. Here the chief justice circulates an assignment sheet, a list of cases to show which justices are assigned the responsibility of writing a majority opinion for the Court. If the chief justice is in the majority at the conference, he assigns the writing of the majority opinion to another justice in the conference majority. Conversely, if the chief justice is in the minority at the conference, the senior associate justice assigns the writing of the majority opinion.

The assigned justice writes a draft majority opinion which, after completion, is circulated to other justices. At this point, memoranda are circulated among the justices to gauge their positions on the draft opinion. Memoranda circulated to all justices, called conference memoranda, offer justices a chance to join the draft opinion (termed a "join memo"), to express doubts about the draft opinion, or to dissent from the draft opinion. The circulation of conference memoranda as well as memoranda from one justice to another offers the justices an opportunity to highlight supporting viewpoints, to clarify ideas, or to disagree courteously with the draft opinion. At the end of this process, the justices join, or concur, with the draft opinion or dissent. Once four justices join the draft opinion of a justice, a majority of five justices has been formed and the draft opinion becomes the opinion of the Court.

The private papers of the justices analyzed in this chapter and in chapter 3 contain many references to clerks. A clerkship is a "highly prized . . . [and] once-in-a-lifetime opportunity to observe the judicial system from the judge's side of the bench" and to help judges decide real cases.[11] Each justice has four clerks. The general role of clerk is to read, assess, comment, and advise the justices, and their specific duties often involve drafting and commenting on majority opinions, dissents, and concurrences and writing bench memoranda and post–oral argument memoranda. A "bench memorandum" is written by a clerk and helps the justice prepare for a case the Court is about to hear.

Williams v. Lee (1959)

In *Williams v. Lee* (1959), the Supreme Court had the option to support or discard the Indian sovereignty doctrine in favor of using federal authority to protect the tribes from state law.[12] The case involved Hugh Lee, a federally approved nonmember shop owner on the Navajo reservation, who brought an action in the Arizona state court against Navajos Paul and Lorena Williams to collect payment for goods sold on credit. The Navajo couple appealed because they thought that the Navajo tribal court had the relevant authority to hear the case. The main question addressed by the Court was whether the Navajo Nation or the State of Arizona had authority over the claim of the nonmember. The justices relied on the principles of inherent tribal sovereignty and territorial sovereignty to strike down the opinion issued by the lower court, which had supported the exercise of state law on the reservation. Furthermore, in contrast to the position adopted by the federal government (represented by the U.S. solicitor general, arguing in favor of the Navajos), which wanted the Court to address questions of tribal authority within the parameters of a federal versus state government framework, the interpretation of the *Williams* Court allowed tribal governments to coexist as a third level of government alongside state governments and the federal government.

The Supreme Court recognized the importance of addressing the uncertainty of the law in the modern context of post–World War II America. The justices had the choice of applying either the Indian sovereignty doctrine or the law that reflected the significant changes in federal policy and Supreme Court case law from the late nineteenth century; this was the first case in a contemporary situation to involve Native Americans, and the outcome was significant to the future of the tribes and the states.[13] The importance of the *Williams* case to the Navajos and to Native America was observed in a clerk's memorandum to Justice Douglas: "Petitioners [the Navajos] contend that this is the most important Indian case in ma[n]y years," and "It appears that this question has not been . . . decided by this Court or by Congress."[14] In addition, the *Williams* court had to settle conflicting strands of law, because, as Chief Justice Earl Warren noted, "the law is unsettled."[15]

The contradictory developments in federal Indian law from the nineteenth century resulted in neither of the two parties being able to "point to precedents in this Court which are decisive."[16] Despite the overwhelming divergence in the precedents and case law, the Court had to rule on the issues and, as Justice Charles Evans Whittaker pointed out, "how to do it."[17] This conflict was simply between the application of the sovereignty doctrine, pointed out in a clerk's memorandum to Chief Justice Warren to mean that "state courts have no jurisdiction over a civil action involving an Indian on a reservation unless Congress so authorizes," and the rationale used by the Arizona Supreme Court (the lower court), which ruled that states had jurisdiction on the reservation unless federal authority existed to prohibit state law. The principle used by the lower court was explained in the same clerk's memorandum: "Unless Congress denies such jurisdiction, state courts have jurisdiction in civil suits involving Indians for transactions arising on reservations within the state."[18]

The Opposing Viewpoints in *Williams v. Lee*

The Navajos, who vehemently disagreed with the ruling of the lower court, wanted the Supreme Court to use the sovereignty doctrine to sanction exclusive tribal authority over nonmembers and to prohibit state law on their reservation unless Congress legislated to allow state authority there. This was described in a clerk's bench memorandum to Warren as the merits of the "broad attack," which was "directed to the contention that state courts lack jurisdiction over suits brought against reservation Indians arising out of transactions taking place on the reservations." The Navajos wanted tribal sovereignty to prevent state courts from having jurisdiction over suits brought by nonmembers against reservation tribal members. Furthermore, the Navajos, who wanted the Court to clarify the law in their favor, suggested the reinvigoration of the sovereignty doctrine and the annulment of any state law on the reservation. As the same bench memorandum explained, the tribe was more "concerned with making law [and] . . . is determined to win on the broad ground that there is no jurisdiction at all in the state courts in any case involving Indians on a reservation."[19] The exclusion of state law from the reservation was fundamental to the tribe's position, as was the principle that explicit congressional authority was required to allow state authority onto the reservation: as explained in a clerk's memorandum to Chief Justice Warren, "The state courts have no jurisdiction over a civil action involving an Indian on a reservation unless Congress so authorizes."[20] In other words, the Navajo position supported exclusive Navajo authority on the reservation until it was reversed by Congress.

The legal position of the tribe also countered the opinion of the Arizona Supreme Court, which ruled that state courts had civil authority on the reservation unless Congress, turning the Indian sovereignty doctrine on its head, restricted state power.[21] The lower court had relied on the principle derived from *Draper v. United States* (1896), which held that states had authority to punish crimes committed by one non-Indian on another on the reservation because state power had not been restricted by congressional legislation. The lower court thought it was reasonable to extend this principle into civil law, stating that Congress had not acted to prevent this extension of state law. The lower court's interpretation of the law, pointed out in a clerk's memorandum to Warren, "relied on a general rule . . . from *Draper v. United States* . . . [which] held that a crime committed by a non-Indian on a reservation was to be tried by state, not federal court. Congress has not denied state jurisdiction in the situation. From this case, the Ariz. SC determined that since Congress has never denied jurisdiction in civil suits, the state courts had it."[22]

The understanding of the lower court was also based on other case law opinions that applied the same rationale. This was pointed out by a clerk to Justice William O. Douglas: "The court below cited some . . . authorities for the proposition that . . . state civil law could be applied to Indians unless Congress prohibits it and Congress has not so prohibited the application of . . . Arizona law here."[23]

The *Williams* Court Uses the Indian Sovereignty Doctrine

The Supreme Court rejected the extension of *Draper* into a general rule, instead preferring to apply tribal sovereignty.[24] One reason used to support the principle of tribal sovereignty was the veto of the Navajo Rehabilitation Bill by President Harry S. Truman in 1949. This bill would have allowed the states to gain authority on the reservations. A bench memorandum read: "In 1949, Congress passed the Navajo Rehabilitation Bill which provided in part that

Navajos on reservations were subject to state laws and that nothing was to be deemed to take away Federal or tribal jurisdiction but that Federal, state and tribal courts were to have concurrent jurisdiction in all cases." In vetoing the bill, Truman had confirmed the sovereignty of the Navajo Nation and reversed the explicit actions of Congress that would have allowed state authority onto the reservation. As the bench memorandum explained, the 1949 bill

> was vetoed by President Truman solely because of this provision concerning jurisdiction. In his veto message the President stated that the bill would "extend State civil and criminal laws and court jurisdiction to the Navajo-Hopi Reservations which are now under Federal and tribal laws and courts." He noted that the Navajo were probably the Indian group least prepared to go out and mingle with their neighbours and be governed by state law. He further stated that it "would be unjust and unwise to compel them [Navajos] to abide by State laws written to fill other needs than theirs," and noted that the Navajos requested a veto for this reason.[25]

In 1950 a revised Navajo rehabilitation bill became law, but it did not contain the provision sanctioning state law on the Navajo reservation.

In addition, the Supreme Court's analysis of the historical background to a 1953 act, Public Law 280, involved the presumption of inherent tribal sovereignty on the reservation. In accordance with this idea, tribes retained sovereignty on the reservation until Congress reversed it and allowed in state authority. The same bench memorandum explained this position:

> In 1953, Congress undertook some major legislation in this area. It passed a bill giving state courts jurisdiction over civil and criminal matters involving Indians on reservations but it specified the states involved—and Arizona was not included. . . . The legislative history of the bill is most informative. In discussing the bill the House Committee stated: As a practical matter, the enforcement of law and order among the Indians in the Indian Country has been left largely to the Indian groups themselves. . . . This would appear to be persuasive proof of Congress' intent and understanding of the present state of the law.[26]

Even with congressional permission, the state still had to legislate to gain control on the reservation. If the Arizona state legislature did not pass a relevant act, then the state forfeited an opportunity to gain a foothold on the Navajo reservation: "No action has been taken by the state to comply with the provisions of the 1953 Congressional Act," and therefore "this history should control any general propositions such as implying jurisdiction in the absence of Congressional restriction."[27] Some justices supported this presumption regarding the 1953 act. Important for the Navajo Nation, Chief Justice Warren and Justice William J. Brennan supported the presumption of inherent tribal sovereignty.[28]

Without the introduction of state legislation to confirm the actions of Congress, Chief Justice Warren said, "[the] 1953 Act gave jurisdiction conditionally—Arizona does not want to carry expense of that change."[29] Therefore, Arizona had to be willing to take the burdens of the 1953 act. Warren pointed out that "the 1953 statute gives Arizona its chance if it will assume burdens that go with it."[30] Because the states did not take the responsibilities established by the 1953 act, Warren believed that the question was to be answered in favor of the tribes and tribal jurisdiction. The question, he said, should "come out with the Indians," and it "goes on tribal forum."[31] Justice Brennan concurred with Warren, observing that the Court "must get to 1953 Act."[32] Nevertheless, the solicitor general cautioned the Supreme Court against using the principle of inherent tribal sovereignty and the "broad attack" to decide the case.

The opinion of the Supreme Court may have been informed by the pro-Indian interpretations and compassionate beliefs of certain justices. Justice Hugo Lafayette Black was generally supportive of Native American rights, as was Justice William O. Douglas.[33] In a letter to Murray Lincoln, chief justice of the Navajos, Justice Black wrote, "You know, I am also sure, the great interest and sympathy I feel for the Tribes that seek to preserve their ways of life."[34]

Black's pro-Indian stance may have helped convince wavering justices such as Felix Frankfurter, who did not support tribal sovereignty in early November 1958 but was doing so by the end of the month.[35] On the *Williams* opinion circulated on December 23, 1958, Justice Frankfurter wrote a response to Justice Black noting the importance of *Worcester* (1832): "And I duly note your carom against 'rites position' . . . in recalling the *Worcester v. Georgia* affair."[36]

Justice Black may, then, have helped with the resurgence of Native American rights in 1959. The position of Chief Justice Warren also seemed to be conciliatory and considered. In a memorandum to Justice Black, Warren asked for an early draft opinion to be changed: "In the middle of page 4, I am wondering if the words, 'sufficiently high stage of economic and social development' might not be softened a bit so far as the Indians are concerned by saying 'acceptable stage' or 'acceptable standard of economic and social development.'"[37]

The Opinion in *Williams v. Lee*

At an internal meeting to discuss the case, on November 21, 1958, the Court was unanimous and voted to reverse the lower court's decision to apply state law rather than tribal sovereignty.[38] The interpretations of the individual justices were reflected in the *Williams* opinion authored by Justice Black. The Court's unanimous opinion outlined how the sovereignty doctrine had changed from its foundations in *Worcester v. Georgia* (1832). From the outset, Justice Black praised Chief Justice Marshall's *Worcester* opinion, describing it as "one of his most courageous and eloquent opinions" and observing its legal importance: "Despite bitter criticism and the defiance of Georgia which refused to obey this Court's mandate in Worcester the broad principles of that decision came to be accepted as law." In fact, though, in the 127 years from *Worcester* to *Williams* the sovereignty doctrine had been modified by congressional policies and Supreme Court case law. In 1832 the tribes had exclusive authority over the reservations; by 1959 this exclusivity had given way to the application of state law on the reservations only on certain and specialized occasions, described by Justice Black as the areas where "essential tribal relations were not involved and where the rights of Indians would not be jeopardized, but the basic policy of Worcester has remained." Only specific parts of the *Worcester* policy had changed, but there was still deference shown by the Court toward tribal sovereignty: "Thus, suits by Indians against outsiders in state courts have been sanctioned. . . . And state courts have been allowed to try non-Indians who committed crimes against each other on a reservation. . . . But if the crime was by or against an Indian, tribal jurisdiction or that expressly conferred on other courts by Congress has remained exclusive."[39] Despite the modifications to *Worcester,* the Indian sovereignty doctrine had survived.

In 1959, the Navajos and all Native American tribes retained inherent sovereignty on the reservation unless Congress revoked parts of that sovereignty or the Supreme Court limited the legal protections afforded by *Worcester.* These principles were summed up by the introduction of what has become known as the "infringement test" by the *Williams* court: "Essentially, absent governing Acts of Congress, the question has always been whether the state action infringed on the right of reservation Indians to make their own laws and be ruled by them."[40] In essence, the tribes retained sovereignty on the reservation until either Congress took it away or it was proved that state authority did not infringe on tribal government, and only then was state authority applicable on the reservation. This test was not as strong as the *Worcester* principle, but as William C. Canby observed, "In theory, at least, this test precludes state interference with tribal self-government no matter how important the state's interest may be."[41] Although the test did give rise to the interpretation that state law existed on the reservation until it infringed on tribal government (see below), the *Williams* court applied the Indian sovereignty doctrine.

The *Williams* opinion overruled the primary rationale of the lower courts and rejected the extension of *Draper v. United States* into a general rule to allow state jurisdiction over civil suits on the reservation.[42] Members were allowed to sue outsiders in state court, but it did not follow in *Williams* that the states had authority on the reservation.[43] Instead, tribal sovereignty existed unless it was removed by an explicit act of Congress.[44] In the most important part of the opinion, Justice Black summed up the application of the sovereignty doctrine by the Supreme Court: "It is immaterial that respondent is not an Indian. He was on the Reservation and the transaction with an Indian took place there. The cases in this Court have consistently guarded the authority of Indian governments over their reservations. Congress recognized this authority in the Navajos in the Treaty of 1868, and has done so ever since. If this power is to be taken away from them, it is for Congress to do it."[45]

In language reminiscent of Chief Justice John Marshall, the opinion of Justice Black applied inherent tribal sovereignty on the reservation where tribal authority was dominant over state law and only Congress had the authority to take it away.[46] The words of Justice Black had returned the principles and presumptions of federal Indian law and the Indian sovereignty doctrine firmly back to those articulated in the time of *Worcester*. This line of thinking matched the general assessment of the powers of the tribe described by Cohen in the 1941 *Handbook*. In an attempt to reconcile the development of Supreme Court case law and divergent federal policies from 1832, Cohen, in a seminal passage of his work, defined the powers of the tribe this way:

> The whole course of judicial decision on the nature of Indian tribal powers is marked by adherence to three fundamental principles: (1) An Indian tribe possesses, in the first instance, all the powers of any sovereign state. (2) Conquest renders the tribe subject to the legislative power of the United States and, in substance, terminates the

external powers of sovereignty of the tribe, *e.g.*, its power to enter into treaties with foreign nations, but does not by itself affect the internal sovereignty of the tribe, *i.e.*, its powers of local self-government. (3) These powers are subject to qualification by treaties and by express legislation of Congress, but, save as thus expressly qualified, full powers of internal sovereignty are vested in the Indian tribes and in their duly constituted organs of government.[47]

The tribes had authority, power, and sovereignty, termed inherent sovereignty, over all lands and people on the reservation unless authority was explicitly withdrawn, divested, or annulled by a clear and plain act of Congress or by treaty. In addition, Cohen's definition was a reminder that the tribes had always had inherent sovereignty over lands and people on those lands.

Moreover, the *Williams* court ruled that tribal authority was concomitant with territorial sovereignty. Navajo criminal and civil authority was applicable to every person on the reservation: "Today the Navajo Courts of Indian Offenses exercise broad criminal and civil jurisdiction which covers suits by outsiders against Indian defendants. No Federal Act has given state courts jurisdiction over such controversies."[48] Alison Dussias points out that the actions of the Supreme Court "treated tribal authority as being geographically-based, referring to the authority of tribal governments over their reservations; the lack of tribal membership of the individual being required to seek redress only in tribal court was irrelevant."[49]

Williams v. Lee (1959) and State Sovereignty

Despite the positive nature of the *Williams* opinion for the Navajos and the rest of Native America, during the *Williams* case the justices considered moving away from the sovereignty doctrine. The Court examined the idea of weakening tribal sovereignty by focusing on federal authority as a way to prohibit the application of state law on the reservation. This would have moved the focus of deciding federal Indian law cases from acknowledging the sovereignty of the tribes to basing decisions on a purely federal-versus-state basis.

Throughout the processes involved in the *Williams* case, members of the Court considered using the principle relied on by the lower court, which held that state law existed on the reservation until it was prohibited by congressional authority; congressional silence on the subject was considered to sanction state law on the reservation—and the foundation of the silent revolution was thereby laid.[50] This principle relied on one primary factor, the inherent sovereignty of the state on the reservation. Against this background, a clerk's memorandum to Justice Douglas read, "I do not feel any alarm at requiring Indians to submit to state court jurisdiction in civil suits until Congress decrees otherwise."[51] This position led Chief Justice Warren to question the role of state authority on the reservation.

The total exclusion of state law over nonmembers on the reservation was a concern to Warren, particularly the indefinite prohibition of state authority: "[I] don't want to say never any [state] jurisdiction on the reservations," and "[I am] not for [going] all the way and say[ing the] . . . state can't have any jurisdiction."[52] This general concern about prohibiting all state law to operate on the reservation fed into the justices thinking of using only federal authority to decide issues of tribal versus state authority.

Several justices mooted using congressional authority to decide the question of state law on the reservation. At conference on November 21, 1958, Justice Frankfurter wanted to use federal regulations exclusively to prevent state law from being applied on the reservation, noting that he "would rely on [regulations] . . . but [wouldn't] go further."[53] This reliance on the federal trader statutes was based on a provision that encouraged nonmembers to trade on the reservation at their own risk. A clerk's bench memorandum read, "A trader may extend credit to Indians, but such credit will be at the trader's own risk."[54] This provision was also explained in a clerk's memorandum as "a regulation which applies to respondent [nonmember] since he was granted permission to open his store on the reservation states that all credit shall be at the trader's risk."[55] In other words, congressional legislation automatically prohibited nonmembers from acting against tribes because they consented to trade at their own risk. Individual justices such as Frankfurter supported this interpretation of federal authority, stating that the "regulation holds up," as did Warren, who "thinks traders do so at own risk."[56] Federal government lawyers arguing the case also supported the use of federal statutes to prevent the general application of state law in the reservation.

The *Williams* court recognized the conflicting ideological positions taken by the federal government and the tribes. A 1958 bench memorandum from one of the chief justice's clerks showed that the federal government wanted the Court to use congressional authority rather than inherent tribal sovereignty to decide the merits of the case. The position adopted by the federal government lawyers, termed the "narrow attack," was "based upon interpretation of the

Federal regulation stating that Indian traders sold on credit at the trader's own risk. This was asserted to deprive the state court of jurisdiction." This strategy was in direct conflict with the position adopted by the Navajos, described in the bench memorandum as "an unusual position" in which the tribe "has not pressed the second, limited attack hoping to prevail on the broad ground. However, the govt . . . has adopted the narrow attack and urges this Court to reverse on the limited ground without reaching the broad ground pressed by the [tribe]."[57]

The government was concerned with the broad position taken by the Navajos and urged the Court to rely on federal authority to oust state law from the reservation rather than reinvigorate the sovereignty doctrine: "The govt argues that the question of jurisdiction may well depend upon the type of subject matter involved and other factors so that this Court should not lay down a broad rule covering all possible case[s]." Despite this conflict, the bench memorandum explained that the government's reliance on statutes was a viable way to decide the merits of the case: "Here the federal policy is clearly set forth in the regulation and an argument can be made that a state court may not take jurisdiction of a case in which the plaintiff [nonmember] is seeking relief barred by federal law." Furthermore, the government wanted the Court to use regulations because this was considered stronger than using tribal sovereignty and was consistent with the historic relationship between the federal government and the tribes: "Indians are traditionally wards of the Federal govt and this regulation gives the Indians greater protection if it is interpreted to be a jurisdictional bar." This position was also favorable because numerous state courts were applying the rationale that states had jurisdiction on the reservation unless Congress precluded state authority. It was clear that the federal government wanted tribal cases to be analyzed and decided within a federal-versus-state framework, so that federal law would protect tribal claims.[58]

Importantly, the federal government wanted the Court to prevent the reinvigoration of the sovereignty doctrine because of federal policy concerns. The government believed that reliance on statutes would prevent broad tribal jurisdiction on the reservation and urged the Court to avoid laying down a rule broad enough to cover all possible cases. The "narrow attack" suited the aims of the federal government, described in the clerk's memorandum as "the policy considerations behind the regulations." The government position was presented to the justices as the stronger argument, because reliance on tribal sovereignty would not result in "winning the particular case before the Court—which involves $82 [the outstanding debt owed by Paul and Lorena Williams to Hugh Lee]."[59] Indeed, many justices initially relied on the use of federal regulations and openly questioned using exclusive tribal authority on the reservations.

Thus, a close inspection of the documents used in the *Williams* case shows that the seeds of the silent revolution were planted by arguments from federal government lawyers and actively considered by many of the serving justices. Indeed, many justices were initially swayed by the idea of using federal statutes to prohibit the application of state law on the reservation. Despite the overwhelming success of the published *Williams* opinion, beneath the surface and within the corridors and offices of the Court the justices were considering the erosion of the sovereignty doctrine and inherent tribal sovereignty. In cases involving state versus tribal claims, the movement away from inherent tribal sovereignty was primarily based on the use of federal authority, not the sovereignty doctrine, to protect tribes from state law.

Kake v. Egan (1962)

Only three years after a ringing endorsement of tribal sovereignty, the Supreme Court in *Kake v. Egan* and *Metlakatla Indians v. Egan* used the idea mooted by the *Williams* court and determined that congressional authority and not tribal sovereignty ousted general state law from tribal lands and the reservation. These were the first cases of the modern era to apply the rationale that states had authority on tribal lands and reservation lands unless it was precluded by congressional legislation. Tribal sovereignty was not considered in either case.

Kake v. Egan (1962) involved a question of whether federal law prevented the application of state law over tribal members on tribal lands.[60] The case asked whether the State of Alaska, pursuant to a statute, could prohibit the use of the salmon traps operated by the incorporated communities of the Thlinget Indians. The use of the traps was sanctioned by permits from the Army Corps of Engineers and the U.S. Forest Service and by regulations issued by the U.S. Department of the Interior. The tribe involved did not have a designated reservation, and the case therefore concerned tribal lands but not reservation lands. Despite this, the Supreme Court used the ruling to extend the general presumption that state law applied over tribal members on reservation lands, in direct conflict with *Worcester* and *Williams*. The *Kake* court justified this process by using case law from the late nineteenth century.

The *Kake* case applied the line of thinking discussed but finally rejected by the *Williams* court that congressional legislation be used to either allow or prevent claims of state authority on the reservation. A clerk's bench memorandum to Chief Justice Warren showed that the Court assessed the merits of the case purely on a federal-versus-state basis: "The basic question involved is whether the federal govt or the State of Alaska has the exclusive authority to regulate the fishing rights of certain Indian communities situated in Alaska." The evidence presented in the case pointed toward the protection of the Alaskan tribes through government regulations. The bench memorandum pointed out that the tribes "were organized as an Indian community under federal law, and have been dependent upon federal protection and regulation for many years. . . . they are the type of Indians the federal govt has traditionally regulated and protected." This emphasis on federal control led to the presumption that tribal fishing rights would be protected against state law. The bench memorandum read that these fishing rights "have been strictly regulated by the Sec. of Interior since the villages were organized. Moreover, since 1948, the Indians have been permitted to use fish traps."[61] This exclusive use of federal regulations meant that questions of tribal sovereignty were ignored.

The case did not involve the issue of state law on a reservation, but the *Kake* court treated tribal lands as reservation lands in order to support its rationale. It argued that state law on reservations was justified by the development of nineteenth-century case law, which fundamentally weakened the principle of *Worcester*.[62] The development of case law contrary to *Worcester* forced the modern-day Court to reassess the general presumption that state law was totally excluded from the reservation. In his opinion, Justice Frankfurter noted, "The general notion drawn from Chief Justice Marshall's opinion in Worcester v. Georgia . . . that an Indian reservation is a distinct nation within whose boundaries state law cannot penetrate, has yielded to closer analysis when confronted, in the course of subsequent developments, with diverse concrete situations." He also interpreted this general weakening of *Worcester* as leading the Court in 1880 to declare that "the Court no longer viewed reservations as distinct nations. On the contrary, it was said that a reservation was in many cases a part of the surrounding State or Territory, and subject to its jurisdiction except as forbidden by federal law."[63] This interpretation of historic case law undermined modern-day tribal sovereignty.[64]

The *Kake* court also analyzed the development of congressional legislation from the 1920s to the 1950s, which allowed more state authority onto the reservations, and noted that "the influence of state law increased rather than decreased." During the 1920s, Congress allowed the states to enforce both compulsory school attendance and sanitation laws on the reservations. A small number of states during the 1940s applied criminal jurisdiction on some of the reservations, and in the 1950s the federal policy of termination abolished the Klamath and Menominee reservations and sanctioned numerous states to have full civil and criminal authority on certain reservations. "Thus Congress has to a substantial degree opened the doors of reservations to state laws, in marked contrast to what prevailed in the time of Chief Justice Marshall."[65]

The *Kake* opinion allowed the application of state law over the tribes because there was no tribal reservation with defined boundaries. The Court associated this set of facts with a case dealing with an off-reservation setting and applied the rule that state law applied unless prohibited by Congress.[66] The Court did not consider the purchase of tribal lands by the federal government and the presence of explicit federal regulations and permits that sanctioned the use of tribal fishing traps on the purchased lands to be relevant to the case: "Congress has neither authorized the use of fish traps at Kake and Angoon nor empowered the Secretary of the Interior to do so."[67] It seems that the opinion should have been limited in principle to cases dealing only with state law over tribes in off-reservation settings. However, the Supreme Court significantly broadened the case to include the application of state law in on-reservation settings, in significant contrast to *Williams*.

Thus, the *Kake* court undermined *Williams* and its infringement test in order to allow state authority into Indian country. The test could have protected tribal interests, but the Court interpreted it in a manner unfavorable to the tribes and tribal sovereignty; as Canby notes, the test "was capable of being interpreted to permit increased exercise of state power within Indian country."[68] In fact, this test was turned on its head. The *Kake* court applied the presumption that state law was applicable on the reservation until it was proved that it adversely influenced tribal authority: "[State law] may be applied to Indians unless such application would interfere with reservation self-government or impair a right granted or reserved by federal law."[69] Only then would state law be nullified. The *Kake* court "clearly suggested that state law and state court jurisdiction could be extended to Indians as well as non-Indians in Indian country, so long as there did not seem to be a direct interference with the tribal government itself."[70]

The 1962 Supreme Court had, then, created the impression that inherent state sovereignty existed on the reservations. This position was made clear by the words chosen by Justice Frankfurter to highlight the inherent right of the states on the reservations: "In the absence of a limiting treaty obligation or Congressional enactment each state had a right to exercise jurisdiction over Indian reservations within its boundaries."[71] The *Kake* court dismissed the broad *Williams* decision, observing that "decisions of this Court are few as to the power of the States when not granted Congressional authority to regulate matters affecting Indians." The *Williams* case was not viewed by the *Kake* court as authoritative; instead, it was regarded simply as "the latest decision" in federal Indian law.[72]

Metlakatla Indians v. Egan (1962)

The companion case to *Kake, Metlakatla Indians v. Egan* (1962), applied the issue of congressional authority versus state authority to decide whether state law was applicable over tribal members on a reservation.[73] The case considered whether the secretary of the interior had the authority to grant regulations allowing the Metlakatla Indian Community to build and use salmon traps on lands Congress had set aside as a reservation under an 1891 act. The presence of a reservation led the Supreme Court to apply the presumption that congressional authority and not tribal sovereignty protected tribal members from state law.

A 1961 bench memorandum to Chief Justice Warren noted that the tribe wanted "freedom from state control inside of a properly defined reservation." But such freedom relied on the primacy of congressional authority over state law. The bench memorandum read, "The US can exercise all of the regulation of the reservation."[74] The protection of the tribes from state law relied on federal statutes and the historic guardian/ward relationship between the United States and Native America. Chief Justice Warren supported the use of federal authority to prohibit state law on the reservation, pointing out that the "cases come down to stat[utory] construction—US now confines its power territorially."[75] In contrast to the *Kake* case, the Supreme Court and in particular Chief Justice Warren supported the principle of the trust relationship to protect the tribes from state law. The trust relationship involved an exclusive relationship between the federal government and Native America and endorsed federal protection over the tribes. The states were excluded from this relationship. As Warren described the situation, "Congress intended to retain wardship over Indians and preserve and protect them—to hold contrary would be to cast Indians adrift," and "Indians get rights in addition to [illegible] generally because of wardship. Think Congress intended to retain wardship and regulate them by its laws."[76] In contrast to the *Kake* case, the Metlakatla Tribe successfully relied on federal authority. The primary reason for this success was the presence of a tribal reservation, considered to be dispositive. As the bench memorandum to Warren noted, the tribe "claim[s] only the freedom from state control inside of a properly defined reservation. This, I believe, is a reasonable claim regardless of the merits."[77]

The *Metlakatla* opinion, written by Justice Frankfurter, explained that the reservation was the fundamental difference between this and the *Kake* case. The Court ruled that a reservation allowed federal authority to protect tribal fishing rights against state law: "The reservation itself was Indian property," and congressional authority through a statute "clearly preserves federal authority over both the reservation and the fishing right then existing." Senator Gruening of Alaska saw the presence of a reservation as a unique characteristic that directly influenced the outcome of the case: "The Court's decision in the Metlakatla case differs in its conclusion from the Kake and Angoon cases only because of Metlakatla's historically different and unique legal status." Thus, in this case federal authority formed an important role in deciding whether state law was applicable on the reservation.[78]

❖ Despite the presence of a reservation in one case and only tribal lands in another, both *Metlakatla* and *Kake* relied exclusively on congressional or federal authority to prohibit the application of state law over tribal affairs and tribal lands. No party to these cases relied on tribal sovereignty. Taken together, *Metlakatla* and *Kake* ensured that state law was applicable over reservations and tribal lands unless it was explicitly precluded by the actions of Congress.

The primacy of federal legislation and authority, considered in *Williams* and applied in *Metlakatla* and *Kake*, became an idea with which the Court felt comfortable. After 1962 it had the option of applying the Indian sovereignty doctrine or using federal authority to determine whether state law was applicable on the reservation. This choice of case law meant that the justices could and would use the law to suit their own ideas about the correct use of tribal sovereignty. As Blake A. Watson points out, "The ability to manipulate presumptions, and transform doctrinal law sub silentio, contributes greatly to the thrust and parry of federal Indian law."[79] *Williams, Kake,* and *Metlakatla* were the clear beginnings of an ideological battle between the Indian sovereignty doctrine and integrationist principles.

Warren Trading Post v. Tax Commission (1965)

The cases of *Warren Trading Post v. Tax Commission* (1965) and *Kennerly v. District Court of Montana* (1971) demonstrate that the Supreme Court was torn between the use of tribal sovereignty and the idea of congressional authority to determine the authority of the tribes or the states on the reservations.

The *Warren Trading Post* court relied primarily on federal authority to prohibit the application of state law over a nonmember trader on a reservation.[80] The case addressed whether the State of Arizona had the right to impose a 2 percent sales and income tax on a nonmember trading business, Warren Trading Post Company, on the Navajo reservation; the trader was there pursuant to a federal license granted by the commissioner of Indian affairs.

Congressional authority predominantly informed the thinking of the justices in this case. Chief Justice Warren viewed congressional legislation, also known as federal preemption, as the correct tool to decide the case, stating that "there's preemption in Cong[ress] leg[islation] which appoints Indian traders."[81] Federal regulations governed nonmember traders on the reservation, and this reliance on federal authority was communicated in a clerk's memorandum to Justice William O. Douglas: "The tax is inconsistent with a comprehensive system of . . . federal regulation of commerce with the Indians occupying and pre-empting the field."[82] This process of thinking appeared to weaken the Court's reliance on tribal sovereignty. A clerk's bench memorandum symbolized this movement away from the sovereignty doctrine: "Since it appears that Congress has occupied this area, I recommend that the Court reverse the decision of SC Ariz. on this ground, and leave, to another time, the issues . . . whether these state taxes interfere with Indian self-government."[83]

The guardian of tribal sovereignty in the post-1959 period was the *Williams* case. So when Justice Hugo Black removed the single reference to *Williams* in a revised draft opinion, it further moved the thinking of the justices toward the use of congressional power. The initial draft, dated April 1 read,

> As this Court recognized *Williams v. Lee,* 358 U.S. 217, 222–223, Arizona had not, and apparently still has not, chosen to assume any burdens of providing for the welfare of the Indians on the reservation. It obviously would be a marked departure from the long standing,

firmly established federal policy in this field to allow the State to tax transactions on the reservation involving Indians when their most vital government services are provided not by the State out of state revenues, but by the Federal Government or out of tribal resources.[84]

But in his revised draft of April 27, Black omitted the first sentence. Thus, the Supreme Court used the trader statutes to strike down a state tax imposed on a nonmember trader. The Court "based its decision on federal pre-emption grounds . . . [where] Congress had the legislative authority to control any subject matter."[85]

Reliance on federal authority undermined the *Williams* infringement test and created the presumption that state law existed on the reservation until removed by Congress. This continued the line of thinking introduced by the *Kake* court, which limited the broad interpretation of the *Williams* infringement test. A clerk's bench memorandum to Chief Justice Warren described the presumption that was beginning to guide the justices: "Unless Congress has actually regulated, by specific statutory enactment, or unless there is interference with tribal self-government . . . the state may tax a trader as it taxes all other businesses in the state." The weakening of the *Williams* test and the movement of the Court away from the sovereignty doctrine was seized upon by the states in their courtroom battle over jurisdiction on the reservations. The bench memorandum went on to point out that the state relied on the counterinterpretation of the *Williams* test to highlight that a state tax "in no way impinges on the right of reservation Indians to make their own laws and be ruled by them."[86] Despite the clear reliance of the Court on federal authority, there was also reliance, in part, on the Indian sovereignty doctrine.

Individual justices were concerned about ignoring the sovereignty doctrine, and the final *Warren Trading Post* opinion addressed this issue. Chief Justice Warren was concerned about the idea that state taxation on the reservation was justified if the state provided for the welfare of the tribe. His argument explicitly revolved around the idea of tribal sovereignty on the reservation, which existed to prevent state taxation there until Congress authorized the state tax. A bench memorandum to Warren summed up the concerns of the chief justice: "It is clear that Arizona could not impose a gross receipts tax on Indian traders simply by assuming responsibility for the Indians, at least not in the absence of additional federal legislation."[87] On April 27, Justice Hugo Black removed the overriding concern of Chief Justice

Warren from his draft opinion.[88] Concerns over unchecked state authority on the reservation ultimately led the final opinion to acknowledge the importance of the sovereignty doctrine: "We think the assessment and collection of this tax would to a substantial extent frustrate the evident congressional purpose of ensuring that no burden shall be imposed upon Indian traders for trading with Indians on reservations except as authorized by Acts of Congress or by valid regulations promulgated under those Acts."[89] State law was not valid until Congress acted to allow the states to tax.

The *Warren Trading Post* court opinion relied on federal authority and acknowledged the importance of the sovereignty doctrine in post-1959 case law. Justice Black addressed these two factors when he wrote of the changes regarding state law on the reservations. He observed that the reservations were once free from state control but that "certain state laws have been permitted to apply to activities on Indian reservations, where those laws are specifically authorized by acts of Congress, or where they clearly do not interfere with federal policies concerning the reservations."[90] Congressional authority and tribal sovereignty were present in the thinking of the justices and in the opinion of the Court, a dual strand from which the Court could chose to prohibit the application of state law on the reservation.

Kennerly v. District Court of Montana (1971)

In *Kennerly v. District Court of Montana* (1971), the Supreme Court primarily used congressional legislation to prevent the application of state law over tribal members on a reservation.[91] In 1964, Blackfeet members bought food on credit from a shop located in a town incorporated under the laws of the State of Montana on the exterior boundaries of the Blackfeet reservation. An action was brought in the courts of Montana against the tribal members for the debt incurred from the purchases. The tribal members appealed, arguing that the state courts had no authority because the transaction took place on the reservation. Although a 1953 act allowed Montana to assume civil jurisdiction on the reservation, the state had not explicitly legislated to assume jurisdiction. However, in 1967 the Blackfeet tribal council passed an act allowing concurrent jurisdiction so that tribal and state courts were allowed to hear civil suits against tribal members. This tribal action had to comply with the Indian Civil Rights Act of 1968. Unfortunately for the Blackfeet, the actions of the tribal council did not follow the demands set out in the 1968 act and the Montana courts did not have jurisdiction over tribal members. The Blackfeet tribal council used tribal sovereignty and consented to the application of state law over tribal members in certain circumstances.

Issues concerning the impact of state law over tribal members on the reservation were controlled by the *Williams* infringement test. Because *Kennerly* involved a fundamental jurisdictional and legal change to tribal authority on the reservation, the Supreme Court opinion addressed the purpose of the test: "The Court in Williams, in the process of discussing the general question of state action impinging on the affairs of reservation Indians, noted that 'essentially, absent governing Acts of Congress, the question has always been whether the state action infringed on the right of reservation Indians to make their own laws and be ruled by them.'"[92]

In a gradual movement of the Court away from tribal sovereignty, the presumption grew that states had jurisdiction on the reservation and over tribal members unless congressional legislation ousted state law or until state law infringed on the tribe in question. The *Kennerly* court applied the *Williams* test. Because an act of Congress existed to prevent the tribal council from allowing concurrent jurisdiction on the reservation, the principle of the test required that the presence of an act automatically nullified state law over tribal members on the reservation, regardless of whether it affected tribal government. Although this decision supported tribal sovereignty and the independence of the Blackfeet from state law, the Supreme Court used the idea of congressional authority to oust state law from the reservation.

The Federal Policy of Tribal Self-Determination

The federal policy of tribal self-determination ended the termination period and symbolized a victory for Native America over the federal government. Throughout the termination era, much of the Native American population wanted the federal government to reinvigorate tribal rights. Through political protest and legal battles, Native America succeeded in reestablishing the importance of tribal sovereignty and tribal rights in the American political system. The new era of tribal self-determination was confirmation that the federal government once again recognized the importance of tribal sovereignty. In 1970, President Richard Nixon recognized the need for tribes to make their own decisions, sanctioning the idea of a more autonomous and culturally free Native America: "The time has come to break decisively with the past and to create conditions for a new era in which the Indian future is determined by Indian acts and Indian decisions." Nixon viewed the new policy era as one that "would explicitly affirm the integrity and right to continued existence of all Indian tribes and Alaska native governments."[93] The underlying principle decreed by Congress was the preservation of the tribes within the boundaries of the United States guided by the process of self-determination.

In 1948, Congress had introduced a definition of Indian country and simultaneously codified existing case law.[94] The original definition of Indian country covered only tribal criminal jurisdiction on the reservation, but in *DeCoteau v. District County Court* (1975) the Supreme Court extended it to cover tribal civil jurisdiction on the reservation.[95] Title 18, Part I, Chapter 53, Section 1151 of the United States Code defines Indian country as

(a) all land within the limits of any Indian reservation under the jurisdiction of the United States Government, notwithstanding the issuance of any patent, and, including rights-of-way running through the reservation,

(b) all dependent Indian communities within the borders of the United States whether within the original or subsequently acquired territory thereof, and whether within or without the limits of a state, and

(c) all Indian allotments, the Indian titles to which have not been extinguished, including rights-of-way running through the same.

McClanahan v. Arizona State Tax Commission (1973)

Warren Trading Post and *Kennerly* had mainly relied on congressional authority to prevent the application of state law on the reservation, but the sovereignty doctrine also informed these decisions. Despite the general movement of the Supreme Court toward congressional authority and the presumption that state law applied on the reservation unless it was revoked by an act of Congress or until it infringed on the tribes, the Court continued to value the sovereignty doctrine. In 1973, however, the Court began to favor congressional authority to restrict the application of state law on Native American reservations— particularly in *McClanahan v. Arizona State Tax Commission* (1973), *Mescalero Apache v. Jones* (1973), and *Tonasket v. Washington* (1973)—in so doing counteracting policies of Congress and the "era of tribal self-determination" established by President Nixon.

The case of *McClanahan v. Arizona State Tax Commission* involved a Navajo member living on the Navajo reservation who had to pay $16.20 in taxes to the State of Arizona for work done exclusively on the reservation.[96] The tribal member filed for a refund and appealed. The Supreme Court ruled that the State of Arizona did not have jurisdiction to impose a tax on income earned by a Navajo exclusively on the reservation because it was forbidden by federal statutes and an 1868 treaty.[97]

In this case the justices supported the principle of general state authority on the reservation and the corollary principle that state authority also applied over nonmembers on the reservation. *McClanahan* was the first case of the modern era, post-1959, to discuss openly and actually apply the idea that state law existed on the reservation until removed by Congress. Justice William Rehnquist supported this right of the states, pointing out that his "own position leaves room for State to tax non-resident Indians—unless stat[ute] prohibits."[98] Indeed, he concluded that states "should be able to impose a general tax [and] our cases do not foreclose this."[99]

Justice Potter Stewart also supported the rights of the states and believed that the diminishment of the *Worcester* principle had allowed the integration of state and tribal land boundaries. He pointed out that the "pendulum has swung from Worcester v. Georgia to integration of Indians—Indian always win unless he's against a [illegible]."[100]

Justice Thurgood Marshall definitively summed up the position of the Court in a memorandum to conference in 1973.[101] The memorandum explained the difference between the imposition of state law over tribal members in *McClanahan* and the imposition of state law over nonmembers in *Kahn v. Arizona State Tax Commission* (1973). Marshall supported the presumption that states had authority over nonmembers on the reservation in contrast to *McClanahan*: "In *McClanahan,* we held that Arizona lacked jurisdiction to tax the appellant in that case for income earned within the reservation. However, our holding was expressly limited to *Indians* who derived their income from reservation sources. Since appellants here [in *Kahn*] are non-Indians, *McClanahan* is not controlling. This Court's prior cases suggest that the State may tax the activity of non-Indians within a reservation except in cases where the federal government has acted to preempt the field."[102]

The Supreme Court dismissed the *Kahn* case and the original verdict stood. Although Justices Douglas and Brennan dissented, their rationale was based on the same interpretation of the case as that of Justice Marshall. Marshall's *Kahn* comment ignored the sovereignty doctrine and the *Williams* case, which supported inherent tribal sovereignty on the reservation, and symbolized the movement of the Supreme Court toward the use of federal authority to protect tribal interests. As N. Bruce Duthu suggests, in the *Khan* memorandum it was clear that the Supreme Court recognized "protectible state interests in Indian Country, at least where non-Indians are involved" and took "a surprisingly solicitous view of state power in Indian Country with no apparent protection for tribal sovereignty outside of affirmative federal legislation."[103]

The appellants (the representatives of the tribes) in *McClanahan* adopted a legal position that was informed by the movement of the Supreme Court toward limiting the influence of *Worcester* and *Williams*. Their position was outlined in a clerk's bench memorandum. The appellants described how the broad rule of *Worcester* had been modified where state interests over nonmembers on the reservation were concerned. The modification of *Worcester*, the memorandum read, "upholds the power of the state to tax the property of non-Indians located on an Indian reservation . . . [and recognizes] an abandonment of the notion that reservations were not physically within a state."[104] The weakening of *Worcester* also allowed the appellants to point out that the Supreme Court could interpret the *Williams* test in a way that sanctioned state law on the reservation. The appellants argued that the test was ambiguous, observing that "the-interference-with-tribal-government test is very broad, and it will lead to state inherent jurisdiction even when the Court and Congress have not considered the issue."[105] Thus, although tribal sovereignty as a stand-alone principle was not strong enough to oust state law over nonmembers on the reservation, it was strong enough to protect tribal members from state law.

Individual justices supported a reinvigoration of the sovereignty doctrine to protect tribal members against state law. Chief Justice Warren Burger was adamant that state law could not be used to obstruct the right of tribal governments to collect taxation revenues from its members: "In depriving Indian tribes of source, this infringes on self government and Congress has not granted state this authority."[106] Justice Byron White agreed that Congress had not granted permission for the states to tax tribal members and pointed out that "on reservation activities unless Congress expressly permits, states can't tax."[107] Justice Harry Blackmun summed up the questions related to the application of state law over tribal members on the reservation when he noted that "precedent favors the Indian."[108]

The protection of tribal members from state law did not rely on the application of federal authority; instead, it was inherent tribal sovereignty. A clerk's memorandum to Justice Blackmun set out this position: "If Congressional authorisation was the test for state jurisdiction, there would have been no need to formulate the *Williams v. Lee* test."[109] Only congressional authority could remove the protections offered by tribal sovereignty against the imposition of state law over tribal members on the reservation. The position taken by many of the justices regarding state law over tribal members was summed up in a clerk's memorandum: the state "cannot (in the absence of specific congressional authorisation) tax income earned within the reservation by Indian residents of the reservation."[110] The justices viewed this interpretation of the law as a way to balance the protections available to the tribes against state law with the states' rights to more authority over nonmembers on the reservation where "the Court and Congress have moved to integrate Indians into white society."[111] The protections of tribal sovereignty over tribal members reversed the development of a presumption from 1959 that states had authority over tribal members on the reservation until it infringed on tribal government.[112]

Clearly, the justices were relying on Navajo sovereignty and not federal authority to protect tribal members against state law. Still, one justice wanted the Court to continue with the presumption developed from 1959. Justice Rehnquist supported the right of state law to apply over tribal members on the reservation until prohibited by congressional legislation. Rehnquist wanted to affirm the decision of the lower court, which allowed the state to tax the tribal member involved, because no congressional legislation existed to prevent the state from doing so.[113] He pointed out that "so long as State doesn't coerce the reservations to collect tax but can reach every-layer if base [illegible]. State can tax unless Congress says can't."[114] A memorandum from Rehnquist to Justice Marshall confirmed his position: "I voted the other way at Conference, but do not plan to write a dissenting opinion," but if the problems of the opinion were amended, "I will reluctantly climb aboard."[115] Rehnquist wanted the same principle to apply to both tribal members and nonmembers.

Initially, Justice Lewis Powell supported the Rehnquist position. He noted on a memorandum: "I see no constitutional limitation on power [of] a state to tax Indians (but will defer to Rehnquist)."[116] But soon after the oral argument on December 12, Powell changed his position and tentatively supported the Navajos.

The memoranda of the *McClanahan* court also supported limitations to the *Worcester* principle. Memoranda from several clerks archived in the Blackmun papers highlight how the Supreme Court limited the broad scope of tribal sovereignty established in *Worcester* in order to pursue integrationist principles. The limitation of *Worcester,* as indicated above, took place between the relationship of tribes and nonmembers. The Court recognized that tribal "relations with non-Indians" was "an area in which the Court has limited *Worcester.*"[117] The Court limited the principle of *Worcester* by restricting the powers of tribal government over nonmembers, addressed as a policy issue in a 1972 clerk's bench memorandum to Justice Blackmun: "The problem becomes one of policy. An ascertainable trend is present toward limiting *Worcester.* Some lower federal courts have (at least in dicta) pared *Worcester* down to its core: tribal government." This process was one of integration where state and reservation boundaries were opened up to allow the states greater authority over nonmembers on the reservation. The same memorandum read, "The narrowing of *Worcester* has reflected the growing belief that Indians . . . be integrated into American society." In stark contrast to the *Worcester* principle of 1832, the modern-day Supreme Court wanted to integrate state law into the reservations. This process of integration, the memorandum noted, meant that "*Worcester* lost its territorial case and became a doctrine related to the Indians as a person."[118]

The Supreme Court underlined this new direction in the *McClanahan* opinion itself. In his opinion, Justice Marshall limited the *Worcester* principle by using case law from the outmoded federal government policy of assimilation and allotment, as the *Kake* court had previously done in 1962.[119] The Marshall language established that *Worcester* and the sovereignty doctrine had changed so much that it could no longer prohibit state law on the reservations: "This is not to say that the Indian sovereignty doctrine, with its concomitant jurisdictional limit on the reach of state law, has remained static during the 141 years since Worcester was decided. Not surprisingly, the doctrine has undergone considerable evolution in response to changed circumstances [and] . . . notions of Indian sovereignty have been adjusted to take account of the State's legitimate interests in regulating the affairs of non-Indians."[120] This rationale underpinned the *McClanahan* opinion. The limitations placed on *Worcester* by the *McClanahan* opinion in 1973 were significantly different from the limitations placed on *Worcester* by the *Williams* opinion of 1959.

In its new integrationist mode, the *McClanahan* court fundamentally modified and eviscerated the rationale used by the *Williams* court to define the authority of *Worcester* in the post-1959 era.[121] It began from the presumption that state law was permitted on the reservation until it affected tribal government:

"Over the years this Court has modified [the Worcester principle] in cases where essential tribal relations were not involved and where the rights of Indians would not be jeopardized."[122] Although the *McClanahan* court seemed to begin its analysis with *Worcester,* it declared that the principle did not apply in the modern era unless state law affected "essential" tribal relations. The interpretation adopted by the *McClanahan* court therefore extended the scope of state authority over nonmembers on the reservation from specific to much broader circumstances.

In contrast to the language used by Justice Black supporting tribal authority over nonmembers in the *Williams* case, the *McClanahan* court viewed tribal sovereignty as a "backdrop" to inform the primary concerns of treaty and statutory interpretation. Conflicts between state and tribal law were to be decided by using tribal sovereignty as "merely as a tool of statutory construction,"[123] a factor secondary to federal authority. The opinion of the Court sanctioned the presence of state law on the reservation and state law over nonmembers as a direct result of the fact that tribal sovereignty was limited to tribal members only unless Congress expressly legislated to enhance tribal authority. This integrationist stance indicated a movement toward the use of federal authority to decide issues of state law on the reservation. This position was pointed out by Justice Marshall:

> The trend has been away from the idea of inherent Indian sovereignty as a bar to state jurisdiction and toward reliance on federal pre-emption. . . . The modern cases thus tend to avoid reliance on platonic notions of Indian sovereignty and to look instead to the applicable treaties and statutes which define the limits of state power. . . . [As a result] the Indian sovereignty doctrine is relevant, then, not because it provides a definitive resolution of the issues in this suit, but because it provides a backdrop against which the applicable treaties and federal statutes must be read.[124]

Federal preemption (authority), then, and not inherent tribal sovereignty barred the application of state law on the reservation.[125]

One factor that may have influenced the justices to favor using congressional authority rather than tribal sovereignty to decide conflicts between tribal and state law was the Red Power movement of the early 1970s.[126] A memorandum from Justice Powell's clerk highlights the impact of the Red Power movement: "Moreover, it does seem that as a phase of resurgent Indian militancy, more and more of these Indian land tax cases [McClanahan, Mescalero Apache Tribe and Tonasket] are coming up. Finally, as anyone who glances at the cases in this area can testify, they are a mess."[127] Consideration of the *McClanahan* case coincided with the Trail of Broken Treaties protest, the occupation of the Bureau of Indian Affairs (BIA) headquarters in Washington, D.C., on November 3, 1972, and the seizure of Wounded Knee on February 27, 1973. The Trail of Broken Treaties protest, from October to November 1972, involved the American Indian Movement (AIM) and other Native American groups. A caravan of nearly a thousand Native Americans from all over the country traveled from the West Coast to Washington D.C. The Trail brought attention to Native American treaty rights and long-standing social problems, which included poor housing and substandard living conditions.

Activists created a twenty-point position paper, a manifesto that highlighted the modern-day problems faced by Native Americans and how these could be alleviated by the government. Moreover, they demanded the abolition of the BIA and more investment in issues such as Native American education, health, and housing. While in Washington, D.C., nearly a thousand Native Americans took over and occupied the headquarters of the BIA for six days in November 1972. One of the most infamous events during the period unfolded at Wounded Knee, a small village on the Pine Ridge Indian Reservation in South Dakota, for seventy-one days from February 27 to May 8, 1973. After Wesley Bad Heart Bull, a Lakota who lived on the reservation, was killed, AIM and several Lakota members clashed with police. Tensions had been increasing between AIM and tribal chairman Richard Wilson, and when Wilson banned AIM from the reservation the BIA called for federal troops. Soon, FBI agents, federal marshals, and U.S. troops arrived with heavy artillery and armored vehicles. Meanwhile, more than two hundred Native Americans, with the support of Oglala elders, occupied Wounded Knee, the historic site of the massacre of Native Americans by American troops in 1890, and declared that the Fort Laramie Treaty of 1868 had sanctioned the independence of the Oglala Sioux Nation as a sovereign state.[128]

The federal government was deeply suspicious of AIM. During the standoff two Native Americans, Frank Clearwater and Lawrence Lamont, were killed and many others were injured, with hundreds of thousands of rounds of ammunition fired by federal authorities at the village of Wounded Knee. Vine Deloria and Clifford Lytle argue that the Supreme Court moved away from inherent tribal sovereignty as a justification of territorial power over nonmembers because of Wounded Knee, noting that the application of the sovereignty doctrine "would have been politically explosive . . . for the Supreme Court."[129]

McClanahan was argued before the Court on December 12, 1972, and the opinion was handed down on March 27, 1973. Given the sensitive political climate of the time, it is possible that the Court did not want to allow the tribes or representatives of AIM to have authority over state citizens on the reservation and to have authority to prevent the assertion of state law on the reservation. The Court was aware of the activities in Washington and Wounded Knee. A clerk's memorandum to Justice Blackmun in December 1972 read, "The recent Trail of Broken Treaties demonstration argued the federal government should remember its undertakings in these past events."[130] In addition, in an "Indian" file kept by Justice Douglas, one newspaper article referred to the takeover of the BIA headquarters and noted that AIM represented "477,000 Indians living on 263 reservations and 300,000 'urban Indians' who have left the reservation for the cities."[131] Another newspaper article in this file discussed what should be done about the Indians at Wounded Knee: "Before we weep too much or too long for the Indians we should ask ourselves how much we really are prepared to do for them, at Wounded Knee."[132] These events may well have influenced the rationale of the opinion.

Mescalero Apache Tribe v. Jones (1973)

The sister taxation case to *McClanahan*, *Mescalero Apache Tribe v. Jones* (1973), supplemented the presumption that states had authority over nonmembers on the reservation.[133] The *Mescalero Apache Tribe* case considered whether the State of New Mexico had authority to impose a nondiscriminatory tax on a ski resort owned by the Mescalero Apache Tribe located outside the reservation on adjacent lands leased from the federal government, pursuant to the Indian Reorganization Act of 1934. New Mexico had the right to impose a gross receipts tax on the annual sales of the ski resort but not the authority to impose a use tax on certain personal property purchased outside the state and used in connection with the resort.[134] Consistent with the developing integrationist principles, the justices used federal authority to decide a question of state law over tribal activities in an off-reservation situation. This opinion also addressed the importance of allowing state law to exist on the reservations.

The underlying issue of the case was whether congressional legislation or tribal sovereignty undermined state law within the boundaries of the state.

Because the case involved an off-reservation setting, the Court preferred to analyze it as a federal-versus-state conflict. A clerk's bench memorandum clarified this line of thinking: "Must Congress allow taxation before the state has power, or does the state have power unless Congress prohibits taxation."[135] The Court was influenced by the presumption developed between *Williams* and *Kennerly*; tribal sovereignty did not prevent state law from applying on the reservation. The corollary principle was that tribal sovereignty did not prohibit state law from applying in an off-reservation setting, and only Congress had the authority to limit state authority. As Justice White observed, when the Supreme Court was "dealing with off reservation activities, state can tax unless Congress says can't."[136] A memorandum from Justice White to Justice Marshall supported the nonapplication of tribal sovereignty (the *Williams* test) outside the reservation. White believed the *Williams* test applied only to conflicts between states and tribes on the reservation: "I had thought the [*Williams*] test had arisen in connection with efforts to control reservation-based activities."[137] If the *Williams* test did not apply off-reservation, then it did not affect tribal government. As Justice White noted, "It is perfectly apparent that taxation of this off-reservation activity does not interfere with tribal self-government."[138] Chief Justice Burger agreed with this assessment and concluded, "Congress probably could lay down rules but it has not."[139] In contrast, Justice Douglas directly opposed this rule: "What Chief says may be good policy, but not in accord with law."[140] The Supreme Court had, then, limited tribal sovereignty outside the reservation and implicitly precluded tribal sovereignty over nonmembers outside the reservation. Eventually, this simple notion would help the Court develop the idea that tribes did not have authority over nonmembers on the reservation.

The *Mescalero Apache Tribe* opinion also supported state authority over nonmembers on the reservation and used the facts and language of *McClanahan* to justify this stance. Although Justice White believed that federal authority was the appropriate source of power to decide questions of state law on the reservation, federal law could not prevent state law from being applied on the reservation at all times: "At the outset, we reject—as did the state court—the broad assertion that the Federal Government has exclusive jurisdiction over the Tribe for all purposes and that the State is therefore prohibited from enforcing its revenue laws against any tribal enterprise 'whether the enterprise is located on or off tribal land.' Generalizations on this subject have become particularly treacherous."[141]

The importance of state sovereignty emasculated *Worcester* and the principle of tribal sovereignty on the reservation. Justice White thought that the "conceptual clarity" of *Worcester* had "given way to more individualized treatment of particular treaties and specific federal statutes, including statehood enabling legislation, as they, taken together, affect the respective rights of States, Indians, and the Federal Government. . . . The upshot has been the repeated statements of this Court to the effect that, even on reservations, state laws may be applied unless such application would interfere with reservation self-government or would impair a right granted or reserved by federal law. Organized Village of Kake . . . Williams v. Lee."[142] Tribal authority was powerless to prevent state law on the reservation because the *McClanahan* case had limited it specifically to tribal members. Set against the facts of *McClanahan*, Robert Clinton argues that the *Mescalero Apache Tribe* court "was attempting to forge a greater change in federal Indian law" and allow states to gain a foothold on the reservations.[143] Although *Mescalero* has been relied on to authorize taxation and regulation of off-reservation tribal enterprises, it is also clear that it established a principle, set against the facts and language of *McClanahan*, that allowed state authority onto the reservation and over nonmembers there.[144]

Tonasket v. Washington (1973)

The sister taxation cases *McClanahan* and *Mescalero Apache Tribe* significantly changed the way the Supreme Court viewed the application of state law on reservations. The Court began to view conflicts between tribal and state authority in terms of their "Indianness," dividing cases into "Indian versus Non-Indian" and "Indian versus Indian." These two cases also confirmed the Court's position that state law was applicable on the reservation unless it was barred by congressional authority and, importantly, could not be applied to tribal members on the reservation unless authorized by Congress.

These cases began the trend of deciding Native American case law in terms of who was involved. The justices' thinking on questions involving tribal members differed from those involving nonmembers. A *McClanahan* bench memorandum pointed out the influence that a nonmember had on the Court's interpretation of "Indianness": "This is relevant to the Indianness of the case. If she [a tribal member] earned the money from tourists, her case is weaker than if she earned it from other Indians."[145] This understanding of "Indianness" informed the thinking of the justices and led them to limit tribal sovereignty to tribal members on the reservation.

This division between tribal members and nonmembers was discussed and made explicit in *Tonasket v. Washington* (1973).[146] Leonard Tonasket, a member of the Confederated Colville Tribes and resident of the Colville Indian Reservation, opened a retail store within the exterior boundaries of the reservation on allotted trust lands. Tonasket sold cigarettes to Native Americans and nonmembers. In 1967 the Washington State Tax Commission seized cigarettes from the store and arrested Tonasket. The Supreme Court had to decide whether the State of Washington, pursuant to Public Law 280, had civil and criminal jurisdiction over the reservation and whether that law allowed the state to tax tribal members who sold cigarettes and goods to both tribal members and nonmembers on the reservation.

The justices in *Tonasket* discussed the reasons why the application of state law on the reservation depended on the involvement of tribal members or nonmembers. From the facts of the *McClanahan* case, tribal sovereignty protected tribal members from state law unless Congress explicitly removed this protection. In the opinion of Justice Blackmun, Public Law 280 did not remove the protections of tribal sovereignty over tribal members: "Congress did not intend to remove Indian tax exemptions [and] . . . did not intend to extend taxing jurisdiction to the States."[147] Justice John Paul Stevens concurred with this interpretation of tribal sovereignty, pointing out that those issues of "I [Indian] to I [Indian] [were] exempt."[148] The importance of excluding state taxes from tribal members was explained in a clerk's bench memorandum: "If [state] tax jurisdiction is extended, then all jurisdiction is extended. This will end the Indian tribe . . . and the traditional governmental function of the tribal unit will end."[149] The legislation was not specific and it did not reverse tribal sovereignty over tribal members.

Opinions regarding state law over nonmembers were different. The justices considered whether the facts involved in the *Tonasket* case allowed the states to tax nonmembers. The involvement of nonmembers on the reservation automatically defined the limitations of tribal authority. The memorandum from Blackmun's clerk read, "This is *McClanahan* with a twist. Arguably this case deals with relations with non-Indians, an area in which the Court has limited *Worcester*." It explained the Court's limitation of tribal authority when cases involved tribal members and nonmembers: "A line of cases has imposed tax liability on non-Indian activities (e.g., railroads) on Indian reservations. Crimes of non-Indians against non-Indians have been exempted from *Worcester*. This is a non-Indian buyer/Indian seller case." The memorandum also offered a solution to the problem. The application of state law over non-Indians and the exclusion of state law over tribal members was "a nice dividing line. . . . From a policy standpoint this would control the problem of Indian enterprises competing with non-Indian businesses by using the Indian tax preferences."[150] A memorandum to Justice Powell suggested the limitations of tribal sovereignty over nonmembers when state interests were implicated: "Tribal sovereignty is of doubtful legal significance, but is always asserted in keeping with the new Indian militancy. It is doubtful that it overrides state laws."[151] Integration had limited tribal sovereignty. Powell noted: "If I write, I should look at maps used in oral argument which show location of Reservation and extent to which Indians and non-Indians have been integrated in living and doing business in same community."[152]

Compared to the application of state law over nonmembers, tribal authority was adjudged to be limited over nonmembers. Consistent with the general integrationist trend, state law applied on the reservation and could be reversed only by federal authority. The solicitor general agreed with the Court's interpretation: "The SG [solicitor general] notes that this case is unusual because appt [tribe] sells primarily to non-Indians and sells a product not related to Indian activities. . . . The SG also seems to lean toward federal preemption even when non-Indians are the buyers."[153] The Supreme Court was comfortable with dividing the law between exclusive tribal matters and tribal member-versus-nonmember cases. As Justice Blackmun noted, "The I [Indian]–non I [Indian] is a good ÷ line" and "leaves to Congress" the right to allow tribal authority over nonmembers and the right to prohibit state law over nonmembers in the reservation.[154]

✦ Only fourteen years had passed from the pro-tribal words written by Justice Hugo Black in *Williams* in support of the Indian sovereignty doctrine. In 1973, the Indian sovereignty doctrine no longer supported tribal authority over nonmembers on the reservations. Instead, state law existed over nonmembers on reservations unless Congress acted to divest this power.

The two sister taxation cases and *Tonasket* ended the presumption that allowed state law to apply to tribal members on the reservation. The *McClanahan* court confirmed the inherent sovereignty of the tribes over tribal members on the reservation, as did the *Tonasket* court. This principle was reaffirmed by the *Mescalero Apache Tribe* court: "Even so, in the special area of state taxation, absent cession of jurisdiction or other federal statutes permitting it, there has been no satisfactory authority for taxing Indian reservation lands or Indian income from activities carried on within the boundaries of the reservation, and McClanahan v. Arizona State Tax Comm'n, lays to rest any doubt in this respect by holding that such taxation is not permissible absent congressional consent." [155] Important for all Native American tribes, the sister taxation cases and *Tonasket* confirmed that the sovereignty doctrine protected them against state law.

Even though these were separate and independent cases, the Supreme Court treated them as a single case in order to facilitate a change in the law. Individually, *McClanahan* involved tribal sovereignty over tribal members on a reservation, *Mescalero Apache Tribe* involved the issue of tribal affairs outside the reservation, and *Tonasket* involved the taxation of nonmembers on a reservation. Nevertheless, these three cases set the foundations of the silent revolution and the integrationist trend, which permanently established the authority of the state on the reservation, allowed state power over nonmembers on the reservation, and in time diminished tribal authority over nonmembers on the reservation.

The Silent Revolution, 1973–2001

The Supreme Court's erosion of tribal sovereignty described in chapters 1 and 2 relied on an ideological change by the justices toward the use of federal authority, known as federal preemption, to protect the interests of the tribes. This change was based on the justices' attempts to reconcile the presence of tribal government and its concomitant sovereignty within a constitutional framework that addressed only the powers of the federal government and the state governments.

This chapter builds on the analysis of the previous two by showing that after 1973 the Supreme Court continued to use federal authority to determine both tribal authority over nonmembers and the application of state law on the reservation. This is not to say, however, that the sovereignty doctrine was nullified; some justices still used it in particular circumstances, leading to ideological tensions. In contrast to the period 1959–73, from 1973 onward the Supreme Court generally protected exclusive tribal rights on the reservations against state law, a protection established in *McClanahan v. Arizona State Tax Comm'n* (1973).[1]

Those protections notwithstanding, this chapter traces the gradual erosion of the key attributes of tribal power and the gradual elaboration of what I term the "integrationist trend" in taxation, criminal, and civil case law from 1973 to 2001. Indeed, the Supreme Court has continued to exhibit integrationist principles to the present day. Central to this chapter is a detailed and comprehensive look at individual cases and the disparate viewpoints of the justices within the areas of taxation, criminal, and civil case law in this period, as well as several other cases from 2001 to 2015.[2] I argue that the silent revolution was supported by the integrationist principles applied in these cases. The conclusions of the 1973 cases created a set of Supreme Court presumptions that limited tribal authority over nonmembers and allowed state law onto the reservations. These presumptions led the Court to question how much authority the tribes and the states had over nonmembers on the reservations. It also led to questions about whether the sovereignty doctrine prohibited the application of state law on the reservations or whether state law was applicable on the reservations until prohibited by Congress.

Growth of the Integrationist Trend, 1975–1978

The integrationist trend is identified by four key principles:

- If the tribes relied on congressional authority to oust state law from the reservations, then by default the state had general authority on the reservations.
- If the states had general authority on the reservations, they also had authority over nonmembers on the reservations.
- If the tribes had authority over only tribal members on the reservations, then by default they had no power over nonmembers on the reservations.
- If the tribes did not have inherent sovereignty over nonmembers on the reservations, then the inherent sovereignty of the state automatically applied to nonmembers on the reservations.[3]

I argue that these integrationist principles worked in tandem to overturn the sovereignty doctrine. From 1973 on, the justices viewed federal authority as the tool that would decide questions of tribal authority over nonmembers and questions about state law on the reservation. They delegated federal authority to the tribes and allowed them to have authority over nonmembers on the reservations while allowing state law to exist on the reservations and over nonmembers on the reservations unless it was reversed by Congress.[4] Thus, congressional authority confirmed the power of the tribes and the limits to which state authority existed on the reservation.

United States v. Mazurie (1975)

The first cases to apply the integrationist principles after 1973 were *United States v. Mazurie* (1975) and *Moe v. Salish & Kootenai Tribes* (1976). In these cases, the Supreme Court applied the new ideas and began the erosion of the sovereignty doctrine and the key attributes of tribal power.

United States v. Mazurie concerned a nonmember who operated a bar on fee lands on the outskirts of the Wind River Reservation and who was prohibited from selling alcohol on the reservation by the Wind River Tribes, pursuant to a congressional statute.[5] The Supreme Court had to decide whether the congressional delegation of power allowed the tribal council the authority

THE SILENT REVOLUTION 69

to prevent him from selling alcohol. The case was the first after 1973 to build on the presumption established by the *McClanahan* court and to apply the ruling in law that tribal authority over nonmembers was limited until Congress delegated the appropriate authority. Despite being briefed on the merits of tribal sovereignty and congressional authority, many of the justices discussed only the idea of congressional authority in the course of their deliberations and in the Court's final opinion.[6]

The foundations of the silent revolution from 1959 to 1973 were key in the outcome of the *Mazurie* case and further weakened the broad ruling of *Williams v. Lee*, which held that tribes had inherent sovereignty over nonmembers. Tribal sovereignty after 1973 appeared to be limited to tribal members, and the Supreme Court did not want to reverse this principle. A clerk's memorandum to Justice Blackmun explained the limitations imposed on tribal sovereignty and the development of congressional authority as a bona fide principle: "In short, the delegation of authority seems to be both desirable and sufficiently limited to pass muster under this Court's prior views of Indian sovereignty." The issue of congressional delegation was the principal theme of the case, but there were concerns, even if Congress granted it, about delegating too much authority to the tribes for them to have control over nonmembers. The memorandum read, "What are the limits on Congress' authority to delegate to Indians the power to govern non-Indians' conduct on the Indian reservation?" Moving away from tribal sovereignty, the Court did not want Congress to sanction all kinds of tribal control over nonmembers. Fundamentally, the justices were limiting the broad rationale of the *Williams* case. Indeed, the *Williams* case relied not on tribal sovereignty but on a delegation of congressional power: "This Court has approved the grant of jurisdiction to Indians to deal with non-Indians in certain matters of importance to the reservation. See, e.g., Williams v. Lee, 358 U.S. 217, 223."[7] Despite this erroneous interpretation of the bold and clear opinion of Justice Hugo Black, *Williams* was now limited to a congressional authority case.

In the *Mazurie* case, the justices had the option of using the sovereignty doctrine or congressional authority to authorize tribal authority over nonmembers. In memoranda to the Court, both options were presented as viable approaches. The arguments for the sovereignty doctrine were contained in references to *Buster v. Wright*, which held that a tribe had inherent sovereignty to tax nonmembers on the reservation. This case had been decided by the U.S. Court of Appeals for the Eighth Circuit in 1905, and an appeal to the Supreme

Court was dismissed in 1906. Therefore, the original *Buster* opinion, a court of appeals case and not a Supreme Court precedent, supported the inherent sovereignty of the tribes to tax the business activity of nonmembers. In *Buster,* the court of appeals wrote:

> The authority of the Creek Nation to prescribe the terms upon which noncitizens may transact business within its borders did not have its origin in an act of Congress, treaty, or agreement of the United States. It was one of the inherent and essential attributes of its original sovereignty. It was a natural right of that people, indispensable to its autonomy as a distinct tribe or nation, and it must remain an attribute of its government until by the agreement of the nation itself or by the superior power of the republic it is taken from it.[8]

In stark contrast to integrationist principles, this ruling simply stated that tribal power to tax nonmembers and their businesses is inherent until removed by Congress. Interestingly, in this case the Creek Nation had inherent sovereignty over fee lands. A clerk's memorandum to Justice Blackmun stated that the *Buster* case "did hold that the Creek Indian Nation had authority to tax non-citizens of the Tribe for the privilege of transacting business within its borders, despite the fact that the business was conducted on fee patented lands. The authority was said to be 'one of the inherent and essential attributes of its original sovereignty.'" The argument was also presented to the Court that Congress had plenary power over Indian affairs, which included allowing the tribes to sell alcohol to nonmembers on the reservation. Referring to the case of *Perrin v. United States* (1914), the clerk's memorandum explained this principle, which allowed Congress exclusive control over matters involving alcohol in the reservation: "In that case Congress had imposed a restriction on ceded lands within the vicinity of lands retained by Indians which prohibited sale of intoxicating liquors. The Court noted that Congress had broad discretion to control the sale of liquor . . . as part of its protective concern for the Indians. That decision seems broad enough to sustain the constitutionality of 18 U.S.C. 1154."[9]

Some of the justices explicitly supported the delegation of congressional power in order to give the tribe authority over nonmembers. Harry Blackmun was one justice who believed that Congress had plenary power over Indian affairs, especially those involving alcohol, and that the outcome of *Perrin v. United States* supported the facts of the *Mazurie* case: "Congressional power under Art. I, §8 to regulate commerce with Indian tribes is broad indeed.

There is little doubt left that it has the right to regulate the sale of alcohol in Indian country. This is clearly established by *Perrin* v. *United States*, 232 U.S. 478 (1914) with respect to sales of alcohol on non-Indian lands even though non-Indians are the sellers."[10]

Justice Blackmun suggested that the plenary authority of Congress over Indian affairs allowed Congress to delegate its authority to the tribes, noting that the "delegation of power may not be unlimited, but I am not disturbed about what delegation we have here, when it relates to the sale of liquor within the boundaries of a reservation. This is surely a localized concern." However, Blackmun's language suggested that issues of greater or broader concern involving tribes and nonmembers did not support tribal jurisdiction over nonmembers. He continued to observe that the justification of using congressional authority was to protect the interests and welfare of the tribes involved: "The alcohol problem among Indians, together with the desire to foster responsibility on the part of the Indian councils should support the statute."[11] Justice Potter Stewart agreed that the case revolved only around the issue of congressional authority: "Think sufficient notice given by this statute and that's all there is to this case"; Justice Byron White concurred with Stewart, noting "agree with PS."[12] Chief Justice Warren Burger also supported the congressional authority analysis, but he did not believe that the legislation involved in the case supported tribal authority over nonmembers and pointed out that "this statute is just too vague."[13]

Thus, the *Mazurie* judgment continued the post-1973 judicial shift in relying on congressional authority and not inherent tribal sovereignty, applying the principle set in the sister taxation cases and *Tonasket*.

Tax Law: *Moe v. Salish & Kootenai Tribes* (1976)

The process adopted by the *Mazurie* court led directly to *Moe v. Salish & Kootenai Tribes* (1976), the first case of the modern era (from 1959) to allow state law onto the reservation and state law over nonmembers on the reservation.[14] The argument in *Moe v. Salish & Kootenai Tribes* was whether the State of Montana had the right to impose cigarette sales taxes on transactions between tribal members and nonmembers on the reservation and have a tribal member collect the tax for the state. In addition, the state wanted to impose a cigarette tax on cigarettes sold by tribal members to other tribal members and to tax the personal property of tribal members on the reservation. I consider only the cigarette tax issue in the context of this chapter.

Limitations placed on tribal sovereignty and the *Williams* principle by the Court had allowed general state law onto the reservation. During *Moe* discussions, this development was summed up by Justice Blackmun: "As to acts between an Indian and a non-Indian, the state has jurisdiction where that jurisdiction does not infringe on the right of reservation Indians to make their own laws and be ruled by them. Having stated these principles, where do they take us? The application always is the difficult task." The Court had to consider whether a state tax on nonmembers on the reservation, which had to be collected by tribal members, affected tribal government. The mindset of the justices had moved away from the principle of inherent sovereignty used by the *Williams* court to prohibit state law on the reservation. Justice Blackmun went on to explain what the outcome of the *Moe* case would have been if the Court had adhered to the *Williams* principle: "The cigarette tax on Indian to non-Indian on reservation sales. This, of course, is the tough issue. Does the tax infringe on the right of tribal members to make their own laws and be governed by them? On a formal legalistic approach the answer would be that it does interfere. And *Williams v. Lee* stands for the proposition that mere involvement of outsiders is not sufficient to grant jurisdiction."[15]

Blackmun's language clarified the legal approach of *Williams* but also indicated his reluctance to use the sovereignty doctrine. The general movement of the Court away from tribal sovereignty undermined what Blackmun termed the "formal legalistic approach." His reluctance to use inherent tribal sovereignty was confirmed when he pointed out that "the normal solution" would have been "to hold that Montana does not have jurisdiction to force the Indian vendor to precollect the tax with respect to sales to non-Indians."[16]

Justice Brennan acknowledged the legal approach of *Williams* but supported the move away from those principles. He illustrated the movement of the Court away from the tribal sovereignty doctrine when he was thinking about ways to allow the state to have control inside the reservation: "As I noted in my bench memo, traditional theories would hold that the Indian could not be required to collect the tax. . . . I have no great policy difficulties, however, with the result reached here (although it does reduce the concept of the reservation as a separate sovereignty)."[17] According to Brennan, the process of integration and the interests of the state on the reservation were preferred to the traditional approaches of federal Indian law. Indeed, the "normal situation" and the "traditional theories" had not existed within the mindset of the justices for many years. The movement of the Court away from the sovereignty doctrine was reflected in its approach to devising a new theory to allow state law to apply on the reservation. A clerk's memorandum to Blackmun explained, "Under the presently accepted legal analysis the state does not appear to have the jurisdiction. . . . The involvement of the state in internal reservation affairs is too great. I suggest, however, a new theory to cover the situation."[18] Once the Supreme Court agreed not to apply the *Williams* principle, state law was sanctioned on the reservation.

The Court's new practice of allowing states authority over nonmembers grew from the idea that the purchase of cigarettes by a nonmember on the reservation was a criminal act under state law. Justice Blackmun believed that once the Court justified Montana's interests on the reservation then the state automatically assumed control of the nonmembers: "One theory that might well support the tax is that the state has a definite interest, with respect to its general criminal jurisdiction over the reservation, in not permitting the Indian vendor to cause the non-Indian vendee from violating another Montana statute that prohibits one's use of an untaxed cigarette." The process of undermining the sovereignty doctrine had removed the barrier prohibiting the application of state law inside the reservation boundary. The interests of the state were now important, especially in the minds of the justices. Blackmun continued, "Of some interest, of course, is the theory suggested above that the state may properly have an interest, and assert it."[19]

Justice Brennan concurred with the new theory. He pointed out in a draft proposal of the opinion that, "in regard to the sales of cigarettes by Indians to non-Indians, I think that the draft is correct to focus on the fact that use of unstamped cigarettes by non-Indians is a crime." In this way, the Court blurred the distinction between the reservation boundary and the state line. It interpreted a criminal act outside the reservation to involve a crime on the reservation. As Brennan explained: "Once it is established that the use by non-Indians is a crime, there are two ways of dealing with the role of the Indian preventing that use. First, the Indian can be viewed as 'causing' the non-Indian's crime, and therefore reachable under a sort of 'aider and abetter' theory. Second, the Indian can simply be made an 'agent' of the state in this particular circumstance and required to prevent the crime from occurring."[20] The state had authority over the activities of a nonmember in two ways, and the Court had to choose one of them.

Ultimately, the Court used this new interpretation to allow state tax onto the reservation on the grounds that state law applied on the reservation because no congressional legislation existed to preclude state authority; to prevent state taxation of nonmembers on the reservation, Congress had to legislate. The Court held that the states had authority over nonmembers because Congress did not regulate the area of tribal cigarette selling to nonmembers and the state tax did not burden federal legislation. In other words, the Court rejected the application of *Warren*. The authority of the state on the reservation was considered "a minimal burden" that did not "frustrate tribal self-government or run afoul of any federal statute dealing with reservation Indians' affairs." Furthermore, the tribe had to collect the state tax from the sales to nonmembers.[21] This case opened the floodgates; once state law was applied in certain circumstances, it was also applied in others.

Even though the *Moe* case did not involve tribal authority over nonmembers, the developments in law from *McClanahan* over whether the ruling involved questions of state authority or tribal authority turned on the intent of congressional authority. The connection between *Moe* and *Mazurie* was shown by arguments made by the State of Washington, presented in a 1973 clerk's memorandum to Justice Blackmun, about the limitations of tribal sovereignty over nonmembers unless Congress sanctioned the relevant authority: "[The state] argues that 'Indian sovereignty' is not inherent in the tribes, but is something bestowed by Congress. It reads *McClanahan* as stating that the particular statutes and treaties there 'read against the *background* of traditional Indian sovereignty' required tax immunity. . . . 'tribal sovereignty' is something within the control and creation of Congress, and . . . therefore the burden is on the Indians to show that Congress intended to give them the particular sovereignty claimed."[22]

In sum, in 1976 the Supreme Court believed in the primacy of congressional legislation to decide the issue of tribal authority over nonmembers and relied on the principle that state law existed on the reservation until prohibited by specific congressional legislation. In contrast to nonmembers, though, tribal members did not have to pay state taxes. A majority of the justices in the deliberations of this case reaffirmed the principle established by *McClanahan* that tribal sovereignty protected tribal members against state law; however, a few justices wanted to reverse this principle. Justice Blackmun supported the *McClanahan* rule: "The cigarette tax on Indian to Indian on reservation sales. This seems clearly to be barred by *McClanahan*. It is an attempt to force something on the Indian buyer that is governed by tribal law unless the state has assumed jurisdiction."[23] Justice Brennan concurred with the Blackmun interpretation and pointed out that this was a settled principle of Supreme

Court case law: "The general and settled principles are that a state has no jurisdiction to enforce a civil tax law with respect to an act purely between Indians on the reservation."[24]

Justices Rehnquist and Powell fundamentally opposed protecting tribal members from state tax. Rehnquist believed that in instances like this, when the reservation population contained so many nonmembers, the Court should reverse the *McClanahan* rule: "Some day [the Court] may want to reconsider the law . . . as applied to reservations like this one . . . which is reservation only in a technical sense." Powell believed that all Native Americans were part of the state and supported this position: "Could reconsider own cases on this . . . as Is [Indians] really assimilated."[25]

Powell disagreed with the *McClanahan* principle because it treated tribal members and nonmembers differently under state law, and he observed, "I'd be willing to reconsider exemptions there [of] Indians from state taxes. But makes no sense to exempt sales by Indians to Indians but not to non-Indians."[26] Despite these considerations, the final opinion on the *Moe* case was unanimous and denied the right of the state to tax tribal members.

The Supreme Court ruled that the state cigarette tax was barred in relation to tribal cigarette sales to tribal members on the reservation. The *Moe* opinion confirmed the principles established by *McClanahan*. The involvement of exclusive tribal issues resulted in the application of the sovereignty doctrine. The *Moe* court held that inherent tribal sovereignty protected tribal members until Congress legislated to remove this barrier to state law, explaining that "McClanahan . . . lays to rest any doubt in this respect by holding that such taxation is not permissible absent congressional consent."[27] The state was also federally preempted from asserting a tax on the sale of cigarettes from tribal members to tribal members only.[28]

Although *Moe* has been referred to as "an insignificant Indian tax dispute in Montana,"[29] the case built on the principle of sanctioning general state law on the reservation unless revoked by Congress, thereby limiting tribal sovereignty to tribal members and further weakening the *Williams* judgment. The Court's decision to use congressional authority connected *Moe* and *Mazurie*.

Criminal Case Law: *Oliphant v. Suquamish Indian Tribe* (1978)

The Supreme Court's silent revolution continued to weaken the Indian sovereignty doctrine. Only three years after *Mazurie*, the principles that underpinned that case were used in *Oliphant v. Suquamish Indian Tribe* (1978) to extinguish tribal criminal authority over nonmembers on the reservation.[30] The primary consideration of the Court was using the power of Congress to determine the outcome of the cases. The issue of state law was not involved in the case.

In 1973, the Suquamish Tribe adopted its Law and Order Code, which extended its inherent criminal authority over both tribal members and nonmembers on the Port Madison Indian Reservation. Then in 1978 the tribe claimed jurisdiction over the criminal actions of two nonmembers on the reservation. Mark David Oliphant assaulted a tribal police officer, and Daniel B. Belgrade collided with a tribal police car after a high-speed chase through the reservation. At the time, there were many more nonmembers (63 percent) living on the reservation than tribal members. The *Oliphant* case examined whether the tribe had inherent criminal authority over nonmembers on the reservation. The *Oliphant* court relied on the principle that tribal authority extended over tribal members but did not extend over nonmembers unless explicitly delegated by Congress. Without the necessary legislation, the tribes did not have sovereignty over nonmembers in tribal court.[31]

The limitation of tribal sovereignty to tribal members and the movement of the Court toward allowing tribal authority over nonmembers only through the delegation of congressional power were combined by the Court to decide the issues of the case. Justice Blackmun believed that these two factors were integral in the Court's modern-day thinking:

I am satis[fied] that history . . . does not support the Indians.

1. The assumption 1850–1950 just the other way.
2. Modern "thought" . . . has changed, but that does not change the history.
3. Congress, probably, could effect a change if it so deserved . . .
5. Fax [facts] here are tough . . .
6. No inherent Indian sovereignty . . .
7. No clear Congress action.[32]

This interpretation clearly linked tribal authority over nonmembers to congressional legislation. Based on his interpretation of historical events, Justice Blackmun concluded that the "Indians no deserve to win."[33] The reference to modern thought may have been to *Williams* and tribal sovereignty, or it may have been to the development of the idea that tribal sovereignty now relied on congressional legislation. However, it was pointed out in a clerk's memorandum to Justice Blackmun that the modern-day Court now relied on the primacy of congressional authority: "The trend of . . . *McClanahan* is unmistakably away from former concepts of residual sovereignty."[34]

The combination of *McClanahan* and *Mazurie* influenced the interpretation of the Court. A clerk's memorandum to Justice Blackmun discussed the similarity between *Mazurie* and *Oliphant* but noted that *Mazurie* delegated federal authority whereas the facts of *Oliphant* did not suggest that there was legislation to allow the tribes authority over nonmembers:

> Perhaps the closest case is *United States* v. *Mazurie* . . . in which the Court upheld the enforcement of a federal law that incorporated by reference a tribal ordinance that had prohibited the operation of the nonIndian defendant's liquor store on the reservation. This case as well as being the closest factually, includes the strongest statement in favor of the the tribes' independent authority over matters that affect the internal and social relations of tribal life. But the case is distinguishable on two very significant points: Congress was said to have delegated to the tribe the regulatory power exercised, and the case involved enforcement of Indian law by the federal courts, not by Indian courts.[35]

Despite the acknowledgment of the independent authority of the tribes, it was clear that the reliance of the Court on congressional authority was the decisive factor in its interpretation of the case. As this same clerk's memorandum to Justice Blackmun observed, "The case therefore boils down to the strength of the presumption of retained power by the Indian tribes in the face of evidence to the contrary, I do not think it is strong enough."

Justice Lewis Powell also supported the idea of tribal sovereignty over tribal members only, thus limiting the Indian sovereignty doctrine:

> I realize that Indian law is indeed "a law unto itself," and often seems incompatible with broader public interests. I am inclined to accept a large measure of autonomy where the issue involves the preservation of tribal history, culture and the rights of Indians. But this case involves the attempt by a handful of Indians to exercise criminal jurisdiction over non-Indians in a manner, and for purposes, unrelated to the preservation of tribal integrity. . . . My guess is that, as the Attorney General of Washington argues, the fundamental error of CA 9 was in viewing "tribal sovereignty" as a geographic concept rather than a personal concept.[36]

Interestingly, the limitation of the sovereignty doctrine was informed by policy considerations contrary to congressional policy supporting tribal self-determination. Powell noted, "In terms of policy considerations, it makes no sense to allow 50 to 150 Indians to set up a 'tribal court' and assume jurisdiction—whether concurrent or not—over more than 2,800 non-Indians who live within the technical boundary of the reservation, and who own in fee most of the land."[37]

Although the application of state law was not involved in this case, Powell principally supported the interests of the states and non-Indians on reservations: "The case is one of considerable importance, perhaps more to the states in which Indian reservations continue to exist than to Indian tribes such as the Suquamish Tribe. . . . If this case is to turn on policy considerations, rather than some firm conclusion drawn from relevant federal law, I would be inclined to weigh heavily the policy arguments in favor of the states."[38]

Many justices supported this reliance on congressional authority. Justice White believed that tribal sovereignty was limited and only Congress could address this issue: "[I] do not buy residual sovereignty [and] Congress has the power." Justice Powell agreed, noting, "Let Congress carve out the *exceptions*. This case a farce factually, a non-case." Justice Stewart explained that, without congressional or treaty power, tribes did not have any control over nonmembers: "It was unknown in 1854 'unless sighted by Treaty,' neatly left Parker and [his] opinions. Therefore no power to try non-Indians for offenses on reservation not unless Is [Indians]."[39] Justice Stevens thought it was a good idea if Congress addressed this issue and not the Court.

The interpretations of the justices, then, relied on the presence of concrete and visible acts of Congress rather than the Indian sovereignty doctrine or other conceptual factors. In the *Oliphant* oral arguments, the Court wanted evidence of a relevant statute that authorized tribal power over nonmembers, and it wanted to know what sources the tribe relied on other than opinions of the Supreme Court:

Mr. Ernstoff: It is impossible to point—

Question: Then actually, you do not have anything.

Mr. Ernstoff: The answer is that Congress has never—

Question: The answer is, you do not have anything.

Mr. Ernstoff: That is correct because, Your Honor, it is very difficult to prove a negative. Congress has never enacted a statute giving a

Tribe power and this Court has recognized the power, how can I point to a statute which gave the Tribe that power? All I can point to is this Court's analysis of the fact that one does not need a statute or a treaty in order to determine that there is a power.[40]

The principles involved in the oral argument of the *Oliphant* case, mainly the presence of congressional authority to sanction tribal power over non-members, underpinned the draft opinion and final opinion of the Court. One draft opinion relied on congressional authority and also distinguished tribal powers over tribal members and those over non-Indians, thereby turning the sovereignty doctrine on its head: "The opinion draws a distinction between true sovereignty and the limited sovereignty of the Indian tribes, which allowed them to govern themselves but did not include the power to try non-Indians. The opinion does not state that although Indian tribes once might have been sovereign, Congress explicitly took away criminal jurisdiction over non-Indians either through §1152 (the interracial crimes statute) or otherwise."[41]

This integrationist thinking, as noted by Justice Powell's clerk, allowed Justice Rehnquist to limit the application and presumption of the sovereignty doctrine: "And because of the problems that would attend an attempt to say that Congress actually withdrew Indian criminal jurisdiction over non-Indians, I do not think I could write a decent concurrence along those lines. Buzz [Justice Rehnquist's clerk] told me that he read every word of every 19th century treaty, in addition to all the legislative history of the 19th century Indian statutes, before concluding that the opinion could not be written to say that there was such a withdrawal of jurisdiction."[42] Thus, the Court's draft opinion began from a presumption contrary to the sovereignty doctrine. Now, tribal criminal authority had to be authorized by Congress.

Tribal sovereignty did not authorize criminal authority or tribal court authority over nonmembers. Justice Rehnquist believed that only Congress could delegate such power and wrote in the final *Oliphant* opinion that the tribes "did not have such jurisdiction [over nonmembers] absent a congressional statute or treaty provision to that effect." Without congressional permission, then, "Indian tribal courts do not have inherent criminal jurisdiction to try and to punish non-Indians, and hence may not assume such jurisdiction unless specifically authorized to do so by Congress."[43]

In contrast to the majority, Justice Marshall declined to accept the concept of congressional authority. Marshall accepted the presumption that tribes had sovereignty over nonmembers unless specifically removed by Congress. In his interpretation, the application of the Indian sovereignty doctrine was guided by a historical duty to protect the tribes: "Could go either way. Is [Indians] need sovereignty manhood—have to protect selves. Therefore with the St. [Suquamish Tribe]—matter of decency."[44] Chief Justice Burger supported Justice Marshall. In a memorandum to Justice Stewart, Burger wrote, "The *Oliphant* dissent having persuaded only one (myself), it is now 'gospel.'"[45] Justice Marshall's resolute opinion about the principles of the sovereignty doctrine was reflected in a memorandum to conference on March 3, 1978:

> I have sent to the printer the following short statement of my reasons for dissenting in this case. . . . Mr Justice Marshall, dissenting. I agree with the court below that the "power to preserve order on the reservation . . . is a sine qua non of the sovereignty that the Suquamish originally possessed." 544 F. 2d 1007, 1009 (CA9 1976). In the absence of affirmative withdrawal by treaty or statute, I am of the view that Indian tribes enjoy as a necessary aspect of their retained sovereignty the right to try and punish all persons who commit offenses against tribal law within the reservation. Accordingly, I dissent.[46]

This statement was also the final Justice Marshall dissent with which Chief Justice Burger joined. Justice Marshall agreed with the opinion of the lower court and with the traditions of the sovereignty doctrine.

Criminal Case Law: *United States v. Wheeler* (1978)

Despite the clear ideological differences between certain members of the Court, only sixteen days after *Oliphant* the Court upheld the principle of inherent tribal sovereignty in *United States v. Wheeler*.[47] The *Wheeler* case considered whether a Navajo man could be prosecuted for an offense against a minor in federal court after being sentenced by the Navajo court for the same crime. The Supreme Court had to assess whether the double jeopardy clause of the Fifth Amendment barred a subsequent federal prosecution. To do this, it had to examine the source of Navajo sovereignty and whether it was delegated by Congress or was inherent and independent of federal authority.

A substantial policy issue confronted the justices in *Wheeler*. If a delegation of congressional power was required by a tribe to prosecute tribal members, then a subsequent federal prosecution was barred. A bench memorandum from Powell's clerk summed up the situation: "The basic problem would be the preclusion of federal prosecutions for major crimes when the defendant had been tried in tribal court on a charge that amounts to a lesser included offense of the federal charge. This strikes me as a problem. It is arguable, as a policy matter, that both the federal and tribal governments have an interest in prosecuting an offender under their respective criminal codes, especially when the definition of offenses is so different (as in the instant case)."[48]

In this case the justices applied the principle that inherent tribal sovereignty had existed over tribal members for many centuries and had not been reversed by Congress. As Justice Marshall explained in a memorandum to conference, "I believe that tribes retain certain rights of self-government through residual sovereignty not deriving from the federal Constitution but pre-existing it."[49] Chief Justice Burger concurred that there were no limitations placed on this historic sovereignty, pointing out that this "200 year old sovereignty still exists, acts as a sov[ereign]," and Justice Stewart also agreed that the tribes had inherent sovereignty over tribal members, noting that "Indians do not come by grant of power but keep until taken away."[50] These interpretations were reiterated in the opinion of the Court, which explained that the tribes "still possess those aspects of sovereignty not withdrawn by treaty or statute, or by implication as a necessary result of their dependent status." The justices considered this Indian sovereignty over tribal members a lesser form of sovereignty, describing it as "primeval sovereignty."[51]

The justices distinguished between the application of tribal sovereignty over tribal members and over nonmembers. Two presumptions existed. Tribal sovereignty over tribal members existed until it was reversed by Congress, and tribal sovereignty over nonmembers had to be delegated by Congress. A bench memorandum to Justice Powell explained: "Tribal sovereignty . . . is not 'full' sovereignty" because of congressional plenary power, and "tribe members owe a kind of allegiance to their tribe that does not exist in other contexts outside of the state or the federal government."[52] The lesser form of tribal sovereignty was applicable over tribal members. Justice Stewart noted: "Tribal Court had jurisdiction to try Indians. This power results from fact federal government had never taken this power away. No conflict with vote in Oliphant."[53] The integrationist principles were summed up in a memorandum from Powell's clerk: "In view of the plenary nature of Congress' control over Indian tribes, it really cannot be said that tribes are sovereign in the way that the federal government or the states are. (This is a slightly different question from the one in Oliphant, where tribal sovereignty—if recognized at all—is recognized only because Congress has chosen to let it continue.)"[54] The type of tribal sovereignty used in *Wheeler* did not include tribal authority over nonmembers. Thus, Justice Rehnquist noted, "No conflict with Oliphant," and Justice Powell wrote, "Agree with Potter [Stewart] and [Chief Justice] Burger. Not inconsistent with my vote in Oliphant."[55]

Although nonmembers were not involved in the facts of the *Wheeler* case, the Supreme Court declared that tribes did not have any authority over nonmembers. Whereas *Oliphant* limited tribal sovereignty over nonmembers in the area of criminal law, the *Wheeler* court expanded this principle into a general rule limiting all tribal sovereignty over nonmembers on the reservation. This general rule was explained by Justice Stewart in the *Wheeler* opinion: "The areas in which such implicit divestiture of sovereignty has been held to have occurred are those involving the relations between an Indian tribe and nonmembers of the tribe."[56]

The reasoning was based on the Court's interpretation of external and social relations. Tribal relations with nonmembers were considered to be external relations, whereas social or internal relations were those among tribal members, over which tribal government had power. The division between these relations and the corresponding limitations on tribal power were explained by the Court: "These limitations rest on the fact that the dependent status of Indian tribes within our territorial jurisdiction is necessarily inconsistent with their freedom independently to determine their external relations. But the powers of self-government, including the power to prescribe and enforce internal criminal laws, are of a different type. They involve only the relations among members of a tribe."[57]

Thus, as part of its integrationist trend, the Supreme Court drew distinctions between external and social relations. The definitions for internal and social affairs changed in the modern era since 1959.[58] The new interpretation allowed external relations to be defined broadly as those between tribal members and nonmembers. As William C. Canby observed, the *Wheeler* case "began a shift in emphasis from tribal power as governmental power over a territory to tribal power as a function of membership."[59] However, historically and certainly up to 1959, external relations were those specifically related to foreign relations with, for example, France or the United Kingdom, and tribal social and internal relations included authority over nonmembers.[60] In 1959, the Court had supported this interpretation, but soon after it determined otherwise.

In sum, the *Wheeler* and *Oliphant* decisions reflected some integrationist principles, but they were not applied in full because state authority was not involved. Both cases reversed the inherent rights of the tribe to prosecute nonmembers on the reservation and continued the trend toward a broader erosion of tribal authority in civil and taxation case law.[61]

Taxation Case Law: 1980–2001

I turn now to taxation case law after 1978, including the influence of criminal case law on the taxation opinions of the Court.[62] I examine case law from 1980 to 1989, reviewing six cases concerning the question of state authority over nonmembers and three cases concerning tribal authority over nonmembers. This analysis ends with a 1989 case, but the principles used by the Court after 1989 did not change until *Atkinson Trading Co. v. Shirley* in 2001.

From 1980 to 1987 the language of the Supreme Court had appeared to reinvigorate the principle of inherent tribal sovereignty as an independent source of power to prohibit state law over nonmembers on the reservations. But the Court never used this principle and instead used congressional preemption to keep state law off the reservation. Moreover, in stark contrast to the period 1959–73, in which general state law was allowed to exist on the reservation, and case law up to 1980, in which the Court delegated authority for the tribes to have control over nonmembers, in 1980 the Court declared that tribes had inherent sovereignty to tax nonmembers—a reversal of the trend toward limiting tribal sovereignty. Thus, taxation case law opened a period of division within the decision-making structures of the Court between using the sovereignty doctrine and using congressional authority.

Washington v. Confederated Tribes (Colville) (1980)

The first Supreme Court case to address these key issues was *Washington v. Confederated Tribes* (1980), often referred to as *Colville*.[63] Integrationist principles informed the discussion in the case, but so too did the traditional sovereignty doctrine. As Justice Blackmun observed, *Colville* was a complicated and "messy" case.[64]

The *Colville* case involved the Colville, Lummi, Makah, and Yakima tribes, which were challenging a range of taxes and laws imposed by the State of Washington over tribal members and nonmembers on tribal reservations. The state wanted to apply a cigarette sales tax and a motor vehicle excise tax as well as civil and criminal jurisdiction over certain reservations. The tribes contended that the imposition of a tribal tax prohibited the states from taxing on the reservations. Ultimately, the Court held that the state could not tax tribal cigarette sales to tribal members but ruled that the state, as well as the tribe, had authority to tax tribal sales to nonmembers.

Justice White was adamant in his belief that Congress had to legislate in an explicit manner to oust state law from the reservation, noting in the first draft of his partial concurrence/dissent that "the majority opinion proceeds on the assumption that federal law requires state tax laws to give way to Indian taxes on transactions between Indians and non-Indians on Indian reservations. I find nothing in our prior cases to support this result. Of course, the tribal tax involved here is a valid tax, but that alone does not warrant pre-empting state taxing power absent more definitive guidance from Congress than we have." Justice White's interpretation came at a time when a tentative majority of justices were thinking about prohibiting the state tax. However, he remained steadfast in his belief about the imposition of the state tax: "Until or unless Congress clearly construes and applies the Indian commerce clause to bar state taxes on reservation sales to non-Indians, I would sustain state revenue measures such as the cigarette and sales taxes involved here."[65]

The entire Supreme Court struggled with the intricacies of the case throughout its duration, but in the end the majority supported Justice White's initial stance. Writing for a majority of seven justices, White noted, "We do not believe that principles of federal Indian law, whether stated in terms of pre-emption, tribal self-government, or otherwise, authorize Indian tribes thus to market an exemption from state taxation to persons who would normally do their business elsewhere."[66] Congressional legislation such as the Indian Financing Act of 1975 and the Indian Self-Determination and Education Assistance Act of 1975 as well as the federal trader statutes were not relevant to granting power to the tribes.[67]

Justice Stevens concurred with White's interpretation. He believed that a state tax was valid even though the tribe also taxed the same transaction, noting, "It is perfectly clear that Washington's taxation of the tribal sales of cigarettes to non-Indians would be valid if the Tribes did not also tax those sales." Tribal authority was not strong enough to oust state law from the reservation: "I am unable to accept the Court's conclusion that the Tribes have the power, by their own action, to render an otherwise valid state tax invalid."[68] Justice Stevens was fundamentally opposed to the principle of inherent tribal sovereignty, and he favored the interests of the states.

Justice Rehnquist supported the right of the state to tax on the reservation until reversed by Congress. His support was based on a strong regard for the inherent right of the states to control all lands, including reservation lands, inside the boundaries of the state. The Rehnquist position was summed up in a clerk's memorandum to Justice Blackmun: "WR [Rehnquist] says that the state can do anything it wants."[69] This presumption about state rights was coupled with the fact that Justice Rehnquist considered tribal sovereignty to be anathema: "It is even more difficult to see why the state must necessarily reduce the scope of its taxing authority to accommodate any such taxing authority by the tribes." According to Rehnquist, tribal authority was exclusively "dependent upon congressional intent," and the tax existed until Congress said otherwise.[70] The importance of state rights and the limitations placed on tribal sovereignty by the Court from 1959 was explained by Rehnquist in a memorandum to Justice Brennan: "I, for one, am simply unwilling to see this Court step in as a surrogate for Congress unless the state taxation is discriminatory or subjects tribes to undue interference with tribal self-government—neither of which are present in this case."[71] This Rehnquist interpretation would prohibit a legal state tax only if it affected tribal government or was interpreted to be discriminatory against the person.

This Rehnquist viewpoint, termed "the Rehnquist test" by Ralph Johnson and Berrie Martinis, was "contrary to the Indian law doctrine disfavoring the application of state laws on a reservation where Congress has expressed no clear intent,"[72] but it clearly highlighted the movement of the Supreme Court away from the sovereignty doctrine. The principles or doctrine of state law on the reservation that Rehnquist spoke of in his first draft were based on congressional power and had developed before 1973 and been applied subsequently in the *McClanahan, Mescalero Apache Tribe,* and *Moe* cases: "Since early in the last century, this Court has been struggling to develop a coherent doctrine by which to measure with some predictability the scope of Indian immunity from state taxation. In recent years, it appeared such a doctrine was well on its way to being established. That doctrine, I had thought, was at bottom a pre-emption analysis based on the principle that Indian immunities are dependent upon congressional intent."[73]

In the sister taxation cases of *McClanahan* and *Mescalero Apache Tribe* (1973), the integrationist trend was reflected in a set of principles that allowed state law onto the reservations unless prohibited by Congress. Justice Rehnquist noted in his final opinion that the principles necessary for the resolution of this case are readily derived from our opinions in McClanahan and Mescalero. McClanahan confirmed the trend which had been developing in recent decades towards a reliance on a federal pre-emption analysis. Congress has for many years legislated extensively in the field of Indian affairs. . . . The companion case to McClanahan, Mescalero Apache Tribe v. Jones . . . established the corollary principle: When tradition did not recognize a sovereign immunity in favor of the Indians, this Court would recognize one only if Congress expressly conferred one. In Mescalero, the State of New Mexico asserted the right to impose a tax on the gross receipts of a ski resort owned and operated by an Indian tribe.[74]

In sum, Rehnquist thought that congressional power controlled the application of tribal authority over nonmembers and also allowed state law onto the reservation unless legislated otherwise by Congress: "I am satisfied that McClanahan and Mescalero were doctrinally correct, I dissent from the Court's failure to adhere to their teaching."[75]

Rehnquist directly conflicted with Justice Brennan, who supported the Indian sovereignty doctrine. In a memorandum to Brennan, Rehnquist wrote, "I agree that our differences on the principles applicable to adjudication of Indian tax immunities are fundamental."[76] These differences were made all too clear by the Rehnquist first draft: "It must, therefore, be solely by judicial intuition that the Court finds that Congress prohibited the States from taxing (at least to the full extent) cigarette purchases by non-Indian purchasers on the reservation. Just at the point of doctrinal development . . . [the Court] . . . pulls out of the closet a judicial immunity wand which may be used at will without regard to the intent of Congress." The attack on the beliefs and original opinion of Justice Brennan was scathing, and he ended his tirade by explaining that Brennan and the Court "had no choice but to devise a new set of rules in order to reach the result it does in this case."[77] In Justice Rehnquist's mind, the idea of inherent tribal sovereignty was irrelevant.

Justice Powell and Chief Justice Burger concurred with Justice Rehnquist, thinking that the sovereignty doctrine was not strong enough to oust state law from the reservation. Instead, they believed that state law existed on the reservation until reversed by congressional legislation. Although Powell appeared to agree with Justice Brennan in January 1980, he was clearly uncomfortable with the application of tribal sovereignty to oust state law. In addition, he wanted clarification of the relevant federal legislation that could be utilized to oust state law: "While I continue to agree with most of what you have written, I think that WHR's dissent makes a point when it says that the Court has not fully identified the source of the pre-emption in this case. Since it is no mere stroke of the tribal pen, but federal power that ousts the state tax, perhaps it would be well to address the gap that Bill identifies."[78]

Powell's view was clarified when he completely rejected Brennan's use of the sovereignty doctrine to oust state law from the reservation, explaining, "I had rather thought the Indians had the better of it on the preemption argument. I have not thought, however, that the principle of tribal self-government was strong enough in itself to prevent the state from taxing cigarette sales to non-Indians. I note that Bill Brennan now rests his view primarily on this ground."[79] Supporting the views of Justice Powell, Chief Justice Burger also dismissed the relevance of tribal sovereignty. Burger explained that the states had the right to tax on the reservation because the tribes had gained tax revenue from their ability to tax their own tribal members, noting that "Moe controls. . . . Indians can still tax their own."[80]

Justice Harry Blackmun followed the same process as Justice Powell and vacillated between the application of the sovereignty doctrine and integrationist principles, but in the end he joined the majority and allowed state law onto the reservation. Blackmun knew about the case for tribal sovereignty and initially supported the exclusive rights of the tribe over nonmembers. Support of the sovereignty doctrine relied on a principle derived from *Williams*. A clerk's memorandum to Justice Blackmun set out the position of *Williams* and the sovereignty doctrine: "The 'economic' activity of the tribe might be more reasonably be considered 'governmental' within the meaning of *Williams*—especially in light of the tribes' desperate need for revenue."[81] To justify using the sovereignty doctrine, Blackmun had to distinguish the facts of the *Colville* case from the *Moe* judgment, which neglected to use the sovereignty doctrine and allowed the application of a state tax on the reservation. The biggest difference between the *Moe* case and the *Colville* case was the involvement of tribal government. A memorandum from a Justice Blackmun clerk to Blackmun explained: "I think there is an important distinction between this case [*Colville*] and *Moe*. . . . In this case, we have a clear indication of the intent of the tribal government, acting in its legislative capacity, to develop an exclusive tribal taxing system. To my knowledge, there was no such tribal attempt to preempt in *Moe*." The tribes argued that the state tax was automatically ousted because it interfered with the process of tribal government. The same memorandum explained that the state tax "is an invalid interference with tribal autonomy, since the tribe has moved to create its own exclusive sovereign taxing program in the field of cigarette sales."[82] On this evidence, Justice Blackmun supported the use of congressional authority and tribal sovereignty to oust state law from the reservation, noting, "I am inclined and say preemption. . . . Tax is interference—tribes need all . . . help they can get—it impinges to a degree on self-government."[83]

Nevertheless, Blackmun understood the merits of state law on the reservation and eventually changed his mind about the application of the sovereignty doctrine. He elected to join the majority *Colville* opinion of Justice White for three reasons. First, he wanted to follow the principle he helped encourage in the *Moe* case, noting that "*Moe* may control but I am not settled yet."[84] Second, he was influenced by a clerk's memorandum that was concerned about the exact federal legislation that ousted state law from the reservation: "I continue to be troubled by exactly what law provides the basis of the decision in these cases."[85] His concern over legislation was similar to that expressed by Justice Powell. Third, Justice Blackmun's biggest fear was that, if the state tax was prohibited, it would allow the tribes to set up all kinds of businesses within the reservation boundaries, depriving the states of much needed revenues. This was reflected in the questions to be asked by Justice Blackmun of the *Colville* case: "If the tribes prevail here on the tax issues, will they not be able to immunize any business from state taxation within the borders of the reservation?"[86] As the clerk had written, "The danger of such a holding is that tribes might start marketing tax exemptions on every saleable item—*e.g.*, cars, trucks, helicopters. In light of this danger, you may see things differently than I, and wish to await the dissent."[87] For Justice Blackmun the overriding interest was the right of the state to enter the reservation. A memorandum Justice Blackmun received from his clerk had outlined the way to decide the issues of the case: "The Court should strive to retain as much of Wash's law as is legally possible."[88] In the end, Justice Blackmun believed in the right of the state to tax and supported Justice White's majority opinion because, as one of Blackmun's clerks wrote, he "handles the problem that most concerned you—i.e., the tribe's argument that even a de minimus tribal tax could completely eradicate the whole state tax."[89]

After addressing the merits of state law, the Court turned to examine the merits of tribal authority over nonmembers. The resulting viewpoint about the inherent right of the tribes to tax nonmembers was significantly different from rulings in criminal case law. The limitation of tribal sovereignty from 1973 appeared to influence the position of the justices regarding inherent tribal sovereignty over nonmembers. In *McClanahan,* tribal authority was limited to tribal members, and it appeared that the *Colville* court would apply the principle adopted in *Mazurie* of giving tribes authority over nonmembers, pursuant to a delegation of congressional power. A memorandum from Justice Powell to Justice Brennan confirmed that the Court had the option of applying the precedent of *Mazurie* and delegating congressional authority: "Our decisions show that such expressions of federal authority and policy can confer additional authority upon the Tribes and pre-empt inconsistent state laws. *United States v. Mazurie,* 419 U.S. 544 (1975), recognizes that the federal government can give the Indians authority over non-Indians who come within the reservation because the tribes traditionally have had substantial independent authority over non-Indians within their territory."[90]

The development of the integrationist principles that allowed state law onto the reservations weighed heavily on Powell's personal viewpoint in this case. He explained that the Court had to address these integrationist principles in its deliberations: "Perhaps some reference to these factors would emphasize the continuity in our Indian law decisions."[91] This was an acknowledgment of the movement of the Court away from tribal sovereignty over nonmembers. A clerk's memorandum supported Powell's position: "Tribal power to tax on-reservation transactions with nonmembers is federally delegated and an essential element of tribal sovereignty."[92] However, despite the support of federal authority, the majority of justices in the *Colville* opinion did not adopt this position and used *Mazurie* to confirm that only congressional authority was strong enough to oust state law: "The Tribes themselves could perhaps pre-empt state taxation through the exercise of properly delegated federal power to do so . . . United States v. Mazurie."[93] Rather than apply the presumption used in *Mazurie* and *Oliphant,* the Court applied the sovereignty doctrine, which allowed tribal taxation of nonmembers on the reservations.

Only Justices Brennan and Marshall supported the exclusive use of the sovereignty doctrine to tax nonmembers and to oust state law from the reservations, countering the Court's integrationist tendencies. In addition, the majority opinion supported the inherent sovereignty of the tribes to tax nonmembers, but as previously discussed tribal sovereignty did not oust state law from the reservation. Justice Brennan began from the presumption that the tribe had inherent sovereignty until divested by Congress. The imposition of the state tax endangered tribal authority. As he observed in his third draft of the original *Colville* opinion, "When the tribal government chose to tax the distribution of cigarettes, the Washington taxing scheme was brought into conflict with the Tribes' federally sanctioned functions and activities. The effect was to jeopardize tribal authority."[94] In Brennan's mind the *Colville* case was simply one where the action of the state interfered with tribal government; it did not call for an in-depth analysis of the history of federal Indian law: "In our view, these questions are considerably more narrow than some of the briefs suggest. We are not required to reconstruct the foundations of Indian sovereignty, locate the precise source of Indian power to assess taxes on non-Indians or finally define the relationship between State and Indian revenue-raising authority."[95] The sovereignty doctrine implied the exclusivity of tribal jurisdiction on the reservation. Justice Brennan viewed the state tax as an impediment to tribal government that "leads to an actual conflict of jurisdiction and sovereignty because the imposition of the Washington tax would inject state law into an on-reservation transaction which the Indians have chosen to subject to their own laws."[96] He interpreted the facts of *Colville* to be similar to those in *Williams*, and therefore the outcome should be the same. Justice Marshall supported this position.[97]

Despite an acknowledgement of the limitations on tribal sovereignty, which Brennan himself developed in *Mazurie* and *Moe*, he refused to dismiss its principles: "I do not read *McClanahan*, *Mescalero* and *Moe* to seal off [the] evolution of the sovereignty doctrine at some arbitrary point in the past or to deprive it of any effect in new situations. Accordingly, I do not intend to alter my position on the cigarette tax."[98]

The conflict between the two camps was symbolized by the divisions between Rehnquist and Brennan, with the latter pointing out that "Bill [Rehnquist] and I disagree substantially as to the applicable legal principles." Rehnquist's position stemmed from the presumption that the tribe had authority when sanctioned by Congress, and until Congress delegated power, any doubts on tribal authority were to be resolved against tribal interests. This principle infuriated Brennan, who considered it to be ignorance of the deep-seated traditions of the sovereignty doctrine used by the Supreme Court: "I find the suggestion that until we do we should resolve doubtful cases against the Indians extraordinary. Rather, I would think, we must attempt to fill in the interstices in existing laws and treaties as best we can. That process inevitably involves appropriate reference to broad federal policies and notions of Indian sovereignty, however amorphous."[99]

Brennan's position reflected the ideas of tribal sovereignty and deference to federal policy and formed the basis of his partial dissent and concurrence in the *Colville* opinion. In the final opinion, he confirmed his view that the sovereignty doctrine prohibited state law on the reservation: "There is a significant territorial component to tribal power . . . and tribal laws will often govern the on-reservation conduct of non-Indians." This was taken from his original written opinion in this case, which was not supported by a majority of the Court. Furthermore, Justice Brennan believed that the underlying reasons of the decision had to be based on "a presumption of sovereignty or autonomy that has roots deep in aboriginal independence." In his view, the majority opinion had taken no consideration of tribal interests and in fact "erodes the Tribes' sovereign authority and stands the special federal solicitude for Indian commerce and governmental autonomy on its head."[100]

Despite the internal differences, the Court ruled that tribes had inherent sovereignty to tax nonmembers on the reservation. Although some justices wanted to apply a delegation of congressional power to sanction tribal authority over nonmembers, in the end the *Colville* court applied the opposite principle: "The power to tax transactions occurring on trust lands and significantly involving a tribe or its members is a fundamental attribute of sovereignty which the tribes retain unless divested of it by federal law or necessary implication of their dependent status."[101] This opinion was in stark contrast to the underlying principles used by the Court in *Oliphant* and *Mazurie*. The *Colville* rationale, in part, held that tribal powers were not implicitly divested because of the dependent status of the tribes, whereas *Oliphant* held that tribal powers over nonmembers were precluded because they were "inconsistent with their [dependent] status."[102] This contrast was explicit in the *Colville* opinion: "In these respects the present cases differ sharply from Oliphant v. Suquamish Indian Tribe."[103]

Although the Court recognized the dichotomy, it has never resolved the issue.[104] One thing was certain, though: the right of the tribes to tax was considered more important than their right to prosecute nonmembers, as shown in *Oliphant*. The difficulties of the *Colville* case were resolved, then, with a compromise. The Supreme Court sanctioned general state authority on the reservations and over nonmembers on the reservations until reversed by Congress. It also ruled that tribes had the inherent right to tax nonmembers on the reservations. Therefore, the principles of state and tribal taxation of nonmembers on the reservations were both confirmed by the Court. These principles would be put to the test in a series of taxation cases from 1980 to 1989.

White Mountain Apache Tribe v. Bracker (1980)

White Mountain Apache Tribe v. Bracker (1980) examined whether state law applied to the activities of a nonmember company on a reservation.[105] Nonmember Pinetop Logging Company was employed by the White Mountain Apache Tribe to fell trees on the Fort Apache Reservation. The State of Arizona imposed its taxes on the activities of Pinetop on the reservation. Pinetop paid the taxes under protest from 1971 and brought an action claiming that the state could not tax it while it worked on tribal and Bureau of Indian Affairs (BIA) roads and exclusively inside reservation boundaries. Ultimately, the Supreme Court held that congressional authority prohibited the state from taxing the nonmember company while it traveled on tribal and BIA roads. The Blackmun and Powell papers reveal that discussions between the justices in the leadup to the decision of the Court rested on the use of congressional authority and not the sovereignty doctrine to oust state law from the reservation. In fact, some references to the sovereignty doctrine were deleted from the opinion.

In this case, Justice Marshall confirmed the Court's use of federal authority in a memorandum to Justice White: "It is the Federal regulatory scheme in general, that leads to the result we reach."[106] Justice Powell believed that the federal statutes and the precedent of *Warren Trading Post* were important factors in the case: "Regulation of timbering is pervasive, Warren Trading Post seems controlling. Even maybe a W/P [Warren Trading Post] argument. State conferred no benefit for these taxes."[107] This reliance on federal statutes was in Justice Blackmun's view similar to the facts of *Warren Trading Post*: "Preemption . . . Warren TP [Trading Post] again controls."[108] Blackmun based his interpretation on a memorandum he received from his clerk: "This case, like *Warren Trading Post* and the pending decision in *Central Machinery,* involves preemption by a federal statute specifically addressing the subject matter taxed by the state." In addition, Blackmun was concerned that his viewpoint in this case contradicted the position he took in *Colville,* but the clerk alleviated Blackmun's predicament: the current case involved the power of Congress and not issues of tribal sovereignty: "Nothing in this opinion would seem to run against your positions in *Confederated Tribes* [*Colville*]. That case involves only the *Williams* principle of tribal self-government. This case, like *Warren Trading Post* and the pending decision in *Central Machinery,* involves pre-emption by a federal statute."[109]

Justice White also agreed that the Court could use congressional authority to oust state law from the reservation and considered the use of tribal sovereignty to be redundant. He was concerned about the language used in a draft opinion, which he believed appeared to support the use of the sovereignty doctrine: "While I agree that federal policies are relevant, this statement might suggest an inquiry into the broad policies of encouraging Indian self-government and strengthening reservation economies without due attention to the specific language and provision of the relevant statutes."[110] The statement to which Justice White referred was from *Bryan v. Itasca County* (1976), which addressed inherent tribal sovereignty and the presumption that states did not have the authority to tax reservation Indians unless Congress passed specific legislation.[111] This position influenced Justice Marshall to delete this reference to inherent tribal sovereignty from the final opinion. Justice White believed, "This statement was unexceptional in *Bryan*," and that the Supreme Court in *Moe* allowed the states to tax nonmembers influenced the *Bracker* case: "It is questionable whether the same rule [in *Bryan*] applies in cases involving State taxation of non-Indians doing business on the reservation. Indeed, *Moe* seems to the contrary, since the State was there permitted to tax non-Indian purchasers from Indian-operated reservation smoke shops despite the absence of federal statutes clearly intended to allow State taxation."[112] Justice White was also concerned about the broad language limiting state jurisdiction over non-Indians: "As you note, generalizations in Indian law are treacherous. I am concerned that some of the broader statements in parts of the opinion, taken out of context, might be applied in an inappropriate way in future cases."[113]

In the end, Justice White dissented from the majority opinion because he believed that the Court should have followed the *Moe* judgment and ruled that an explicit congressional act was required to oust state law from the reservation. This viewpoint contrasted with Justice Marshall's view and the opinion itself, which relied on congressional authority and was informed by the Court's recognition of tribal sovereignty. Marshall agreed with the Court's use of federal preemption, which was informed by the traditions of tribal sovereignty, and underlined that *Williams* was also relevant in cases concerning tribal versus state power: "A number of our cases recognize the principle that the exercise of state authority over the reservation may be impermissible, not because it is 'preempted' in the ordinary sense, but because it infringes on tribal self-government. See *Williams v. Lee*."[114]

This interpretation of *Williams* did not, however, support the inherent sovereignty of the tribes but instead supported the interpretation used by the Supreme Court after 1959, which allowed state law onto the reservation unless the tribes could prove that it infringed on their rights. In the final opinion, Justice Marshall appeared to revive the sovereignty doctrine, but it was in language only: "The 'semi-independent position' of Indian tribes" gave rise to a barrier that prevented "the assertion of state regulatory authority over tribal reservations and members" if it unlawfully infringed "on the right of reservation Indians to make their own laws and be ruled by them." This barrier was "a sufficient basis for holding state law inapplicable to activity undertaken on the reservation or by tribal members."[115]

Although this statement was true, the *Williams* test had changed drastically from 1959, and it no longer prohibited state law from the reservation. Justice Marshall acknowledged his *McClanahan* opinion of 1973 and mentioned that tribal sovereignty in that case was used within the broader context of federal preemption. Preemption worked on the presumption that "traditional notions of Indian self-government are so deeply engrained in our jurisprudence that they have provided an important 'backdrop' . . . against which vague or ambiguous federal enactments must always be measured."[116] Considerations of tribal sovereignty helped inform the federal preemption process, which prohibited state law over nonmembers: "In a number of cases we have held that state authority over non-Indians acting on tribal reservations is pre-empted even though Congress has offered no explicit statement on the subject."[117] This analysis reduced the arguments of the state "to a claim that they may assess taxes on non-Indians engaged in commerce on the reservation whenever there is no express congressional statement to the contrary"—of which Marshall said, "That is simply not the law."[118]

This statement may appear to have revitalized the tribal sovereignty argument, but the opinion of the Court was considered only within the framework of federal preemption.[119] The opinion did not consider the use of the sovereignty doctrine. It held that federal preemption was a barrier that prohibited the application of state law on the reservation, and for state law to be preempted there had to be not only congressional legislation but also broad considerations for the interests of the tribe.[120]

In the end, the *Bracker* court held that the state tax did not apply to a nonmember company. Justices Rehnquist, Stewart, and Stevens dissented and believed that state law existed on the reservation until explicitly removed by Congress. This was a reaffirmation of the position adopted by a majority of the Court in *Colville*. As Justice Stevens said, "Shouldn't let people who do business with Indians escape state tax."[121] This principle of the inherent right of the states to tax influenced the position of the dissenters.

Central Machinery Co. v. Arizona Tax Comm'n (1980)

Central Machinery Co. v. Arizona Tax Comm'n (1980) followed the same rationale as *Bracker*, and the justices were similarly divided.[122] This case considered whether a nonmember company that sold eleven tractors to an enterprise operated by the Gila River Indian Tribe, called Gila River Farms, had to pay a state tax. All business transactions between the nonmember company and the tribe, involving the initial business dealings to obtain the tractors, contracts, payment, and delivery, were completed exclusively on the reservation. The State of Arizona sought to tax these transactions. The Supreme Court ruled that because the business deal took place on the reservation and was controlled by federal regulations, the state tax was prohibited.

The majority of justices used congressional preemption, the same principle used in *Bracker*, to prohibit a state tax on a nonmember company on the reservation. Interestingly, the majority recognized the influence of integrationist principles but did not apply them, whereas the dissent recognized and used them. The key difference between the two positions was that the majority used tribal sovereignty to influence its analysis and was intent on protecting the interests of the tribe. In fact, a memorandum to Justice Blackmun criticized the majority for the lack of evidence to support its position, pointing out that "the opinion is barebones."[123] The majority recognized the impact of the sister taxation cases, *McClanahan* and *Mescalero Apache Tribe*, and *Moe* and *Colville* on the law but refused to apply that integrationist conclusion: "It may be that in light of modern conditions the State of Arizona should be allowed to tax transactions such as the one involved in this case. Until Congress repeals or amends the Indian trader statutes, however, we must give them 'a sweep as broad as [their] language' . . . and interpret them in light of the intent of the Congress that enacted them."[124]

The majority relied on the broad holding of *Warren Trading Post*, which declared that congressional statutes ousted a state tax on a nonmember trader. Even though *Warren* did acknowledge tribal sovereignty, the *Central Machinery* case did not. Justice Marshall followed the advice of a bench memorandum, which read that a state tax was "impermissible because . . . it interferes with tribal self-government by taxing tribal conduct on the reservation. There is no need for the Court to reach . . . these contentions."[125] Chief Justice Burger agreed with the outcome and noted, "All transactions were on reservation. In 1604 [Central Machinery] federally approved . . . sale on Reservation is enough. Federal Government has preempted all trading on Reservation. Purpose is to protect Indians. 1604 is stronger for preemption than Warren Trading Post."[126]

The positions of Justices Rehnquist, Stevens, Stewart, and Powell throughout the case relied on integrationist principles and fundamentally rejected the sovereignty doctrine and tribal sovereignty. Rehnquist determined simply that congressional authority was not explicit, noting that "Congress has not preempted this."[127] Justice Stevens concurred with this viewpoint and added that nothing in the legislation prevented the state from taxing, pointing out that "state can tax even versus a federal statute" and "preemption arg.—no merit—no evidence of federal interests to preempt. Warren not pertinent here because no federal license here."[128] Justice Powell agreed, noting, "Unlike the situation in Warren Trading, petitioner was not in business of trading on Reservation. No pervasive federal regulations of isolated transactions of sale of these tractors. No preemption. Only Indian interest was not to be taken advantage of. But result here would have been same if Indians had bought tractors in Phoenix."[129]

The majority took issue with the "existence of the Indian trader statutes, not their administration" to preempt state law.[130] For the dissent, this was not explicit evidence of congressional authority as there was in *Warren Trading Post*. As Justice Stewart said, "Warren relates to licensing of I [Indian] traders—none such here."[131] Justice Stewart confirmed his position when he wrote in dissent that "the Court's construction of the trader statutes" was too sweeping and "no portion of [them] indicates a congressional intention to immunize anybody from state taxation."[132] The dissent argued that the *Central Machinery* opinion contradicted the philosophy and decree of *Moe* and *Colville*.[133] Based on the movement of the Court toward congressional authority and the rulings in those two cases, the dissent argued that allowing states to tax on the reservation was commonplace: "The Court has on more than one occasion sustained state taxation of transactions occurring on Indian reservations."[134]

Ramah Navajo School Bd. v. Bureau of Revenue (1982)

Only two years after *Central Machinery*, the justices again had to decide a case that involved the right of the state to tax a nonmember company on a reservation. In *Ramah Navajo School Bd. v. Bureau of Revenue* (1982), the Court followed a similar path to the *Bracker* case, on virtually identical principles.[135] In this case, the Court had to decide whether federal law prohibited the State of New Mexico from taxing a nonmember company, Lembke Construction, which had received funds from the Ramah Navajo Chapter of the Navajo Indian Tribe and the federal government to build a tribal school on the reservation. From 1974 to 1977, the nonmember company paid the state tax, and the tribe reimbursed these payments of $232,264.38, but both Lembke and the tribe protested the imposition of state taxes.

A memorandum written by a Justice Blackmun clerk discussed the general movement of the Court away from the sovereignty doctrine and toward integrationist principles. The clerk discussed the views of the solicitor general, who argued that the justices should use the sovereignty doctrine to preempt state law over nonmembers on the reservation: "The SG's suggestion, which relies strongly on the tradition of Indian sovereignty, is almost as unsatisfactory. As the Court noted some years ago, 'the trend has been away from the idea of inherent Indian sovereignty as a bar to state jurisdiction and toward a reliance on federal preemption. . . .' McClanahan, 411 U.S. at 172." The limitations put on tribal sovereignty supposed that the Court, as it had done before and after *Williams* in 1959, the clerk continued, could not use the sovereignty doctrine as a rule prohibiting state law on the reservation: "I am not much impressed by the parties' suggestions that the Court develop a broad rule that will dispose of a substantial number of cases. It may well be that this area of the law is confused, and that the Court therefore is forced to hear entirely too many Indian cases." On this view, congressional authority was the only appropriate tool to protect the tribes from state law. The shift away from the sovereignty doctrine did not show any signs of being diminished or reversed: "I would not adopt the general rule proposed by the SG, which seems inconsistent with several of the Court's decisions."[136] At the conference, Justice Powell tentatively supported the tribe but was unconvinced with the use of preemption in these cases: "Inclined to think White Mountain and Central Machinery come close to controlling. There probably is federal preemption—though I don't think this should be the law and could be persuaded not to reverse [the holding below]."[137]

Ramah court memoranda show that many of the justices agreed with the use of congressional authority in the case. Indeed, some justices relied specifically on federal preemption to prohibit state law over nonmembers on the reservation. The presence of general legislation was enough for Justice

Blackmun to support the preclusion of the state tax, who noted that "regulation not so pervasive as in WM [White Mountain] . . . but Preemption . . . federal supervision."[138] Justice Sandra Day O'Connor agreed that *White Mountain Apache* was the relevant case and supported the use of federal regulations: "WM depends on fed regul if we stick with that we [apply federal regulations in *Ramah*]."[139] Justice Brennan was explicit about using congressional authority as had previously been done in *White Mountain Apache* and *Central Machinery*: "WM + Central Mach reg use."[140]

Although the *Ramah* opinion of the Court relied on federal authority, it again underlined tribal sovereignty as a principle to prohibit state law on the reservation. The Court once again declared that inherent tribal sovereignty and the *Williams* test of 1959 were principles capable of prohibiting state law on the reservation, but it used these principles only to inform the process of federal preemption.[141] The language used to support tribal sovereignty was based on the "infringement test" from *Williams*, but, as the above discussion of *Bracker* makes clear, the Court's interpretation of this test changed dramatically after its use in *Williams* and had not relied on inherent tribal sovereignty. The Court's use of tribal sovereignty was contained within its federal preemption analysis of the case: "Ambiguities in federal law should be construed generously, and federal pre-emption is not limited to those situations where Congress has explicitly announced an intention to pre-empt state activity."[142] The presumption of tribal sovereignty, where tribal authority prevailed unless specifically removed by Congress, continued to be used within the framework of federal preemption. This interpretation of tribal sovereignty was highlighted in Justice Marshall's opinion: "The Bureau of Revenue argues that imposition of the state tax is not pre-empted because the federal statutes and regulations do not specifically express the intention to pre-empt this exercise of state authority. This argument is clearly foreclosed by our precedents. In White Mountain we flatly rejected a similar argument."[143] Limitations placed on tribal sovereignty by the Court, especially when issues of state law were involved, meant that the majority opinion did not interpret or use this statement to support the independence of the sovereignty doctrine.

In contrast, the position of the three justices in the *Ramah* dissent showed the movement of the Court toward congressional authority and the irrelevance of the sovereignty doctrine that prohibited state law over nonmembers on the reservation. At conference, Justice Stevens supported the rights of the states, noting, "No reason why State can't tax contractor."

Justice Rehnquist agreed and explained that "prior cases do not control. Can distinguish White Mountain and Central Machinery. Regulations in there were more specific."[144] The presumption of the dissent was that tribal sovereignty applied only to tribal members. The dissent, written by Justice Rehnquist, was virtually identical to the position he adopted in *Colville*; once again, he believed that the Supreme Court was following an identified trend, one that allowed the state to tax nonmembers on the reservation unless explicitly prohibited by Congress and ultimately eviscerated the sovereignty doctrine: "I believe the dominant trend of our cases is toward treating the scope of reservation immunity from nondiscriminatory state taxation as a question of pre-emption, ultimately dependent on congressional intent. In such a framework, the tradition of Indian sovereignty stands as an independent barrier to discriminatory taxes, and otherwise serves only as a guide to the ascertainment of the congressional will."[145]

In the minds of the dissenters, the sovereignty doctrine and inherent tribal sovereignty were irrelevant in the face of "the sovereign prerogatives of the State of New Mexico." The limitations placed on tribal sovereignty resulted from the involvement of the states and their laws. In some instances, however, "a state law may be invalid because it infringes 'the right of reservation Indians to make their own laws and be ruled by them.'" But this applied only in instances where "the State attempts to interfere with the residual sovereignty of a tribe to govern its own members[;] the 'tradition of tribal sovereignty' merely provides a 'backdrop' against which the pre-emptive effect of federal statutes or treaties must be assessed."[146] The principle of tribal sovereignty was insufficient to prevent state law from being applicable to nonmembers on the reservation. In fact, Justice Rehnquist connected the limitations of tribal sovereignty when confronted with state power with the limitations of tribal authority over nonmembers—thereby reflecting nearly all of the aspects of the integrationist trend.

Merrion v. Jicarilla Apache Tribe (1982)

Although in *Ramah* Justice Rehnquist did not consider tribal sovereignty to be a bona fide principle to govern nonmembers on reservations, this was the critical issue in *Merrion v. Jicarilla Apache Tribe* (1982), where the question was whether the Jicarilla Apache Tribe had inherent sovereignty to tax a nonmember company that extracted oil and gas on the reservation.[147] In 1953 the tribe had given a nonmember company leases to remove oil and gas from the reservation, but the tribal constitution did not allow the tribe to impose a tax. This changed in 1969 when the Jicarillas amended their constitution to allow the imposition of a tribal tax, and in 1976 they imposed a tax on the nonmember company. The Supreme Court held that the Jicarilla Apaches had inherent power to impose the tax. In contrast to *Bracker, Central Machinery,* and *Ramah,* this case did not involve state interests of authority over a nonmember company.

In contrast to earlier case law that had weakened the sovereignty doctrine, in *Merrion* many justices reaffirmed the sovereignty doctrine as a viable source of tribal government power over nonmembers. Justice Brennan considered taxation to be an integral part of tribal government, noting that "the power to tax derives from their retained power of sovereignty. The power to tax is necessary to the vestiges which remain of Indian self-government."[148] Justice Blackmun concurred with the importance of raising revenue from nonmember taxes: "I agreed with Thurgood at Conference that the Jicarilla possess the sovereign power to levy the challenged tax."[149] Justice Marshall began from the presumption he adopted in his *Oliphant* dissent that tribes retain sovereignty until divested by Congress: "I am convinced that the Tribe retained the power to impose the severance taxes involved here," and "I would confirm the Tribe's authority to tax as necessary to self-government and territorial management."[150] These principles formed the basis of the *Merrion* majority opinion.

The underlying principle used by Marshall in formulating his opinion began from the presumption that tribes have inherent sovereignty until removed by Congress. He reiterated that only Congress could reverse the tribes' inherent right to tax, explaining that a tribe "did not surrender its authority to tax the mining activities of petitioners, whether this authority is deemed to arise from the Tribe's inherent power of self-government or from its inherent power to exclude nonmembers. Therefore, the Tribe may enforce its severance tax unless and until Congress divests this power, an action that Congress has not taken to date."[151]

This was a strict application of the sovereignty doctrine, one that contrasted significantly with the developing integrationist trend and, in particular, the *Mazurie* and *Oliphant* rulings. In those cases, criminal authority over nonmembers was not considered important to tribal government and was not protected by the sovereignty doctrine. In *Merrion,* the majority considered taxing nonmembers a fundamental right essential for generating government revenue: "The power to tax is an essential attribute of Indian sovereignty because it is a necessary instrument of self-government and territorial management. This power enables a tribal government to raise revenues for its essential services. The power . . . derives from the tribe's general authority, as sovereign, to control economic activity within its jurisdiction, and to defray the cost of providing governmental services by requiring contributions from persons or enterprises engaged in economic activities within that jurisdiction."[152] Clearly the Court was considering the everyday economic pressures on the tribes to be relevant to tribal sovereignty. Tax revenue was important for tribal government to provide services to both tribal members and nonmembers.

Within the Court, though, there were definitive movements to further the integrationist trend and to limit the *Colville* precedent. Justice Rehnquist believed that tribal authority over nonmembers and the use of tribal authority to prohibit state law from the reservation were no longer viable principles to be supported. He viewed these two aspects of tribal sovereignty to be connected, and tribal authority, regardless of the facts of the case, was dependent on congressional intent: "I wonder if you could cite somewhere in the opinion Byron's *Mescalero Apache Tribe* v. *Jones*, 411 U.S. 145 (1973), and Thurgood's *McClanahan* v. *Arizona State Tax Commission*, 411 U.S. 164 (1973). They are more or less the 'flip side' of this case, but since they are fairly recent opinions dealing with *state* authority to tax income of a tribe or individual Indians residing on a reservation I think they are consistent with your analysis."[153]

Justice Rehnquist believed that tribal authority in any situation was limited to tribal members and that Congress had to sanction tribal authority over nonmembers. He noted that it "takes something more than residual sovereign power to tax non-members" and "takes > residual sovereign power for Is [Indians] to tax non Is."[154] This position was supported by Chief Justice Burger, who believed that Congress had to delegate authority to the tribes and asked, "Is there inherent authority? None reserved in lease."[155] The views of Justice Marshall had attracted a majority following, but Justice Stevens remained resolute about the limitations placed on tribal sovereignty by Supreme Court case law, explaining that the "cases clarify a def. btro [definite breakthrough] powers of Tribe over its members and over nonmembers."[156] Stevens disagreed with the principles of tribal sovereignty used by Marshall, noting that "it will come as no great surprise that I intend to circulate a dissent." The reason for the dissent was made clear in a memorandum to Justice Marshall that pointed out that the opinion did "not adequately confront the critical distinction between an Indian tribe's power over its own members, which is a good deal greater than the power possessed by many sovereigns, and its much more limited power over nonmembers."[157] Justice Stevens believed that there was a "real difference between [tribal] powers over tribe and powers over non-members."[158]

Justice O'Connor agreed with the three justices who would form the *Merrion* dissent, but she had issues regarding the *Colville* case: "Do not like the broad conclusions in this draft," but "Colville said tax can be levied and not positive I can do that."[159] In the end, O'Connor joined the majority opinion, whereas the three dissenters maintained the presumption that the tribe did not have power over nonmembers until delegated authority by Congress. For Justice Stevens, this was "consistent with this Court's recognition of the limited character of the power of Indian tribes over nonmembers in general."[160]

Throughout considerations of this case, the justices had difficulties reconciling the movement of the Court away from tribal sovereignty with the precedent of *Colville,* which allowed tribes to tax nonmembers, and came perilously close to prohibiting the right of the tribe to tax. But in the end the ideological differences were reflected in a six to three majority opinion in favor of inherent tribal sovereignty.[161] The dissent again reflected the integrationist trend, which relied on congressional authority to sanction tribal authority over nonmembers on the reservation.

Kerr-McGee Corp. v. Navajo Tribe (1985) and
California v. Cabazon Band of Mission Indians (1987)

Although *Merrion* reaffirmed the inherent right of the tribes to tax nonmembers on the reservation, that right had been weakened by the position taken by the three dissenters. Toward the latter part of the 1980s, the Court once again addressed the question of inherent tribal sovereignty and the rights of state authority on the reservation.

The *Kerr-McGee Corp. v. Navajo Tribe* (1985) case again considered the sovereignty doctrine and the presumption that tribes enjoyed the sovereign right to tax nonmembers until reversed by Congress.[162] In 1978 the Navajo Tribe had enacted ordinances taxing tribal members and nonmember companies with leasehold interests on the reservation and taxing the receipts of the property extracted from the reservation. These ordinances had been submitted for federal approval, but the BIA told the Navajos that no federal act required the BIA to approve them. A nonmember company that extracted minerals from the reservation disapproved of these ordinances and appealed their imposition.

The deliberations of the justices during this case reveal the importance of *Merrion* to the outcome. Justice Stevens stated that the current case was "controlled by Merrion."[163] Justice Blackmun agreed about the application of inherent tribal sovereignty. He noted "I [Indian] sovereignty recgd in Merrion and Colville. Cong can divest this power but it must do so clearly and affirmably. Sovereignty exists and silence [of Congress] confirms it."[164] In other words, tribal inherent sovereignty existed because it had not been removed by explicit congressional legislation. In its opinion, the Court confirmed that the tribes did not require the consent of the secretary of the interior to tax nonmembers on the reservation.

Only two years after *Kerr-McGee*, the Court had to decide another case that involved state authority over nonmembers. In *California v. Cabazon Band of Mission Indians* (1987), the Supreme Court had to decide whether to prohibit a state from taxing reservation activities.[165] The Cabazon and Morongo Bands of Mission Indians operated federally approved reservation bingo games and card games on their reservation in Riverside County, California. The State of California and Riverside County wanted to impose their statutes governing bingo and card games on the reservation because the tribal gaming enterprises attracted large numbers of nonmember users to the reservation.

Once again the justices had to balance the interests of the tribe and the state over nonmembers. A bench memorandum from a Justice Blackmun clerk set out an argument that excluded state law from the reservation because the activity involved a tribal enterprise: "The state is not only attempting to exercise jurisdiction over Indians, but it is trying to exercise jurisdiction over the Tribes," and because the tribal nation was involved in the activity state law was excluded.[166] This position was supported by Justice White, who had circulated an opinion, and Justice Blackmun's clerk sent a memorandum to Blackmun urging him to "form a court." The reasons were set out as follows: "The Tribe here is acting in its capacity as a tribal unit or nation raising revenue for tribal health and welfare programs. In such a situation, the tribal immunity is much stronger and it is arguably appropriate for the Court to require an express congressional statement authorizing the State's jurisdiction in such situations." The interests of the tribe outweighed the interests of the state. In sum, "he [Justice White] applies the Federal Common Law balancing approach and simply recognizes that the tribal sovereignty interests weigh heavily in situations where the traditional goals of Indian self-government and economic development are involved."[167] Interestingly, Justice Stevens circulated a dissent that supported state law on the reservation until Congress explicitly acted to preclude it. Another memorandum to Blackmun acknowledged that the position adopted by Stevens was misleading: "The legal analysis is very cursory and does not present a fair reading of the Court's treatment of cases involving tribal activities even when non-Indians are involved."[168] Blackmun was urged to join Justices Brennan, Marshall, and Powell, who had already joined the Justice White draft opinion.

The ruling of the *Cabazon* court followed a path similar to those of *Bracker, Central Machinery,* and *Ramah* and prohibited the state tax on grounds of federal preemption, reflecting the historical traditions of tribal sovereignty. The three dissenters argued that there was no explicit congressional authority prohibiting the states from taxing nonmembers. Once again, the integrationist trend was evident in the thinking of the justices in a case dealing with state law over nonmembers.

Cotton Petroleum Corp. v. New Mexico (1989)

After *Cabazon,* the personnel of the Supreme Court changed and it became more unified in its expression of the integrationist trend. In 1986, Justice Rehnquist replaced Warren Burger as chief justice, and Antonin Scalia filled the empty seat.[169] Justice Scalia was a vigorous integrationist, as was Justice O'Connor during the late 1980s and into the 1990s. Then, in 1988 with the appointment of Anthony Kennedy, the Court shifted further away from the ideas of tribal sovereignty toward integration.[170] In 1989 the Court demonstrated this shift in its handling of the *Cotton Petroleum Corp. v. New Mexico* (1989) case.[171]

The *Cotton* case again tested whether a state could tax a nonmember company on the reservation. The Jicarilla Apache Tribe leased lands to the Cotton Petroleum Corporation, a nonmember company, for the production of oil and gas, which was subject to both tribal and states taxes. The company paid the states taxes under protest and appealed, arguing that they were preempted by federal law. The majority opinion of the *Cotton* court was the first to apply integrationist principles in the 1980s.

The majority opinion applied the principles found in the Rehnquist concurrence/dissent in *Colville* and in the *Bracker, Central Machinery, Ramah,* and *Cabazon* dissents. Six justices ruled that a state could tax a nonmember company on the reservation because no explicit congressional legislation existed to prevent the tax.[172] The majority opinion used federal preemption to decide the outcome of the case, but not in the same way as in the majority opinions in *Bracker, Ramah,* and *Cabazon,* which had relied on the traditions of tribal sovereignty. Instead, the *Cotton* majority relied on the interests of the states and the idea that states had the right to tax nonmember companies unless it was removed by explicit congressional legislation.

Chief Justice Rehnquist, who had been demanding some consistency in the tax cases, believed that no federal legislation existed to bar the state tax, noting to "reject fed. preemption point."[173] Justice Stevens concurred with Rehnquist and argued that the case law during the 1980s had been too "pro-Indian": "I [Indians] have been out of step in I [Indian] cases."[174] Justice Stevens reinforced his views in his opinion, explaining, "Under this Court's modern decisions, on-reservation oil and gas production by non-Indian lessees is subject to nondiscriminatory state taxation unless Congress has expressly or impliedly acted to pre-empt the state taxes."[175]

The *Cotton* case involved the issue of federal preemption, but it did not follow the principles laid down in the precedent of *Bracker,* which required federal preemption to be informed by tribal sovereignty.[176] The use of federal preemption in *Cotton* relied exclusively on whether specific congressional legislation existed that prohibited state law over nonmembers on a reservation.[177]

Ultimately, the *Cotton* majority applied the rationale of the *Ramah* dissent, which at the time included Rehnquist, White, and Stevens.[178] As Justice Stevens explained, federal preemption was "primarily an exercise in examining congressional intent."[179] The Court had examined whether a congressional act limited state sovereignty over nonmember activity on the reservation. In the opinion of the Court, there were no explicit regulations that prohibited state law and, therefore, congressional silence on the issue meant that state sovereignty was not preempted by federal legislation.[180] This process did not allow tribal sovereignty to influence the Court's assessment of congressional legislation. The *Cotton* court viewed tribal sovereignty, as had the *Ramah* dissent, merely as a test to prevent the imposition of a discriminatory tax, thereby reducing tribal authority to authority over tribal members only.[181] In the view of the *Cotton* majority, the state tax on a nonmember company was lawful and not considered to be discriminatory. Limitations on tribal sovereignty were consistent with the Court's philosophy that the boundary between the reservation and the state no longer existed. The Court summed up this process of integration, explaining that this was "an area where two governmental entities share jurisdiction."[182]

Since 1989, the Supreme Court has not once ruled in favor of exclusive tribal jurisdiction over nonmembers or prohibited state taxation authority over nonmembers on a reservation.[183] The integrationist trend was evident in state law and state authority over nonmembers sanctioned on the reservation. Concurrent tribal and state taxation of nonmembers became the accepted standard. Then, in 2001, the same integrationist principles directly began affecting the inherent right of the tribe to tax nonmembers on the reservations, as we see in the next section.

Civil Jurisdiction Case Law, 1981–2001

The shift of the Supreme Court away from the sovereignty doctrine and toward integration happened gradually in civil case law between 1981 and 2001. Although the archival evidence of the Blackmun papers ends in 1994, the general trend of the Court was still apparent in its opinions after 1994.

In civil case law, the justices exhibited the integrationist principles seen in the *Mazurie* and *Oliphant* opinions, which ruled that a congressional delegation of authority was required for tribes to have authority over nonmembers on a reservation. This principle was unanimously applied by the Court in *Montana v. United States* (1981), but only to nonmembers on nonmember or fee lands on the reservation. Conversely, the *Montana* court also applied the principle of inherent tribal sovereignty over nonmembers on tribal or trust lands on the reservation. The status of land was important to determine jurisdiction. Interestingly, in 1983 the Court used a preemption test, similar to that used in taxation case law, to determine the scope of state authority versus tribal authority over nonmembers on a reservation; this test was not used by the Court again in civil case law.

Between 1989 and 1993, the diverse views of the justices regarding tribal sovereignty over nonmembers on nonmember lands led to an ideological battle. Some justices wanted to apply the sovereignty doctrine; others stressed integration. In 1993 the Court was still bound by its own *Montana* precedent, which ruled that tribes had inherent civil authority over nonmembers on tribal and trust lands, and set about circumventing this principle. It extracted an idea from *Montana* whereby any tribal or trust land appropriated by Congress or any involvement of nonmembers on the lands in question resulted in the divestiture of exclusive tribal authority and therefore the loss of tribal trust status and inherent tribal sovereignty over those lands. This eroded the sovereignty doctrine and strengthened the integrationist trend over tribal lands.

In 2001 the Court was fully integrationist for the first time in civil case law: tribes were prevented from exercising civil authority over nonmembers on tribal lands on a reservation and, as a result, the state had inherent sovereignty over nonmembers there. This process all began with the case of *Montana v. United States*.

Montana v. United States (1981)

The integrationist principles visible in *Mazurie* (1975) and *Oliphant* (1978), cases within which tribal authority over nonmembers required a delegation of congressional power, and the revival of inherent tribal sovereignty in *Colville* (1980) directly influenced *Montana v. United States* (1981).[184] In this case, the Crow Tribe of Montana introduced a regulation preventing nonmember hunting and fishing on the reservation, which included nonmember/fee lands and tribal lands. The tribe relied on its ownership of the bed of the Big Horn River, its treaties, and its inherent sovereignty to prove that it had civil authority over nonmembers on the entire reservation. In contrast to the arguments of the Crow Tribe, the State of Montana contended that it had authority to regulate nonmember hunting and fishing.

During deliberations, several justices dismissed inherent tribal sovereignty as a principle that allowed the tribes regulatory power over nonmember activity. The basis of tribal authority had to be sanctioned by Congress. Justice White believed that the "Indians can't regulate fee owner residents." This interpretation was supported by Justice Stevens, who argued that the tribes "can't regulate [fishing and hunting] done by non-Indians on their own land." Justice Stewart's view went further, arguing that the tribe "doesn't have it [authority] over land of allottees whether Indian or non-Indian and whether resident or non-residents." Without inherent sovereignty over nonmembers on fee lands, the tribes had to rely on the goodwill of Congress. Chief Justice Burger believed in the use of congressional authority, noting that the "Indians do not have [authority] absent act." In the mindset of the justices, the principle of inherent tribal sovereignty over nonmembers on nonmember lands was invalid. Matters of tribal authority over tribal members and nonmembers depended on the status of the land involved.[185]

Although the justices believed that the tribes did not have authority over nonmembers on nonmember and fee lands on the reservation, the majority argued that tribes did have authority over tribal members there. In addition, the tribes had authority over tribal members and nonmembers on tribal and trust lands. This point was summed up by Justice Powell: "Tribe has some regulatory authority power but not to regulate non-members on own land."[186] Powell reasoned: "I cannot agree with CA9 [court of appeals] that a non-Indian owner on River can't fish," and thus the tribal regulation over non-Indians "goes too far."[187] Justice Stewart found the dividing line between the two to be a comfortable idea, noting that the tribe had authority to "regulate H[unting] and F[ishing] over *its* members" but "no regulate H[unting] and F[ishing] over allotees (W[hites] on I[ndians])" and summed up the idea of the Court when he said, "Tribe has sovereignty over own members and own property, not over fee owners."[188]

Justice Blackmun was briefed by his clerks on the arguments for inherent tribal sovereignty but instead took the integrationist tack because of concerns regarding tribal authority over nonmembers on fee lands. The position of the tribe was to support the use of the sovereignty doctrine, and they argued that the federal government supported tribal authority over nonmembers. A memorandum from a clerk explained this position: "Federal authorities consistently have upheld the right of Indian tribes as sovereigns to regulate the conduct of non-Indians within the boundaries of a reservation, even if those non-Indians own land within the reservation." Given this prior federal knowledge supporting broad tribal authority, the tribes argued that "it may be that persons who purchase land within an Indian reservation should be on notice that the Indian tribe will exert governing authority over it." Despite the merits of tribal sovereignty, Justice Blackmun decided to support the interests of nonmembers and the states. This position was influenced by advice given in the same clerk's memorandum: "I am troubled, however, by the situation faced by some *amici* states in which there are reservations where 80 or 90 percent of the land is owned by non-members of the Tribe. It seems difficult to find any justification for allowing those tribes to exercise sovereignty over such lands."[189] In the end, Blackmun was concerned about allowing large populations of nonmembers on several reservations to be governed by tribal law. He ruled against the tribes, stating that the tribal "regulation is troublesome and may not be valid."[190]

Justice Powell was also briefed on the merits of inherent tribal sovereignty over nonmembers but found no interest in these arguments. A bench memorandum explained that the Crow tribe "retains the authority to regulate hunting and fishing by non-members" because "Regulating hunting and fishing are even more central to the interests of the tribe than taxing [granted in the *Colville* case], as is indicated by the hunting rights granted them under the 1868 Treaty." The clerk summed up this point by noting, "In my view, the Tribe may regulate hunting and fishing by non-residents within the reservation without regard to who owns the land within the reservation. This seems most consistent with the notion of a limited Indian sovereignty and allows the Tribe to protect its most precious group asset, its natural resources."[191]

The limitations placed on tribal sovereignty allowed the Court to support the right of the state to regulate nonmembers on nonmember lands. Justice Rehnquist, a staunch proponent of states' rights on the reservation, pointed out that the state "can regulate hunting and fishing by allottees and people who can hunt and fish without trespassing on Indian land." State authority filled the vacuum left by the removal of tribal authority over nonmembers. Justice Stewart believed that state authority filled the void, noting that "Montana owns property, can say *all* can come in." This idea was supported by Chief Justice Burger, who stated that "Montana has the authority and [can] regul[ate] freely."[192] Without tribal control of the land, Justice Powell observed, the state "can control fishing on it."[193] The state had primary authority over nonmembers on nonmember fee lands. Justice White considered the court of appeals decision to be "silly" and pointed out that the state controlled nonmembers but not tribal members: "State can set seasons and limits on non-members, but not for Indians."[194] The internal position of the Court heavily suggested that the state had sovereignty over nonmembers on nonmember lands on the reservation. A memorandum from Justice Powell to Justice Stewart highlighted policy issues arising from the draft opinion issued on February 5, 1981: "I have never been clear as to the extent of a tribe's civil jurisdiction within a reservation with respect to use of land owned by non-Indians. A tribe certainly needs some powers to further its collective welfare, but on some reservations a majority of the land is owned by non-Indians. I assume your opinion does not go beyond anything we have said in the past with respect to a tribe's general civil jurisdiction."[195] Thus Powell was concerned about allowing tribal authority over nonmembers on nonmember lands in light of previous Court decisions.

For a short time, Justices Brennan and Marshall believed that it was not the states but the tribes that had inherent sovereignty over the nonmembers in question. On December 5, 1980, Justice Blackmun noted that the position of the Court on the issue of tribal regulation was "7–2 Regs," indicating that Brennan and Marshall supported inherent tribal sovereignty.[196] However, the final *Montana* opinion was unanimous, with both men supporting the principle that Congress had to enact legislation in order to allow the tribes authority over nonmembers on nonmember lands on the reservation.

In its opinion, the Court relied on the principle used in the *Oliphant* and *Wheeler* criminal cases to justify its integrationist movement in this civil case:[197] "Though *Oliphant* only determined inherent tribal authority in criminal matters, the principles on which it relied support the general proposition that the inherent sovereign powers of an Indian tribe do not extend to the activities of nonmembers of the tribe."[198] Unlike the case of criminal law, this did not apply to tribal authority over nonmembers on tribal lands. The rule over nonmembers was qualified by two exceptions:

> To be sure, Indian tribes retain inherent sovereign power to exercise some forms of civil jurisdiction over non-Indians on their reservations, even on non-Indian fee lands. A tribe may regulate, through taxation, licensing, or other means, the activities of nonmembers who enter consensual relationships with the tribe or its members, through commercial dealing, contracts, leases, or other arrangements. Williams v. Lee . . . Morris v. Hitchcock . . . Buster v. Wright . . . Washington v. Confederated Tribes of Colville Indian Reservation. . . . A tribe may also retain inherent power to exercise civil authority over the conduct of non-Indians on fee lands within its reservation when that conduct threatens or has some direct effect on the political integrity, the economic security, or the health or welfare of the tribe. See Fisher v. District Court . . . Williams v. Lee . . . Montana Catholic Missions v. Missoula County . . . Thomas v. Gay.[199]

The tribe had to prove one of these exceptions to be granted authority over nonmembers on nonmember lands.[200] With these newly constructed exceptions, the justices had codified the case law and deliberately excluded most cases that relied heavily and almost exclusively on inherent tribal sovereignty. They had cleverly emasculated almost a century of opinions reliant on inherent tribal sovereignty into exceptions that contradicted the fallacy of the newly created general rule.[201] A new legal history had been created.

Although the exceptions appeared to contradict the general rule, they were within the rubric of the integrationist trend, which sanctioned tribal authority over nonmembers through a delegation of congressional authority. This interpretation turned the definition of inherent sovereignty on its head. The Court had devised a new test and a general rule to erode the sovereignty doctrine, and this legal precedent was something the tribes did not know about until the *Montana* decree itself.[202] The *Montana* court reaffirmed its integrationist leanings and further limited tribal sovereignty when it explained, "Exercise of tribal power beyond what is necessary to protect tribal self-government or to control internal relations is inconsistent with the dependent status of the tribes, and so cannot survive without express congressional delegation."[203] It now required explicit legislation by Congress to authorize tribal authority, and without this there could be no authority over nonmembers: "There is simply no suggestion in the legislative history that Congress intended that the non-Indians who would settle upon alienated allotted lands would be subject to tribal regulatory authority."[204] The Court made it clear that the tribes did not have authority over nonmembers on nonmember and fee lands until Congress authorized such power.

In contrast, the Court ruled that the tribes retained inherent sovereignty over nonmembers on tribal and trust lands of the reservation. It clarified the sovereignty of the tribes on tribal lands when it reaffirmed the opinion of the court of appeals: "The Court of Appeals held that the Tribe may prohibit nonmembers from hunting or fishing on land belonging to the Tribe or held by the United States in trust for the Tribe, and with this holding we can readily agree. We also agree with the Court of Appeals that if the Tribe permits nonmembers to fish or hunt on such lands, it may condition their entry by charging a fee or establishing bag and creel limits." The confirmation of the court of appeals decision led the Supreme Court to address only "the power of the Tribe to regulate non-Indian fishing and hunting on reservation land owned in fee by nonmembers of the Tribe."[205]

Despite this application of inherent tribal sovereignty, the *Montana* court also ruled that it was possible to overturn the protections of tribal sovereignty over tribal lands. Its opinion held that the General Allotment Act of 1887 had opened up tribal and trust reservation lands to nonmembers and in doing so removed the exclusive authority of the tribes over parts of the reservation.[206] The justices interpreted nonmember-owned lands to be fee land that was not subject to tribal jurisdiction. Therefore, the movement of nonmembers onto the land, precipitated by the 1887 act, was an important factor of the opinion: "What is relevant in this case is the effect of the land alienation occasioned by that policy."[207] The removal of inherent tribal sovereignty over those lands resulted in the status of the lands being removed from the tribal and trust status. Consequently, without the protections of tribal sovereignty, the tribes required a delegation of congressional power to have authority over those lost lands.[208]

A memorandum to conference from Justice Stewart highlighted the integrationist trend in *Montana* on civil case law. The memorandum concerned the decision made by the Court of Appeals for the Tenth Circuit in *Mescalero Apache Tribe v. State of New Mexico* (1980).[209] This case considered whether the tribe could assume authority over nonmember hunting and fishing on tribal and trust lands of the reservation, in which the tribe had invested years of planning and funding and designed tribal regulations around tribal needs. In addition, the federal government had heavily supervised the project. The case was factually similar to *Montana,* but in contrast the decision of the court of appeals in *Mescalero Apache Tribe v. New Mexico* was that the tribe had inherent sovereignty over its territory. Justice Stewart believed that the difference in viewpoint between the court of appeals and the Supreme Court revolved around the issue of inherent tribal sovereignty as a principle to allow tribal authority over nonmembers: "Nevertheless, in discussing several of the grounds for its decision, the CA [court of appeals] here takes views of tribal authority at odds with *Montana.* For example, the CA found inherent authority to regulate hunting and fishing without strong evidence of the tribe's dependence on wildlife for its subsistence." This interpretation highlighted the Court's movement away from inherent tribal sovereignty and toward congressional authority. Despite the general limitations put on tribal sovereignty, in civil case law tribal sovereignty still applied over tribal lands. Justice Stewart believed that the fundamental difference between the *Mescalero Apache Tribe v. New Mexico* court of appeals case and *Montana* was the status of the lands involved: "In *Montana,* the issue was the power of the Tribe to regulate hunting and fishing on lands technically within the reservation, but alienated in fee simple to nonIndians. . . . Nothing in the present case suggests that any of the reservation lands at issue have been allotted or alienated out of tribal or federal hands." The *Montana* case became the standard through which the Supreme Court would consider whether tribes had authority over nonmembers. Despite the presence of tribal lands, Justice Stewart considered *Montana* to be the relevant case against which to judge whether tribes had authority over nonmembers: "The Mescalero Apache Tribe's claim of exclusive autho[r]ity may therefore pass muster under the language in *Montana* recognizing tribal authority over matters demonstrably affecting the economic welfare of the Tribe or the proper exercise of its self-government."

This memorandum showed how important the integrationist theme and the *Montana* decision were to the ideology of the Supreme Court.[210]

In sum, the *Montana* opinion established three contradictory holdings: (1) the tribes did not have general jurisdiction over nonmembers; (2) tribes did not have inherent sovereignty over nonmembers on nonmember lands on the reservation unless it was authorized by Congress or was proved within one of the exceptions;[211] (3) the tribes had inherent sovereignty over nonmembers on tribal and trust lands of the reservation. It reflected, then, a midway point between the nullification of inherent tribal sovereignty in criminal case law and the reaffirmation of the inherent right of the tribes to tax in taxation case law.

New Mexico v. Mescalero Apache Tribe (1983)

Only two years after *Montana,* the justices were faced with a case that involved the application of state law over nonmember hunting and fishing on a reservation: *New Mexico v. Mescalero Apache Tribe* (1983).[212] The Mescalero Apache Tribe had established a comprehensive scheme for managing fish and wildlife resources on their 460,000-acre reservation in New Mexico. The scheme had been extensively supervised by the federal authorities, and federally approved tribal ordinances detailed the hunting and fishing conditions of tribal members and nonmembers. Nevertheless, the State of New Mexico wanted to restrict the tribe's regulation of hunting and fishing on the reservation and to apply state laws over nonmembers there.

The principle focus of the justices was on the use of congressional authority and the preemption test to oust state law from the reservation. Justice Marshall supported the primacy of Congress in this case, noting "White Mountain, preemption OK," that is, he wanted to use the precedent of *Bracker* to determine the outcome of this case.[213] Chief Justice Burger agreed with the Marshall position: "We are balancing. . . . Wildlife is basis for tribal support, do this on preemption" and the "state concedes efficiency of management."[214] Justice Brennan concurred with both the chief justice and Marshall on the importance of the preemption test and the regulations involved: "Can use recog[nized] exclusion of St[ate] v. Tribe and regul[ate] natural life on the Reservation?" In his written notes, Justice Blackmun also supported preemption: "This is federal basket and premption. . . . The tribal-fed[eral] combo here = preemption."[215]

Other justices were less sure about preemption. Justice Rehnquist thought, "On balance, +. Difficult. Agree with JPS [Stevens]."[216] Interestingly,

Justice O'Connor was also ambivalent. She thought the Court "c[oul]d use White Mountain [v. Bracker],"[217] but she also supported Justice Stevens. A conference memo written by Justice Brennan's clerk argued that the use of the "case-by-case balancing test articulated in *White Mountain Apache Tribe*" in *Mescalero Apache Tribe* favored the tribe because the state regulatory interest was minimal, the "Indian interest here is substantial," and "the federal interest here is also significant."[218] In the end, the justices placed heavy emphasis on the preemption test, used in taxation case law, and not on the *Montana* precedent.

The lands involved in this case were tribal lands owned by the Mescalero Apache Tribe. Justice Blackmun believed the facts of the *Mescalero Apache* case were different from those in *Montana* and noted that "Montana v. US has little to do with this case" because "Tribe has no jurisdiction to regulate non I[ndians] on reservation land owned by nonmembers."[219] In a conference memorandum, Brennan's clerk argued that "when Potter Stewart recommended that we GVR this case in light of *Montana* v. *United States*, he acknowledged in his memo that the two cases were quite different, and that 'the CA [court of appeals] here may well be able to distinguish or even apply *Montana* in reaffirming its initial judgment. I think that Potter's assessment has been confirmed, and that this is a clear case in which exclusive tribal authority must be recognized.'"[220] Indeed, the justices in *Montana* affirmed inherent tribal sovereignty over tribal lands of the reservation. The reservation lands involved in *Mescalero Apache* were tribal lands, and therefore the justices had the option of applying the sovereignty doctrine. A bench memorandum written by Marshall's clerk read, the Montana court "readily agree[d]" as to Indian-held lands that the Tribe 'may prohibit nonmembers from hunting and fishing' on tribal lands. . . . This authority is fully confirmed by federal treaties and laws purporting to reserve the regulation of wildlife to Indian tribes, subject only to the plenary power of the national sovereign."[221] In the opinion itself, Justice Marshall condemned inherent tribal sovereignty as a bar to state authority to a footnote.[222] The justices had ignored the option of inherent tribal sovereignty in favor of the preemption test, a test very much reliant on federal authority to protect the interests of the tribe.

Integrationist principles informed the considerations of many of the justices in this case, particularly the application of state law on reservations. Justice White inextricably related the interests of the state with its people, observing "State interest . . . very important here" and "What if St[ate] said can go on the Res[ervation]?"[223] Justice Stevens questioned the use of federal preemption because of the negative effects of the tribal regulations on the state; accordingly, state law applied until it harmed the tribal system of regulations. Stevens thought, "*N* preemption. I[ndian] activities more harmful to larger terr[itory] v the State. So not 100% preemption. Therefore reject preemption. Tribal sovereignty theory we parted I[ndian]s unless it harms the sys[tem]. OK if try let activities b[e] "Temp[orary] I[ndian]s."[224] In addition, Stevens wanted clarity in resolving cases between state authority and tribal authority on the reservation, arguing that the Court "can't decide these cases on an ad hoc basis."[225] O'Connor agreed with Stevens and supported state laws over nonmembers on the reservation: "But use JPS [Stevens] theory v tribal sovereignty. Spread out effect can be great—if so, some st[atute] for State regulation."[226]

A memorandum from Justice Powell to Justice Marshall on May 27, 1983, highlighted the significance of state interests on the reservations and the limitations placed on tribal sovereignty. Powell disagreed with a sentence in the first draft that limited the application of state authority in a preemption test: "A State seeking not merely to tax but to regulate a tribal activity is under a greater burden to advance a significant State interest, since duplicative and potentially conflicting regulation is generally more disruptive than double taxation." Powell wanted an approach more cautious than one that expanded tribal interests. In conclusion, he noted: "Moreover, as a general proposition I would think that some types of regulation could be less 'disruptive' of tribal activity than heavy double taxation. The extent of interference with tribal activity would depend on the facts and circumstances. Thus, it seems unnecessary—certainly in this case—to draw a distinction between the burden of justification required by the state."[227]

A memorandum from Justice O'Connor to Justice Marshall on May 31, 1983, shows the significance of the state over reservation activities and the limitations that had been imposed on the sovereignty doctrine. O'Connor was unhappy with parts of the language used by Marshall concerning state law on the reservation:

> On page 8, in the first full paragraph, you quote *Mescalero* and *Confederated Tribes* for the proposition that Indians on reservations have been historically immune from all state control, and that they retain this immunity insofar as it is consistent with federal objectives. I

think it would be more accurate to say that "Because of their sovereign status, tribes and their reservation lands have, in some circumstances, possessed 'historic immunity from state and local control,' . . ." This would avoid conveying the impression that Indians have enjoyed a tradition of immunity from state law in all areas.[228]

In response to O'Connor, rather than demonstrate that tribal sovereignty was a strong element and, indeed, a fundamental factor in determining congressional preemption, Marshall used O'Connor's suggestions in his opinion and strengthened the presumption of state law on the reservations.

In addition, O'Connor disagreed with the way Marshall phrased the preemption test in his draft opinion because it severly limited the interests of the state:

On page 12, in the carryover paragraph, you state: "Thus, when a tribe undertakes an enterprise under the authority of federal law, an assertion of state authority is preempted to the extent that it 'threaten[s] the overriding federal objective' of promoting 'tribal self-sufficiency and economic development.'" I think the implication of this statement is too broad and contrary to the balancing structure for preemption analysis established in *Bracker*. The threat to a federal policy is only one factor to be considered. There is no preemption "to the extent" there is a threat, as the option suggests. In short, some financial burdens imposed by state regulation may be perfectly permissible depending on the outcome of balancing federal and tribal interests against state interests.[229]

Justice Marshall included these suggested changes in his final opinion, and as a result the presumption of state authority on the reservation was strengthened and the *Bracker* test weakened.[230] Justice O'Connor wrote to Justice Marshall saying, "Thank you for accommodating my suggestions."[231]

The opinion of the Court declared that the laws of the State of New Mexico were preempted by federal law. Justices Marshall argued that the exercise of concurrent jurisdiction (tribal and state laws at the same time) would have nullified the tribal authority to regulate the resources by tribal members and nonmembers, interfered with the comprehensive tribal regulatory scheme, and threatened the objective of Congress to encourage tribal self-government and economic development.[232] The reliance of the Court on congressional preemption demonstrated the movement away from the Indian sovereignty doctrine and toward a more integrationist position. Although tribal interests informed the preemption test, it was merely a test between federal and state authority over nonmembers on the reservation.

Brendale v. Confederated Yakima Indian Nation (1989)

Whereas the status of lands in *Montana* was crucial to the application of the sovereignty doctrine, it was not paramount in *New Mexico v. Mescalero Apache Tribe*. Interestingly, the *New Mexico v. Mescalero Apache Tribe* opinion was the only time the Supreme Court used the preemption test in civil case law. From 1989 to 2001 the justices used *Montana* to begin their determination of state or tribal jurisdiction—a stance we see in several more cases, all of which fundamentally eroded tribal civil jurisdiction over nonmembers on the reservation.

Brendale v. Confederated Yakima Indian Nation (1989) considered whether the Yakima Tribe or Yakima County, Washington, had zoning authority over nonmember lands in what were defined as the "open" and "closed" areas of the reservation.[233] Over half of the open area consisted of fee lands, which contained commercial and residential developments, and agricultural lands. The population of the open area was also overwhelmingly non-Indian. The closed area was mainly 807,000 acres of forestland, including 25,000 acres of fee lands. This area had been closed to the public by the tribes since 1972. The *Brendale* case was an "extremely important case for Native Americans" because the standard for tribal authority over nonmembers was "in flux."[234]

The majority of the Court in this case supported the general presumption established in *Montana* that congressional authority was required for a tribe to have authority over nonmembers on nonmember and fee lands. Because this authority was absent, the Yakimas did not have authority over nonmembers, the state did. Chief Justice Rehnquist believed tribal authority had been replaced, noting that the county had "authority to zone fee lands owned by non-I[ndians]," and Justice White concurred, observing that "zoning means exclusive"[235]—that is, the county and not the tribe had zoning authority over nonmembers. Justice Stevens agreed with Rehnquist and White that the county and state had the authority in the open area. But Stevens drew his opinion from the *Merrion* dissent from 1982, holding that the authority of a tribe was not inherent sovereignty but was based solely on the power of tribes to exclude nonmembers from their reservations.

Stevens, along with Justice O'Connor, differed from Rehnquist and White about the closed area of the reservation. Although they supported the presumption that the tribes had no inherent authority over nonmembers, they believed that the tribes could exclude nonmembers from the closed part of the reservation. Stevens was unequivocal in his belief that the tribes did not have inherent sovereignty over nonmembers, pointing out that the *Brendale* case was "not controlled by Montana, [as that case] depended on inherent sovereignty." Nevertheless, he believed that the tribes still had the right to exclude nonmembers from the reservation: "Is [Indians] have power to exclude non-Is from Reservation. Therefore can control what happens on the land."[236] Essentially, then, tribal sovereignty amounted only to the power to exclude and was therefore not territorial or inherent.[237] Justice O'Connor favored an integrationist position but was initially unsure whether to support Stevens or Rehnquist and White—"May go with CJ [chief justice] but for now sympathetic to JPS"—thus rejecting the principle of inherent tribal sovereignty.[238]

Justices Blackmun, Marshall, and Brennan applied the sovereignty doctrine to sanction tribal authority. Brennan was adamant in this position, noting that the "tribe retains its inherent authority," and "no checkerboard."[239] His opinion indicated that the tribes had exclusive authority to zone all of the reservation lands unless explicitly revoked by Congress. Marshall received a bench memorandum from his clerk arguing that the *Montana* case was an aberration: "This Court's decisions, the notable exception of *Montana* v. *United States,* have held that Indian tribes have civil jurisdiction over the Reservation-based activities of nonmembers absent congressional or treaty limitation. There is no such limitation here; rather congressional policy favors tribal self-governance, particularly where land matters are at stake."[240]

In this case, Justice Blackmun made a laudable attempt to undermine the radical change he had helped establish in *Montana*. A clerk's bench memorandum explained the difference between the Court's interpretation of tribal sovereignty in civil case law before and after *Montana*: tribal sovereignty before *Montana* existed "unless affirmatively limited by a special treaty provision or federal statute. In *Montana* . . . , however, the Court reversed the inference."[241] A memorandum from his clerk explained that his and the Court's position in *Montana* disregarded tribal sovereignty: "With respect to the inherent sovereignty issue, the Court was unanimous."[242] But Blackmun determined that this discrepancy did not pose any problems for his dissent. The *Montana* case, he wrote, was "only 1 v. many cases and I am not sympathetic to it, PS [Potter Stewart] went too far."[243]

Therefore, Blackmun had to find a way to distinguish and diminish the effect of *Montana*. He did this by analyzing case law after *Montana* and concluded that post-*Montana* case law supported tribal sovereignty. A memorandum from his clerk pointed out the way Blackmun approached his dissent: "*Montana* is only one of many opinions dealing with civil jurisdiction and inherent tribal authority to exercise that jurisdiction over fee lands and over non-Indians. . . . None of the cases post-dating *Montana* make reference to that opinion's presumption against inherent tribal authority."[244]

To excuse himself from "*Montana*'s anomalous presumption against finding inherent tribal authority," Blackmun had to reinvigorate the sovereignty doctrine. He circumvented the *Montana* ruling by arguing that once tribal interests were implicated and affected in any way a tribe automatically had authority: "*Montana* should be read as a case in which the tribe made no showing, indeed did not even allege, that the non-Indian conduct sought to be regulated in any way interfered with the political or economic interests of the tribe, or the tribe's health and welfare."[245] In the end, Justice Blackmun declared support for inherent sovereignty and that the "Montana case should not control."[246]

The ideological differences between the justices are illustrated by the divergent positions adopted by Justice White and Justice Blackmun in their reading and interpretation of the *Wheeler* case of 1978. White attacked the dissent circulated by Blackmun, and the ideological conflict was discussed in a memorandum between Blackmun and his clerk: "[In] the revised majority, Justice White accuses the dissent of ignoring relevant passages in *Wheeler* to the effect that all tribal authority over non-Indians is inconsistent with their dependent status and, therefore, necessarily divested. Frankly, I am surprised and disappointed that Justice White has given this reading to *Wheeler*. His interpretation rests on a single clause, severed from a single sentence, wrenched totally out of context."[247] Whereas White was taking the integrationist position, which rested tribal authority over nonmembers exclusively on congressional legislation, Blackmun was applying the sovereignty doctrine and declared that *Wheeler* had not divested all inherent tribal sovereignty over nonmembers. Blackmun concluded that *Wheeler* had clarified the circumstances where tribal sovereignty had been divested from the tribe and over nonmembers. He argued that in adopting White's position the Supreme Court had merely misinterpreted *Wheeler*.

Originally, the *Brendale* court had a majority of six justices against the three dissenters, Blackmun, Marshall, and Brennan. This was highlighted by text that had been penciled out in the third draft of the Blackmun dissent: "Because I believe that the majority's reading of *Montana* is at odds with our jurisprudence of tribal sovereignty . . . I dissent."[248] Ultimately, though, the court was divided into three camps of judges, two opinions, and two opposing presumptions regarding tribal sovereignty. Justice White delivered the first opinion of the Court, an exclusively integrationist opinion joined by Scalia, Kennedy, and Rehnquist. To make a majority, Justices Stevens and O'Connor joined them. The rationale of the first opinion was supported by the general proposition that a tribe did not have civil jurisdiction over nonmembers on fee lands unless it could prove one of the two *Montana* exceptions or provide evidence of congressional authorization, as had occurred in *Mazurie*. This development of the integrationist trend meant that tribal sovereignty "generally extends only to what is necessary to protect tribal self-government or to control internal relations . . . unless there has been an express congressional delegation of tribal power to the contrary." The *Mazurie* case first changed the presumption of tribal authority over nonmembers from inherent tribal sovereignty to a delegation of congressional power, prior to it being used in civil case law. Therefore, for the tribe to have authority over nonmembers, a congressional delegation was required, and according to Justice White "there is no contention here that Congress has expressly delegated to the [Yakima] Tribe the power to zone the fee lands of nonmembers."[249]

The second camp sanctioned tribal authority over nonmembers within the closed area of the reservation but did not allow tribal authority over nonmembers in the open area. These two justices began from the presumption that the powers of the tribe did not include inherent sovereignty and were restricted to the power to exclude nonmembers from the reservation. They determined that the tribe had authority to exclude nonmembers from the closed area. This part of the decision was joined by the third camp, which held that tribes had inherent sovereignty over nonmembers on the reservation.

Overall, the two opinions and presumptions regarding tribal sovereignty reflected adherence to both an integrationist position and the sovereignty doctrine. The first and second camps leaned integrationist, the third applied the sovereignty doctrine. A majority had begun from the presumption that tribes did not have inherent sovereignty unless it was delegated by Congress and that, without inherent sovereignty, the state assumed jurisdiction over nonmembers on the reservation. This followed the pattern of the law established in criminal case law (*Oliphant* and *Wheeler*) and civil case law (*Montana*).

South Dakota v. Bourland (1993)

Only four years after *Brendale*, a majority of the Supreme Court justices limited the application of the sovereignty doctrine in civil case law. *South Dakota v. Bourland* (1993) addressed whether the Cheyenne River Sioux Tribe still maintained authority over 104,420 acres of tribal lands that were conveyed to the United States, pursuant to the Cheyenne River Act, for the Oahe dam and reservoir project.[250] The dispute started when the tribe no longer recognized the right of the state to regulate nonmembers, declaring that only it could regulate nonmember hunting. The state argued that the taking of the lands by congressional act transferred the status of the lands from tribal to fee and that therefore the tribe had lost its inherent authority to regulate nonmember hunting and fishing on the taken lands.

The presumption used by the majority of the justices in their deliberations was that an explicit congressional delegation was required to allow the tribe authority over the taken lands. Justice Scalia believed that the Court had to examine whether Congress allowed tribal authority to exist over nonmembers, pointing out that the "regulation issue is before us." Originally, Scalia had agreed that federal regulations allowed tribal authority over nonmembers, noting that "'local' includes 'tribal' for now."[251] In the end, though, he voted against the tribe's right to claim authority over the taken lands. Chief Justice Rehnquist also changed his position about the use of federal regulations. A memorandum from Justice Blackmun's clerk to Blackmun pointed out that "the Chief [Rehnquist] has, not surprisingly, changed his vote in this case."[252] A majority of justices believed that tribes did not have sovereignty over nonmembers on nonmember lands.

Although the final opinion did not rule on whether state law applied to nonmembers, the Blackmun papers reveal that the Court had wanted to sanction state authority over nonmembers on the lands in question. As a direct result of the tribes being denied inherent sovereignty over nonmembers on fee lands, the private view of the Court was that the state had the sovereign right over nonmembers. Justice Kennedy believed that state law replaced tribal authority, noting "State access to all," and Justice O'Connor agreed, pointing out that "state law applies."[253] With the application of state law, Justice White believed that nonmember rights were no longer limited and that "non-Is [non-Indians] have complete rights," and Justice Stevens "[agreed] with BRW [Byron White]."[254] Despite this support for state law, the *Bourland* court could not address or rule on this issue because the issue was not even before the Court.

Once any lands were removed from tribal and trust status and thereby were out of tribal control, the Supreme Court prevented tribal authority over nonmembers on those lands. Justice O'Connor argued that once lands were designated fee lands the status of the lands could not be changed: "If you let them [tribes] change a fee, this is contrary to the statute."[255] The transfer of land status meant that the tribes lost authority over nonmembers. This view was supported by Justice White, who believed that a general rule should be applied to deny any kind of tribal authority over nonmembers on fee lands, noting that it was "silly to give Tribes this fee right."[256] Justice White wanted tribal authority to cease completely once tribal and trust lands were changed to fee lands.

Taking an integrationist stance, the *Bourland* opinion inferred a broad rule that lands appropriated by Congress, whether or not it was for the process of allotment, were automatically transferred in status from tribal to fee lands, and thus the tribes lost inherent sovereignty over nonmembers on those lands.[257] But the *Montana* ruling still protected tribal authority over nonmembers on tribal lands, so the Court began the process of changing the status of lands from tribal to fee in order to circumvent the *Montana* holding. Whereas *Montana* used the process of allotment to justify the removal of tribal authority over lands, the *Bourland* court reasoned that a modern-day congressional act, which required the lands for a dam project, justified the removal of tribal control over the lands. Essentially, the tribe lost exclusive control and therefore lost the tribal and trust status of the lands. The *Bourland* court declared that Congress had deprived the tribe of exclusive authority, and this was enough to transfer the status of lands from tribal to fee; it was no longer the underlying principle (e.g., allotment) that changed the status of the lands. After *Bourland,* any appropriation of lands by Congress was sufficient to transfer the status of lands from trust to fee, regardless of the underlying rationale: "When Congress has broadly opened up such land to non-Indians, the effect of the transfer is the destruction of preexisting Indian rights to regulatory control."[258]

In addition, the *Bourland* opinion relied on the general proposition of *Montana* that prohibited tribal sovereignty over nonmembers. Justice Clarence Thomas believed that tribes did not have inherent sovereignty over nonmembers and declared, "The reality . . . after Montana, [is] tribal sovereignty over nonmembers 'cannot survive without express congressional delegation,' . . . and is therefore not inherent."[259] "Inherent tribal sovereignty" had become a term dependent on a congressional delegation of power; for the tribes to have authority over nonmembers, a relevant treaty or congressional delegation was required.[260]

In stark contrast to the viewpoints of other justices, Justice Blackmun supported the sovereignty doctrine and justified his position by reaffirming his partial concurrence and dissent from the *Brendale* case. The ideological differences between Blackmun and the majority of the Court regarding the interpretation of *Montana* and the sovereignty doctrine were summed up in a memorandum from Justice Blackmun's clerk to Blackmun: "Given your understanding of *Montana* and your view of tribal authority over non-members generally, as expressed in your concurring and dissenting opinion in *Brendale,* I recommend you vote to affirm CA8 [court of appeals]."[261] In direct contrast to the Court's integrationist tendencies, Blackmun had begun from the presumption that the tribes had inherent sovereignty unless removed by Congress. He considered the application of the sovereignty doctrine the appropriate way to weaken the integrationist trend. A memorandum from a Blackmun clerk read: "This would be the best way to respond to Justice Thomas' [analysis] . . . which accuses the dissent of shutting its eyes to the fact that inherent tribal sovereignty is subject to complete defeasance."[262]

The divergence between the majority and the dissent was profound, with no middle ground. Indeed, with the insistence that Congress had to act to revoke tribal sovereignty, Justice Blackmun explained that within the congressional act there was "no clear Explanation of Congress intent to divest tribal authority."[263] Furthermore, the position adopted by Justice Blackmun in *Brendale* was once again used in *Bourland.* A memorandum from Justice Blackmun's clerk outlined Blackmun's interpretation of the law: "Your views on tribal civil jurisdiction are well spelled out in your *Brendale* opinion."[264]

Once again, Justice Blackmun relied on the interpretation that case law before and after *Montana* supported tribal authority over nonmembers unless removed by Congress. A memorandum from Justice Blackmun's clerk to Blackmun read, "In *Brendale,* you noted that *Montana* was part of a long line of cases establishing that 'tribes retain their sovereign powers over non-Indians on reservation lands unless the exercise of that sovereignty would be "inconsistent with the overriding interests of the National Government.""[265]

In his dissent, Blackmun explained that the sovereignty doctrine was a "fundamental principle," and because of this tribal authority had been limited only in specific circumstances: "only 'where the exercise of tribal sovereignty would be inconsistent with the overriding interests of the National Government, as when the tribes seek to engage in foreign relations, alienate their lands to non-Indians without federal consent, or prosecute non-Indians in tribal courts which do not accord the full protections of the Bill of Rights.'"[266]

Despite the cases that followed, Justice Blackmun believed that *Montana* did not preclude inherent tribal sovereignty over all external relations between tribal members and nonmembers.[267] To attach greater significance to his position, Blackmun was advised by his clerk to add a quotation from *Wheeler*, which summed up the principle of the sovereignty doctrine: "Inherent tribal sovereignty 'exists only at the sufferance of Congress and is subject to complete defeasance. *But until Congress acts, the tribes retain their existing sovereign powers.* In sum, Indian tribes still possess those aspects of sovereignty not withdrawn by treaty or statute, or by implication as a *necessary* result of their dependent status.'"[268]

Strate v. A-1 Contractors (1997)

Justice Blackmun had fought against the integrationist trend, but after his retirement in 1994 integration became the primary rationale of the Supreme Court in civil case law. The unanimously assumed irrelevance of the sovereignty doctrine in civil case law was shown in the case of *Strate v. A-1 Contractors* (1997).[269] The case considered whether the tribe or the state had authority to rule on an accident that occurred between two nonmembers on a 6.59-mile section of a North Dakota state highway within the Fort Berthold Reservation. The stretch of road was open to the public and maintained by the state under a federally granted right-of-way, but the road was on trust land held by the United States for the Three Affiliated Tribes.

The *Strate* opinion redefined the way the Supreme Court decided future civil cases. The justices unanimously agreed that cases involving tribes and nonmembers must begin with analysis of the *Montana* principles and not *Williams*, indicating the dramatic integrationist shift. *Montana* was "the pathmarking case concerning tribal civil authority over nonmembers." The Court agreed that *Montana* was correct when it enunciated that tribes lack authority over nonmembers on fee lands, noting that after *Montana* "the civil authority of Indian tribes and their courts with respect to non Indian fee lands generally 'do[es] not extend to the activities of nonmembers of the tribe.'" The only way tribes would have authority over nonmembers was if Congress delegated power or the tribes provided evidence to support one of the *Montana* exceptions: "Absent a different congressional direction, Indian tribes lack civil authority over the conduct of nonmembers on non Indian land within a reservation, subject to two exceptions." The integrationist position became much stronger, and in general tribal authority over nonmember conduct was allowed "only in limited circumstances" without express congressional legislation. This restriction on tribal authority also applied to tribal court authority over nonmembers.[270]

The principles relied upon by the *Strate* court were a direct contrast to the language used by Hugo Black in *Williams v. Lee* (1959) and explicitly demonstrated how the thinking of the justices had changed over a thirty-eight-year period. The *Williams* court had judged that state authority impinged on tribal court authority and tribal government, and therefore that tribal sovereignty existed unless divested by Congress: "To allow the exercise of state jurisdiction here would undermine the authority of the tribal courts over Reservation affairs and hence would infringe on the right of the Indians to govern themselves. It is immaterial that respondent is not an Indian. He was on the Reservation and the transaction with an Indian took place there. . . . this Court [has] consistently guarded the authority of Indian governments over their reservations. . . . If this power is to be taken away from them, it is for Congress to do it."[271] Over only thirty-eight years, the Supreme Court had moved from supporting the sovereignty doctrine to supporting the precedent of *Montana* and integrationist priniciples.

The *Strate* opinion undermined the Blackmun position that civil case law both before and after *Montana* relied explicitly on the sovereignty doctrine and the presumption that inherent tribal sovereignty applied over nonmembers until legislation by Congress precluded such authority.[272] In the *Strate* case, the tribe's argument was based on Blackmun's position in *Brendale* and *Bourland*. The tribe argued that the cases of *National Farmers* and *Iowa Mutual* explicitly sanctioned inherent tribal sovereignty over nonmembers until removed by Congress.[273] The *Strate* court disagreed with the arguments of the tribe and decided that *National Farmers* and *Iowa Mutual* did not sustain tribal court authority over nonmembers on the reservation.[274]

The loss of tribal sovereignty and tribal court authority over nonmembers on fee lands resulted in the state assuming authority over nonmembers, based on the Court's interpretation regarding the transfer of tribal lands to fee lands. The justices applied the rule used in *Bourland* that once exclusive tribal authority over lands was lost the status of the lands automatically transferred from tribal to fee and the tribes lost inherent sovereignty over the lands. Todd Miller explains that the justices in *Strate* "had to find that the Tribe had alienated the land underlying the highway right-of-way to fit the case into the nonmember fee property model that would allow for the use of the Montana rule."[275] The Court believed that the federal right-of-way removed the exclusive rights of the tribe over the road and so changed the status of the lands involved from tribal to fee: "The right of way North Dakota acquired for its highway renders the 6.59 mile stretch here at issue equivalent, for nonmember governance purposes, to such alienated, non Indian land."[276] Consequently, the tribe lost authority over the lands and nonmembers on the lands.

Because it misjudged the status of the right-of-way, the *Strate* court struggled to fit the facts of the case into one that denied inherent tribal sovereignty over the tribal lands in question.[277] According to Miller, an easement interest in land, which the state of North Dakota had, should not have affected tribal authority over the land: "The easement holder has neither the permanent possession of even a single molecule of the land itself, nor the exclusive time-bound possession granted by a lease. Instead the easement holder has the right to make or control a particular use of the land that remains owned by another."[278]

In its opinion, the Court ruled that once the tribe lost exclusive authority over the lands in question it lost authority in general: "[The] state forum [was] open to all who sustain injuries on North Dakota's highway. Opening the Tribal Court . . . is not necessary to protect tribal self government," and "this commonplace state highway accident claim in an unfamiliar court" was unnecessary.[279] The justices believed that it was imperative for nonmembers to be tried in state courts rather than tribal courts. Overall, the effect of *Strate* reinforced the general presumption of *Montana* and the integrationist trend in civil case law.

Atkinson Trading Co. v. Shirley (2001)

The strength of the integrationist trend in the thinking of the Supreme Court justices was demonstrated when they announced their decisions in *Atkinson Trading Co. v. Shirley* (2001), a tax case, and *Nevada v. Hicks* (2001), a civil case. As Sarah Krakoff observed, the *Strate* justices "opened the door to Hicks and Atkinson by taking the tack that Montana was the 'pathmarking' case involving all questions of jurisdiction over non-Indians."[280]

Atkinson Trading Co. v. Shirley questioned whether the Navajo Nation had the authority to impose a hotel occupancy tax on nonmembers on the exterior boundaries of the reservation, classified by the Supreme Court as fee lands.[281] The Atkinson Trading Company owned the hotels and collected the tax for the tribes, but it challenged the authority of the Navajo Nation to impose the tax. The *Atkinson* case did not rely on the principles used in previous tax cases but instead relied specifically on the *Montana* civil case to determine the outcome. Since 1989, taxation case law has applied both integrationist principles and the sovereignty doctrine to allow concurrent tribal and state taxation of nonmembers on the reservation. The *Atkinson* court ruling moved away from the established principle of concurrent taxation to the presumption that tribes did not have inherent sovereignty to tax nonmembers on nonmember lands of the reservation. This reversed the broad assumptions of historic and modern-day case law that determined that tribes had inherent sovereignty over nonmembers on any part of the reservation.

The influence of civil case law allowed the *Atkinson* court to abandon the principle of concurrent taxation. The Court accepted that tribal authority over nonmembers and the right to tax them on fee lands relied on a congressional delegation of power.[282] Before 2001 the Court had readily applied the sovereignty doctrine and allowed the tribes to tax nonmembers on the reservation, but this principle was changed because the *Atkinson* justices considered *Montana* to be the dominant precedent: "*Montana*'s general rule applies to tribal attempts to tax nonmember activity occurring on non-Indian fee land. Tribal jurisdiction is limited: For powers not expressly conferred them by federal statute or treaty, tribes must rely upon their retained or inherent sovereignty. Their power over nonmembers on non-Indian fee land is sharply circumscribed."[283]

From the outset, the justices applied the *Montana* ruling, because the tax in question fell on nonmembers on fee lands. The status of the lands was crucial to the case, and because fee lands were involved it implicated the "*Montana-Strate* line of authority" and precluded tribal authority over nonmembers.[284] Despite the existence of previous case law that supported the inherent right of the tribes to tax nonmembers—*Colville, Merrion,* and *Kerr-McGee Corp. v. Navajo Tribe*—the *Atkinson* court was unanimously integrationist: "Congress has not authorized the Navajo Nation's hotel occupancy tax through treaty or statute. . . . it is incumbent upon the Navajo Nation to establish the existence of one of *Montana*'s exceptions."[285] The actions of the tribe could not be reconciled by one of the exceptions, so the ability of the Navajos to tax was prohibited.[286]

The use of *Montana* and the application of integrationist principles had also limited the sovereignty doctrine and the ruling of *Merrion*, which held that tribes had inherent sovereignty to tax nonmembers anywhere on the reservation. Although *Merrion*, a taxation case, did not fit within the line of civil cases that followed *Montana*, the *Atkinson* court ruling reconciled and realigned *Merrion* to fit the integrationist framework: "Incorporating *Merrion*'s reasoning here would be tantamount to rejecting *Montana*'s general rule."[287] The *Atkinson* decision confirmed the movement of the Court away from inherent tribal sovereignty, which had been established as the principle of *Merrion*. To reconcile the two cases the Court examined the status of the lands involved. The *Merrion* case had involved only trust lands, whereas *Atkinson* involved fee lands. Trust lands were owned and controlled by the tribes; fee lands were not controlled by the tribes. This clear division allowed the justices to conclude that "an Indian tribe's sovereign power to tax—whatever its derivation—reaches no further than tribal land."[288] In fact, the *Atkinson* court pointed out that the views of the *Merrion* justices supported a tribal tax on tribal lands: the *Merrion* court "was careful to note that an Indian tribe's inherent power to tax only extended to '"transactions occurring on *trust lands* and significantly involving a tribe or its members."'"[289]

Interestingly, the lands involved in *Merrion* were established by an executive order in 1887, and the 742,315 acres of reservation were by default tribal trust property.[290] It was clear to the justices that tribal authority was precluded over fee lands, for the *Merrion* case "did not address assertions of tribal jurisdiction over non-Indian fee land."[291] Ironically, the *Merrion* dissent cited *Buster v. Wright*, a 1905 case from the U.S. Court of Appeals for the Eighth Circuit, which held that the Creek Nation had inherent sovereignty to tax nonmembers on fee lands.[292] The justices' conclusion came despite the concession that tribal power to tax was derived from an "Indian tribe's 'general authority, as sovereign, to control economic activity within its jurisdiction.'"[293] Moreover, the *Atkinson* opinion considered the *Merrion* dissent, which held that tribes only had the right to exclude nonmembers from the reservation, rather than the *Merrion* opinion.[294] Thus, the reassessment of *Merrion* by the justices in the *Atkinson* case limited tribal sovereignty over fee lands.

As part of the movement of the Supreme Court away from inherent tribal sovereignty, the *Atkinson* court questioned the *Montana* ruling that protected tribal sovereignty over nonmembers on tribal lands. The concurrence of Justice David Souter,[295] joined by Justices Kennedy and Thomas, expanded and explicitly incorporated tribal and trust lands into the *Montana* ruling, so the tribes did not have any authority over nonmembers unless authorized by Congress or evidence was found to support the *Montana* exceptions:

> If we are to see coherence in the various manifestations of the general law of tribal jurisdiction over non-Indians, the source of doctrine must be *Montana* v. *United States*. . . . Under *Montana,* the status of territory within a reservation's boundaries as tribal or fee land may have much to do (as it does here) with the likelihood (or not) that facts will exist that are relevant under the exceptions to *Montana*'s "general proposition" that "the inherent sovereign powers of an Indian tribe do not extend to the activities of nonmembers of the tribe." That general proposition is, however, the first principle, regardless of whether the land at issue is fee land, or land owned by or held in trust for an Indian tribe.[296]

These views established a new precedent to define future cases involving tribal sovereignty over nonmembers on a reservation. Regardless of the status of the lands, for tribes to have authority over nonmembers it had to be legislated by Congress.

Nevada v. Hicks (2001)

Only twenty-seven days after *Atkinson,* the Supreme Court decided *Nevada v. Hicks* and applied integrationist principles in full for the first time.[297] This case considered whether the Fallon Paiute-Shoshone Tribal Court had jurisdiction to hear civil claims against state officials who entered tribal lands to execute a state court and tribal court search warrant against Floyd Hicks, a tribal member, for an off-reservation crime.

The integrationist principles established in criminal case law heavily influenced the thinking of the justices in the *Hicks* case. The *Oliphant* and *Wheeler* cases had not looked at the status of lands involved but instead had looked at the people involved, tribal members versus nonmembers, and had subsequently ruled that tribes did not have authority over nonmembers. This rationale was used by the *Hicks* court to undermine *Montana,* which determined the application of tribal authority over nonmembers by the type of lands involved. The *Hicks* court believed that the general trend established in civil case law by *Montana* was created by the *Oliphant* court, which had concluded "the general proposition that the inherent sovereign powers of an Indian tribe do not extend to the activities of nonmembers of the tribe."[298] The justices saw *Oliphant* as a critical case in the development of civil case law.[299] They applied the *Oliphant* rationale to inform their interpretation of the *Montana* case and thereby eroded tribal authority over nonmembers on tribal lands.

This reliance on *Oliphant* by the *Hicks* court signaled the intent of the justices to undermine the protection offered to tribal authority on tribal lands by the *Montana* precedent. This integrationist approach in civil case law was consistent with the general movement of the Court away from using tribal sovereignty when nonmembers were involved. As Singer explains, the *Hicks* court went "substantially beyond the Montana line of cases to hold that the tribe has no jurisdiction over a nonmember who enters tribal land. This comes close to extending Oliphant to civil jurisdiction, limiting tribal regulatory power to tribal members and non-members who agree to such jurisdiction."[300] The *Hicks* court believed that it was up to Congress to allow tribal authority over nonmembers: "Where non-members are concerned, the 'exercise of tribal power *beyond what is necessary to protect tribal self-government or to control internal relations* is inconsistent with the dependent status of the tribes, and so cannot survive without express congressional delegation.'"[301] The Court's interpretation of internal relations did not constitute tribal authority over nonmembers and was therefore dependent on Congress. Generally, tribal sovereignty applied only to tribal members: "Internal relations can be understood by looking at the examples of tribal power to which *Montana* referred: tribes have authority '[to punish tribal offenders,] to determine tribal membership, to regulate domestic relations among members, and to prescribe rules of inheritance for members.' . . . These examples show, we said, that Indians have 'the right . . . to make their own laws and be ruled by them.'"[302]

The *Hicks* court believed that the views expressed by the *Montana* general presumption regarding tribal authority over nonmembers actually undermined the *Montana* ruling, which protected tribal authority over nonmembers on tribal lands.[303] Justice Scalia pointed out that directly after the *Montana* proposition the Court "cautioned that, 'to be sure, Indian tribes retain inherent sovereign power to exercise some forms of civil jurisdiction over non-Indians on their reservations, even on non-Indian fee lands,' . . . clearly implying that the general rule of *Montana* applies to both Indian and non-Indian land."[304] The undermining of tribal sovereignty over nonmembers on tribal lands in civil case law confirmed that the Supreme Court wanted to align civil case law with the principles established in other areas of the law. In effect, this opinion overruled *Williams* and the sovereignty doctrine[305] and conflicted with the precedent and "parthmarking case" of *Montana*.

The *Hicks* court was influenced by the Justice Souter concurrence in *Atkinson*. The justices believed that the involvement of nonmembers anywhere on the reservation required that the general presumption of *Montana* be applied to fee and tribal lands: "The rule that, where nonmembers are concerned, 'the exercise of tribal power beyond what is necessary to protect tribal self-government or to control internal relations . . . cannot survive without express congressional delegation,' *Montana* v. *United* States . . . applies to both Indian and non-Indian land."[306] For the first time in civil case law during the modern era, inherent tribal sovereignty did not apply to nonmembers on trust lands: "Tribal ownership is not alone enough to support regulatory jurisdiction over nonmembers."[307] Souter echoed his previous concurrence in *Atkinson*. He explained that under the *Montana* principle tribal authority over nonmembers on fee and tribal lands did not exist:

> I would go right to *Montana*'s rule that a tribe's civil jurisdiction generally stops short of non-member defendants. . . . *Montana* applied this presumption against tribal jurisdiction to non-member conduct on fee land within a reservation; I would also apply it where, as here, a non-member acts on tribal or trust land, and I would thus make it explicit that land status within a reservation is not a primary jurisdictional fact, but is relevant only insofar as it bears on the application of one of *Montana*'s exceptions to a particular case.[308]

This Souter interpretation applied *Montana* to deny inherent tribal sovereignty over nonmembers on both fee and trust lands.[309]

Without general civil authority over nonmembers, the tribal court also had no authority over nonmembers. The *Hicks* court deferred to the application of the *Montana-Strate* line of authority.[310] Because inherent tribal sovereignty over nonmembers was limited, it followed that the adjudicatory power of the tribe was limited in the equivalent manner. As Justice Souter observed, "The path marked best is the rule that, at least as a presumptive matter, tribal courts lack civil jurisdiction over nonmembers." The Supreme Court ruled that tribal courts did not have authority to hear civil cases in relation to the misconduct of state officials (nonmembers) in pursuit of an off-reservation crime. Although the civil suit was against "state officials in their *individual* capacities," the Court explained that "the distinction between individual and official capacity suits is irrelevant."[311]

Again, inherent tribal sovereignty over all nonmembers on the reservation was precluded. The implication was that an individual state officer acting either in an official capacity or individually, pursuant to state authority, could enter the reservation without tribal consent and did not need to consult the tribal government.[312] The limitations placed on tribal court, Souter argued, not only apply "the animating principle behind our precedents, but fits with historical assumptions about tribal authority and serves sound policy."[313]

Integrationist principles and assumptions had resulted in tribal authority being replaced by inherent state sovereignty on the reservation. The use of state law on the reservation had developed within the decision-making structures of the Court since 1959, and the application of state law on the reservation by the *Hicks* court significantly eroded the Indian sovereignty doctrine, making it clear that the sovereignty doctrine no longer protected the reservation from state law:

> Our cases make clear that the Indians' right to make their own laws and be governed by them does not exclude all state regulatory authority on the reservation. State sovereignty does not end at a res-ervation's border. Though tribes are often referred to as "sovereign" entities, it was "long ago" that "the Court departed from Chief Justice Marshall's view that 'the laws of [a State] can have no force' within reservation boundaries. *Worcester v. Georgia,* 6 Pet. 515, 561 (1832)," *White Mountain Apache Tribe v. Bracker,* 448 U.S. 136, 141 (1980). "Ordinarily," it is now clear, "an Indian reservation is considered part of the territory of the State." . . . see also *Organized Village of Kake v. Egan.*[314]

The now fully developed integrationist trend allowed state law onto the res-ervation and allowed state authority over nonmembers on the reservation. The justification for using inherent state sovereignty on the reservation was based on the right of the state to assert jurisdiction for "off-reservation violations of state law."[315] The Court argued that Congress had not withdrawn inherent state sovereignty on the reservations for pursuing off-reservation crimes: "The States' inherent jurisdiction on reservations can of course be stripped by Congress, see *Draper* v. *United* States. . . . But with regard to the jurisdiction at issue here that has not occurred. The Government's assertion that '[a]s a general matter, although state officials have jurisdiction to investigate and prosecute crimes on a reservation that exclusively involve non-Indians, . . . they do not have jurisdiction with respect to crimes involving Indian perpetrators or Indian victims,' . . . is misleading."[316]

The Supreme Court had fundamentally prevented the application of the tribal sovereignty doctrine in the face of state sovereignty. The presumption of the sovereignty doctrine had also been reversed; now, an explicit act of Congress was required in order to remove the inherent right of the state from the reservation. Analysis of federal legislation by the Court did not preclude state law: "Nothing in the federal statutory scheme prescribes, or even remotely suggests, that state officers cannot enter a reservation (including Indian-fee land) to investigate or prosecute violations of state law occurring off the reservation." Therefore, the "state's interest in [the] execution of process is considerable."[317] In addition, Justice Scalia specifically supported general limitations on tribal authority: "We do not say state officers cannot be regulated; we say they cannot be regulated in the performance of their law-enforcement duties. Action unrelated to that is potentially subject to tribal control depending on the outcome of *Montana* analysis."[318] The last sentence appeared to preclude any kind of inherent tribal sovereignty over nonmembers on the reservation unless the tribes met one of the two *Montana* exceptions, and therefore Congress had to legislate to preclude state sovereignty on the reservation.

✤ In sum, the *Atkinson* ruling eroded the rights of the tribes to tax nonmembers on fee lands, and the *Hicks* decision fundamentally eroded tribal authority over nonmembers on tribal and trust lands. The two cases demonstrated the dramatic integrationist shift of the Supreme Court, which fundamentally eroded inherent tribal civil and taxation authority over nonmembers on fee and tribal lands of the reservation and thus reversed the principle of *Montana*. The *Atkinson* court mooted the idea of extending the integrationist trend to cover tribal lands, and the *Hicks* court duly obliged and applied the rationale that tribes did not have inherent sovereignty over nonmembers on tribal and trust lands in civil cases. The loss of tribal sovereignty over nonmembers was subsequently replaced by inherent state sovereignty. Taken together, the

Atkinson and *Hicks* rulings can be construed to have dramatically undermined the authority of the tribes to tax nonmembers on fee and tribal lands of the reservation and to have caused the loss of tribal civil authority over nonmembers on the reservations.[319]

Civil and Taxation Case Law from 2001 to the Present

Since 2001 the Supreme Court has been consistently integrationist. Only two relevant cases have been decided by the Court in the areas of taxation and civil case law since 2001—the tax case *Wagnon v. Prairie Band Potawatomi Nation* (2005) and the civil case *Plains Commerce Bank v. Long Family Land and Cattle Co.* (2008). Beyond those two, *Dollar General Corporation v. Mississippi Band of Choctaw Indians* (Docket No. 13–1496), a civil case, is expected to be decided in the 2015–16 term. This paucity reflects the hard work carried out by the Native American Rights Fund and its Supreme Court Project, which seeks to keep cases away from the Court (see chapter 4).

Wagnon v. Prairie Band Potawatomi Nation (2005)

The context of *Wagnon v. Prairie Band Potawatomi Nation* is that the Prairie Band Potawatomi Nation operated a gas station on tribal land within reservation boundaries and imposed a tax on fuel sold at the station.[320] In addition, the State of Kansas imposed a tax on the non-Indian gasoline distributors when they initially received the fuel and then passed it on to the gas station.

Justice Thomas, in his majority opinion, ruled that the Kansas fuel tax was permitted because the transaction occurred off-reservation and the legal incidence of the tax fell on the non-Indian distributor. This was despite the fundamental and important issue of the tax being passed on to the Potawatomi Nation. The dissent argued that there were strong federal and tribal interests against the imposition of the state tax, effectively double taxation, and they held that the Kansas tax was preempted and thus invalid.

The *Wagnon* case ruling maintained the integrationist trend in taxation case law and very much limited and ignored the Indian sovereignty doctrine and inherent tribal sovereignty. The Court sided with the ideas used in the *Cotton Petroleum* opinion of 1989 as well as the Rehnquist concurrence/dissent in *Colville* and the dissents in *Bracker, Central Machinery, Ramah,* and *Cabazon.* The *Wagnon* majority relied, first and foremost, on the interests of the state and the idea that states had the right to tax nonmember companies unless that right was removed by specific congressional legislation.

The twist in the case involved the legal incidence of the tax, and the Court ruled that this occurred outside the reservation. Thus, taking integrationist principles a step further, the Court had found a small detail of state interest that pointed toward off-reservation activity. The justices did not analyze the activities on the reservation and thereby simply nullified the use of tribal sovereignty. Instead they concentrated on the activity outside the reservation and concluded that an off-reservation activity turned the case into a federal-versus-state issue. The Court used the rationale in *Mescalero Apache Tribe v. Jones* (1973) to determine the outcome of this case. A majority failed to use the federal preemption principles laid down in the *Bracker* precedent of 1980, which required federal preemption to be informed by tribal sovereignty.[321] Put simply, the application of integrationist principles protected the rights of the states, and the majority opinion was unconcerned about tribal sovereignty and the effects of the tax on the tribe and its business.

Plains Commerce Bank v. Long Family Land and Cattle Co. (2008)

In *Plains Commerce Bank v. Long Family Land and Cattle Co.* (2008), the Supreme Court considered a case involving the Long Company, including Ronnie and Lila Long (members of the Cheyenne River Sioux Tribe), who owned a majority of the company's shares, and the Plains Commerce Bank, located twenty-five miles off the reservation.[322] The bank had provided operating loans to the Long Company. However, one year the Longs leased (mortgaged) 2,230 acres of fee lands to the bank in order to secure money for the company. The Longs had the option to purchase the fee land at the end of the lease, but soon after they suffered financial hardship and defaulted on their loan and could not purchase that land. Then, the bank sold the land to non-Indians.

The Supreme Court opinion, authored by Chief Justice John Roberts, held that the Cheyenne River Sioux Tribal Court did not have jurisdiction over a claim of discrimination made by the Longs against the Plains Commerce Bank, which sold fee lands to non-Indians on more favorable terms than it did to the Longs.[323] He held that the claim of discrimination was over the sale of fee lands on the reservation and, consequently, that the tribe did not have authority to adjudicate claims on such lands. In contrast, the dissent held that the Cheyenne River Sioux Tribal Court had adjudicatory authority over the matter.

Once again, in the *Plains Commerce Bank* case the Court exhibited its integrationist outlook and ignored the Indian sovereignty doctrine and inherent tribal sovereignty. In addition, the Court's opinion clearly limited the

Montana exceptions to such an extent that they almost seem inapplicable as a base to prove the existence of inherent tribal sovereignty over nonmembers and on fee lands of the reservation. As Matthew L. M. Fletcher puts it, "It is exceptionally difficult for a tribe to meet the *Montana* test on nonmember land."[324] If the facts of the *Plains Commerce Bank* do not fit the *Montana* exceptions, then nothing ever will.

Dollar General Corporation v. Mississippi Band of Choctaw Indians

On June 15, 2015, the Supreme Court granted review to the petition of certiorari in the case of *Dollar General Corporation v. Mississippi Band of Choctaw Indians*. The issue before the Court will be "whether Indian tribal courts have jurisdiction to adjudicate civil tort claims against nonmembers, including as a means of regulating the conduct of nonmembers who enter into consensual relationships with a tribe or its members."[325]

The facts of the case involve John Doe, a thirteen-year-old member of the Mississippi Band of Choctaw Indians Tribe, who was placed on work experience pursuant to the Youth Opportunity Program (YOP) at the Dollar General Store in the Choctaw Town Center. The supervisor at the store was Dale Townsend, a non-Indian adult who resided outside the reservation in Philadelphia, Mississippi. The Dollar General Store had a commercial lease with Dolgencorp, a nonresident corporation, which had leased the store from Choctaw Shopping Center Enterprise. Choctaw Enterprise was owned by the Mississippi Band of Choctaw Indians. Dollar General possessed a tribal business licence. The store was located on tribal lands, which in turn are lands held in trust by the U.S. government, on the reservation. The plaintiffs alleged that during the time of John Doe's placement at the store Dale Townsend made repeated sexual advances toward the boy.[326]

In 2005, the family of John Doe brought a civil action against Dale Townsend and Dollar General in the Mississippi Band of Choctaw Indians Tribal Court. The attorney general of the Mississippi Band of Choctaw brought an action in Tribal Court excluding Mr. Townsend from the reservation. Dale Townsend and Dollar General filed a motion to dismiss the action because the court lacked subject matter jurisdiction.[327]

The appeal was heard in the Supreme Court of the Mississippi Band of Choctaw Indians.[328] In the discussion about subject matter jurisdiction, that court declared that, because Dollar General voluntarily signed a commercial lease with the Choctaw Shopping Center Enterprise and entered the reservation for commercial activities, a consensual relationship was formed between the tribe and Dollar General under the first *Montana* exception. In addition, Dollar General had a written lease with Choctaw Enterprise and also a business license granted by the tribe. Moreover, the court ruled that the second *Montana* exception was justified because to protect the health and welfare of its tribal members a tribal forum to adjudicate disputes was necessary, especially in light of the circumstances. The health and welfare of tribal members were considered as important as the health and welfare of the tribe as a whole.

Dolgencorp and Townsend filed an action in the U.S. District Court for the Southern District of Mississippi against the tribal defendants.[329] In 2008 the district court adjudged that the facts of the case were not supported under the second *Montana* exception. However, the court ruled that John Doe and Dolgencorp had entered into a consensual relationship with the Choctaws because John Doe was working under the supervision and control of Dollar General and the supervisor, Dale Townsend. The first *Montana* exception had been addressed. Conversely, the court ruled that the tribes had no jurisdiction over Townsend because there was no consensual relationship between him and the Doe family and the tribe.

Dolgencorp and the tribal defendants filed cross motions for summary judgment in the U.S. District Court for the Southern District of Mississippi.[330] In 2011 that court ruled that Townsend had on behalf of Dolgencorp agreed to participate in the YOP program, and through that agreement John Doe was placed under the supervision of Townsend. Simply, the court agreed that the alleged molestation of John Doe (tort claims) had occurred as a direct result of a consensual relationship and the tribe therefore had successfully met the criteria of the first *Montana* exception.

Dolgencorp appealed, and on October 3, 2013, the U.S. Court of Appeals for the Fifth Circuit announced its decision. The appeals court ruled that a relationship "of a commercial nature" occurred when John Doe performed limited work in exchange for job experience and training.[331] Therefore, Dolgencorp's participation in the YOP and the placement of John Doe in Dollar General formed the appropriate nexus. Moreover, the appeals court suggested that the regulation of the health and safety of its tribal members was fundamental to the authority of tribal government. This principle took notice of the *Plains Commerce* case, within which the *Montana* consensual relationship exception was, in theory, narrowed to specific relationships that "implicate tribal governance and internal relations."[332]

On March 14, 2014, less than a year after its opinion, the court of appeals announced that a panel rehearing of the case en banc was denied.[333] The en banc poll of judges declared that nine judges voted against rehearing en banc and five judges voted in favor. Consequently, a petition for a writ of certiorari was filed by Dolgencorp at the Supreme Court on June 12, 2014, and after lengthy consideration the Court granted review. The Court heard oral arguments on December 7, 2015, and a decision is expected before the end of the 2015–16 term.[334]

The Supreme Court justices have a broad question to consider. The Court may concentrate on the specific issue of what forms a consensual relationship under the first *Montana* exception, or it may examine, once and for all, tribal court jurisdiction and tribal jurisdiction over nonmembers on the reservation. One suspects that the Court will choose the latter, because it has been some time since it has had the opportunity to address tribal sovereignty over nonmembers. In light of the uncertainty caused by *Hicks* (2001) and *Atkinson* (2001), which contradict *Montana,* the Court may unearth a new precedent, founded on presumptions and principles contrary to hundreds of years of history, legislative debate, treaties, inherent sovereignty, and the Indian sovereignty doctrine, to sweep away tribal civil jurisdiction over nonmembers on reservations and unearth an *Oliphant* ripe for the twenty-first century.

✤ 4

Native America, Congress, and the Silent Revolution

The principles of the silent revolution have become embedded in the case law of the Supreme Court, and the legal paradigm established therein has begun to appear in congressional legislation as well, particularly after 2001. In that year, the Supreme Court decided two cases, *Atkinson Trading Co. v. Shirley* and *Nevada v. Hicks*, which unsettled many individuals and organizations both within and outside Indian country. In response to the *Hicks* decision, probably the last straw in a series of Court decisions that undermined the principles of inherent tribal sovereignty, Native America began a process to undo much of the damage and to prevent further setbacks to the Indian sovereignty doctrine and inherent tribal sovereignty. This chapter reviews that watershed response to *Atkinson* and *Hicks* by Native America and by Congress.

Native America Responds

The Supreme Court opinions in *Atkinson* and *Hicks* forced Native America to find various strategies to claim back the initiative and resurrect the traditional guiding principles of federal Indian law. These two decisions were described by the Native American Rights Fund (NARF) as "devastating in that they struck crippling blows to tribal sovereignty and tribal jurisdiction—the most fundamental elements of continued tribal existence."[1]

To defend what remained of the Indian sovereignty doctrine and tribal authority within Indian country, many Native American leaders and organizations—the National Congress of American Indians (NCAI), Native American Rights Fund (NARF), National American Indian Court Judges Association (NAICJA), and the National Indian Gaming Association (NIGA)—convened for a meeting in Washington, D.C., on September 11, 2001. During this time, the foundations of the Tribal Sovereignty Protection Initiative were planned, effectively a "Strategic Plan to Stop the Supreme Court's Erosion of Tribal Sovereignty." The meeting was wide ranging and incorporated "legislative, governance and litigation strategies" to protect and reinvigorate tribal jurisdiction and sovereignty. The meeting concluded with consensus for the future direction of the Tribal Sovereignty Protection Initiative, expressed in six strategic plans:

    I. Develop federal legislation to reaffirm tribal jurisdiction.

    II. Form a Supreme Court project to support and coordinate tribal advocacy before the Supreme Court.

    III. Promote strategies for tribal governance that will protect tribal jurisdiction.

    IV. Increase tribal participation in the selection of the federal judiciary.

    V. Develop a media and advocacy strategy to inform Congress, the public, and tribal leadership about tribal governance and that will promote the overall initiative.

    VI. Implement a fundraising campaign to support NCAI and NARF and their related expenses in promoting the initiative.[2]

One of these plans was quickly established in the form of the Tribal Supreme Court Project. The underlying rationale of this project was to strengthen legal coordination and resources between Native American nations and to minimize the number of times the Supreme Court granted review of petitions for certiorari (a formal request for the Court to hear a case) in Indian law cases. Indeed, there was a fear that the legal situation of all Native American tribes would get worse: "Most lawyers work hard to keep their lower court victories out of the Supreme Court, but sometimes, fearing hostile justices, they look to avoid the high court even when they have lost." Indeed, if some justices had an agenda in federal Indian law cases ("Chief Justice John Roberts Jr. has been quoted as asking what is so special about Indian tribes and their relationship to the United States")—then a sensible option was to circumvent the institution.[3] Today, the Tribal Supreme Court Project, having grown substantially over the years, has a working group of over two hundred attorneys and academics who specialize in all aspects of federal Indian law.

Critically, one of the tactics adopted by the Initiative was to set up its Legislative Committee, cochaired by John Echohawk, NARF executive director, and lawyer Susan M. Williams to draft legislation to "reconfirm the Congressional recognition of tribal sovereignty in a manner that will cause the Supreme Court to support tribal jurisdiction." To create such an important proposal required many drafts and countless working hours of deliberation and counterargument. From the outset, the committee had to choose between two options. They were going to either draft legislation with specific content to "narrowly target certain areas, such as jurisdiction over trust land," or address general and wide-ranging issues to "broadly support tribal regulatory, judicial and criminal jurisdiction on a territorial basis." In addition, the advice of Hawaii senator Daniel K. Inouye, chairman of the Senate Committee on Indian Affairs, was requested to address this pressing and substantive issue. The proposed legislation was to function on two levels: it would reaffirm inherent tribal sovereignty and confirm it through a congressional delegation of power; it would "seek the full federal laws that are necessary to protect tribal rights."[4]

The development of the proposed legislation began in late 2001 and continued until the introduction of Senate Bill 578 in 2003. Throughout the eighteen months of consultation over the Tribal Sovereignty and Economic Enhancement Act, the language and appearance of the bill changed but the intention and guiding principles, anchored to the Indian sovereignty doctrine and inherent tribal sovereignty, were resolute. The creation of a bill that met the interests of hundreds of Native American nations, lawyers, and scholars was no small challenge.

The first draft of the bill, written by Charles Wilkinson, professor of law at the University of Colorado Law School, appeared on October 2, 2001. Over the course of the next few days the Legislation Options Subcommittee, also known as the Legislative Drafting Workgroup, chaired by Echohawk and Williams, met to review and amend the Wilkinson draft. Its purpose was clear: to develop a discussion draft bill to affirm tribal jurisdiction in Indian country, including civil, criminal, judicial, and territorial jurisdiction. Williams wrote: "I received a number of proposals suggesting language for the various sections of the bill. Because Charles drafted a complete bill that hits all the issues, I thought it made the most sense to use Charles' work as a starting point for our discussions. Accordingly, this memorandum adopts the form of Charles' bill and sets out the alternative proposals under the relevant section headings."[5]

In the findings part of the draft bill, a section that appears in many bills to provide context and historical background to the specific information of the bill itself, the information was specific to tribal sovereignty and, accordingly, proposed "a comprehensive set of findings that traces the legal history of tribal sovereignty and federal Indian policy from the Nation's birth to the present."[6] These findings, twelve in all, examined the issue of sovereign nations before contact with the Europeans, the sovereign-to-sovereign relationship, recognized in hundreds of treaties and underpinned by inherent sovereignty between Native American nations and the United States, and the limitations imposed by the Marshall trilogy. The upshot was that the tribes essentially "retained all other sovereign powers not expressly relinquished by the tribes or expressly limited by Congress."[7]

The findings also briefly examined negative congressional policy, including allotment and termination, and positive congressional legislation such as the Indian Reorganization Act of 1934 and the Indian Self-Determination and Education Assistance Act of 1975, as well as the role of tribal governments on reservations and their powers and the problems caused by the long and difficult relationship with the United States. Importantly, the findings ended with reference to Congress's current policy of tribal self-determination, which had enabled numerous statutes that enhanced strong and stable tribal governments, and the inconsistency of Supreme Court opinions vis-à-vis that congressional policy. Historically, it had been Congress that defined the nation's relationship with Native America and not the Supreme Court. Accordingly, the authors of the draft bill concluded that, "in order to fulfill Congress' constitutional responsibility to implement federal Indian policy as trustee, it is Congress' duty to clarify the nature and extent of the powers of sovereign tribal governments."[8]

The section titled "Tribal Powers" contained a general statement of tribal powers followed by specific tribal powers, notably legislative powers, civil regulatory powers, civil judicial powers, criminal powers, and territorial jurisdiction. There was also a discussion about whether to recognize these powers as inherent only or to obtain a congressional delegation of power too, and about whether to address tribal powers in a general or a specific way. One position, expressed in a memorandum, read, "[The tribal powers] are recognized as inherent, but Charles' draft also would have Congress delegate the aforementioned powers so there would be no question about the tribes' right to exercise them. The various categories of powers are described broadly to encompass all of Indian country and all persons found therein. Charles also defines tribal territorial jurisdiction as coextensive with Indian country as defined at 18 U.S.C. §1151 as amended to include a definition of dependent Indian communities." However, the memorandum continued, committee member Eric Eberhard took a different approach and was very specific about the powers of the tribes: "Eric takes a somewhat different approach, grounded in Nathan Margold's 1934 Solicitor's Opinion on the powers of Indian tribes. Eric's proposal lists the regulation of property and specific types of transactions as within a tribe's legislative and regulatory authority. . . . In addition, Eric's draft provides that a tribe's judicial and administrative authority is coextensive with its legislative authority, and sufficient to effectuate its inherent powers or those delegated by Congress."[9]

Despite the divergence in opinion, both authors firmly addressed and believed in the inherent nature of these powers and the need for their reaffirmation by Congress. Moreover, the proposed bill wanted Public Law 280 to be repealed one year after its passage in Congress. However, two other members had a contrary opinion and wanted Public Law 280 to be amended so that the United States "must reassume civil and/or criminal jurisdiction when either a state *or* a tribe so requests."[10] In that case, if a tribe demanded the retrocession of jurisdiction then the United States would have no choice but to carry out the demands of the tribe in question. Other sections included the provision of intergovernmental agreements between tribes and states and the use of federal money to allow tribes to acquire lands, to improve tribal courts, and as payment in lieu of taxes.

A fortnight later and tribal leaders as well as the full Sovereignty Protection Steering Committee and Workgroup met to discuss the changes set forth to the original Wilkinson draft bill. At the outset of the meeting, the importance of the Initiative process was clarified as a means to guard against and to vigorously contest "this new direction in the Court's Indian law cases," which posed "a very serious threat to the ability of tribal governments to provide needed governmental services and authority on Indian lands and in the long term, to maintain the culturally separate identities of Indian communities."[11]

Despite the simple and clear focus of reaffirming tribal jurisdiction, there were many problems. Hundreds of Native American nations were involved in the process. Many had divergent histories and cultures as well as modern-day needs that included a myriad of different problems. It was difficult for the committee to reconcile sometimes obvious divergences into a workable and specific goal. In addition, this process was overwhelming in scope, including as it did a centuries-old relationship with thousands of treaties, statutes, and complex case law. Despite the complexity, the rationale of the bill was simple in the eyes of the committee. Rather than address federal policy limitations placed upon tribal jurisdiction, the committee "intended to fashion a legislative remedy that focuses specifically on the problems caused by the recent line of Supreme Court cases."[12] The Indian sovereignty doctrine was based on the presumption that tribes had inherent sovereignty over the lands and people on their reservations unless Congress acted to reverse attributes of that sovereignty. Unfortunately, the rationale in the recent line of Supreme Court opinions began from the presumption that tribes required congressional legislation to acquire sovereignty in the first place. In view of this recent development, the committee wanted the draft bill to reaffirm the original purpose of the Indian sovereignty doctrine—to reestablish that only Congress, under Article I of the Constitution, and the U.S. president, under the treaty-making power in Article II, had the authority to limit tribal sovereignty.

The committee had three basic reasons for concentrating exclusively on affirming inherent tribal sovereignty in order to undo recent Supreme Court cases. First, this simple focus would make it easier to attract supporters and sponsors instead of creating opponents. Second, a more comprehensive bill would be too complex and impossible to explain to members of Congress. Third, the inclusion of all manner of issues in the draft bill would "bring out many of the distinctions among tribes and . . . run the risk of losing the unified tribal support for the bill."[13]

With these decisions in place, the committee asked everyone involved to consider five important tasks while drafting the bill:

1. Tribes needed to show practical evidence and advance socially compelling arguments that having jurisdiction over non-Indians was critical for tribes to govern effectively.
2. Tribes needed to counter the response of opponents by changing the public perception of tribal jurisdiction over non-Indians to one that was necessary for effective tribal governance.
3. Tribes needed to consider the practical reality of additional jurisdictional responsibilities. Did they have the necessary revenues and infrastructure to implement these responsibilities?
4. All of those involved were required to develop policy and legal arguments to support the draft bill in such a way that it reaffirmed inherent tribal sovereignty and ensured that Congress adhered to the policy of tribal self-determination.
5. Everybody involved needed to assess the feasibility of the bill within the federal and state political environments.[14]

These five activities would allow all tribes to demonstrate to the nation's population that tribes had governments and that these provided all manner of services to Native Americans and non-Indians. In addition, evidence of the regional differences in jurisdictional issues would be acquired by the committee so that these could be addressed in the draft bill. The committee discussed the draft bill section by section, with much debate over the definitions of "Indian country" and "reservation."

Over a month later, on November 20, 2001, draft materials were available for the Tribal Sovereignty Protection Initiative. Among these materials was a memorandum explaining the draft legislation, similar to the bills over the past few weeks, the draft legislation itself, and a resolution from the NCAI supporting the advancement of the legislation. These documents were to be considered at the NCAI annual meeting during the last week of the month.

During these meetings the reality of this mammoth task was apparent to those involved. Generally, the involvement of hundreds of tribes made "it especially hard, if not impossible, to develop a bill that will provide sovereignty protection for all tribes."[15] One key problem was that not all tribes wanted to assume full authority over nonmembers, particularly criminal jurisdiction. These tribes were offered legal and political advice to address their situations, including the use of tribal constitutions to affirm authority over people on reservations or federal legislation such as the Indian Reorganization Act of 1934 to deal with local and regional issues. This enabled discussions of the legislation to move forward. Furthermore, the bill had to address the simple focus of reaffirming tribal jurisdiction. If it wavered from this position, "it will be difficult to push a single, one size fits all bill through Congress on such a potentially controversial issue."[16] Problems such as federal court review of tribal court decisions, as well as those already noted, were discussed and amended for over a year and a half.

Only a few months after the NCAI meeting, on February 27, 2002, the Senate Committee on Indian Affairs held a hearing specifically regarding the recent Supreme Court opinions and their impact on Native America.[17] During these proceedings many individuals gave evidence and presented written statements regarding the severe limitations placed on tribal jurisdiction within Indian country. The evidence was sobering and reinforced plainly to the American people and legislators that the Court had created many insolvable problems and jurisdictional limitations for Native American tribes. For the next year, the Tribal Sovereignty Protection Initiative continued to work on its draft bill and organized meetings throughout Indian country. The plan for all involved was to develop a structured bill by 2003, and to accomplish this target the tribes planned to educate Congress, appeal and educate the public about the role of tribal government, and resolve disputes on a local level.[18] Indeed this strategy was firmly developed in October 2001 and was being implemented in 2002. In that year, the draft proposed:

> First, that Congress should reaffirm the principle that Indian tribes are the primary governments within Indian country and retain their inherent right to govern all people and places unless that power has been specifically limited by treaty or federal statute. Second, recognizing that any serious legislative effort must address the issue of civil rights, the bill would have provided for federal judicial review of tribal court decisions to guard the civil rights of non-Indians, while specifically protecting the right of tribes to create and maintain their own forms of government and their traditions, religions, cultures, languages and ways of life. Third, recognizing that tribal consent is critical, each tribe would have the right to opt in or out of the legislation and whether to exercise any or all aspects of jurisdiction offered in the bill.[19]

Although the primary focus of the Initiative was to reaffirm inherent tribal sovereignty, other considerations developed through the process. Analysis of Supreme Court case law showed that the process of federal review of tribal court decisions was an essential concept that had to be addressed in the draft bill. In addition, the commonsense concept of tribal consent was critical to those tribes who had concerns about aspects of the bill. Indeed, they could cherry-pick aspects of the bill that suited their position. By December 2002, the Initiative had completed its legislative proposal.[20]

Congress and Precedent: Authority to Reverse Supreme Court Opinions

On February 25, 2003, Senator Inouye announced at an executive council winter session of the NCAI that the Senate would be introducing "historic legislation" to protect tribal sovereignty. He declared that a "discussion bill," designed to undo recent Supreme Court opinions in the field of federal Indian law, would be formally introduced to the Senate to allow time for legislation to be developed and passed in a number of years.[21]

Generally, Congress has the authority to reverse Supreme Court decisions and had exercised this right in federal Indian law on several occasions between 1884 and 2004.[22] However, to this day, Congress has yet to intervene and directly reverse Supreme Court decisions dealing with inherent tribal sovereignty and state authority over nonmembers on the reservations. Even the recent Tribal Law and Order Act in 2010 and the Violence Against Women Reauthorization Act in 2013 did not undermine the silent revolution.

Ex parte Crow Dog (1883)

In *Ex parte Crow Dog* (1883), the Supreme Court held that the United States did not have criminal authority to try a tribal member for the killing of another tribal member on a reservation and reversed the conviction of Crow Dog (Kan-gi-shun-ca) by the First District Court of Dakota.[23] Indeed, the inherent sovereignty of tribes ousted federal law from the reservation.[24] Then, in 1885, Congress introduced the Major Crimes Act and explicitly overruled the *Crow Dog* opinion. The act read:

> *Be it enacted, &c.* * * * That immediately upon and after the date of the passage of this act all Indians, committing against the person or property of another Indian or other person any of the following crimes, namely, murder, manslaughter, rape, assault with intent to kill, arson, burglary, and larceny within any Territory of the United States, and either within or without an Indian reservation, shall be subject therefor to the laws of such Territory relating to said crimes, and shall be tried therefor in the same courts and in the same manner and shall be subject to the same penalties as are all other persons charged with the commission of said crimes, respectively; and the said courts are hereby given jurisdiction in all such cases; And all such Indians committing any of the above crimes against the person or property of another Indian or other person within the boundaries of any State of the United States, and within the limits of any Indian reservation, shall be subject to the same laws, tried in the same courts and in the same manner, and subject to the same penalties as are all other persons committing any of the above crimes within the exclusive jurisdiction of the United States. [*March 3, 1885.*][25]

Congress had thereby passed legislation that allowed the U.S. legal system to try a Native American who committed certain crimes against another Native American.[26]

Duro v. Reina (1990)

The process of overruling Indian-related case law through congressional legislation occurred once again in the twentieth century. In *Duro v. Reina* (1990), Duro, an enrolled member of another tribe, allegedly shot and killed a Native American on a reservation.[27] He was charged with firing an illegal weapon under the tribal criminal code. Duro appealed to the federal district court because he believed that the tribal court had no jurisdiction over him. The district court ruled that the tribal court had no jurisdiction because it was discriminatory and in violation of the equal protection guarantees of the Indian Civil Rights Act of 1968. In addition, it ruled that, after *Oliphant*, non-Indians were exempt from the criminal jurisdiction of tribal courts. The court of appeals reversed the decision of the lower court.

In 1990, the Supreme Court opinion of *Duro*, authored by Justice Anthony Kennedy, ruled that "an Indian tribe may not assert criminal jurisdiction over a nonmember Indian." The justification for the decision was that "the rationale of *Oliphant, Wheeler*, and subsequent cases compels the conclusion that Indian tribes lack jurisdiction over nonmembers" and that tribal court authorities "embody only the powers of *internal* self-governance." In other words, tribal courts had authority over tribal members only. Additionally, the Court declared that Duro was a citizen of the United States and that "this case must be decided in light of the fact that all Indians are now citizens of the United States."[28]

Then, in 1991, Congress passed specific legislation explicitly reversing the *Duro* decree and restored tribal criminal jurisdiction over non-member Indians.[29] Congress specifically amended the language defining the "powers of self-government" in the Indian Civil Rights Act of 1968 to include "the inherent power of Indian tribes, hereby recognized and affirmed, to exercise criminal jurisdiction over all Indians."[30]

United States v. Lara (2004)

The impact of the 1991 legislation was the focus of a 2004 Supreme Court case that tested the limits of inherent tribal sovereignty and whether it could be recognized by Congress. In *United States v. Lara* (2004), Billy Jo Lara, a member of the Turtle Mountain Band of Chippewa Indians, lived on the Spirit Lake Reservation with his wife and children.[31] After assaulting a BIA officer, he was convicted by the tribal court of the Spirit Lake Tribe. Thereafter, the federal government charged him for the same incident, and Lara argued that the Fifth Amendment protection against double jeopardy prevented a new prosecution. The *Lara* court held that "Congress has the constitutional power to lift the restrictions on the tribes' criminal jurisdiction over nonmember Indians." The 7–2 majority confirmed that congressional legislation had overruled *Duro* and clarified that Congress had plenary power over tribal affairs. Consequently, Congress had the authority to restrict or relax the limitations imposed on tribal sovereignty.[32] The action of Congress, as Initiative Legislative Committee cochair Echohawk stated, "was an adjustment of the status of tribal sovereign authority," and if "Congress wants to adjust that, they can do that and that's all this was."[33]

The key question answered by the Supreme Court was whether the legislation extended congressional authority to allow the tribes to prosecute tribal nonmembers or whether the legislation reaffirmed inherent tribal sovereignty. As Justice Stephen Breyer explained, "Section 1301(2) 'recognize[s] and affirm[s]' in each tribe the 'inherent power' to prosecute nonmember Indians, and its legislative history confirms that such was Congress' intent. Thus, it seeks to adjust the tribes' status, relaxing restrictions, recognized in *Duro*, that the political branches had imposed on the tribes' exercise of inherent prosecutorial power."[34]

Justice Breyer concluded that the source of tribal power was inherent sovereignty, a source independent of Congress rather than a congressional delegation of power, which was an extension of congressional authority. In the practical sense, if congressional legislation allowed tribes to do something, whether with inherent sovereignty or not, it appeared to agree with the rationale of the modern-day Supreme Court that argued that Congress must act to allow tribal authority over nonmembers.

Senate Bill 578 and Inherent Tribal Sovereignty

Despite the congressional steps to overrule certain Supreme Court cases, Congress had yet to reverse any of the case law from the period of the silent revolution—such as *Oliphant v. Suquamish Indian Tribe* (1978), *Montana v. United States* (1981), *Brendale v. Confederated Yakima Indian Nation* (1989), *South Dakota v. Bourland* (1993), *Strate v. A-1 Contractors* (1997), *Atkinson Trading Co. v. Shirley* (2001), or *Nevada v. Hicks* (2001). Similarly, Congress did not pass S. 578, a bill that would have reinvigorated tribal sovereignty and reversed this case law.

After many years of detailed negotiation to develop a coherent and simply focused bill by the Tribal Sovereignty Protection Initiative, in 2003 the Senate introduced bill S. 578 and the House of Representatives introduced bill H.R. 2242, both of which were called Tribal Government Amendments to the Homeland Security Act. This bill was the closest Congress had come to completely reversing recent Supreme Court federal Indian case law. The language used in the 2003 bill was similar to those words read by Native Americans in 2001, guided by the simple focus of reaffirming tribal jurisdiction and undoing several recent Court opinions.

The S. 578 bill, developed in coordination with the Senate Government Affairs Committee, was announced in a Senate session on March 7, 2003, by Senator Inouye and on behalf of Senator Ben Nighthorse Campbell (Colorado), Senator Daniel Akaka (Hawaii), and Senator Maria Cantwell (Washington).[35] S. 578, also known as the "Hicks fix," was designed to amend existing statutes—the original Homeland Security Act of 2002—to allow the tribes the appropriate jurisdiction and authority on the reservations to respond appropriately to acts of terrorism. As Senator Inouye explained, the purpose of the bill was to "amend the Homeland Security Act of 2002 to include Indian tribal governments amongst the governmental entities that are consulted with respect to activities carried out by the Secretary of the Department of Homeland Security."[36]

The bill had two objectives. In the original Homeland Security Act of 2002, tribes were defined as local governments, which was both politically and legally inaccurate.[37] The 2003 bill would rectify the situation and acknowledge tribes as equivalent to any one of the states of the Union. Senator Inouye presented this important issue to the Senate when he introduced the bill:

> In the Homeland Security Act of 2002, tribal governments are included in the definition of "local governments." As we all know, local governments are political subdivisions of the States. In contrast, tribal governments are recognized as separate sovereigns under the United States Constitution that do not derive their sovereign status from the States, and accordingly, we believe that Federal law should continue to reflect the legal distinction between local governments that are political subdivisions of the States and tribal governments. Accordingly, these amendments would remove tribal governments from the definition of "local governments" as currently set forth in the Act, and insert tribal governments in the appropriate and relevant sections of the Act.[38]

For the tribes to be viewed as government entities under the auspices of the Homeland Security Act, they had to have the requisite authority to counter terrorism on their reservations. Therefore, the bill would allow tribes to access and receive funding and technical expertise to combat terrorism.[39]

Along with redefining the tribal government, Senator Inouye believed that Congress had to reinstate tribal sovereignty to counter acts of terrorism. S. 578, he stated, "makes clear that for purposes of homeland security, the United States recognizes the inherent authority of tribal governments to exercise jurisdiction currently with the Federal government to assure that applicable criminal, civil and regulatory laws are enforced on tribal lands."[40] Senator Inouye's words were in direct conflict with the Supreme Court and formed the underlying principles of Section 13 of Bill S. 578, titled "Congressional Affirmation and Declaration of Tribal Government Authorities":

> (a) in general—For the purpose of this Act, Congress affirms and declares that the inherent sovereign authority of an Indian tribal government includes the authority to enforce and adjudicate violations of applicable criminal, civil, and regulatory laws committed by any person on land under the jurisdiction of the Indian tribal government, except as expressly and clearly limited by—
>
>> (1) a treaty between the United States and an Indian tribe; or
>>
>> (2) an Act of Congress.
>
> (b) scope—The authority of an Indian tribal government described in subsection (a) shall—
>
>> (1) be concurrent with the authority of the United States; and
>>
>> (2) extend to—
>>
>>> (A) all places and persons within the Indian country (as defined in section 1151 of title 18, United States Code) under the concurrent jurisdiction of the United States and the Indian tribal government; and
>>>
>>> (B) any person, activity, or event having sufficient contacts with that land, or with a member of the Indian tribal government, to ensure protection of due process rights.

Clearly, Section 13 supported the extension of tribal sovereignty over reservation lands and all of the people on those lands, subject only to federal law.

Section 13 also reaffirmed the congressional definition of "Indian country." In 1948, Congress had introduced a definition and simultaneously codified existing case law.[41] In the original definition, only tribal criminal jurisdiction on the reservation was relevant. However, as a direct result of the opinion issued in *DeCoteau v. District County Court* (1975), the Supreme Court made tribal civil jurisdiction on the reservation relevant.[42]

Title 18, Part I, Chapter 53, Section 1151 of the United States Code defines "Indian country" as

(a) all land within the limits of any Indian reservation under the jurisdiction of the United States Government, notwithstanding the issuance of any patent, and, including rights-of-way running through the reservation,

(b) all dependent Indian communities within the borders of the United States whether within the original or subsequently acquired territory thereof, and whether within or without the limits of a state, and

(c) all Indian allotments, the Indian titles to which have not been extinguished, including rights-of-way running through the same.[43]

In this 1948 definition, Congress had recognized the jurisdictional definition of tribal authority within Indian country. However, during the silent revolution the Court had undercut this definition; thus, by reaffirming the status of Indian country in Section 13 of S. 578, Congress had introduced a bill that conflicted with and was antithetical to the principles of the judiciary.

Reactions to S. 578

Ultimately, Senate bill 578 was withdrawn, and the primary reason for the withdrawal was its controversial Section 13. Indeed, it was widely acknowledged by both Native Americans and non-Indians that this particular section threatened to overrule Supreme Court case law, which had protected nonmembers from tribal sovereignty and allowed state law to operate on the reservations. Interestingly, the opposing views about this section were not exclusively Native American versus non-Native American; on the contrary, opinions varied with individuals as well as with the real-life, day-to-day situations of individual tribes.

Much of the disagreement about Section 13 centered on whether it would be a good thing or a bad thing for Section 13 to undo the Supreme Court's erosion of inherent tribal sovereignty—for example, in *Oliphant v. Suquamish*

Indian Tribe and *Nevada v. Hicks*. Opinions from the U.S. attorney for the District of Minnesota and the Congressional Research Service (CRS) supported claims that Section 13 was aimed at directly overruling Supreme Court case law. Thomas B. Heffelfinger, U.S. attorney for the District of Minnesota, testified before the Senate that Section 13 overruled case law and was "a legislative overturn" of *Oliphant* and "an attempt to deal with the *Oliphant* issue head-on." Furthermore, according to Heffelfinger, the Native American Issues Subcommittee's (NAIS) Oliphant Working Group had concluded that "section 13 as currently written is too broad" and that to overrule *Oliphant* in "a broad and isolated manner could result in complicated legal and practical law enforcement issues such as those of due process concerns, double jeopardy, resources and appellate rights." Therefore, due process issues such as separation of powers, provision of defense counsel for indigent defendants, makeup of jury pools, and appellate and habeas corpus relief needed to be addressed by the tribes themselves if *Oliphant* was to be overruled.[44]

M. Maureen Murphy, of the CRS, noted that Section 13 "raised concern in some quarters that it would overturn Nevada v. Hicks . . . or otherwise expand Indian tribal sovereignty." Murphy was also concerned that the expansion of tribal sovereignty in S. 578 was contrary to the limitations imposed by the Supreme Court in criminal and civil case law. She noted that Section 13 "appeared to endorse a view of tribal criminal and civil jurisdiction inconsistent with Supreme Court rulings on the subject of tribal jurisdiction" and that "some language in the legislation that appears to endorse a view of tribal sovereignty . . . seems inconsistent with Supreme Court rulings on the subject."[45]

The CRS believed that this conflict arose from the fact that the draft legislation allowed the tribes to have authority over nonmembers on the reservations, contrary to recent case law; Section 13 appeared "to confer, reinstate, or delegate to tribes authority over nonmembers and non-Indian fee land that the courts have found to have been divested." Yet the CRS was ambivalent about the overall effect, for it also noted that Section 13 was limited by the words "For the purpose of this Act" and intimated that Section 13 "may be found to be limited, should the courts be called on for interpretation."[46]

For some tribes, the implementation of Section 13 would have caused everyday practical problems on the reservations. Writing many years later, James Hawkins, a lawyer with the Great Lakes Inter-Tribal Council, an organization of twelve tribes located in Wisconsin and upper Michigan, reported that S. 578 and Section 13 would have "swept away" cases such as *Oliphant* and

Montana and "erected reservation boundary barriers to criminal and regulatory law enforcement," particularly in states where cooperation between tribal, state, and local law enforcement was ambiguous.[47] The reality of present-day circumstances in Wisconsin, a Public Law 280 state, was, however, different because state and tribal criminal jurisdiction was concurrent. Therefore, Hawkins continued, if the Wisconsin tribes had the "entirety of reservation law enforcement," then as a result "off-reservation agencies have so much less reason to cooperate and the prospects for adequate training, development, coverage, and continued funding would probably have been extremely limited for the tribes." Moreover, one tribe had "substantive concerns" over the language used in the bill. Some commentators, according to Hawkins, had indicated that overall "there was no great groundswell of support from tribes from across the country."

In 2003, many Native Americans supported Section 13, precisely because it would have reversed case law that in turn had eroded tribal authority on the reservations. On August 21, 2003, the Governors' Interstate Indian Council (GIIC), a forum for delegates appointed by the governors of individual states and who represented state Indian affairs agencies and organizations, presented a resolution (adopted by unanimous vote of the delegates present) in support of S. 578 and H.R. 2242, including Section 13. Indeed, the GIIC supported the explicit language, described to be "tribal inherent sovereignty jurisdictional statements in their respective sections 13," and therefore urged Congress to pass the bills with these statements "that provide for tribal inherent civil and criminal jurisdiction for homeland security purposes."[48] W. Ron Allen, chairman of the Jamestown-S'Klallam Tribe, also supported Section 13 and its purpose.[49]

All the while the Tribal Sovereignty Protection Initiative was working on a draft bill, giving Native Americans and non-Indians the opportunity to examine and understand the issues at stake, there were always strong, almost impenetrable factors at work to prevent the passage of S. 578 into law. One factor was that Native Americans are a small percentage of the overall American population and form small populations within the individual states. Therefore, in political terms—or realpolitik—the so-called controversial issues could never gather the support required in Congress. The introduction of the bill was not auspicious; there were only three cosponsors. Ultimately, the bill failed to move out of committee to the Senate floor. W. Ron Allen suggests simply that "the votes were not there."[50] The political reasons for inaction are too strong when a grant of authority would allow a minority population to control a majority population upon reservation lands and within Indian country. As Kevin K. Washburn, former assistant secretary of Indian affairs for the U.S. Department of the Interior, puts it: "American Indians are only about 2% of the population in the US, and I am not sure that the other 98% will ever be willing to ask its congressional representatives to force them to submit to the criminal authority of the tribal 2%. Indeed, why would they?"[51]

Many years later, legal representative Tom Schlosser eloquently summed up the impossible task faced by Native Americans around 2003, outlining three reasons why Congress did not act to implement tribal jurisdiction over non-Indians:

> First, the physical and demographic situations among reservations (technically, the areas in question are Indian country, a term broader than reservations) vary so widely. Some reservations are almost completely owned by non Indians who also overwhelmingly outnumber the Indians. Most reservations look nothing like Monument Valley (which featured in many Westerns). Second, giving to the Indians the criminal prosecution authority over a group of citizens who cannot vote in tribal elections (and often can't serve on tribal court juries) would seem to many congressmen to be unfair and undemocratic. Third, there are thousands of separate tracts of Indian country, ranging from parcels the size of a home lot, to reservations larger than some of our smaller states. No single solution would work for them all, another reason Congress is unlikely to act.[52]

In other words, members of Congress would not vote for legislation for tribal jurisdiction over nonmembers because a majority population on many reservations would be under minority rule, nonmembers would not be able to participate in regional elections, and legislators might well be voting for something that might harm their local area, because of the vastly different issues faced by over five hundred tribes. In sum, Schlosser stated, "few congressmen are likely to sponsor legislation that is opposed by many of their constituents. So if you have a reservation in your congressional district, and its voters don't outnumber the rest of your district, why would you push such a bill?"

Section 13 would have overturned much of the silent revolution, but the fierce debate focused on the impact on non-Indians. Much of the vitriol was propagated by anti-tribal groups such as the Citizens Equal Rights Alliance

(CERA). Indeed, they interpreted Section 13 as an overturn of Supreme Court case law that they believed protected the constitutional rights of American citizens on the reservations. CERA argued that Section 13 would allow arbitrary tribal authority to exist over state and American citizens and pointed out that Congress was avoiding its moral and legal duty to protect approximately 500,000 nonmembers living on the reservations. Notwithstanding this myopic standpoint, a reading of the entire S. 578 bill (as well as Section 13) would have informed them about the specific built-in federal law protections against such infringements of rights. In addition, such tribal authority, in certain areas of the law, already existed; non-Indians were currently brought before tribal forums for minor acts that contravened tribal law.

The specific concerns raised by the prospect of tribal authority over non-Indians included non-Indians not being able to vote in tribal elections or participate in tribal or reservation life. Indeed, CERA was raising an issue over which the Supreme Court was concerned in *Oliphant* and had ruled against the tribes. Unfortunately, CERA's general assumptions used fear as a tool to destabilize non-Indians living within reservation boundaries. On May 16, 2003, a CERA press release stated, "There's a civil rights nightmare waiting to happen with Senator Inouye's S. 578 amendment to the Homeland Security Bill." Essentially, the S. 578 bill would "deprive several million people, some of whom live near—and others that legally own property in—'Indian Country' of their constitutional rights, under the guise of making Indian Tribes a part of Homeland Security because some reservation land is on U.S. borders." Indeed, CERA summed up the entire congressional process of S. 578, in addition to proclaiming its own right-wing political and philosophical bias, by declaring that media representatives attend meetings "to learn how racist tyrannical Federal Indian policies are harming the lives of tribal and non-tribal United States citizens that live in or near areas newly defined as 'Indian Country.'"[53] In addition, CERA equated Native Americans with terrorists, to which Senator Daniel Inouye replied, "To suggest that tribal governments are terrorists, or that citizens of this country are subject to attack by Native people is to make one of the most outrageous assertions I've ever heard."[54]

Contrary to the assertions of CERA, participation in governance, such as voting in an election, has never been a prerequisite for the determination of jurisdiction over a person or a reason to deny authority based on due process and equal protection rights. In the case of *Duro v. Reina*, Justice Brennan, in his dissenting opinion, categorically stated, "Nor have we [Supreme Court] ever held that participation in the political process is a prerequisite to the exercise of criminal jurisdiction by a sovereign. If such were the case, a State could not prosecute nonresidents, and this country could not prosecute aliens who violate our laws."[55] For example, if a citizen from Wales visited Pennsylvania, the jurisdiction and authority of the state and the country would not be extinguished purely because a citizen of the United Kingdom cannot vote in a U.S. state or national election.

Additionally, opponents of S. 578, including anti-tribal groups, argued that tribal governments lacked the sophistication to assume authority over non-Indians.[56] Scholars have observed that the political and legal elite of America did not view tribes and their institutions as their equals. One example: "Neither the Court nor the Congress is willing to grant true equal parity to tribal courts because a number of these policymakers do not view them as being fully legitimate bodies. . . . Tribal courts are viewed through very racialized eyes and several of the justices do not feel that they are fully equipped to address the needs of non-tribal citizens."[57]

Clearly, such generalizations about tribal "sophistication" were ill founded. There are more than 550 tribal governments within the United States, and they vary considerably in history, culture, and opinion. With so much variation, how would one assign a measurable value for sophistication? Sophistication differs from person to person, from county to county, and from state to state. Some tribal governments have developed legal systems similar to that of the United States; others have not. This does not mean that any one of these tribal legal systems would not offer impartial justice, at least as vigorously as the states do. One need only look at the justice systems of some of the states and the miscarriages of justice that have occurred, many of them founded precisely on questionable due process and the provision of incapable lawyers.[58] Indeed, the purpose of tribal government systems is to protect the communities in which they serve, and who would deny their importance? The purpose of Section 13 was to allow tribal governments to decide whether the reversal of Supreme Court case law and reassertion of inherent tribal sovereignty was a legal and workable possibility for them. If it was, then they would act upon it, in accordance with the unequivocal protections offered by federal law.

Tribes, tribal courts, and their practitioners throughout the United States have strived to educate non-Indians about their legal systems. Yet many Americans continue to be skeptical about the standards of tribal courts. As Dorma L. Sahneyah, chief prosecutor of the Hopi Tribe, put it in Senate testimony,

"Seemingly, no matter how dedicated tribal courts are to their function, they are doomed to being perceived as substandard, even when compared to local justice courts in some States like New York, where part-time plumbers and retirees who lack any understanding of law, have authority to sentence wrongdoers up to two years."[59] Undoubtedly, Section 13 did not conform to the political reality in the early twenty-first century.

The fiction created by some anti-tribal groups was mirrored at times by inaccurate reports in local and national media to prevent the passage of S. 578. A *Washington Times* article reported that "opponents of this move—who include some non-Indians living on reservations—say it would overturn a 25-year-old Supreme Court decision 'limiting and defining Indian sovereignty' and could lead to tribal power grabs affecting hundreds of thousands of non-Indians"; a Republican committee staffer claimed that groups of non-Indians feared the snowball effect of "other jurisdictional grabs" by tribal governments.[60] If many non-Indian communities had negative images of tribal governments and discriminatory views about tribal authority, then by stating that these standards would be forced onto them only further caricatured those stereotypes. In the same news article, the negative publicity was eloquently explained by Patricia Zell, a legal staffer for Senator Inoyue, who declared that "some groups hit the panic button, claiming this change would mean tribal governments would be able to exercise control over all people for all purposes. That's just not true." The anti-tribal perspective was supported in a 2003 *New American* article in which the author declared that S. 578 was "a quiet power grab" by Native Americans that would have led to "literally hundreds of small, self-contained sovereign nations on American soil" and could "be permitted to establish any form of government they please."[61] Borrowing such negative stereotypes of Native Americans, anti-tribal groups were and continue to be strong. W. Ron Allen emphasizes that S. 578 was derailed by the potency of such groups: "If you check the web sites of such groups as the Citizens Alliance Organization, which opposes tribal sovereignty, you get a pretty good sense of what we were up against in trying to get this legislation passed."[62]

Despite the concerns expressed by many people, in fact Section 13 was limited by its own terminology and did not sanction unchecked tribal sovereignty over nonmembers on reservations. Although Section 13 appeared to return tribal authority over nonmembers to pre-1973 standards, it was explicitly qualified: tribal authority existed "except as expressly and clearly limited by" two important caveats, a treaty or an act of Congress. This qualification undermined the dominant perception of exclusive tribal authority over parts of American society. Inherent tribal authority over state and American citizens on the reservations would have worked alongside the authority of the United States. As Senator Maria Cantwell commented in 2004, "The bill affirms general tribal sovereignty and provides that federal and tribal court have concurrent jurisdiction over Indian crimes on tribal lands, within the Homeland Security Act of 2002."[63] In fact, Section 13 was explicit about the concurrent nature of the law where nonmembers were concerned: tribal authority over reservation lands and the people on those lands was guaranteed to be "under the concurrent jurisdiction of the United States." The importance of concurrent tribal and federal jurisdiction was "to ensure protection of due process rights." Thus, not only was inherent tribal sovereignty limited by treaty and acts of Congress, it was to be exercised concurrently with federal laws to ensure the protection of the rights of due process. The fears of unabridged tribal authority over nonmembers on the reservations with little or no due process rights should have been calmed by the explicit terminology within Section 13 to the contrary.

The specific reference to concurrent jurisdiction contained within this section merely demonstrated the continuation of the trust relationship and adherence to tribal self-determination policy that had been adopted by the U.S. government in 1970. That policy contained no reference to usurpation by state authority or states' rights within the borders of Indian country. Historically, the relations between the federal government and the tribes had been exclusive and barred interference from the states. It is only a relatively modern phenomenon—issued from the Supreme Court—that gave states a larger say in the affairs of non-Indians on tribal lands. Section 13 was merely to clarify and, within the context of Supreme Court opinions over the previous fifty years, reinvigorate the relationship between the legislature and executive of the United States with the hundreds of Native American tribes. The arguments that Section 13 would allow unfettered tribal authority over non-Indians were clearly invalid. Section 13 had merely highlighted a glaring problem and sought to rebalance the difficulty in a way that allowed tribes to counter terrorism in an equitable way based on accurate histories and relations.

The End of S. 578 and the Aftermath

Senate Bill 578 was introduced in the Senate and referred to the Committee on Governmental Affairs, but because of a lack of congressional support it was never reported out of committee. Soon after, the Tribal Sovereignty Protection

Initiative amended its legislative focus from a broad and simplistic one to a focus "addressing specific jurisdictional issues and problems in Indian country."[64] These specifically included homeland security, criminal jurisdiction, violence against women and domestic violence, alcohol and drug abuse, and sales taxes. This broad strategy change took place at the 2003 NCAI Midyear Session. The primary reason was that "NCAI member tribes expressed a lack of consensus to support the introduction of the comprehensive sovereignty legislation that has been developed by the TSPI drafting committee."[65] Rather, these tribes supported specific measures in Indian country. NCAI member tribes wanted "more politically feasible" measures produced in a much quicker period of time.

On March 1, 2005, Congress introduced bill S. 477 as a direct replacement for S. 578.[66] As a result of the conflict between Congress and the judiciary and the diverse interpretations of Section 13, this new bill did not include the contentious wording found in Section 13 of S. 578.

The introduction of S. 477 solved the conflict between the two institutions of government. In contrast to S. 578, M. Maureen Murphy of CRS pointed out, S. 477 did not contain a "direct statement specifically granting or delegating a particular law enforcement authority to tribes or overruling any named Supreme Court case." The purpose of the new bill was not to overrule Supreme Court case law but to ensure the participation of the tribes in the protection of the United States against terror. The CRS report read, "S. 477 differs from the earlier version both by including authority for direct funding, rather than indirect funding through individual states, of Indian tribal homeland security projects, and by eliminating the provisions in the earlier bill that appeared to endorse a view of tribal criminal and civil jurisdiction inconsistent with Supreme Court rulings on the subject of tribal jurisdiction."[67]

Although Congress bowed to pressure to withdraw Section 13 of S. 578, by introducing the new bill it still retained the ultimate authority to overrule Supreme Court case law. Unfortunately, writes Matthew L. M. Fletcher, Congress "is slowly vacating the field of Indian affairs, rarely addressing important national Indian affairs issues and, with tribal support, leaving internal Indian affairs to tribes themselves. Despite efforts by Indian nations to persuade Congress to legislate in response to the Supreme Court's *Oliphant* and *Hicks* decisions, as well as a recent statutory interpretation case going against both Indian nations and the United States, Congress usually does not respond to tribal efforts to enact omnibus legislation."[68]

The defeat of bills S. 578 and H.R. 2242 was a considerable setback for Native Americans, and particularly the Tribal Sovereignty Protection Initiative. Nevertheless, in June 2005 the Initiative planned a follow-up meeting to their previous meeting in February 2005 to implement the next step in its battle to reaffirm tribal jurisdiction and to undo the recent Supreme Court opinions in federal Indian law. The tribal strategy, as a NCAI document read, was to pursue "legislation to restore and enhance tribal civil and criminal jurisdiction as well as explore other legislative vehicles such as the reauthorization of the Violence Against Women Act."[69] The development of draft bills to address specific and singular issues continued.

Ultimately, the failure of Congress to introduce S. 578 and its Section 13 into legislation supported the silent revolution of the Supreme Court and its integrationist priniciples. In *MacArthur v. San Juan County* (2005), the plaintiffs argued that Congress had revived inherent tribal civil authority over non-Indians by enacting the 1968 Indian Civil Rights Act, as amended by Pub. L. No. 101–511 (1990), the 1975 Indian Self-Determination and Education Assistance Act, the 1993 Indian Tribal Justice Act, the 1994 Indian Self-Determination and Education Assistance Contract Reform Act, the 1994 Tribal Self-Governance Act, and the 2000 Indian Tribal Justice Technical and Legal Assistance Act. But the district court, in its opinion dated December 15, 2005, disagreed and brought an end to congressional reinforcement of Indian sovereignty in the period: "[*United States v.*] *Lara* establishes that Congress may redefine the scope of tribal authority over non-members by legislative adjustment, as it did in response to *Duro v. Reina* concerning tribal criminal jurisdiction. Congress has not yet done so with reference to *Montana* or its progeny, including *Strate, Atkinson,* and the problematic *Nevada v. Hicks,* decided in 2001. So *Montana* continues to govern inherent Indian tribal civil authority over non-Indians conducting activities on non-Indian lands within reservation boundaries."[70]

Tribal Law and Order Act, 2010

Overall, the congressional response to S. 578 suggests that the Supreme Court's silent revolution has taken hold in Congress as well. More recently, however, Congress has passed legislation, including the Tribal Law and Order Act in 2010 and the Violence Against Women Reauthorization Act in 2013, which prima facie takes a stand for tribal self-governance.

On July 29, 2010, President Barack Obama signed the Tribal Law and Order Act into law. The purpose of this act was to reduce violent crime in

Indian country and to combat the huge problems of sexual and domestic abuse faced by Native American women. In addition, the act intended to clarify the responsibilities of tribal, state, and federal agencies and to promote cooperation.[71] Though this 2010 act was an essential tool to begin the long and hard struggle to reduce crime on tribal reservations, one important issue was not addressed: tribal criminal authority over non-Indians.

Within Indian country, centuries of congressional legislation and Supreme Court decisions have resulted in a maze of jurisdictional problems faced by local, state, tribal, and federal law enforcement agencies on a day-to-day basis.[72] This maze, described in the findings section of the 2010 act as a "complicated jurisdictional scheme," does not provide public safety to tribal communities because the system requires a "high degree" of cooperation among tribal, state, and federal agencies.[73] Criminals have exploited this situation; congressional legislation certainly created it. The Major Crimes Act of 1885 transferred the authority to punish a crime committed by one Native American on another from the tribes to the federal government.[74] In 1953, Public Law 280 granted certain states (California, Minnesota, Nebraska, Oregon, Wisconsin, and Alaska) extensive criminal jurisdiction over tribal lands within those specific states. The Indian Civil Rights Act of 1968 forced tribes to observe the U.S. Bill of Rights and limited the length of sentences and fines that could be declared by tribal courts.[75] And in 1978 the Supreme Court exacerbated the situation with its ruling in *Oliphant v. Suquamish Tribe,* which held that tribes do not have criminal authority over nonmembers on their reservations.

Today, this complex jurisdictional blanket involves many procedures before justice is served in Indian country. One must examine the type of crime, the location of the crime, the race of the victim, and the race of the perpetrator; when all of these jigsaw pieces are in place, one must then determine whether the tribe, state, or federal government (or indeed a combination or combinations) has jurisdiction to arrest and prosecute these crimes.[76] In Senate testimony, Thomas B. Heffelfinger pertinently summed up the problems of this piecemeal system: "For the last 122 years of Supreme Court decisions and stop-gap legislative actions, criminal jurisdiction in Indian Country has become a mess. It is a patchwork quilt of decisions and stop-gap legislation . . . a mess which means law enforcement is more difficult, delay is normal, respect for the law is deteriorated. The losers in that situation are tribal governments and tribal people."[77]

Law enforcement problems in Indian country have been well documented over the past forty years. In 1975 the Report of the Task Force on Indian Matters, conducted by the U.S. Department of Justice, acknowledged that "law enforcement on Indian reservations is in serious trouble."[78] Over twenty years later the Report of the Executive Committee for Indian Country Law Enforcement Improvements stated that "there is a public safety crisis in Indian Country."[79] More than a decade later, "little ha[d] changed in either the makeup of the system of justice in place on Indian lands or the consistency of funding for the system."[80] Despite countless reports, recommendations, and promises, the criminal justice system in Indian country had not improved at all.

The process to combat the broken criminal justice system in Indian country, the origins of the Tribal Law and Order Act, began in May 2007 when North Dakota senator Byron Dorgan, chairman of the Senate Committee on Indian Affairs, held an oversight hearing on law enforcement in Indian country. Only six months later he released a concept paper that recommended changes to the criminal justice system in Indian country. After many hearings, meetings, and discussions between Native Americans and legislators, on July 23, 2008, Senator Dorgan introduced bill S. 3320, which was viewed by many as an opportunity to improve the delivery of law enforcement in Indian country. Unfortunately, by the end of 2008 Congress had not enacted Dorgan's bill.

On April 2, 2009, Senator Dorgan introduced bill S. 797, called the Tribal Law and Order Act of 2009. This bill was referred to the Senate Committee on Indian Affairs, and hearings were held during which numerous witnesses presented evidence that included agreement on the need for increased numbers of law enforcement officers on reservations, more federal deputation, additional funding to build more detention and correctional facilities, and federal prosecution of more crimes, including low-level crimes, occurring on reservations.[81] The 2009 bill was crucial because it provided the blocks to begin improving the lives of Native Americans within their own homes and communities.

Many in Indian country believed the Tribal Law and Order Act bills in both 2008 and 2009 would be panaceas to the myriad jurisdictional problems. M. Brent Leonhard, deputy attorney general for the Confederated Tribes of the Umatilla Indian Reservation, lauded the 2008 initiative, stating that the bill was "probably one of the most important Indian Country crime bills in the last 30 or 40 years, primarily because it gets at systemic fixes to a completely broken system."[82] In a Senate hearing in 2009, Thomas J. Perrelli, associate attorney general, stated that the "Tribal Law and Order Act of 2009 . . . is comprehensive and important legislation."[83] Yet, despite the optimism created by the successive bills, by the end of 2009 neither the Senate nor the House of Representatives had passed any one of them.

Then suddenly on June 23, 2010, Illinois senator Richard Durbin, on behalf of Senator Dorgan, proposed S.A. 4391, a Senate amendment to include the Tribal Law and Order Act of 2010 within H.R. 725, an act to protect Indian arts and crafts. This new Tribal Law and Order Act of 2010 explicitly would not affect non-Indians. Under Section 6, "Effects," the bill read, "Nothing in this Act confers on an Indian tribe criminal jurisdiction over non-Indians."[84] On the same day, the Senate agreed to the amendment by unanimous consent.

When the amended H.R. 725 was presented to the House of Representatives on July 21, 2010, in what Congress terms the suspension calendar, there was some consternation. The Tribal Law and Order Act of 2010 was a last-minute addition to H.R. 725. Some members disagreed with the Senate process to incorporate a last-minute addition to another bill. Congressman Doc Hastings, of Washington's 4th District, explained the problematic situation: "Violence and crime against Indians is a serious problem deserving the attention of this Congress. Such an important issue as this should not be relegated to the suspension calendar where innocuous bills are often given just cursory consideration. The process being used today to consider this legislation is normally reserved for bills such as naming post offices and congratulating sports teams on winning championships. Addressing crimes against Indians deserves to be considered in a much more serious, thorough process."[85]

Congressman Hastings objected and believed that the process was unfair to members of the House and to everyone in Indian country. All in all, H.R. 725 changed from a ten-page document with little funding costs to a bill over one hundred pages long that was to cost over a billion dollars. Nevertheless, many members supported the amendment. For example, Congressman Tom Cole, a representative from Oklahoma's 4th District, believed, "This bill isn't a cure all but it's an important start in moving in the right direction. . . . A vote against this bill, in my opinion, is a vote to continue the status quo of rampant violence and drug abuse in Indian Country, which we have an opportunity to make significant progress on."[86] In the end, the House voted 326 in favor (248 Democrats and 78 Republicans) and 92 against (all Republicans).[87] The Tribal

Law and Order Act of 2010 was a laudable and overdue piece of legislation that provided the foundations for Native Americans to address problems faced by the justice system in Indian country.

One important factor was missing from the 2010 act: the issue of tribal criminal authority over non-Indians. In 1978 the Supreme Court had declared in *Oliphant v. Suquamish Tribe* that Native American tribes did not have criminal authority over non-Indians. Interestingly, during the nascent development of what was to become the Tribal Law and Order Act of 2010, the issue of overturning *Oliphant* was a considered option. In a U.S. Senate Committee on Indian Affairs concept paper, dated November 2007, one of the recommendations for proposed legislation was to expand "the arresting authority of tribal and federal officers over all crimes committed on Indian lands regardless of the nature of the offense (tribal, federal, or state crime) or the status of the offender as Indian or not."[88] Included in this paper was a recommendation that tribes have all relevant criminal authority over domestic and sexual violence crimes, even if the perpetrator was a non-Indian. In addition, according to Kevin K. Washburn, during this period "there was a limited Oliphant-fix in an early version of what became the Tribal Law and Order Act, but no one wanted to sponsor (or presumably vote for) the bill with that language in there. It was deemed too controversial."[89] Ron His Horse Is Thunder, chairman of the Standing Rock Sioux Tribe, questioned why this partial *Oliphant* fix was not contained in the bill to introduce the Tribal Law and Order Act of 2008: "The Tribe strongly supported the jurisdictional pilot project outlined in your 2007 concept paper. This project would have permitted certain tribes, after adopting specific due process protections, to exercise criminal jurisdiction over non-Indians for domestic violence offenses where the offender was in a consensual (married or cohabiting) relationship with an Indian victim."[90] Interestingly, Senator Dorgan, in an Indian Committee Senate hearing dated March 17, 2008, commented on tribal jurisdiction and the associated political problems: "The jurisdictional questions are real and serious. We are talking about tribal jurisdictions. Those are always controversial issues."[91]

During the fifteen Senate Indian Committee hearings held between 2007 and 2010 on improving criminal justice in Indian country, numerous witnesses called for the rule of *Oliphant* to be overturned. After all, Congress was the institution with the power to undo *Oliphant*. As Bonnie Clairmont of the Tribal Law and Policy Institute argued, "Congress should recognize that tribal authorities have jurisdiction over all offenders who commit crimes on tribal land, regardless of their Indigenous or other identity."[92] Recognizing tribal authority would reduce the complexity of the system and ensure a quick response to emergency calls. As Alaska senator Lisa Murkowski stated, "You shouldn't have to sort through the jurisdiction table before they send somebody to help."[93]

The reaffirmation of tribal criminal authority would also reduce the controversy surrounding declinations—cases not prosecuted by the federal authorities. The severity of federal declinations has caused consternation and presented an enormous problem in Indian country. Because of federal agency reluctance, many non-Indians were escaping punishment for horrific crimes. Kelly Gaines Stoner, director of the Native American Legal Resource Center and Clinical Programs at Oklahoma City University, expanded on this point: "In the case of Federal declinations involving a Native American victim and a non-Indian accused, no other population in the United States is told that no criminal justice consequences will be imposed on the non-Indian rapist, child molesters and murderers. These perpetrators continue to walk free in tribal communities. And these non-Indian perpetrators are free to re-offend and actually do re-offend, because they know that nothing will happen to them."[94]

Furthermore, recognizing tribal authority would allow the institutions with an interest and ability in protecting communities—tribal governments—to do so while lessening the responsibility on federal and state governments, which had not protected Indian country and in theory had little motivation to do so. This argument was expanded upon by Washburn:

> Only the tribe is primarily concerned for the Indian reservation. The tribe is the government that is concerned most with what is going on in an Indian reservation. If we make it a State responsibility under Public Law 280, or we make it a Federal responsibility under the Indian Country system, we have taken the responsibility for the problem away from the government that has the most serious interest in correcting the problem. So that is a fundamental problem, and we are not going to get anything corrected, ultimately, until we make sure that tribal governments have primacy on these issues. Anything else, I think, is a half solution or a partial solution.[95]

Overruling *Oliphant* was important because it would address critical conditions in Indian country. Diane Enos, president of the Salt River Pima–Maricopa Indian Community, wanted criminal jurisdiction restored over non-Indians because "the viciousness and frequency of crimes committed today by both non-Indians and Indians has increased greatly since the Oliphant, Wheeler and Duro Era" and because the tribes would be accountable to their own people, in contrast to state and federal officials who did not live there and did not have to live without public safety.[96]

All in all, there was a general reluctance to take on the issue of *Oliphant* as a guiding principle that defined tribal criminal authority between Native Americans and non-Indians in Indian country. As Elbridge Coochise, a member of the Independent Court Review Team conceded, "It may be unrealistic to overturn *Oliphant*" but, overall, "If this bill has a major failing, it is the failure to deal with *Oliphant*."[97] In July 2008, despite the concerns raised over the negative impact of *Oliphant* in the Indian Committee Senate hearings, the bill introduced in Congress as the Tribal Law and Order Act of 2008 did not even attempt to address any of the problems created by the *Oliphant* ruling. A year later and the same bill was introduced without any recognition of the problems created by *Oliphant*. In a hearing to discuss the 2009 bill, Chad Smith, principal chief of the Cherokee Nation, believed that "crime committed by non-Indians must also be addressed" and, "while all improvements to tribal law enforcement agencies are greatly appreciated, until tribes have the authority to combat all crime in Indian Country, and not just those crimes committed by Indians, no amount of money will fully fix the problems we are facing."[98]

The will of Congress, in particular the Indian Senate Committee, must be applauded for introducing and passing the Tribal Law and Order Act in 2010. Nevertheless, the overall bill tended to support the silent revolution of the Supreme Court and in some ways justified it. Congress did not want to take on the difficult task of addressing the *Oliphant* conundrum, despite numerous statements supporting and offering ways to overrule this 1978 decision.

Indeed, throughout the process to introduce the Tribal Law and Order Act in 2010, it became apparent that more fundamental issues had to be addressed before *Oliphant*. In Indian country there was a desperate need for resources to address shortcomings in the tribal criminal system. Funds were required to employ more police officers to patrol smaller areas of territory and to build the infrastructure (e.g., police stations, jails and detention facilities) necessary to house suspected criminals and to deal with the tragic events occurring in Indian country. That reality was highlighted by Senator Byron Dorgan when he said, "tribal detention facilities and jails are in shambles."[99]

Moreover, the Senate hearings heard evidence that convinced them to sidestep *Oliphant* and develop solutions. For one thing, in Indian country there appeared to be a greater need for cooperation between the tribes and state and federal governments in order to bring more prosecutions and to convict more individuals, particularly non-Indians. The high declination rates were a major concern for many witnesses before the Senate Indian Committee, but Senator Dorgan contended that this might well be due to a lack of resources reaching the U.S Attorney's Office and the FBI.[100] This was a reason to circumvent the *Oliphant* conundrum. Quite simply, after the introduction of the 2010 act, one could wait and see whether federal declinations decreased, cooperation increased, and public safety improved in Indian country—without acting on *Oliphant*.

Additionally, *Oliphant* could not be addressed because of the constitutional concerns that would exist if the tribes assumed criminal authority over non-Indians. If the proposed legislation addressed the question of the constitutional rights of non-Indians in tribal courts, it would be severely delayed or, more likely, reached an impasse without passing. Non-Indians would have required the protection of the Constitution, equal protection, and procedural safeguards. Such issues included the right of review in federal courts (appellate review process), the provision of legal counsel (free of charge) for indigent defendants, the right to participate in jury pools, and the independence of the judiciary. Voting in tribal elections was also an issue raised within the hearings. In addition, tribes needed a better appellate process. All of these issues would need to be addressed properly and precisely in a bill. For tribal courts to assume jurisdiction over non-Indians, Senator Dorgan stated, "we have to make certain that all of the constitutions are guaranteed, due process and so on would be certain there."[101]

One relevant piece of evidence was presented to the Indian Senate Committee about the "jurisdictional gap" created by *Oliphant*, whereby tribes generally relied on other authorities to punish non-Indians. Diane Humetewa, U.S. attorney for the District of Arizona, testified that there was no gap, despite ample evidence to the contrary: "First, I wish to address the misunderstanding often perpetuated about a jurisdictional gap in Indian Country. It is important to understand that for every crime in Indian Country, there is a court of justice, be it tribal, state, or federal. For every criminal who commits an offense in Indian Country, there is a venue for justice. In some cases, there are in fact multiple courts with jurisdictions over the matter."[102] Humetewa's argument was, then, another reason to avoid dealing with *Oliphant*. If resources and money were given to the tribes, states, and federal authorities, then simply and in theory there would be no jurisdictional gap.

Taking a different tack, Thomas B. Heffelfinger testified that Congress should form a Congressional Indian Country Criminal Jurisdiction Commission to develop and provide "a comprehensively new body of criminal law in Indian Country," primarily to "remove confusion [by simplifying criminal jurisdiction in Indian Country] and improve public safety." Heffelfinger trusted the "clout of Congress" to "bring about a long-term change in the quality of life and fight against crime in Indian Country." Simply addressing the *Oliphant* conundrum was not comprehensive enough: "Continued isolated judicial decisions and legislative 'fixes' simply will not do the job."[103] Senator Dorgan concurred: with the "fractionalization of all this jurisdiction, we need to find our way through this. Perhaps a commission is the right recommendation."[104]

Ultimately, the introduction of the Tribal Law and Order Act of 2010 allowed for more funding and for the tribes to address pressing concerns regarding the infrastructure and personnel of their criminal systems in Indian country.[105] Washburn summed up the importance of the act when he said, "I always argued . . . that obtaining jurisdiction over our own members was much more of a necessity [than fixing *Oliphant*]. In other words, it is far more important to obtain full jurisdiction again over our own members for purposes [of] self-government (and the TLOA went toward this direction), and then maybe down the road we can demonstrate that our justice systems are fair and maybe we can justify resumption of jurisdiction over non-members."[106] And to that end, the process that led to the 2010 act had presented the required notice for the tribes to amend their constitutions and ensure that they met all constitutional and due process rights, particularly those of non-Indians. Having done that, tribes who wanted authority over non-Indians would be better situated to one day take on *Oliphant* and have it overturned.

Violence Against Women Reauthorization Act of 2013

On February 3, 2009, the appointment of Eric H. Holder as the U.S. attorney general represented a watershed moment in Indian country. From the outset his staff, specifically Associate Attorney General Thomas J. Perelli, recognized the unprecedented criminal problems in Indian country and the need to do more.[107] More funding was needed to address domestic violence in Indian country. In June 2009, Perrelli testified, "We acknowledge that more needs to be done, and we are undertaking a comprehensive review of what we are doing in Indian Country with an eye towards what would be appropriate to propose to the President in the 2011 budget."[108] Then on July 14, 2011, at an Indian Senate Committee meeting, Perrelli announced that "to protect, shield, and safeguard Native women from violent crime" was "a very high priority for the Department of Justice as we work in anticipation of the reauthorization of the Violence Against Women Act this year"; the Justice Department recognized these deplorable problems, and Perrelli argued that "something must be done to end this cycle of violence."[109]

Unbelievably, only a week later a legislative proposal, containing much of the evidence previously presented by Perrelli, directly confronted the opinions and ideology of the Supreme Court. The proposal outlined support for the inherent authority of tribes over domestic violence cases, regardless of whether the defendant was Indian or non-Indian.[110] Furthermore, the proposal was meant to "clarify that tribal courts have full civil jurisdiction to issue and enforce certain protection orders against both Indians and non-Indians." Because of "epidemic rates" of crime committed against Native American women, the Department of Justice had "placed a high priority on combating violence against women in tribal communities," and federal legislation was required. Critically, the Justice Department recognized that the tribes would be "exercising an inherent tribal power" and not only "a delegated Federal power" when they were prosecuting domestic violence crimes.[111] In sum, the proposed legislation was in direct conflict with the opinions, ideas, and assumptions of the Supreme Court.

Interestingly, the legislative proposal took on board much of the evidence presented by witnesses at the Tribal Law and Order Act hearings. The constitutional rights and due process rights of the defendants were protected such as to provide indigent criminal defendants with a licensed lawyer at no cost, and jurors were to be selected in accordance with other courts. In addition, the proposal contained the "constitutional catch-all provision" to address concerns over the lack of constitutional rights and to enable the tribes to exercise criminal jurisdiction over all individuals.[112] This provision encompassed those rights not protected under the Indian Civil Rights Act and the Tribal Law and Order Act. In addition, the proposal recognized tribes as best placed to tackle violence in their communities, and with sufficient resources they could opt in to have further powers to prosecute, which included establishing procedural protections.

Less than a year had passed since the Tribal Law and Order Act of 2010, and the Department of Justice now felt that "the current legal structure for prosecuting domestic violence in Indian country was not well-suited to combating this pattern of escalating violence" because federal resources were "often far away and stretched thin" and tribal governments could not prosecute non-Indians. Therefore, the Justice Department adjudged that "tribal governments . . . should be essential parts of the response to these crimes."[113]

In a 2012 article, M. Brent Leonhard, attorney for the Confederated Tribes of the Umatilla Indian Reservation, examined the political necessity and legality of the Department of Justice's legislative proposal. He observed that politically the proposal was necessary because of the unprecedented levels of domestic abuse and the numbers of non-Indians in Indian country who committed such offenses. Many offenses went unpunished and perpetrators were free to harm again. The legality of the proposal to partially overrule *Oliphant,* Leonhard argued, was valid because the *Oliphant* decision was grounded in common law and not decided on constitutional law. In addition, Leonhard addressed the concerns and skepticism surrounding the rights that would be required to prosecute non-Indians and concluded that the specific rights granted in the proposal were "significant" and those granted to "non-Indian defendants [were] greater rights than are enumerated in the United States Constitution."[114]

Clearly, action was required to address this issue; a plethora of evidence existed to substantiate the horrendous levels of domestic violence committed against Native Americans in Indian country and the inefficiency of the system in place to protect them. In addition, the language of the legislative proposal made it crystal clear that non-Indians would have substantial rights, including those guaranteed by the U.S. Constitution:

> (e) RIGHTS OF DEFENDANTS.—In a criminal proceeding in which a participating tribe exercises special domestic-violence criminal jurisdiction, the tribe shall provide to the defendant
>> (1) all rights protected by the Indian Civil Rights Act;
>> (2) if a term of imprisonment of any length is imposed, all rights described in paragraphs (1) through (5) of section 1302(c); and
>> (3) all other rights whose protection would be required by the United States Constitution in order to allow the participating tribe to exercise criminal jurisdiction over the defendant.[115]

CRS recognized that non-Indian rights would be protected by the constitutional provision but cautioned that the protections required to be delivered by the tribes were not yet clear.[116]

On November 30, 2011, only four months after the Department of Justice proposal, Vermont senator Patrick Leahy and Idaho senator Mike Crapo introduced the Violence Against Women Reauthorization Act (S. 1925) to the Senate. According to Section 904, "Tribal Jurisdiction over Crimes of Domestic Violence," tribes would have concurrent jurisdiction to prosecute domestic violence committed by non-Indians in Indian country and defendant rights would be guaranteed; in Section 905, "Tribal Protection Orders," tribes would have civil jurisdiction to issue and enforce certain protection orders involving Native Americans and non-Indians. Section 908 declared that tribal jurisdiction would be implemented two years after the legislation was passed to allow tribes to amend tribal codes and for them to ensure the successful application of new procedures. In addition, tribes could fast-track this process and submit to a pilot project.[117] On April 26, 2012, the Senate approved the legislation with 68 voting in favor (51 Democrats, 15 Republicans, and two Independents) and 31 against (all Republicans).[118]

Some Republican senators strongly suggested that the bill "adds new, controversial provisions that we cannot support" and was beyond the spirit of the original Violence Against Women Act. This minority view condemned the Judiciary Committee for a "shockingly cursory" consideration of the tribal provision. The minority were shocked that tribal courts would have jurisdiction over nonmembers. They stated (incorrectly), "S. 1925, for the first time in the nation's history, would extend to tribal courts criminal jurisdiction over non-Indians. That is a significant change."[119] Ironically, the Suquamish Indian Tribe had criminal jurisdiction over Mark David Oliphant in 1973 when he was charged before the Provisional Court of the Suquamish Indian Tribe for assaulting an officer and resisting arrest.[120] This jurisdiction was not invalidated until 1978.[121] If these dissenting senators had read, for example, the Treaty with the Six Nations of 1784, they would have discovered, as Leonhard argued, that "the treaty contains explicit language recognizing that the six nations in fact exercised criminal jurisdiction over United States citizens contemporaneously with the execution of the treaty."[122] Furthermore, "most treaties that the United States entered into with Indian tribes between 1785 and 1795—that is, both immediately before and immediately after the drafting and ratification of the Constitution—expressly provided for tribal criminal jurisdiction over non-Indians residing in Indian country."[123]

The words chosen by the minority senators echoed the legal history outlined by Justice Rehnquist in *Oliphant*, who stated that, "from the earliest treaties with these tribes, it was apparently assumed that the tribes did not have criminal jurisdiction over non-Indians absent a congressional statute or treaty provision to that effect." To justify this broad assertion, Rehnquist had cited a short statement from an 1830 treaty with the Choctaw Indian Tribe, which read "[the Choctaw] express a wish that Congress may grant to the Choctaws the right of punishing by their own laws any white man who shall come into their nation, and infringe any of their national regulations," and wiped out centuries of history and reality.[124]

In contrast to this isolated statement, one not need look far to find a statement that supported tribal criminal jurisdiction over non-Indians. For example, only forty-four years previously, Article 4 of the Treaty with the Choctaw of 1786 read, "If any citizen of the United States, or other person not being an Indian, shall attempt to settle on any of the lands hereby allotted to the Indians to live and hunt on, such person shall forfeit the protection of the United States of America, and the Indians may punish him or not as they please."[125] In his article, Leonhard categorically highlighted many other treaties that contain similar language and other supporting language to demonstrate that tribes did have criminal jurisdiction over non-Indians.[126] Rehnquist had used the words "apparently assumed" to support the logic that treaties did not provide tribes with authority to punish non-Indians, presumably because some Indians were ambivalent upon the reading of the treaties. This ambivalence should have forced Rehnquist and the majority to apply the canons of construction to resolve any doubtful language in favor of the tribes.[127] In addition, Rehnquist should have at least examined this language used by the Supreme Court in *Winters v. United States* (1908): "By a rule of interpretation of agreements and treaties with the Indians, ambiguities occurring will be resolved from the standpoint of the Indians. And the rule should certainly be applied to determine between two inferences, one of which would support the purpose of the agreement and the other impair or defeat it."[128]

Despite overwhelming evidence to the contrary, then, a minority of senators relied on *Oliphant* to present as fact that "it has long been understood that they [Indians] have no criminal jurisdiction over non-Indians."[129] This minority believed that tribal courts did not have the ability to protect the rights of non-Indians or, presumably, to be fair and equitable.[130] They asked, "On what basis is the majority report confident that all tribes are able to provide all defendants with all rights guaranteed by the United States Constitution?"[131] This line of argument tied in with concerns expressed by the National Association of Criminal Defense Lawyers (NACDL). A letter sent to the Senate highlighted evidence of some tribes neglecting to protect tribal rights, pursuant to the Indian Civil Rights Act of 1968, in tribal courts. Examples included not appointing counsel for indigent defendants and sentencing Native American defendants beyond the required maximum sentence. The letter concluded that, "regardless of what Congress might put on paper, many tribes have been unwilling or unable to provide adequate protections to the rights of criminal defendants prosecuted in their courts." Accordingly, the NACDL wanted Congress to wait and see whether the resources given under the Tribal Law and Order Act of 2010 to help support the rights of defendants in tribal courts would produce evidence of change in tribal courts and, therefore, hard data to show that the situation had improved.[132] These minority concerns notwithstanding, in the proposed legislation (S. 1925) the rights of defendants in tribal court included "all other rights whose protection is necessary under the Constitution of the United States in order for Congress to recognize and affirm the inherent power of the participating tribe to exercise special domestic violence criminal jurisdiction over the defendant"; in other words, the necessary rights that defendants would have in state and federal courts would be applicable, under statute, in tribal courts too.[133]

The Senate minority was questioning the expertise of the tribal courts and the costs of undertaking the process by tribal courts as well as federal courts, and some of them believed that the states should continue to prosecute non-Indians on reservations. Despite considerable evidence to support the real problem of domestic violence in Indian country, four senators concluded, "There is no good reason not to give states and their local governments jurisdiction to prosecute offenses committed by non-Indians within Indian reservations." Moreover, the minority was unconvinced by the centuries-old concept of inherent tribal sovereignty. They believed "after tribal courts [had] exercised their 'inherent powers' under section 904," many non-Indians would file for a grant of habeas corpus in federal district courts, and that "the law today makes clear that there is no inherent power of tribes to do anything of the sort the bill says. Self-government is not government over 'all persons'— including non-Indians."[134]

Supreme Court opinions had recently dismantled tribal criminal authority over non-Indians, so the minority held that, "because tribes lack this power, it is untrue to say that Congress can recognize and affirm it."[135] In other words, Congress could not interfere with the current law and situation in

Indian country. This position echoed the concurring opinion of Justice Clarence Thomas in *United States v. Lara* (2004), in which he argued that federal Indian law relied on "two largely incompatible and doubtful assumptions": that Congress, and not another part of federal government, "can regulate virtually every aspect of the tribes without rendering tribal sovereignty a nullity"; and that the tribes "retain inherent sovereignty to enforce their criminal laws against their own members." Therefore, Thomas wanted to "reexamine the premises and logic" of Supreme Court cases that focused on sovereignty.[136] The minority senators believed, as did Justice Thomas, the S. 1925 bill "goes much further than changing something for the future. It says that something inherently already exists that does not now exist."[137]

It should be clear, though, that those holding this minority position forgot how the United States itself was formed: "The fundamental premise upon which such a conclusion would rely—that a government cannot possess sovereign powers while subject to the plenary power of another government—is belied by the United States' constitutional structure itself."[138] In addition, relationships between Native Americans and the United States have constantly changed, and this is what has happened with inherent tribal sovereignty. As Chief Justice John Marshall said in *Worcester v. Georgia*, "a weaker power does not surrender its independence, its right to self-government, by associating with a stronger, and taking its protection."[139] Nevertheless, uncomfortable with the language of S. 1925, the House proposed H.R. 4970, a Violence Against Women Act Reauthorization bill, without the critical language supporting tribal criminal authority over nonmembers in limited circumstances.[140]

A majority of the House of Representatives rejected S. 1925 in 2012, and their reasoning was simple. They believed that granting limited tribal criminal and civil authority over non-Indians was unconstitutional and only a political tool for the forthcoming election. They saw the Senate bill as unconstitutional primarily because Native Americans were "not parties to the U.S. Constitution" and therefore "derive neither powers nor obligations from it." The conclusion drawn from this, despite the House report stating they were "domestic dependent nations," was that non-Indians would not have any constitutional rights before tribal courts because the courts were not subject to the Constitution.[141]

At the time, a letter from many preeminent law scholars noted that the legislation set out stringent due process and constitutional protections. For example, tribal courts use the Indian Civil Rights Act "to provide all rights accorded to defendants in state and federal court," which included Fourth and Fifth Amendment rights, and federal courts have jurisdiction to review tribal courts decisions. In addition, tribal courts apply due process rights in civil cases, and tribes must provide "all other rights" in order to exercise their inherent authority. The concerns over non-Indian rights in tribal court were protected because the Violence Against Women Reauthorization Act "provides ample safeguards" and is "consistent" with U.S. Constitutional safeguards.[142]

The NACDL and National Association of Federal Defenders (NAFD) disagreed with the position of these scholars, and in a letter to the House commented that "Congress should seek to ensure that tribal justice systems are equipped to protect the rights of defendants before subjecting a new category of citizens, who have not consented to be governed by the tribes, to deprivation of their constitutional rights in tribal court. H.R. 4970 gets it right here, S. 1925 does not." In sum, the NACDL and NAFD were arguing that there was no jurisdictional gap involving the prosecution of non-Indians in Indian country, that the expansion of inherent tribal sovereignty over non-Indians was unprecedented and unconstitutional, and that non-Indians would not be provided with full constitutional rights. They commented that S. 1925 was not a congressional delegation of power and that non-Indians would not therefore enjoy full constitutional rights. The rights contained in the Indian Civil Rights Act and Tribal Law and Order Act were, they argued, not enough, and there was concern that tribes were not complying with the standards set out in those acts. In addition, there were concerns over due process and equal protection, which included the use of qualified lawyers and a trial by an impartial jury. All of these concerns were based on evidence obtained from tribal courts. The concerns raised were that Native American defendants were denied access to the tribal code of laws, that there was no funding for indigent defendants, that the courts imposed fines which indigent defendants could not pay, and that there were no rules for discovery by defendants of the evidence against them or for the disclosure of evidence likely to exonerate.[143]

The NACDL and NAFD also suggested that non-Indians had to consent to be prosecuted in tribal courts. This rationale, the consent-of-the-governed theory, purports that individuals consent to be governed within the protections of the U.S. Constitution, consisting of the nation and the state, and expect the continued protection of those rights by each sovereign. This viewpoint was articulated by Justice Kennedy (concurring opinion) in *United States v. Lara* (2004): "Each sovereign must respect the proper sphere of the other, for the citizen has rights and duties as to both."[144] He rejected the notion that an American citizen could be prosecuted by a third entity. Nevertheless, in early treaties conducted between Native Americans and the United States it was required that U.S. citizens be prosecuted by the tribes. Even the founders of the Constitution knew about these treaties, with many involved in drafting and negotiating them.[145] Knowing there were other sovereign nations (European powers and Native American tribes) in North America, they must have deliberated about U.S. citizens being tried by judicial systems other than their own. Therefore, it could be argued that the United States, with knowledge and affirmation from the founding fathers of the Constitution, allowed its citizens to be prosecuted by the tribes because the tribes had appropriate authority, namely, inherent tribal sovereignty, and by virtue of treaties the consent passed from one sovereign to another.

Additionally, the consent of non-Indians to be prosecuted was implicit in the terms of those treaties because, as well as knowing of the constitutional protections offered by nation and states, the founding fathers also knew of a third sovereign with inherent sovereignty over its lands and all of the people upon those lands. This understanding was no more apparent than in the Supreme Court case that defined the entire legal justice system of the United States: *Johnson v. McIntosh*. In 1823, Chief Justice Marshall defined the inherent sovereignty of tribes to criminally punish non-Indians when he stated, "The person who purchases lands from the Indians within their territory incorporates himself with them so far as respects the property purchased; holds their title under their protection and subject to their laws."[146] Non-Indians who bought land in Indian country had acquired the land under tribal protection and were therefore subject to tribal law. Ironically, case law from the institution in which Justice Kennedy sits has recognized and affirmed the authority of the tribes to prosecute non-Indians.[147] Put simply, if a non-Indian commits a crime in Indian country, the non-Indian has consented by merely committing such a heinous act in Indian country.[148]

The majority of the House believed that the recognition of inherent tribal sovereignty to prosecute non-Indians under the Indian commerce clause, according to the House report, was a moot point and an "unsettled question of constitutional law."[149] However, the report conceded that tribal courts could prosecute non-Indians with a congressional delegation of authority. In sum, this would allow tribes to prosecute within the full parameters of the Constitution. The report relied on the position taken by the CRS, which noted:

> The dichotomy between delegated and inherent power of tribes has important constitutional implications. If Congress is deemed to have delegated to the tribes Congress's own power to prosecute crimes, the whole panoply of protections accorded criminal defendants in the Bill of Rights will apply. If, on the other hand, Congress is permitted to recognize the tribes' inherent sovereignty, so that the tribes are exercising their own powers, the Constitution will not apply. Instead, criminal defendants must rely on statutory protections under the Indian Civil Rights Act or those protected under tribal law.[150]

Indeed, the House decided that the tribes had no inherent criminal authority over non-Indians, relying on the *Oliphant* opinion, and as a result argued that Congress could not reverse this process and allow tribal courts to punish non-Indians. Despite its reliance on the CRS report for this argument, the House could have also found a counterargument. The CRS acknowledged that Congress had reversed the Supreme Court case *Duro v. Reina* (1990) in 1991, with congressional legislation reaffirming inherent tribal sovereignty to punish non-member Indians in tribal courts. If Congress could move the boundaries of the law to accommodate non-member Indians, then why could it not do the same for non-Indians? "It could be argued that because non-member Indians and non-Indians are both outsiders to the tribe, there appears to be no reason to distinguish Congress's authority to relax restrictions on the tribes' inherent sovereignty to try non-member Indians from its authority to relax restrictions on the tribes' authority to try non-Indians. In other words, if the tribe can exercise inherent authority over non-member Indians, it appears it would be able to exercise inherent authority over non-Indians."[151]

The House report, supported by a majority of representatives, also challenged the usefulness of data purporting high levels of non-Indian crimes against Native American women. Overall, then, the concerns of many in the House were those raised by the minority in the Senate: the constitutional and due process rights of non-Indians in tribal court, the reliability of the data purporting high levels of domestic abuse in Indian country, and the constitutionality of a bill that would partially overrule a Supreme Court ruling—namely, the highly controversial *Oliphant v. Suquamish Tribe* of 1978.

Contained within the House report was a dissenting opinion to the proposed H.R. 4970. This minority opinion supported S. 1925 because it was narrow in focus, aimed to protect vulnerable individuals, and provided adequate guidelines to address past case law (*Oliphant*) and the future legal protections of non-Indians. S. 1925, the minority wrote, was "based on the premise that tribal nations with sufficient resources and authority will best be able to address violence in their own communities, and they should be allowed to do so when the necessary procedural protections are established. Extending this jurisdiction in a very narrow set of cases over non-Indians who voluntarily and knowingly established significant ties to the tribe is consistent with that approach, responsive to the epidemic of violence experienced by Native women, and within the authority of Congress to do."[152]

Congressman Darrell Issa, a representative from California's 49th District, questioned whether the House bill, opposing the extension of limited criminal and civil authority over non-Indians, was based on race: "There is an important issue here about tribal sovereignty and perhaps what one might call race discrimination."[153] Indeed, this observation highlighted, perhaps, the political and legal undertones that led to *Oliphant* in the first place and have continued unabated every time the issue of inherent tribal sovereignty over non-Indians is presented to the Supreme Court or Congress. On May 16, 2012, the House of Representatives voted 222 (216 Republicans and six Democrats) in favor and 205 (182 Democrats and 23 Republicans) against H.R. 4970—Violence Against Women Reauthorization Act of 2012.[154] The impasse between the Senate and the House was not resolved before the August 2012 break.

On January 22, 2013, the Violence Against Women Reauthorization Act was reintroduced in the Senate as bill S. 47. Only a few weeks later, and despite opposition from Republicans, the Senate passed the legislation with 78 voting in favor and 22 against.[155]

The bill moved to the House and S. 47 was debated on February 28, 2013. Concern was expressed about S. 47's constitutionality.[156] This bill used very similar language to the statutory language at issue in the *Lara* case, ensuring that concerns raised in a NACDL letter were specifically addressed. From the NACDL perspective, "in short, the Supreme Court has never stated that the extension of Indian tribes' 'inherent legal authority' to the prosecution of non-Indians would be constitutional."[157] S. 47 also specifically addressed the questions posed by the Supreme Court in *Lara* regarding the constitutional power of Congress to recognize the inherent sovereignty of the tribes to prosecute. There were six considerations at issue in *Lara* that were contained in Section 904 of S. 47:

1. "The Constitution grants Congress broad general powers to legislate in respect to Indian tribes."

2. "Congress, with this Court's approval, has interpreted the Constitution's 'plenary' grants of power as authorizing it to enact legislation that both restricts and, in turn, relaxes those restrictions on tribal sovereign authority."

3. "Congress' statutory goal—to modify the degree of autonomy enjoyed by a dependent sovereign that is not a State—is not an unusual legislative objective."

4. There is "no explicit language in the Constitution suggesting a limitation on Congress' institutional authority to relax restrictions on tribal sovereignty previously imposed by the political branches."

5. "The change at issue here is a limited one . . . [largely concerning] a tribe's authority to control events that occur upon the tribe's own land."

6. The Court's "conclusion that Congress has the power to relax the restrictions imposed by the political branches on the tribes' inherent prosecutorial authority is consistent with [the Supreme Court's] earlier cases."[158]

Importantly, the formation of S. 47 was guided by the opinions of individual justices to ensure that the Supreme Court, if called upon in the near future, would adjudge the legislation to be constitutional. The House thought it was "noteworthy" in *Oliphant* that the Court suggested that Congress had the constitutional authority to restore inherent tribal sovereignty for them to exercise jurisdiction over non-Indians. In addition, the House noted, "the *Oliphant* Court expressly stated that the increasing sophistication of tribal court systems, the Indian Civil Rights Act's protection of defendants' procedural rights, and the prevalence of non-Indian crime in Indian country" were options to weigh before tribes should criminally try non-Indians.[159] On February 28, the House passed the legislation and voted 286 (199 Democrats and 87 Republicans) in favor and 138 (138 Republicans) against.[160] Four days later it was presented to President Obama, and on March 7 the president signed the legislation and it became Public Law No. 113-4, the Violence Against Women Reauthorization Act of 2013.[161] Under Section 904 of Public Law 113-4, inherent tribal sovereignty allows tribes to prosecute Native Americans and non-Indians suspected of domestic violence:

> (b) Nature of the Criminal Jurisdiction.—
>
> (1) In general.—Notwithstanding any other provision of law, in addition to all powers of self-government recognized and affirmed by sections 201 and 203, the powers of self-government of a participating tribe include the inherent power of that tribe, which is hereby recognized and affirmed, to exercise special domestic violence criminal jurisdiction over all persons.

In addition, under Section 905, inherent tribal sovereignty permits tribes to exercise civil jurisdiction over Native Americans and non-Indians in order to enforce protection orders:

> (e) Tribal Court Jurisdiction.—For purposes of this section, a court of an Indian tribe shall have full civil jurisdiction to issue and enforce protection orders involving any person, including the authority to enforce any orders through civil contempt proceedings, to exclude violators from Indian land, and to use other appropriate mechanisms, in matters arising anywhere in the Indian country of the Indian tribe (as defined in section 1151) or otherwise within the authority of the Indian tribe.

The Violence Against Women Reauthorization Act of 2013 therefore reaffirmed inherent tribal sovereignty and, astonishingly, partially limited the opinion of *Oliphant*. In some respects, this legislation prepared foundations from which the grasp of the 1981 *Montana* opinion in cases involving tribal civil jurisdiction over non-Indians might be diminished.

The response of the Department of Justice, after its shocking legislative proposal in 2011, was positive. Attorney General Holder stated that the legislation was a "historic step" because the "loophole that left many Native American women without adequate protection" had been closed. On a practical level the act was simply designed "to address domestic violence against Native American women, who experience the highest rates of assault in the United States."[162]

With a partial reversal of *Oliphant*, for the first time in thirty-five years Native American tribal courts had authority, underpinned by inherent tribal sovereignty, to prosecute non-Indians in tribal courts. Undoubtedly, this is the first time in congressional history that some form of legislation has passed to undermine the process of the silent revolution. Although it was a very small step to retract decades of Court opinions, it showed that tireless Native American activism and education, both legally and politically, supported by Democratic members of Congress (including a few House Republicans), can slowly reverse and undermine the silent revolution.

In the near future, the Supreme Court will have an opportunity to examine and decide upon the merits of the Violence Against Women Reauthorization Act of 2013. When presented with the facts of a case involving this brave and necessary piece of congressional legislation, the Court may well strike it down. It would do so because it relies on inherent tribal sovereignty as a basis of criminal authority over non-Indians in Indian country—the antithesis of the integrationist positions that have dominated the modern Court. Unless in the near future one or more justices are replaced by someone with a better knowledge of the history of federal Indian law, defending the legislation will be enormously difficult. The ideas regarding inherent tribal sovereignty propagated by the current set of justices show no signs of ending.[163]

Given the dominant integrationist trend, there is likely only one way to win a case involving the constitutionality of the Violence Against Women Reauthorization Act of 2013. This would be to take the highly controversial stand that the act is an exclusive federal delegation of congressional power. In contrast to the aforementioned NACDL letter to the Senate, who advanced this idea because it ensured the protection of non-Indian rights, this proposition is advanced here simply because the Supreme Court has tended to judge cases on the basis of federal versus state authority, whereby tribal sovereignty has been incorporated into the parameters of federal power and dramatically undermined.[164]

Notwithstanding the power of the silent revolution, legal counsel for the tribes should strive to reassert the Indian sovereignty doctrine and inherent tribal sovereignty by defining the Violence Against Women Act as congressional legislation that reaffirms inherent tribal sovereignty.[165] With any legislation, the Court will have to examine the legislative intent of the 2013 act. They will read that Congress supported inherent tribal sovereignty in this circumstance and will therefore find it difficult to circumvent this large obstacle of congressional intent in support of tribal rights. To combat the proclivities of the justices and the main thrust of Justice Rehnquist's decision in *Oliphant*, those defending the act must document and introduce in open court the wealth of information proving that tribes did have criminal authority over non-Indians—treaties, case law, archival materials from colonial powers, legislative history (congressional debates). They must also ensure that all points of discontent raised in *Lara* are addressed point by point in order to demonstrate the constitutionality of the legislation.

In advance of such a case, the tribes must address all constitutional rights and due process concerns. In addition, the power of the commerce clause must be examined to advance the constitutionality of the legislation. Therefore, the plenary power of Congress, despite the problems that it has caused, will have to be relied upon too.[166] Conversely, some justices, such as Thomas and Kennedy, might well question the constitutionality of the commerce clause.[167] Therein lies the problem. Without the power of the commerce clause, Congress does not have delegated authority over Native Americans anywhere else in the Constitution.[168] However, to hold the act unconstitutional because of a lack of congressional authority under the Constitution would dismantle hundreds of years of federal legislation and Supreme Court case law. In short, the Court would pull out the land upon which the entire U.S. legal justice system rests. Interestingly, in such a situation Native American tribes would revert to wholly sovereign bodies under the protection and within the borders of the United States, to whom they have not lost any sovereignty.[169] In reality, the Constitution did not abrogate any tribal sovereignty at all. On the contrary, the silence of the Constitution on this matter affirms the enduring and permanent nature of inherent tribal sovereignty.

In sum, inherent tribal sovereignty is a continuous set of principles underpinned by natural law that has existed and continues to exist, despite and contrary to common law decisions of the Supreme Court, which are fleeting precedents to be overruled, challenged, modified, or affirmed at will and dependent on political and ideological affinity.

❖ 5
The Effects of the Silent Revolution

The case law opinions of the Supreme Court have dramatically affected the day-to-day lives of Native Americans and the authority of tribes within their own reservations. With specific evidence from Native Americans and non-Native Americans, this chapter examines the real and damaging effects of tax, civil, and criminal case law opinions on the authority of certain tribes inside their homelands.[1] As John St. Clair, chief justice of the Supreme Court of the Wind River Reservation, observed, the general impact of the U.S. Supreme Court's limitation of "the powers and authorities of Indian tribal governments is that it severely restricts the ability to exercise basic regulatory and adjudicatory functions when dealing with everyday activities on reservations."[2]

Taxation Case Law

Taxation is a key attribute of all tribal governments. The silent revolution has affected the taxation authority of the tribes in two ways. First, from 1980 to 2001 case law sanctioned the idea of concurrent tribal and state taxation of nonmembers and nonmember businesses on the reservations. The effect of concurrent taxation has been large losses of revenue for many Native American nations to the states.[3] Second, in *Atkinson Trading Co. v. Shirley* (2001), the Supreme Court moved away from the idea of concurrent taxation on non-member lands of the reservation to the idea that tribes did not have inherent taxation authority over nonmembers on nonmember lands of the reservation. The effect of *Atkinson* has been additional loss of revenue for some tribes.[4]

Taxation is an important revenue-raising tool for governments to provide for the health, welfare, and survival of society. Taxation provides revenue to support the protection of tribal history as well as the survival of tribal culture and helps provide a government with income to spend on infrastructure, welfare, and social programs and to invest in and sustain an economy.[5] Therefore, the right of a tribe to tax is fundamental. As Justice Thurgood Marshall observed in *Merrion v. Jicarilla Apache Tribe* (1982), "The power to tax is an essential attribute of Indian sovereignty . . . [and] this power enables a tribal government to receive revenues for its essential services . . . by requiring contributions from persons or enterprises."[6] Nevertheless, during the silent revolution the Supreme Court sanctioned concurrent tribal and state taxation of nonmembers on the reservations and limited the exclusive right of the tribes to tax.

Two Supreme Court cases from the 1980s show how concurrent taxation caused tribal revenues to be lost to states.[7] In *Washington v. Confederated Tribes* (1980), also known as *Colville,* the Supreme Court held that both the tribes and the state had authority to tax nonmembers on the reservation.[8] This opinion severely limited the profits made by tribally owned reservation cigarette businesses. The taxation revenue of the four tribes involved in the case, as Justice Byron White noted in his opinion, was made from "non-Indians—residents of nearby communities who journey to the reservation."[9] The profits made by individual tribes varied. From 1972 to 1976, the Colville Tribe earned approximately $266,000 from cigarette taxes, the Lummi Tribe earned $54,000, and the Makah Tribe earned $13,000; in 1975 the Yakima earned $278,000.[10] The Court ruled that the involvement of nonmembers justified the imposition of a state tax as well as the tribal tax, thereby significantly reducing much needed tribal revenue.

The effect of concurrent taxation was again highlighted in *Cotton Petroleum Corp. v. New Mexico* (1989).[11] This case involved a nonmember company that wanted the Supreme Court to prohibit the imposition of a state tax on its on-reservation oil and gas operations. In its arguments to the Court, the company presented evidence to show how much money had been paid in state taxes for on-reservation business operations. From 1981 to 1985, the state received $47,483,306 in taxation revenues.[12] For those five years, the Jicarilla Apache Tribe lost significant amounts of taxation revenue for which it would not be reimbursed, and its future tax earnings would also be lost to the State of New Mexico.

In a 2003 concept paper, the National Congress of American Indians (NCAI) addressed the financial problems put upon some of the tribes with the introduction of concurrent taxation. Economic enterprises established by the Tulalip Tribe were damaged by the reality of concurrent taxation: "The Tulalip Tribe of Washington has established Quil Ceda Village, which includes a business park, parkland, and watershed. The tribe provides comprehensive municipal services, but the state receives a windfall of $11 to $50 million each year in sales taxes while the Tribe—which has 25% unemployment—receives no tax revenue due to the economic impossibility of adding a tribal tax on top of the state tax."[13] The result of the imposition of the State of Washington tax was twofold: it took much needed revenue away from the reservation, and it limited the rights of the tribe to tax nonmembers and further reduced tribal revenues.

The negative effect of concurrent taxation is supported by evidence from the Wind River Reservation in Wyoming. The State of Wyoming was allowed to take a disproportionate amount of taxes from the reservation, which helped contribute to a high unemployment level: "An economic study has found that the state collects $185 million in severance and property taxes from the reservation, but returns only $85 million in services—on a reservation with 70% unemployment."[14] In 2001, concurrent taxation forced tribes in the State of Oklahoma to pay $8.4 million to the state from the tribal collection of tobacco taxes, and thirty tribes divided motor fuel tax collections with the state.[15] In addition, concurrent taxation had led tribes to negotiate more than two hundred compacts with the states to govern state excise taxes that included cigarettes, petroleum, and alcohol and vehicle registration.[16]

The prospect of double taxation provides little if no incentive for non-member businesses to invest on the reservations.[17] As Justice Harry Blackmun explained in *Cotton Petroleum,* "Assuming that the Tribe continues to tax oil and gas production at present levels, on-reservation taxes will remain 75% higher (14% as opposed to 8% of gross value) than off-reservation taxes within the State."[18] Generally, profits drive business, and if a nonmember business has to pay 75 percent more in taxes by investing on-reservation, thereby unnecessarily reducing its profits, it will naturally look to invest off-reservation.

Although concurrent taxation dominated taxation case law from 1980 to 2001, in *Atkinson Trading Co. v. Shirley* (2001) the Supreme Court changed principles and disallowed concurrent taxation.[19] For the first time in the modern era, the Court prohibited tribal taxation over nonmembers on nonmember lands on the reservation.[20] In a 2008 Senate Committee on Indian Affairs hearing, Judge Theresa Pouley of the Tulalip Tribe spoke about the taxation problems faced by her tribe brought on by "constraints on tribal governments raising revenues for public safety" in contrast to state and local governments. Washington State "funds public safety through taxes on retail sales, real property and business activity," but in contrast "[the tribe on the] Tulalip Reservation, (which contains many non-Indian residents and businesses) . . . is effectively precluded by recent Supreme Court decisions from imposing these same taxes to fund this basic government service."[21] The NCAI explained that the 2001 *Atkinson* decision was disastrous.[22] W. Ron Allen, chairman of the Jamestown S'Klallam Tribe, agreed with this interpretation: "The *Atkinson* case with regard to, can we tax? And it's saying absolutely not, you cannot tax non-Indian businesses on Indian lands."[23] Pouley went further and suggested that taxation over nonmembers had in all respects ended. The collection of taxation as a source of revenue, Pouley argued, "is now effectively foreclosed to tribal governments due to land status and de facto limits on taxation of persons and businesses operating in Indian Country."[24] Without the right to tax nonmember businesses, the tribes were losing much needed revenues. As Allen pointed out, "If the Congress says, you need to become self-sufficient but we can't tax, where does Congress think that we're going to start getting revenues?" In addition, without revenue, the tribes were finding it more difficult to provide fundamental reservation-based services.[25]

The *Atkinson* case dramatically affected the economies of the tribes, including the Navajos. Robert Yazzie, chief justice of the Navajo Nation, testified that the *Atkinson* opinion fundamentally changed the Navajo economy and "adversely impacted the economic stability of the Navajo Nation government by jeopardizing future tax returns. The decreased revenues had a direct correlation on the level of essential governmental services that the Navajo government provided to all residents and travellers of the Navajo Nation."[26] The Navajo economy was required to either reduce government services or to provide nothing at all. The NCAI commented on the effects of *Atkinson* on all Native Americans while addressing those on the Navajo Nation in particular: "As at Navajo, where the *Atkinson* case prevents the Navajo Nation from taxing nonmembers to support a reservation population in excess of 200,000 people, tribes nationally are now prohibited from raising revenues to provide residents with governmental services." Overall, the NCAI summed up the impact of *Atkinson* on the provision of tribal government services throughout Native America: "Indian tribes are full-service governments, offering Indians and non-Indians alike a broad range of recreational, economic, education, and health services. Yet this new direction in the Supreme Court's Indian law cases poses a very serious threat to the ability of tribal governments to provide needed governmental services on Indian lands."[27]

The Supreme Court had placed limitations on the capacity of tribal governments to look after the reservation populations and threatened the short-term future of tribal governments in general. Ultimately, Colorado senator Ben Nighthorse Campbell testified, "An Indian tribal government that is unable to levy a tax on a hotel or things of that nature that enjoy the benefits and the amenities of the tribe with the things that the tribe provides certainly cannot survive very long."[28]

Atkinson also resulted in some nonmember businesses refusing to pay tribal taxes, thereby creating disorder and uncertainty on the reservations. For Roland E. Johnson, governor of the Pueblo of Laguna, "the validity of the [tribal] tax has come into question." In 2003 the Pueblo of Laguna, thinking nothing of the limitations imposed by Supreme Court case law, responded to a train crash on the reservation with all of the necessary emergency services. But the Burlington Northern Santa Fe Railroad refused to pay tribal taxes to the tribe in light of *Atkinson,* even after being helped by them. According to Johnson, the railroad "now asserts that these cases would allow them not to pay the tax that Laguna uses to provide essential governmental services when needed. We assert that this is unconscionable and wrong. Congress and Federal agencies have long encouraged tribal governmental and economic self determination but now the Judicial Branch is crippling exercise of this determination by judicial fiat."[29]

Johnson held that the unilateral decisions of the Supreme Court were devastating tribal economies and tribal government authority on the reservation. Yazzie supported this position and stated that the nonpayment of tax by nonmembers was morally wrong; it "also adversely impact[s] economic development within the Navajo Nation. Businesses located on fee land are able to avoid paying tribal taxes while businesses located on trust lands continue to pay. The fee land businesses, for all practical purposes, receive a free ride and the benefits of a civilized society that are assured by the provision of governmental services by the Navajo Nation."[30]

The safety and welfare of nonmember companies are provided by tribal services, and normally the costs of providing tribal provisions are offset by tribal taxes. Now, however, the tribes have to find extra money to provide free services to nonmember companies. Yazzie confirmed the impact of *Atkinson* during the question-and-answer session conducted by the chairman of the Senate Indian Affairs Committee:

> **The Chairman.** Now you have indicated that the Navajo Nation provides services to these utility companies, such as fire protection, police protection, et cetera?

Mr. Yazzie. Yes; the Navajo Nation does provide emergency services in case of accidents, services such as medical, fire protection, and police services to both Indians and non-Indians.

The Chairman. And they are refusing to pay for those services through taxation?

Mr. Yazzie. To our knowledge, that's the case today.[31]

With *Atkinson*, the Supreme Court had created uncertainty over whether nonmember companies had to pay tribal taxes, uncertainty that made the reservations that much less attractive for businesses. As Allen noted, "If the Court starts saying that we can't provide order within our reservation borders, how are we going to invite investors to come into our reservations and invest, if they feel that they have no due recourse or they have no confidence over the order that is supposed to be maintained within the reservation borders?"[32]

Civil Jurisdiction Case Law

Civil jurisdiction is an essential part of society. The silent revolution has affected tribal civil authority on the reservations in two basic ways. From 1981 to 2001 it eroded tribal civil jurisdiction over nonmembers on non-member reservation lands and therefore limited the rights of the tribe to protect elements of tribal culture and welfare on those lands. Then, *Nevada v. Hicks* (2001) went further, eroding tribal civil authority over nonmembers even on tribal and trust lands. From the limited evidence gathered for this work, the *Hicks* ruling has dramatically affected numerous Native American reservations.

Civil jurisdiction protects the culture, identity, and welfare of a society within a defined area of land. Civil authority is an important attribute of tribal government because it maintains "a society's culture and values. . . . A government that loses its right to regulate civil matters eventually loses its identity."[33] Land is an essential part of many tribal cultures and religions, and the exercise of civil authority protects the cultural connection to those lands.[34] For many tribes, the connection with the land is cultural as well as ancestral. Tribes "have a multi-generational, cultural bond to their land that makes that land unique and nonfungible. . . . Without this land base, Indian tribes quite simply cease to exist as culturally distinct societies. Full, undiminished sovereignty over tribal lands and those who occupy or use those lands is thus essential to the continuation of Indian tribes in the United States."[35] Tribal civil authority over reservation lands is fundamental to maintaining tribal cultures and histories as well as the future identity of the tribes: "These cultural and religious ties to the land make the issue of civil regulatory jurisdiction even more crucial. Without the power to zone, tribal governments are stripped of their ability to define a reservation's essential characters based on their cultural and religious ties."[36]

From 1981 to 2001, the Supreme Court held that tribes had generally lost civil authority over nonmember reservation lands. Without authority, the tribes did not have the right to define the culture of those lands or protect tribal members on those lands. This process began with *Montana v. United States* (1981), in which the Court ruled that tribes did not have inherent civil authority to control hunting and fishing by nonmembers on nonmember fee lands of the reservation. Once *Montana* was used to prohibit exclusive tribal zoning jurisdiction over the reservation, the Court extended the limitations placed on tribal civil jurisdiction with *Brendale v. Confederate Yakima Indian Nation* (1989).[37] Zoning ensures that a government has a comprehensive land management policy to define the uses and culture of land. As the U.S. Court of Appeals for the Ninth Circuit observed, zoning "promote[d] the health and welfare of the community."[38] Without zoning power over certain reservation lands, the tribes lost the right to define what happened on those lands. In *Brendale,* Justice Harry Blackmun argued that the tribes were threatened by not having the right to zone and therefore lost the right "of the general and longer term advantages of comprehensive land management."[39] These advantages included the protection of tribal culture associated with those lands. For example, testimony by Michael O. Finley, chairman of the Confederated Tribes of the Colville Reservation, to the U.S. Senate Committee on Indian Affairs in 2011 pointed to jurisdictional problems over culturally important parts of the reservation: "Many of those lands [fee lands owned by non-Indians] are cherished lands around our lakes and rivers and today around many of the larger municipalities that border our reservation. And so with that, we get this checkerboard effect across the Colville Reservation and it has created what I call a jurisdictional conundrum because of the difficulties that we have with exercising our jurisdiction and sovereignty on those lands around these municipalities."[40]

This erosion of tribal civil authority by the Supreme Court continued. In *South Dakota v. Bourland* (1993), the *Montana* rationale was used to prohibit tribal authority over nonmembers on lands removed from tribal status by the federal government. In *Strate v. A-1 Contractors* (1997), the *Montana* rationale was used to prohibit tribal jurisdiction over a road accident that occurred on a reservation road on a federal right-of-way.[41] Once tribes lost exclusive authority over lands on the reservation, they lost the right to define the character of those lands. Yazzie testified that *Strate* affected the right of the Navajo Tribe to regulate and control what nonmember businesses did on the reservation: "Businesses with right-of-ways or leases of Navajo Nation land, such as utilities and pipeline, are now claiming that the Navajo Nation has no authority to regulate or sue them."[42] *Strate* also limited tribal court jurisdiction over nonmembers and tribal protection over tribal members on the reservation. If a situation on the reservation involved a tribal member and a nonmember, the rationale of the Supreme Court was that the state court had the necessary jurisdiction to decide the issue. As John St. Clair, chief judge of the Shoshone and Arapaho tribal court, pointed out, tribal members were no longer protected by a tribal court when the issue involved a nonmember: "In the civil area . . . the non-Indian is at an advantage because he could take the Indian into either the tribal court or the State court, whereas the Indian can only take the non-Indian into the State court, but not into the tribal court. So there's two choices for him or her."[43]

Until 2001, the Supreme Court continuously limited tribal authority over nonmembers on nonmember lands. Then, in *Nevada v. Hicks* (2001), the Court declared that tribes did not have civil authority over nonmembers on tribal and trust lands and therefore lost the exclusive right to culturally define, protect, and control those lands.[44] Now, the state had inherent sovereignty to enter tribal lands in pursuit of an off-reservation crime.

In testimony to the Senate Committee on Indian Affairs, representatives from the Navajo Nation and the Jamestown S'Klallam Tribe discussed the impact of the *Hicks* decision. Yazzie noted that the Supreme Court had severely diminished the power of the Navajos to govern inside the reservation: "In sum, recent U.S. Supreme Court decisions have made it impossible to maintain a functioning civil government in the Navajo Nation to safeguard the public."[45] Allen supported this interpretation, noting that "Indian governments are supposed to be provided the authority, based on our sovereignty, to govern ourselves, to provide for the needs of our people, and to protect our cultures, our unique ways of life that are very unique to our society."[46] *Hicks* had limited the government power of the Jamestown S'Klallam inside their reservation, particularly on matters of cultural protection. Allen feared for the loss of their culture, noting that they could not "maintain the culturally separate identities of Indian communities."[47]

More than ten years after *Hicks*, tribes continue to be burdened by the problem of trust versus fee lands. The Colville Tribe is desperately trying to buy back fee lands upon which it can exercise civil jurisdiction and govern accordingly.[48] Overall, without the cultural protections associated with civil jurisdiction, "the social, cultural, and economic viability of American Indian communities and, perhaps, even identities is untenable over the long run."[49]

The loss of tribal control on the reservations has increased the number of state police entering the reservations without tribal consent. This problem is a direct result of *Hicks*. This issue was addressed in an exchange between Yazzie and Senator Daniel K. Inouye, chairman of the Senate Indian Affairs Committee, during a Senate hearing in 2002. The dialogue confirmed that the issue of state law on the reservation was a concern for the representative of the Navajos but also for the Jamestown S'Klallam Tribe and the Shoshones and Arapahoes:

> **The Chairman.** All three of you have testified that, as a result of the *Nevada* v. *Hicks* case, more and more State and local police depart- ments are coming into reservations. Are you documenting these instances, so we can use it as evidence in our reports? Yes, Chief Justice?
>
> **Mr. Yazzie.** Mr. Chairman, it would be nice to document, give you numbers, but we do not have the ability to do that. We just don't have the resources to maintain, to get statistics. It takes money to buy computers and to develop the data necessary to tell us something.
>
> **The Chairman.** But would you say that these incidents are com- monplace?
>
> **Mr. Yazzie.** Yes.[50]

The effect of increasing levels of state law and state law agencies on the reservation was not specific to just the three tribes represented at the hearing. In the opinion of Allen, the law was adversely affecting the whole of Indian country: "The Hicks decision is causing some of the greatest concerns in Indian country today. Although we think this is a limited decision, there are a number of state and local police departments who have interpreted the decision for themselves. They have decided that they have the authority to come onto reservations and enforce state law. We have a growing number of reports of this happening throughout Indian country, and it is a monumental concern."[51]

The fallout from the *Hicks* case caused concerns for Native America and threatened tribal interests on the reservations.[52] Allen explained the fear within Native America about Supreme Court case law, noting the concerns for "tribal leaders, our lawyers, our counsels, and our people regarding the future of our governments, our reservations, and the welfare of our communities."[53] Civil case law from the silent revolution had detrimentally affected the civil authority of the tribes within the reservations. The erosion of tribal sovereignty was "taking its toll on the ability of tribes to survive as unique cultural and political communities and [was] diminishing their contribution to the vitality of our country as a whole."[54]

Criminal Jurisdiction Case Law

Criminal jurisdiction protects a society within a territorial domain from crime and the fear of crime and sanctions the prosecution of individuals or groups who commit acts contrary to criminal law: "Criminal jurisdiction is the power of a government to establish rules of conduct and to punish those who violate the rules . . . everywhere within its borders."[55] In *Oliphant v. Suquamish Indian Tribe* (1978), the Supreme Court abolished tribal criminal authority and tribal court authority over nonmembers on the reservation.[56] The *Oliphant* case had and continues to have a devastating effect on Native America.[57] However, over many years Native American nations have begun to fight back against the injustice of that legal decision.[58]

Since *Oliphant*, Native Americans have not had the authority to punish nonmembers on the reservations or protect society from crime, thus removing an important attribute of tribal sovereignty. For Christopher B. Chaney, FBI unit chief, the *Oliphant* opinion had "a significant impact on day-to-day life in Indian country" because it affected "one of the most basic tenets of sovereignty: the ability of a government to exercise criminal jurisdiction within its own territory."[59]

In Senate testimony, Thomas B. Heffelfinger, U.S. attorney for the District of Minnesota, stated, "In the view of many, the *Oliphant* decision has created a gap in Indian country law enforcement and negatively impacts tribes' abilities to respond effectively to terrorist incidents and other crimes which may be committed by non-Indians in Indian country."[60] Chaney agrees, pointing out that *Oliphant* "has proven to be a large stumbling block to effective law enforcement and has had an adverse impact on public safety on the reservations for both

Indians and non-Indians."[61] Without criminal authority over nonmembers, tribes have been unable to protect tribal members from nonmember crime.[62]

Many tribes have highlighted this sense of tribal powerlessness. In 2007, Marcus D. Wells, chairman of the Three Affiliated Tribes of the Fort Berthold Reservation, gave testimony in the Senate and highlighted how outrageous the jurisdictional void left by the opinion of nine justices had become and how it could lead to further injustice: "One story comes to mind where one of our members called for help. BIA responded and could not remove the non-Indian. The county would not respond. Officers managed to control the situation and left the residence. Hours later, the officer responded a second time. Things had escalated. The woman, in self-defense, had pulled a knife in an effort to protect herself and her children. The BIA officer removed her and she was booked for the offense. Her children were taken by social services. Where is the justice?"[63]

The category of person involved (tribal member, nontribal member, nonmember) dictates who responds to a call, whether it be a city or county official or a tribal officer or the BIA, but so too do other factors such as the location of the crime—whether it occurred in Indian country on tribal trust land or fee land—and the type of crime. All of these complications exacerbate the jurisdictional quagmire on the reservations. Indeed, Jamestown's Allen testified that tribes could not prevent nonmember crime as a direct result of the opinions of the Supreme Court.[64] St. Clair summed up the despair of the Shoshones and Arapahoes on the Wind River Reservation when issues of domestic violence and drug and alcohol abuse involving nonmembers had arisen: "When both Indians and non-Indians are involved in domestic violence, alcohol and/or drug-related disturbances, or other criminal activity, the tribes can only adjudicate the Indians while non-Indians, even when detained and turned over to State officials, go unpunished. This double standard of justice creates resentment and projects the image that non-Indians are above the law in the area where they choose to live or choose to enter into."[65]

Powerlessness for the Wind River Reservation and its tribal members was seeing nonmembers escape criminal prosecution for illegal acts on the reservation. In fact, the situation created by *Oliphant*, as Earl Old Person from the Blackfeet Tribe explained, had "created a mess."[66] Many tribes had felt the real and everyday effects of the *Oliphant* ruling on the ground in tribal reservations, leaving the tribes helpless in the face of nonmember crime.

One direct result of the nullification of tribal criminal law and tribal court authority over nonmembers on the reservations was an increase in crimes committed by nonmembers on the reservations. Theresa M. Pouley, Tulalip tribal court judge, pointed out a disturbing fact: "When we recognize the alarming level of violent crime in Indian Country, we must not forget that the majority of perpetrators of violent crime against Indians are non-Indian."[67] The volume of nonmember lawlessness was identified in two Bureau of Justice Statistics publications in 1999 and 2004. The first identified nonmembers as the principal perpetrators of crime against Native Americans: "At least 70% of the violent victimizations experienced by American Indians are committed by persons not of the same race—a substantially higher rate of interracial violence than experienced by white or black victims." This report also provided figures for specific crimes, including rape, sexual assault, and robbery, committed by non–Native Americans against Native Americans. Between 1992 and 1996, "American Indian victims of rape/sexual assault most often reported that the victimization involved an offender of a different race. About 9 in 10 American Indian victims of rape or sexual assault were estimated to have had assailants who were white or black. Two-thirds or more of the American Indian victims of robbery, aggravated assault, and simple assault described the offender as belonging to a different race."[68]

These are ominously high figures, and this evidence is supported by a 2004 Bureau of Justice Statistics publication—*A BJS Statistical Profile, 1992–2002 American Indians and Crime*—which recorded nonmember crime statistics between 1992 and 2001, including these: "White or black offenders committed 88% of all violent victimizations, 1992–2001. Victims identified Asians or American Indians . . . as the offender in 13% of the violent acts." The rate of crimes committed by nonmembers against Native Americans far exceeded that committed by Asian or Native Americans on Native Americans: "In 66% of the violent crimes in which the race of the offender was reported, American Indian victims indicated the offender was either white or black. Nearly 4 in 5 American Indian victims of rape/sexual assault described the offender as white. About 3 in 5 American Indian victims of robbery (57%), aggravated assault (58%), and simple assault (55%) described the offender as white." As the report's author pointed out, "American Indian victims were more likely to report the offender was from a different race, compared to blacks and white victims."[69]

These Bureau of Justice Statistics reports were supported by the 2007 Amnesty International report *Maze of Injustice*, which presents the disturbing picture of more than one in three Native American women being raped during their lifetime, often by non-Indians, and of the official statistics' great underestimation of the severity of the problem.[70] Jacqueline Johnson Pata, executive director of the NCAI, testified that nonmembers who commit crimes against Native American women often know about the lack of criminal recourse, and that in real terms *Oliphant* has fueled these crimes; the tribal criminal authority void created by the Supreme Court "feeds the epidemic" of violence against Native American women.[71] A consequence of *Oliphant* was that Native America did not have authority or jurisdiction to prosecute the large number of serious crimes committed by nonmembers against Native Americans.

Many tribal members from different tribes have illustrated how the *Oliphant* decision created or contributed to nonmember crime on the reservations. In a question-and-answer session with Senator Inouye, St. Clair explained the increase in nonmember crime against Shoshones and Arapahoes as a direct result of the *Oliphant* case:

> **The Chairman.** You have indicated in your testimony that non-Indians on your reservation consider themselves to be above the law. Are you suggesting that, as a result of these Supreme Court decisions, the level of criminal activities among non-Indians has gone up?
>
> **Mr. St. Clair.** Yes; I think just crime in general, whether it's Indians or non-Indians, has arisen on reservations. When an incident does occur, even if there is an extradition procedure or agreement or a law enforcement assistance agreement between the tribes and the county or the State government, that just deals with how to handle the incident on the scene. It doesn't deal with adjudication. Most of the time, once that is completed, the non-Indian is not prosecuted. So the result is that only the Indian people are prosecuted.[72]

Incidents of domestic abuse by nonmembers have also affected the Jamestown S'Klallam Tribe. As Jamestown chairman Allen observed, the *Oliphant* case resulted in an increase in domestic abuse over which the tribe had no control: "We have a domestic violence problem with a non-Indian beating up an Indian woman, which we know is a common problem that we have throughout our communities, but we can't do anything about it. So what are we to do? The courts come to us, our courts come to us as politicians and say, 'What are we going to do about this?' So we have some serious problems."[73]

The same problems are seen in the vast population of the Navajo Nation. Navajo judge Yazzie recalled an incident during the mid-1990s: "Bruce Williams, a non-Indian, raced through a community located within the territorial jurisdiction of the Navajo Nation just to demonstrate that the Navajo Nation did not have criminal jurisdiction over his activities." The issue of domestic violence among the Navajos was similar to that of the Jamestown S'Klallam Tribe, with the *Oliphant* ruling allowing many nonmembers to escape punishment for domestic violence crimes. Despite the Violence Against Women Act passed by Congress in 1994, Yazzie explained that it did not protect women against nonmember acts of domestic violence: "Whenever a Navajo woman is beaten by a non-Indian spouse neither the State nor the Navajo Nation is presumed to have jurisdiction over the matter, only the federal government can prosecute." Furthermore, if the victim was not severely injured or killed, the federal government, Yazzie said, "will generally decline the matter."[74]

The everyday problems caused by the *Oliphant* judgment in Native American reservations were also discussed in testimony by Tex Hall, president of the NCAI:

> The jurisdictional problems that were talked about previously created by the *Oliphant* decision denies tribal people the opportunity to protect our tribal people and that must change. . . . it highlights the very real issues that tribes face every day. . . . Tribal police need the tools to address crimes committed by non-Indians in Indian country. Domestic violence and alcohol and drug crimes are our biggest problems in sheer volume alone. The most important civil right we all have is the right to be safe in our homes.[75]

The problems created by *Oliphant* have been exacerbated by the failure of the federal and state governments to prosecute all nonmember crimes. The Bureau of Justice Statistics publication of 1999 records that, in fiscal year 1996, U.S. attorneys investigated 1,927 suspects for crimes committed in Indian country.[76] In fiscal year 2000, U.S. attorneys investigated 2,074 suspects (not all Native Americans) for crimes in Indian country.[77] In each of these years there were approximately 30,000 violent crimes reported by Native Americans victims.[78] Federal authorities were neglecting to investigate thousands of cases—94 percent of reported crimes.

In a 2008 hearing, the U.S. Senate Committee on Indian Affairs released data, provided by Syracuse University, about the declination rates (numbers of cases referred against the number of cases declined) in Indian country over the four-year period 2004–7: there was a 50 percent declination rate on murder, a 58 percent declination rate on aggravated assault, a 72 percent declination rate on child sex crimes, and a 76.5 percent declination rate on adult sex crimes. Obviously, an extremely high number of individuals were escaping punishment for serious crimes. On hearing the figures, Indian Affairs chairman Byron Dorgan stated, "When we see all of that, we have a responsibility. People are hurt. People are victims of crime. People are killed because the system isn't working."[79]

A 2010 U.S. Government Accountability Office report recorded that U.S. attorneys declined to prosecute 67 percent of sexual abuse and related cases and 46 percent of assault matters in Indian country.[80] A 2007 Amnesty International report detailed many instances when state or federal government or a combination of the two failed to act on reported crime.[81] Alvin Windy Boy Jr., chairman of the Chippewa Cree Tribe, described the reluctance of federal authorities to prosecute nonmember crime on the Chippewa Cree Reservation: "If we have a criminal violation by a non-Indian within our reservation, we turn the case over to the federal authorities. . . . But they do not have the time and resources to cover what they already have on their plates."[82] The situation was similar on the Puyallup reservation. In a 2007 Senate hearing, Herman Dillon Sr., chairman of the Puyallup Tribe, highlighted many examples of the reluctance of federal authorities such as the FBI and BIA to help or respond quickly to serious incidents on the reservation.[83]

State governments have also failed to act. The Jamestown S'Klallam Tribes' Allen pointed out that the State of Washington had little motivation to help the tribe and prosecute nonmember crime on the reservation: "Are the county governments or State governments going to help out? No, they're not. They have other priorities. They have no interest in spending their resources to deal with the problems on Indian reservations, and the attitude has not been very encouraging over the years, even though in some areas you will see some constructive success that is going on."[84]

Both federal and state governments have been very reluctant to act within reservations to prosecute domestic violence cases. The NCAI pointed out that the domestic violence arena was "a particularly difficult issue on Indian reservations because federal and state authorities most often decline to investigate or prosecute, and tribal governments have no authority to exercise jurisdiction over non-Indians."[85] *Oliphant* had created a jurisdictional void.

Elements of Native America have called for the reversal of *Oliphant* and the requisite authority of tribal courts to be restored by the Supreme Court or Congress. Only with the reinstatement of tribal criminal authority over nonmembers will the tribes succeed in limiting and addressing nonmember crime on the reservations. In a prepared statement to Congress, Carmen O'Leary, director of the Native Women's Society of the Great Plains, explained the value of restoring jurisdiction to Native women and their communities:

> One important step is a return of criminal jurisdiction to Indian nations over crimes of domestic violence, stalking, dating violence and sexual assault by non-Indians. This type of jurisdictional fix is critical to enhancing the safety of Native women. Many episodes of violence against Native women include perpetrators of another race who know that they can continue to offend without any consequences due to the unique and confusing jurisdictional rules present in Indian country. With a jurisdictional fix that restores tribal criminal jurisdiction over non-Indians for these limited crimes, the offender that goes unpunished under the current system might finally get what he deserves and his victim might finally achieve a sense of peace, knowing that justice was served.[86]

Earl Old Person of the Blackfeet Nation argued that the "tribe should be the one that controls, not BIA, not FBI. . . . The tribe needs to be given back what the United States Supreme Court has taken. Non-Indians choose to live on the Blackfeet Reservation. They must be subject to its criminal laws in order for the Blackfeet Nation to keep the peace."[87] This line of thinking was echoed by a Colville representative: "I have been saying this for some time, that to totally fix the problem, to have criminal jurisdiction over non-members, we need an Oliphant fix, and you don't hear enough of that. We are talking about the welfare and safety of our people. And I think that until we get that, tribes can't truly exercise their sovereign jurisdiction over their lands whether it is fee or trust."[88]

The failure of federal and state governments to support the tribes and prosecute nonmembers led the NCAI to call for the restoration of tribal court authority over nonmembers: "Given the well-documented failure of federal and state officers to prosecute reservation crimes, the court decisions curtailing tribal authority have left a law enforcement void. Visitors, as well as reservation residents, will benefit from improved tribal justice systems where tribal governments are the primary authority."[89] As Kevin K. Washburn, assistant secretary of Indian Affairs for the U.S. Department of the Interior, testified, "Both tribal self-governance and public safety are better served when tribes exercise a central role in providing public safety and criminal justice on Indian reservations."[90] Moreover, the lack of ability to prosecute nonmembers not only disables the tribes from protecting their own communities but fundamentally violates their human rights.

With the 2013 Violence Against Women Reauthorization Act, which undoes some of the damage created by *Oliphant*, tribes can again prosecute nonmembers for domestic violence crimes committed on the reservation (see chapter 4). In addition, many tribes have successfully implemented schemes to circumvent the *Oliphant* decision. To get around the problem of *Oliphant*, tribes have used tribal and state compacts, decriminalized some offenses into civil offenses, and excluded nonmembers from the reservation. Tribal and state compacts have allowed the tribes to arrest nonmembers on the reservation. In 2001, the Winnebago Tribe signed a compact with the State of Nebraska authorizing tribal police and BIA officers to arrest nonmembers on the reservation. This process of cross-deputization had been undertaken between numerous tribes and states, including the Navajo Nation and the State of New Mexico, the Jicarilla Apache Tribe and New Mexico, the Eastern Band of Cherokee and North Carolina, the Cherokee Nation and Oklahoma, and the Choctaw Nation and various Oklahoma cities.[91] Judge Pouley of the Tulalip tribal court explained that the cross-commissioning of tribal officers on the reservation means that they act with the authority of a state officer to respond to incidents that involve both tribal members and nonmembers, providing "seamless law enforcement arrest authority over crimes committed by all persons on the Tulalip Reservation."[92] Cooperation between tribal and state governments, as well as the federal government, has ensured progress in prosecuting criminal activity.[93]

Despite the success of some agreements between tribes and states, many other tribes have not been successful and are still burdened by the practical limitations of *Oliphant*. The lack of cross-deputization has caused a serious practical problem for the Colville Reservation. Michael O. Finley, chairman of the Confederated Tribes of the Colville Reservation, explained that the tribe responds to all calls but that jurisdictional and financial problems are often the result:

In absence of a fast and reliable way to ascertain title of the land prior to responding to a call, the Colville Tribes' police force generally responds to all calls on the Colville Reservation out of an abundance of caution. The lack of cross-deputization agreements is most apparent when calls originate on fee land within these municipalities. . . . In circumstances where the Colville Tribes responds to calls where it is later determined that these municipalities actually possess jurisdiction, it would not be inaccurate to describe these situations as a diversion of tribal resources.[94]

In some places, cross-deputization agreements have not been authorized by relevant parties because of local political factors or "concerns over civil liability."[95]

While some tribes have managed to weaken the stranglehold of *Oliphant* through tribal and state compacts, others have decriminalized some offenses and turned them into civil offenses; the Jicarilla Apache tribal code was rewritten to allow the tribe to enforce the law against nonmember poachers on the reservation, and the Navajo Nation decriminalized its traffic laws.[96] Judge Yazzie explained that the Navajo Nation decriminalized offenses out of necessity and had successfully worked around *Oliphant*.[97] In addition, the Navajo Nation wrote into its legal code the right to exclude nonmembers from the reservation.

Although some tribes have been successful in undermining the ideology of the Supreme Court in *Oliphant*, there are still strong constraints imposed on tribal criminal authority over nonmembers on the reservations. And these constraints do not affect tribal members only; they affect everyone who lives, works, or travels on a reservation. As Judge Pouley testified, "Our law enforcement officers aren't safe. Our Tribal members aren't safe. Our police officers aren't safe. But no citizen of the United States is safe as long as the message we send is run from Tribal police; commit crimes with impunity because you won't be prosecuted."[98]

❖ There is no doubt that the Supreme Court's silent revolution has dramatically affected the everyday and practical authority and workings of tribal governments and tribal councils. As Robert Laurence put it, "Tribes have had increasingly unfettered power to do less and less," and "eventually the tribes will have entirely unfettered power to do essentially nothing."[99] Aside from the congressional testimony and a few government statistics cited in this chapter, it is clear that there is limited evidence and quantifiable data to reflect the true impact in Indian country of modern Supreme Court decisions. This chapter begins the process, but more effort is needed throughout Indian country to document and quantify recurring problems. It is through a concentrated effort of collecting hard data from each and every tribe that the silent revolution can be reversed.

✦ 6
Native American "Nation Building"
during the Silent Revolution

Throughout the storm of the silent revolution, which eroded the inherent sovereignty of the tribes over nonmembers on the reservations, one principle never changed. In *McClanahan v. Arizona State Tax Commission* (1973), *Mescalero Apache v. Jones* (1973), and *Tonasket v. Washington* (1973), the Supreme Court ruled that tribes had authority over tribal members unless revoked by an act of Congress or by a treaty. This principle of tribal sovereignty was confirmation of an old idea. During the 1960s and early 1970s, Native Americans had used their sovereignty to end the federal policy of termination and to support both economic activities on the reservations and a political revival. Indeed, the hope and belief of many Native Americans proved to be the seedlings of opportunity to counteract the silent revolution. Many tribes embraced the limitations imposed by the Court on civil, taxation, and criminal authority over nonmembers by strengthening their identities and economies. Over the course of the past forty-five years, nation building has occurred in Native America.[1]

Tribal sovereignty is a concept not readily defined; these two words mean different things to hundreds of tribes and millions of people. At best, we can suggest that tribal sovereignty is a collective moral and spiritual idea supported by a common culture that can empower groups of people. David E. Wilkins writes that tribal sovereignty is "the spiritual, moral, and dynamic cultural force within a given tribal community empowering the group toward political, economic, and, most importantly, cultural integrity; as well as maturity in the group's relationship with its own members, with other peoples and their governments, and with the environment." Clara Sue Kidwell argues that culture is central to an understanding of sovereignty: "It is also deeply embedded in culture, that is the association between sovereignty and cultural integrity." Vine Deloria and Clifford A. Lytle explain that spirituality rather than the abstract "sovereignty" is central to the cultures of most tribes. They suggest that authority, power, and sovereignty possessed by tribal governments are "privileges," but "such privileges do not assuage the needs of a spiritual tradition that remains very strong within most tribes and that needs to express itself in ways familiar to the people."[2]

Deloria offers the opinion that people should use their recognized sovereignty rather than simply talk about the concept: "Very few [people] will do the hard work to go out and exercise the sovereignty that already exists. They spend all of their time trying to define sovereignty more clearly, and that's absurd if 'sovereignty' means that any political entity can negotiate on an equal basis with any another."[3] Stephen Cornell observes that once a group of people assert sovereignty, they make "a claim to rights and powers" and thereafter they "exercise that sovereignty."[4] Put simply, as it has been by Oren Lyons, Faithkeeper of the Turtle Clan of the Onondaga Council of Chiefs of the Haudenosaunee, "Sovereignty is as sovereignty does."[5] The 1970s represented an opportunity for tribes to use sovereignty to build infrastructures on their reservations and to develop sustainable economies on their reservations. Stephen Cornell and Joseph P. Kalt eloquently sum up the opportunity presented to all Native Americans: "This opportunity is a political and organizational one. It is a chance to rethink, restructure, reorganize—a chance not to start a business or exploit an economic niche but to substantially reshape the future. It is the opportunity for nation-building."[6]

The onset of the silent revolution represented a bifurcation between the congressional policy of tribal self-determination and the opinions of the Supreme Court. Remarkably, while the Supreme Court began to erode the fundamental attributes of tribal criminal, civil, and taxation power, within the political arena there was affirmation of tribal political strength and the recognition of the resurgence of Native America within the United States.[7] In 1970, President Nixon introduced the federal policy of tribal self-determination after President Johnson had mooted the idea in 1968. On March 6, 1968, President Johnson had articulated a new federal policy to be pursued by his administration: "I propose a new goal for our Indian programs: A goal that ends the old debate about 'termination' of Indian programs and stresses self-determination; a goal that erases old attitudes of paternalism and promotes partnership self-help."[8] This statement began the end of termination, and within two years President Nixon had ended the termination policy. In a Special Message on Indian Affairs, Nixon made clear his intentions to end termination and to move toward a federal policy based on tribal self-determination. By adopting tribal self-determination, Nixon pointed out, the "new and coherent strategy" would allow more tribal autonomy and control over Indian lives, and it "must be the goal of any new national policy toward the Indian people to strengthen the Indian's sense of autonomy without threatening this sense of community. We must assure the Indian that he can assume control of his own life without being separated involuntary from the tribal group."[9] These policies of the executive were supported by Congress. The era of tribal self-determination had been determined by Native America.[10]

The Red Power movement of the 1960s and 1970s had forced the U.S. government to end its termination policy in 1970.[11] Red Power was composed of divergent groups with divergent issues and divergent demands. For example, there were differences between urban and reservation Native Americans as well as intratribal differences within both groups.[12] Native American activism was an umbrella movement built on many goals, including recognition of treaty and land rights, sovereignty rights, and cultural rights. Activism and events included the occupation of Alcatraz Island on November 9, 1969, the takeover of Mount Rushmore in September 1970, the Trail of Broken Treaties from October to November 1972, Wounded Knee from February 27 to May 8, 1973, the Pine Ridge shootout in 1975, and the Longest Walk on February 11, 1978.[13] For Stephen Cornell, the activism of Native Americans during the 1970s represented a time of renewal for all in Indian country: "The Indian is back. He lay in wait, biding his time, but now he's back, knocking at the door not only of the White House, but of Congress, the courts, and the American public."[14] According to Cornell, the success of the Red Power movement was an important factor to prove that Native America had not vanished but "had returned to the political arena with unexpected, often defiant force, and in the process had reversed the four-hundred-year trend of declining Indian influence and power."[15]

Federal Contributions to the Revival of Native America

The revival of Native America during the 1970s was evidenced by a greater amount of Native American legislation passed by Congress, expanding tribal authority and granting federal recognition to many tribes. General federal legislation increased the authority and power of the tribes, including the Indian Financing Act of 1974, the Alaskan Native Claims and Settlement Act of 1971, the Indian Self-Determination and Education Assistance Act of 1975, the Indian Child Welfare Act of 1978, and the American Indian Religious Freedom Act of 1978. In the opinion of John Wunder, "By the end of the 1970s, a peace pipe had been figuratively passed between Native Americas and many institutions of the United States. The tobacco was lit."[16] In addition, Congress enacted specific legislation to restore the Menominees, pursuant to the Menominee Restoration Act of 1973, as a federally recognized tribe. During the 1970s, several tribes were federally recognized, including the Alabama Creeks, the Narragansetts, the Ottawas, the Tunica-Biloxis, the Mashantucket Pequots, and the tribes of Maine. These and many more tribes were recognized in the 1970s because of direct action by both Congress and the Department of the Interior.[17] Native American legislation continued to be passed in Congress during the 1980s, but the trend slowed considerably in the 1990s.[18]

The reaffirmation of the government-to-government relationship between the United States and the tribes was a symbol that confirmed the political resurgence of Native America. On January 24, 1983, President Reagan reaffirmed that relationship and continued the policy of tribal self-determination: "This administration honors the commitment this nation made in 1970 and 1975 to strengthen tribal governments and lessen Federal control over tribal governmental affairs. This administration is determined to turn these goals into reality. Our policy is to reaffirm dealing with Indian tribes on a government-to-government basis and to pursue the policy of self-government for Indian tribes without threatening termination."[19]

Confirmation continued with Presidents Clinton, George W. Bush, and Obama. In 2013, Obama signed an executive order that established the White House Council on Native American Affairs:

> This order establishes a national policy to ensure that the Federal Government engages in a true and lasting government-to-government relationship with federally recognized tribes in a more coordinated and effective manner, including by better carrying out its trust responsibilities. This policy is established as a means of promoting and sustaining prosperous and resilient tribal communities. Greater engagement and meaningful consultation with tribes is of paramount importance in developing any policies affecting tribal nations. To honor treaties and recognize tribes' inherent sovereignty and right to self-government under U.S. law, it is the policy of the United States to promote the development of prosperous and resilient tribal communities.[20]

This reaffirmation of federal government policy continuously strengthened the political rights of Native America. Writing in the 1980s, Cornell believed that tribal power and control had grown: "For the first time, tribes today wield considerable control over development decisions and have used that power to launch a variety of development strategies of their own. In other words, their effective power—on the reservations and off—has grown." Cornell added that this sense of strength was the product "of court decisions in favor of tribal control" and "new federal policies of self-determination: a genuine turn to bilateral relations"[21]

Interestingly, while the Supreme Court was eroding civil, criminal, and taxation authority over nonmembers on the reservation in this period, some of their opinions supported tribal sovereignty and treaty rights over tribal members and their reservation lands. Often these decisions protected tribal hunting and fishing rights. In *Choctaw Nation v. Oklahoma* (1970) there was a dispute between the Choctaw Nation and the State of Oklahoma over the title to lands and mineral rights beneath some navigable parts of the Arkansas River.[22] The State of Oklahoma had leased oil and gas and other mineral rights to state corporations. The Cherokees, Choctaws, and Chickasaws argued that they owned the lands. The final opinion of the Supreme Court held that the tribes had title to the lands under the river pursuant to several treaties, including the Treaty of Dancing Rabbit Creek in 1830 and the Treaty of New Echota in 1835.[23]

Other Court opinions supported tribal fishing rights. In *Menominee Tribe of Indians v. United States* (1968), the Menominees brought an action in the Court of Claims to claim compensation over the loss of hunting and fishing rights.[24] The Wisconsin Supreme Court had previously ruled that the tribe lost these rights in the Menominee Termination Act of 1954 because the State of Wisconsin had assumed jurisdiction over the tribes and their lands. But the Wisconsin Supreme Court had failed to consider a provision in Public Law 280 that specifically stated that the Menominees would not be deprived of their hunting and fishing rights. The Court of Claims ruled that the Menominees retained their hunting and fishing rights under the Treaty of Wolf River of 1854 and that the Menominee Termination Act did not extinguish these rights. In the U.S. Supreme Court opinion, Justice William O. Douglas ruled that the treaty language "to be held as Indian lands are held" included Menominee hunting and fishing rights. These rights survived despite the Menominee Termination Act. In summation, Douglas stated that "to abrogate treaty rights of Indians is not to be lightly imputed to Congress."[25]

In the same year, the Supreme Court decided *Puyallup Tribe v. Department of Game*.[26] This 1968 case asked if the language used in the Treaty of Medicine Creek barred the State of Washington from imposing conservation measures to regulate the fishing nets used to catch salmon and steelhead fish by the tribe. The treaty stated that the "right of taking fish at all usual and accustomed grounds and stations, is . . . secured to said Indians, in common with all citizens of the Territory."[27] The Supreme Court ruled that the conservation interests of the state allowed it to regulate tribal fishing, but that the tribe continued to have authority to fish under its treaty rights. Only five years later the Court had to rule again in the situation between the Puyallup Tribe and Washington State. In *Department of Game v. Puyallup Tribe* (1973) the justices considered whether the Washington State game department had the right to prohibit all commercial net fishing by the Puyallups.[28] The opinion of Justice Douglas ruled that commercial net fishing was protected by treaty, and as a result the state regulation prohibiting the fishing was discriminatory. The regulation could be imposed, but it had to balance the interests of the Puyallups and sports fishermen.

The 1973 decision still did not end the problem between the Puyallups and Washington State. Four years later the justices granted review to *Puyallup Tribe, Inc. v. Department of Game* (1977).[29] The case considered whether the Washington Superior Court had jurisdiction over the Puyallup Tribe. The Supreme Court ruled that a state court had no jurisdiction over a tribe but did have jurisdiction over individual tribal members. In addition, the Wolf River treaty failed to grant the Puyallups an exclusive right to take the steelhead that passed through the reservation. Therefore, the tribe had a right to fish in places protected by the treaty, but it had to be done with consideration for state citizens. Tribal members were not allowed to take an unlimited number of fish on the reservation. The state had the right to regulate conservation measures, but it had to be done in a reasonable manner.[30]

The case of *Minnesota v. Mille Lacs Band of Chippewa Indians* (1999) involved the debate of treaty rights and whether they had protected fishing as well as hunting and gathering rights of the Mille Lacs Band.[31] In 1837, several Chippewa bands ceded lands in return for hunting, fishing, and gathering rights on the ceded lands. In 1850 an executive order revoked these rights. In 1855 a treaty between the Mille Lacs Band and the United States set aside reservation lands for the tribe. Then in 1990 the Mille Lacs Band and several members sued the State of Minnesota because of its interference with the treaty rights. The Supreme Court ruled that the Chippewas retained their hunting, fishing, and gathering rights because they were protected by the 1837 treaty. Indeed, the 1855 treaty had not abrogated the rights set out in the 1837 treaty.

In sum, the Supreme Court did rule in favor of tribal interests in a small number of cases concerning treaty rights as well as fishing and hunting rights during the silent revolution. It also supported tribal interests in some cases involving adoption and water rights.[32]

The Success of Tribal Economies

Many tribal economies developed and flourished during the 1970s. Tribes created tribal businesses on the reservations, and the federal government increased direct funding that supported business projects.[33] In addition, broad congressional policy allowed the tribes to build successful and sustainable economies.[34] With sustained federal funding and growing tribal economies, reservation poverty levels improved as well.[35]

One example of tribal success is the Mississippi Band of Choctaw. The economic success of this group began in 1975 when Chief Phillip Martin sent out business proposals to attract private investment to the reservation to develop infrastructure and initiate solutions to the social and educational problems of the tribe. By the late 1970s, the Mississippi Choctaws had attracted business to the reservation and established many reservation businesses. From 1978, they had "entered an era of unprecedented economic growth," and by the twenty-first century "the Mississippi Choctaws have virtually eliminated unemployment on their lands and must turn to non-Indians by the thousands to work in Choctaw-owned factories, enterprises, schools, and government agencies."[36] As Chief Martin explained, the strong tribal economy created by the Mississippi Choctaws was founded on "the strengthening of the tribal government . . . [a gradual process] that took place between the late 60's and 1979."[37]

Another example of tribal success occurred in western Washington. In 1970 the Muckleshoots were a small and impoverished tribe that possessed less than half an acre of common land. To the Muckleshoots, fishing for salmon had always been central to economic life and the survival of the tribe. During the 1960s, state fisheries intervention supressed the catch; fishing people were arrested and their boats and nets seized. Catches fell to levels that forced the Muckleshoots and others to go hungry. Guided by necessity and outrage, the Muckleshoots and other Washington tribes protested and brought attention to the fact that they were being barred from fishing off-reservation by the state, its officers, and its citizens. These protests, known as "fish-ins," drew celebrities such as Marlon Brando and copious press coverage.[38]

After several years of protest and civil disobedience, the resurgence of the Muckleshoots began in early 1974 when Judge George Hugo Boldt of the Federal District Court for the Western District of Washington announced that the Muckleshoots and thirteen other tribes in western Washington, pursuant to a series of treaties in 1854 and 1855 with the United States, "therefore holds for the benefit of its members a reserved right to harvest anadromous fish at all usual and accustomed places outside reservation boundaries, in common with others"[39]—known thereafter as the Boldt decision. Judge Boldt's court assumed direction of the fishery from the state, but the State of Washington refused to recognize the Boldt decision. This impasse was resolved in 1979 when the Supreme Court affirmed the Boldt decision in *Washington v. Fishing Vessel Assn.* (1979).[40]

After the Boldt decision, the Muckleshoots developed their fishing fleet, opened a smoke-shop, and purchased a hatchery. They also opened gambling venues that provided much-needed revenue to build infrastructure on the reservation and to invest in reservation jobs and education. The money provided by the bingo hall and casino allowed the Muckleshoots to build a new tribal school and provided college scholarships. It also resulted in the new Health and Wellness Center, with medical and dental services, as well as sports facilities, a water treatment plant, a business park, a 20,000-seat outdoor concert venue, and new homes for tribal members. In 1970 the Muckleshoots had very little land and money, yet in 2014 the tribe was able to purchase 96,307 acres of land, for which it paid $313 million.[41] Walter E. Echo-Hawk, an attorney and tribal judge, visited the Muckleshoot tribal school and stated, "In my mind, for a smaller tribe . . . I've always looked at Muckleshoot as a model for nation-building. I think all of Indian Country can look to this reservation as a model for tribal development."[42]

The Salish and Kootenai Tribes at the Flathead Reservation provided their people with economic success by attracting investment and developing tribal services. The regeneration of the reservation began during the 1980s, and by the 1990s the Flathead Reservation profited from a "thick private sector economy" in which the tribes owned many reservation industries. Indeed, the Salish and Kootenai Tribes "began building one of the most effective tribal governments in the U.S., reclaiming control of their lands and community and moving the tribe toward sustainable, successful economic development."[43] By 2014, the Salish and Kootenais had created a successful tribal economy, and tribal government was an essential component:

On the Reservation, the Confederated Salish and Kootenai Tribes are the most significant economic actor. Each year the Tribes spend tens of millions of dollars locally. The Tribes own most of the timber, range, and recreation resources, as well as the lands where irrigation waters originate. Tribal members own and operate over one hundred local businesses. The Tribal organization also operates several businesses. In addition, it runs schools and manages the Reservation's electric utility, and will soon own and operate Kerr Dam, a major hydropower generation facility.[44]

The Citizen Potawatomi Nation is another tribe that built economic success within its reservation. In the 1970s the tribe owned less than three acres of trust lands and had $550 in the bank. The headquarters of tribal government was stationed in an old trailer. In 2010 the assets owned by the Citizen Potawatomi Nation included a golf course, a bank, a large discount food retail store, a tribal farm, a casino, restaurants, and a radio station. A strong private-sector economy had developed too. In addition, the Nation had bought over 4,000 acres of land. In a similar system to that operated by the Muckleshoots, the Citizen Potawatomi Nation invested revenue and resources in services for its citizens. These included a small business development program, child development support, health care, and education. Now, the Citizen Potawatomi Nation is the "economic engine of the Shawnee, Oklahoma region."[45]

Many tribes with natural resources such as oil, coal, and natural gas have fueled their economic revival by opening up their lands for exploitation. Among them are the Navajos, Northern Cheyennes, and Jicarilla Apaches.[46] During the 1990s some reservations successfully established tribal enterprises and others attracted multinational corporations. Enterprises owned by the Chickasaw Nation include gas stations, bingo facilities, and numerous shops as well as "motor fuel truck plazas" and a chemical finishing plant; together they contributed $3 million per month to tribal government.[47] The economic success of the Winnebago Ho-Chunk tribal enterprise cut tribal unemployment from 70 percent to 13 percent in six years.[48] Indeed, the businesses of the Winnebago Tribe of Nebraska have competed successfully in the mainstream U.S. economy, and in a decade their annual revenues increased from nothing to $150 million.[49]

Other tribal governments developed gaming enterprises to raise revenue and help support the reservations. The first Native American gaming operation of the modern era was established by the Seminole Tribe of Florida in 1979 when the tribe established a bingo hall on the reservation.[50] During the federal budget cuts of the 1980s, tribal gaming operations steadily increased. Deloria and Lytle have argued that the Republican administration of President Reagan encouraged gaming on the reservations to counteract large federal budget cuts.[51] After the Supreme Court ruling in *California v. Cabazon Band of Mission Indians* (1987), large numbers of tribes developed gaming facilities on their reservations.[52] In response, Congress legislated to control tribal gaming pursuant to the Indian Gaming Regulatory Act of 1988.

The total revenues generated by tribal gaming and the number of tribal operations have increased dramatically from the early 1990s to 2014. In 1995 tribal gaming revenues totaled $5.46 billion, and by 2000 revenues had increased to $10.96 billion. Only five years later, tribal gaming revenues were $22.63 billion, by 2010 they were $26.5 billion, and in 2014 they were $28.5 billion.[53]

Tribal gaming revenues are organized into revenue ranges by the National Indian Gaming Commission: $250 million and over (introduced in 2002), $100 million and over, $50 to $100 million, $25 to $50 million, $10 to $25 million, $3 to $10 million, and under $3 million. From 1996 to 2014 the number of operations in each revenue range increased. For example, in 1996, twelve tribal operations generated revenues of $100 million and over; in 2014 that number had increased to fifty-three. In 2014 twenty-six operations generated revenues of $250 million and over. In 1996, twenty-four tribal operations generated $25 to $50 million in revenues; in 2014 that number totaled seventy. In 1996, forty-two tribal operations generated $3 to $10 million in revenues; in 2014 that number had increased to seventy-six.[54] Tribal gaming is a consequence of tribal sovereignty, and many tribes have succeeded in building large revenues from these enterprises. Tribes such as the Pequots, the Oneidas, and the Mille Lacs Band of Ojibwe have been particularly successful because of their proximity to concentrated population centers.[55]

More tribal capital to spend on reservation infrastructure has led to improved living standards for many Native Americans. Data provided in *The American Indians on Reservations: A Databook of Socioeconomic Change between the 1990 and 2000 Censuses* demonstrate a general increase in the living standards of Native America. From 1990 to 2000, the Native American population rose by 20 percent but still contained a "substantial growth in income per capita," with inflation adjusted figures, of approximately 33 percent, in comparison to 11 percent for the United States as a whole. In the same period, Native American family poverty rates dropped approximately 7 percent in nongaming areas and approximately 12 percent in gaming areas, while in the United States it dropped 0.8 percent; and Native American unemployment decreased by approximately 2 percent in nongaming areas and by approximately 5 percent in gaming areas, while in the United States it decreased by 0.5 percent. The number of Native Americans living in homes with plumbing increased markedly.[56]

Strengthened reservation economies have been highlighted in several recent publications. A 2005 Bureau of the Census publication presents the success of tribal businesses and their profits from 1997 to 2002 and notes that the number of Native American businesses operating in the United States increased from 197,300 in 1997 to 206,125 in 2002. Although the revenues, indicated by total sales and receipts, of Native American businesses decreased from $34.344 billion in 1997 to $26.396 billion in 2002, the Bureau publication holds that those figures are an aberration.[57] In a 2006 Bureau of the Census publication, the estimates for Native American business revenues were updated. The revised figures for 2002 show that 201,387 businesses generated $26.873 billion.[58] These figures were updated once again in a 2011 Census publication; in all, there were 236,967 businesses, an increase of 17.7 percent from 2002, with total generated revenue of $34.4 billion.[59] In August 2015, the Census Bureau released preliminary data about "American Indian- and Alaska Native-owned" businesses in 2012; the number of businesses owned totaled 274,238 and the overall generated revenue was $42.2 billion.[60]

✜ Tribal sovereignty and the federal policy of tribal self-determination have developed tribal economies, promoted political strength, supported tribal ambition, and encouraged tribes and their tribal members to believe in a sustainable future. The empowerment of Native America during the 1970s resulted in greater political and economic autonomy. Indeed, tribal sovereignty instilled a self-belief that has continued to the present day. According to Kalt and Singer:

> The last three decades [ca. 1970–2000] have witnessed a remarkable resurgence of the Indian nations in the United States. After centuries of turmoil, oppression, attempted subjugation, and economic deprivation, the Indian nations have asserted their rights and identities, have built and rebuilt political systems in order to implement self-rule,

and have begun to overcome what once seemed to be insurmountable problems of poverty and social disarray. The foundation of this resurgence has been the exercise of self-government by the more than 560 federally recognized tribes in the U.S.[61]

Although the silent revolution had affected and continues to affect Native America, tribes such as the Muckleshoots, the Mississippi Band of Choctaw, and the Citizen Potawatomi Nation have demonstrated what is possible with tribal sovereignty and tribal self-determination. Tribal sovereignty has been important because the tribes had to decide their own economic futures, and the set of powers allowed local people to decide local issues. The empowerment of local decision making rather than a decree from offices far away and far removed from the cultures and economies of the reservations was critical to the economic success of many tribes during the period of the silent revolution. Jonathan B. Taylor and Kalt eloquently stated:

> Prior research repeatedly indicates that devolution of powers of self-rule to tribes can bring, and has brought, improvements in program efficiency, enterprise competency, and socioeconomic conditions. The reasons are to be found in the fact that self-rule brings decision making home, and local decision makers are held more accountable to local needs, conditions, and cultures than outsiders. On the other hand, prior to the present era of Indian self-determination, decades of distant decision making by federal and state authorities accountable to non-Indian constituents and masters had shown little discernable ability to break repeated patterns of poverty and social disarray.[62]

Conclusion

The erosion of the Indian sovereignty doctrine began in the period 1959–73, when the Supreme Court justices allowed more state law onto the reservations. This process fundamentally undermined the Indian sovereignty doctrine and the principle of *Worcester v. Georgia* (1832), which prohibited all forms of state law on the reservations. Although *Williams v. Lee* (1959) was a victory for inherent tribal sovereignty, the memoranda contained in the private papers of the Supreme Court justices from the *Williams* case reveal that the Court considered moving away from the Indian sovereignty doctrine and the principles established in *Worcester* to a position where congressional legislation was required to oust state law from the reservations.[1] Memoranda from the William O. Douglas, William J. Brennan, and Earl Warren papers show that individual justices including Warren were comfortable with the use of congressional authority but were concerned about the complete absence of state law on the reservations.[2] The movement away from the sovereignty doctrine coincided with the views of the justices who wanted to address the constant power struggles over authority on the reservations between the federal government, tribal governments, and state governments. The justices began to view federal Indian law cases in terms of federal versus state authority, with the welfare of the tribes purportedly being protected by the federal government.

After *Williams,* the Supreme Court continued to move away from the sovereignty doctrine toward the primacy of congressional authority in order to prohibit state law on the reservations. The private papers of Brennan, Warren, and Douglas showed that the *Kake Village v. Egan* (1962) and *Metlakatla Indians v. Egan* (1962) cases revolved exclusively around the idea of congressional authority[3] and that the *Warren Trading Post v. Tax Comm'n* (1965) case used the idea of congressional authority to prevent the application of state law on the reservation.[4] This argument was further developed in *Kennerly v. District Court of Montana* (1971) and applied as a principle in *McClanahan v. Arizona State Tax Comm'n* (1973), *Mescalero Apache Tribe v. Jones* (1973), and *Tonasket v. Washington* (1973). The principle, developed in a line of case law from 1959, was highlighted in a Justice Thurgood Marshall memorandum to conference in 1973 and in a bench memorandum from the *Tonasket* case.[5] Justices William H. Rehnquist and Potter Stewart and the tribal counsel who argued on behalf of the Navajo Tribe in *McClanahan* also supported the application of general state law on the reservation, which in turn sanctioned state law over nonmembers on the reservation.[6] By 1973, then, the views of the justices fundamentally limited the Indian sovereignty doctrine and the *Worcester* principles.[7]

The silent revolution was grounded by an integrationist trend in the application of four principles that worked in tandem to turn the Indian sovereignty doctrine on its head. Rather than the tribes having sovereignty over all people and lands on the reservations, from 1973 the Supreme Court justices believed that tribal authority was limited to tribal members and subsequently that tribal authority over nonmembers on the reservations existed only after an explicit delegation of congressional power. The corollary of this view was that the states had authority on the reservations until it was reversed by Congress. The justices concluded that the removal of inherent tribal sovereignty over nonmembers meant its replacement by inherent state sovereignty. The opening up of the reservations to the application of state law over nonmembers on the reservation served to integrate the reservations into the nation as a whole rather than preserve the notion of separate reservations.

Today, tribal sovereignty over nonmembers survives only through a delegation of congressional power, whereas inherent state authority exists on the reservations and over nonmembers on the reservations until reversed by Congress. The erosion of the key attributes of tribal power continued in the taxation case *Wagnon v. Prairie Band Potawatomi Nation* (2005) and the civil case *Plains Commerce Bank v. Long Family Land and Cattle Co.* (2008). However, the states generally have no authority over tribal members on the reservations because to that limited degree the Indian sovereignty doctrine still protects the tribes from state law and only explicit congressional legislation can remove this protection.

The silent revolution affected three key areas of tribal authority over nonmembers: taxation, criminal, and civil authority. After the sister cases *McClanahan* and *Mescalero Apache Tribe* and the case of *Tonasket* in 1973, the Supreme Court continued with the same integrationist principles in *United States v. Mazurie* (1975) and *Moe v. Salish and Kootenai Tribes* (1976). The *Mazurie* case applied the principle established in the sister taxation cases and *Tonasket* that tribal authority over nonmembers after 1973 was based on congressional authority. The papers of Brennan, Harry A. Blackmun, and Lewis F. Powell Jr. reveal that the Supreme Court considered tribal authority to be limited to tribal members only, and therefore only authorization from Congress allowed the tribes to have authority over nonmembers.[8] The Indian sovereignty doctrine was not considered by the justices to be strong enough to support the idea of inherent tribal sovereignty as a way to control nonmember activity. The justices in the *Moe* case applied the principle that the states had authority on the reservations and authority over nonmembers on the reservations. The Blackmun and Brennan papers show that the justices refused to use the Indian sovereignty doctrine to protect tribal reservations from state law.[9]

In criminal case law, the justices nullified the application of tribal criminal authority over nonmembers on the reservations and limited tribal criminal authority to tribal members only. In *Oliphant v. Suquamish Indian Tribe* (1978) and *United States v. Wheeler* (1978), the Supreme Court developed the principles formed in *McClanahan, Mescalero Apache Tribe,* and *Tonasket.* The private papers of Justices Blackmun and Powell show that the justices believed that the sister taxation cases and *Tonasket* had limited tribal sovereignty to tribal members and that, as a result, tribal sovereignty could not be applied over nonmembers and was dependent on congressional authority.[10] Therefore, in criminal law the justices applied the principle that if tribes were to have criminal authority over nonmembers it would have to be delegated by Congress. The *Oliphant* case ruled that the tribes did not have authority over nonmembers because it was not authorized by Congress. The limitations placed on tribal criminal authority over nonmembers were confirmed in *Wheeler* when the Court reaffirmed that tribes had inherent criminal authority only over tribal members on the reservation.

Taxation case law throughout the silent revolution dramatically affected the tribes by establishing the rights of the states to tax nonmembers and nonmember companies on the reservations unless it was prohibited by congressional authority. Between 1980 and 2001 the Supreme Court had allowed the tribes also to tax nonmembers on the reservations. This contrasted significantly with the development of criminal case law, which had limited tribal sovereignty over nonmembers. However, in *Atkinson Trading Co. v. Shirley* (2001) the Court dramatically changed course and ruled that the tribes did not have inherent sovereignty to tax nonmembers on nonmember lands of the reservations.

The erosion of the Indian sovereignty doctrine in civil case law was a gradual process. In *Montana v. United States* (1981), the Court applied the principle that the tribes did not have inherent civil sovereignty over non-members on nonmember lands of the reservation unless it was authorized by Congress. This was a development of the principles applied in *McClanahan*, *Mescalero Apache Tribe*, and *Tonasket* in 1973 and thereafter used in *Mazurie* and *Oliphant*. Although the Court adopted a broad rationale that tribes did not have any civil jurisdiction over nonmembers unless authorized by Congress, the sovereignty doctrine allowed the tribes to have authority over nonmembers on tribal lands. However, between 1981 and 2001 the Court further eroded the Indian sovereignty doctrine and fundamentally eroded tribal civil juris-diction over nonmembers on the reservations.[11] Then, in 2001, in the case of *Nevada v. Hicks*, the justices denied the application of tribal authority over nonmembers on tribal lands, and consequently the states were ruled to have inherent sovereignty over nonmembers on the reservation. Since *Hicks*, the Court has applied integrationist principles in cases such as *Wagnon v. Prairie Band Potawatomi Nation* (2005) and *Plains Commerce Bank v. Long Family Land and Cattle Co.* (2008).

The silent revolution dramatically affected the practical and everyday workings of tribal authority on the reservations, though obtaining evidence about the effects of Supreme Court case law on tribal authority is difficult and serves as a point of reference for future research. The effect of the silent revolution on tribal taxation authority in such cases as *Washington v. Confed-erated Tribes* (1980) and *Cotton Petroleum Corp. v. New Mexico* (1989) was a loss of tribal revenues to the states and diminished incentive for economic investment.[12] It also limited the amount of tribal revenue available to support tribal government programs and services to both tribal members and non-members on the reservations.[13]

The silent revolution in civil case law—illustrated in *Montana v. United States*, *Brendale v. Confederated Yakima Indian Nation* (1989), *South Dakota v. Bourland, Strate v. A-1 Contractors* (1997), and *Nevada v. Hicks* (2001)—limited the rights of tribes to protect elements of tribal culture and welfare on nonmember lands of the reservations. In addition, it eroded tribal civil authority over nonmembers on tribal and trust lands of the reservations and increased the incidence of state police forces entering reservations without tribal consent.[14] Exacerbating this situation was one of the consequences of criminal case law—a jurisdictional gap created in *Oliphant* that limited tribal criminal authority over nonmembers on the reservations, a gap that federal and state governments were increasingly reluctant to step in and assume responsibility for. This led to a sense of tribal powerlessness on the reservations[15] and contributed to significant amounts of crime committed by nonmembers.[16] In response, many Native American tribes successfully circumvented and ameliorated the limitations imposed by *Oliphant* on their criminal authority over nonmembers.[17]

In response to the unprecedented Supreme Court opinions issued in 2001, Native America and supporters of tribal rights began a process to coordinate the protection of tribal sovereignty through political and legal activism. Native Americans formed the Tribal Sovereignty Protection Initiative to stop further erosion of tribal sovereignty by the Court. Key considerations included developing congressional legislation to reaffirm tribal authority, pursuant to educating legislators and the broader American public about tribal governments, and keeping cases away from the Supreme Court—later called the Tribal Supreme Court Project. Political activism and coordination among tribes led to Senate bill 578 and House bill 2242, which were essentially legislative proposals to undo the silent revolution. But the prospect of tribal authority over nonmembers throughout the United States was highly controversial in Congress, and these bills failed. Then, with continued political activism, Native America was crucial in developing legislation—the Tribal Law and Order Act of 2010—to reduce violent crime and to protect tribal members in Indian country. Only three years later, Congress passed legislation—the Violence Against Women Reauthorization Act of 2013—which allows tribes to exercise inherent sovereignty to prosecute nonmembers in tribal courts for domestic violence crimes on reservations. This act partially undid the effects of *Oliphant.*

The dissonance between the Violence Against Women Reauthorization Act and the silent revolution reflects the crisis in federal Indian law today between the rationale of the Indian sovereignty doctrine, beginning with the presumption that tribes have inherent tribal sovereignty until aspects of this sovereignty are limited by express federal legislation or treaty, and the integrationist trend, beginning with the presumption that tribes do not have inherent sovereignty over reservation nonmembers until Congress expressly acts to allow tribal authority over those nonmembers. As of 2016, then, the federal judiciary and the legislature are doctrinally at odds regarding tribal sovereignty over nonmembers on the reservations.

Although many writings celebrate the political resurgence of Native America from the 1970s, it must be remembered that in the background during this period were the growing number of Supreme Court opinions in federal Indian law that slowly eroded tribal sovereignty and the key attributes of tribal power over nonmembers in terms of civil, criminal, and taxation case law. Nevetheless, in this same period within the political arena the federal executive and Congress have affirmed the political resurgence of Native America. Tribes have used their limited power to build reservation economies, to develop reservation infrastructure, and to improve their collective lives for the future. Indeed, tribal sovereignty resulted in an empowerment that led directly to nation building.

Overall, the silent revolution and its integrationist trend have become embedded in the case law of the Supreme Court, and although Congress passed the Violence Against Women Reauthorization Act in 2013, it can generally be argued that the legal paradigm established by the Court points toward its continued application in congressional legislation. One hopes this latter point will prove to be incorrect, but it will take the resolve of a strong, ethical, and supportive Congress to reverse the Court's trend. Ultimately, Native America has the largest role to play in undoing the silent revolution. The process of educating the American public about tribal governments and their presence in twenty-first-century America will slowly, but undoubtedly, change the nation's ideas and perceptions of Native Americans and lead to a greater understanding and support for protecting tribal sovereignty. In addition, the American public must be educated about the impact of Supreme Court opinions on everyday Native American lives. Once there are hard data, collected and collated by each and every tribal government, to demonstrate the harm that Supreme Court civil, criminal, and taxation case law opinions have brought to reservations, the silent revolution can be driven back and abandoned. In time and with hope, the future will be brighter: "Indian Country is patient and tends to hold the long-view. We keep chipping away at the obstacles on our path and until the way is clear. Our time will come, our issues will be addressed and things will be made right. Clearly, those who oppose tribal sovereignty are on the wrong side of history."[18]

Notes

Introduction

1. The terms "tribe" and "nation" are used interchangeably in this work to refer to Native American groups.
2. The term "nonmember" in this book refers to non-Indians. "Nonmember" and "non-Indian" are used interchangeably throughout the book. The word "state" refers to one or more of the fifty states of the Union.
3. For examples of works that do discuss some of the effects on the tribes, see Jeff Corntassel and Richard C. Witmer II, *Forced Federalism: Contemporary Challenges to Indigenous Nationhood* (Norman: University of Oklahoma Press, 2008); Alex T. Skibine, "The Court's Use of the Implicit Divestiture Doctrine to Implement Its Imperfect Notion of Federalism in Indian Country," *Tulsa Law Journal* 36 (2000): 267–304; and J. P. Lavelle, "Implicit Divestiture Reconsidered: Outtakes from Cohen's Handbook Cutting Room Floor," *Connecticut Law Review* 38 (2006): 731–76.
4. The seminal book in this area of the law is Felix S. Cohen, *Handbook of Federal Indian Law* (Washington, D.C.: Government Printing Office, 1941). Cohen examined the effect of treaties, Supreme Court case law, federal statutes, and U.S. government policy on the tribes up to 1941. This voluminous study thus outlined the powers removed from the tribes and highlighted those remaining with them. This work in essence codified the position of Native America within the U.S. legal system. Over the past few decades, this work has been amended and updated several times to take account of tribal authority, federal legislation, and Supreme Court case law since the 1940s.

   Other books offer contemporary insight into the opinions of the Supreme Court and its effect on the precedents and the principles used in federal Indian law. See Monroe E. Price, *Law and the American Indian: Readings, Notes, and Cases* (Indianapolis, Ind.: Bobbs-Merrill, 1973); William C. Canby Jr., *American Indian Law in a Nutshell* (St. Paul, Minn.: West, 1998); Stephen L. Pevar, *The Rights of Indians and Tribes: The Authoritative ACLU Guide to Indian and Tribal Rights*, 3rd ed. (Carbondale: Southern Illinois University Press, 2002); and David H. Getches, Charles F. Wilkinson, and Robert A. Williams Jr., *Federal Indian Law: Cases and Materials*, 3rd ed. (St. Paul, Minn.: West, 1993). All of these provide a good reference point for the determination of contemporary tribal rights. The writings give detailed accounts of Supreme Court case law and the effect of the case law, federal legislation, and treaties on the law as a whole.
5. Russel Lawrence Barsh and James Youngblood Henderson, *The Road: Indian Tribes and Political Liberty* (Berkeley: University of California Press, 1980); David E. Wilkins, *American Indian Sovereignty and the U.S. Supreme Court: The Masking of Justice* (Aus-

tin: University of Texas Press, 1997); Frank Pommersheim, *Braid of Feathers: American Indian Law and Contemporary Tribal Life* (Berkeley: University of California Press, 1995); Erin Hogan Fouberg, *Tribal Territory, Sovereignty, and Governance: A Study of the Cheyenne River and Lake Traverse Indian Reservations* (New York: Garland, 2000).

6. Charles F. Wilkinson, *American Indians, Time, and the Law* (New Haven: Yale University Press, 1987); Vine Deloria Jr. and Clifford M. Lytle, *American Indians, American Justice* (Austin: University of Texas Press, 1983); Petra T. Shattuck and Jill Norgren, *Partial Justice: Federal Indian Law in a Liberal Constitutional System* (Providence: Berg, 1993).

7. Robert A. Williams Jr., *Like a Loaded Weapon: The Rehnquist Court, Indian Rights, and the Legal History of Racism in America* (Minneapolis: University of Minnesota Press, 2005). The use of racism in Supreme Court decisions is also examined, although not exhaustively, in James E. Falkowski, *Indian Law/Race Law: A Five-Hundred-Year History* (New York: Praeger, 1992); and Robert A. Williams Jr., *The American Indian in Western Legal Thought: The Discourse of Conquest* (New York: Oxford University Press, 1990). See also Sidney L. Harring, *Crow Dog's Case: American Indian Sovereignty, Tribal Law, and United States Law in the Nineteenth Century* (New York: Cambridge University Press, 1994); and David E. Wilkins and K. Tsianina Lomawaima, *Uneven Ground: American Indian Sovereignty and Federal Law* (Norman: University of Oklahoma Press, 2001).

8. David H. Getches, "Conquering the Cultural Frontier: The New Subjectivism of the Supreme Court in Indian Law," *California Law Review* 84 (1996): 1573–655; L. Scott Gould, "The Consent Paradigm: Tribal Sovereignty at the Millennium," *Columbia Law Review* 96 (1996): 809–902; Philip P. Frickey, "A Common Law for Our Age of Colonialism: The Judicial Divestiture of Indian Tribal Authority over Nonmembers," *Yale Law Journal* 109 (1999): 1–85.

9. Philip P. Frickey, "Adjudication and Its Discontents: Coherence and Conciliation in Federal Indian Law," *Harvard Law Review* 110 (1997): 1754–84; Joseph William Singer, "Sovereignty and Property," *Northwestern University Law Review* 86 (1991): 1–56; John Fredericks III, "America's First Nations: The Origins, History and Future of American Indian Sovereignty," *Journal of Law and Policy* 7 (1999): 347–410.

10. N. Bruce Duthu, "The Thurgood Marshall Papers and the Quest for a Principled Theory of Tribal Sovereignty: Fueling the Fires of Tribal/State Conflict," *Vermont Law Review* 21 (1996): 47–110; Sarah Krakoff, "Undoing Indian Law One Case at a Time: Judicial Minimalism and Tribal Sovereignty," *American University Law Review* 50 (2001): 1177–268; Daniel I. S. J. Rey-Bear, "The Flathead Water Quality Standards Dispute: Legal Bases for Tribal Regulatory Authority over Non-Indian Reservation Lands," *American Indian Law Review* 20 (1996): 151–224; Frank Pommersheim, "Coyote Paradox: Some Indian Law Reflections from the Edge of the Prairie," *Arizona State Law Journal* 31 (1999): 439–81; Robert N. Clinton, "State Power over Indian Reservations: A Critical Comment on Burger Court Decisions," *South Dakota Law Review* 26 (1981): 434–46; Robert Laurence, "Symmetry and Asymmetry in Federal Indian Law," *Arizona Law Review* 42 (2000) 861–934; Blake A. Watson, "The Thrust and Parry of Federal Indian Law," *University of Dayton Law Review* 23 (1998): 437–514; Robert A. Williams Jr., "The Algebra of Federal Indian Law: The Hard Trail of Decolonizing and Ameri-

canizing the White Man's Indian Jurisprudence," *Wisconsin Law Review* 1986 (1986): 219–99; Skibine, "Court's Use."

11. The William J. Brennan papers are still, in part, restricted. In 2005 the case files from 1975 to 1985 were opened. Although the Powell papers have been available with required permissions for several years, they are now open due to the death of Justice Antonin Scalia in 2016.

12. Clinton, "State Power," 445.

Chapter 1

1. For a comprehensive and fascinating examination of the period from the eighteenth century to 1959, I recommend Barsh and Henderson, *Road*. These authors also detail federal Indian law opinions of the Supreme Court from 1959 to 1980.

2. John Marshall, born in Virginia, was nominated for office by President John Adams and was sworn in as chief justice in 1801. He served more than thirty-four years and authored more than five hundred opinions; his contribution to American constitutional law is formidable. Oyez Project at IIT Chicago–Kent College of Law, www.oyez.org/justices (hereafter Oyez Project), s.v. "John Marshall."

3. See Dewi Ioan Ball and Joy Porter, eds., *Competing Voices from Native America* (Santa Barbara, Calif.: Greenwood Press, 2009).

4. These ideological differences between the justices during the early nineteenth century formed the beginning of the debate about tribal sovereignty over lands and peoples on reservations in light of federal power and state rights.

5. "Plenary power" in this context means unlimited control over the tribes, with the potential to revoke part or all of the characteristics of tribal sovereignty. This tribal-federal relationship was exclusive and did not involve state authority. See Wilkins, *American Indian Sovereignty*.

6. Ann E. Tweedy, "Connecting the Dots between the Constitution, the Marshall Trilogy, and United States v. Lara: Notes toward a Blueprint for the Next Legislative Restoration of Tribal Sovereignty," *University of Michigan Journal of Law Reform* 42 (2009): 651–717; Gloria Valencia-Weber, "The Supreme Court's Indian Law Decisions: Deviations from Constitutional Principles and the Crafting of Judicial Smallpox Blankets," *University of Pennsylvania Journal of Constitutional Law* 5 (2003): 405–82.

7. See *Talton v. Mayes*, 163 U.S. 376 (1896).

8. *United States Statutes at Large* 16 (1871): 566.

9. Today there is great skepticism about whether the U.S. Constitution granted the United States authority to interfere in Native American affairs. The Supreme Court case *United States v. Lara* (2004) opened a debate about whether Congress has the authority (plenary power) to deal with Native American affairs and whether sovereignty that is extinguished by the Court itself can be delegated back to Native American tribes.

10. Johnson v. McIntosh, 21 U.S. 543 (1823). For an in-depth examination of the case, see Lindsay G. Robertson, *Conquest by Law: How the Discovery of America Dispossessed Indigenous Peoples of Their Lands* (New York: Oxford University Press, 2005); and Blake A. Watson, *Buying American from the Indians: Johnson v. McIntosh and the History of Native Land Rights* (Norman: University of Oklahoma Press, 2012). See also Walter R.

Echo-Hawk, *In the Courts of the Conqueror: The 10 Worst Indian Law Cases Ever Decided* (Golden, Colo.: Fulcrum, 2010).

11. Getches, Wilkinson, and Williams, *Federal Indian Law*.

12. Hope M. Babcock, "A Civic-Republican Vision of 'Domestic Dependent Nations' in the Twenty-First Century: Tribal Sovereignty Re-envisioned, Reinvigorated, and Re-empowered," *Utah Law Review* 2005 (2005): 472.

13. *Johnson v. McIntosh*, 574.

14. Frickey, "Common Law," 9.

15. *Johnson v. McIntosh*, 592.

16. Joseph C. Burke, "The Cherokee Cases: A Study in Law, Politics, and Morality," *Stanford Law Review* 21 (1969): 502–3.

17. *Johnson v. McIntosh*, 572–73.

18. This view is supported by Peter d'Errico in "American Indian Sovereignty: Now You See It, Now You Don't," Legal Studies Department, University of Massachusetts/ Amherst, unpublished paper delivered as the inaugural lecture at the American Indian Civics Project, Humboldt State University, California, October 24, 1997. D'Errico points out that the sophistry of Marshall's opinion cloaked the superiority of the Christian religion over tribal rights within the rhetoric of American expansionism.

19. Cherokee Nation v. Georgia, 30 U.S. 1 (1831).

20. Ibid., 15.

21. Ibid., 16.

22. Ibid., 17.

23. Robert B. Porter, "The Meaning of Indigenous Nation Sovereignty," *Arizona State Law Journal* 34 (2002): 82.

24. Burke, "Cherokee Cases," 514.

25. *Cherokee Nation v. Georgia*, 17.

26. Ibid., 21, 27–28. William Johnson was a Republican who was nominated by President Jefferson and sworn in to office as an associate justice in 1804. Oyez Project, s.v. "William Johnson."

27. *Cherokee Nation v. Georgia*, 39. Henry Baldwin was sworn in to office as an associate justice in 1830 after being nominated by President Jackson. Previously, Baldwin had supported Jackson in his bid for the presidency. Oyez Project, s.v. "Henry Baldwin."

28. *Cherokee Nation v. Georgia*, 47–50.

29. Smith Thompson was nominated by President Monroe and sworn in as an associate justice in 1823. Oyez Project, s.v. "Smith Thompson."

30. Joseph Story was nominated for office by President Madison and served as an associate justice from 1812 until 1845. Oyez Project, s.v. "Joseph Story."

31. *Cherokee Nation v. Georgia*, 53. Justice Thompson cited Emmerich de Vattel, a Swiss jurist who applied a theory of natural law to international relations. Thompson argued that the Cherokees were a foreign state because they met Vattel's description of a state and nation:

    The terms "state" and "nation" are used in the law of nations, as well as in common parlance, as importing the same thing, and imply a body of men, united together to procure their mutual safety and advantage by means of their union. Such a society has its affairs and interests to manage; it deliberates, and takes resolutions in common, and thus becomes a moral person, having an understanding and a will peculiar to itself, and is susceptible of obligations and laws. Vattel 1. Nations being composed of men naturally free and independent, and who, before the establishment of civil societies, live together in the state of nature, nations or sovereign states, are to be considered as so many free persons, living together in a state of nature. Vattel 2, § 4. Every nation that governs itself, under what form soever, without any dependence on a foreign power is a sovereign state. Its rights are naturally the same as those of any other state. Such are moral persons who live together in a natural society under the law of nations. It is sufficient if it be really sovereign and independent—that is, it must govern itself by its own authority and laws. (52–53)

32. Ibid., 74.

33. Justice Thompson wrote:

If we look to the whole course of treatment by this country of the Indians from the year 1775 to the present day when dealing with them in their aggregate capacity as nations or tribes and regarding the mode and manner in which all negotiations have been carried on and concluded with them, the conclusion appears to me irresistible that they have been regarded, by the Executive and Legislative branches of the Government, not only as sovereign and independent, but as foreign nations or tribes, not within the jurisdiction nor under the government of the States within which they were located. (Ibid., 59)

34. Ibid., 70.

35. Burke, "Cherokee Cases," 514.

36. Worcester v. Georgia, 31 U.S. 515 (1832). See Jill Norgren, *The Cherokee Cases: The Confrontation of Law and Politics* (New York: McGraw-Hill, 1996); Shattuck and Norgren, *Partial Justice*; Williams, *American Indian*; and Burke, "Cherokee Cases."

37. John McLean was nominated by President Jackson and sworn in as an associate justice in 1830. Oyez Project, s.v. "John McLean."

38. *Worcester v. Georgia*, 596: "Mr Justice Baldwin dissented, stating that, in his opinion, the record was not properly returned upon the writ of error, and ought to have been returned by the State court, and not by the clerk of that Court. As to the merits, he said his opinion remained the same as was expressed by him in the case of the *Cherokee Nation v. The State of Georgia* at the last term. The opinion of Mr Justice Baldwin was not delivered to the reporter."

39. Ibid., 543–44.

40. Ibid., 544.

41. Ibid., 544–45.

42. Joseph Burke, "Cherokee Cases," 531, writes that the contradiction between the Marshall opinions in *Worcester* and *Cherokee Nation* was based on the view that conditions in 1832 offered a more favorable legal, political, and moral climate to advance Native American rights than in 1831. Vine Deloria and Clifford A. Lytle, *American Indians*, 32, support this notion by arguing that the *Worcester* opinion aligned itself with the dissents of Justices Thompson and Story in *Cherokee Nation* in 1831.

43. Charles J. Kappler, ed., *Indian Affairs: Laws and Treaties*, vol. 2: *Treaties* (Washington, D.C.: Government Printing Office, 1904), 3–5.

44. *Worcester v. Georgia*, 550.

45. Ibid., 551–52.

46. Ibid., 552.

47. Ibid., 556–57.

48. Nell Jessup Newton, "Federal Power over Indians: Its Sources, Scope, and Limitations," *University of Pennsylvania Law Review* 132 (1984): 202.

49. *Worcester v. Georgia*, 561.

50. Ibid., 562–63.

51. David H. Getches, "Conquering the Cultural Frontier," 1582, notes that the *Worcester* case "lays the cornerstone for the legal system's continuing recognition of tribal sovereignty."

52. *Worcester v. Georgia*, 580.

53. Ibid., 581, 592.

54. Although removal forced many tribes to the west of the Mississippi, some tribes stayed east and remain there today.

55. *United States Statutes at Large* 4 (1846): 411.

56. United States v. Rogers, 45 U.S. 567 (1846).

57. Roger B. Taney was nominated by President Jackson and sworn in as chief justice in 1836. Oyez Project, s.v. "Roger B. Taney."

58. *United States v. Rogers*, 572, 567.

59. Theodore H. Haas, "The Legal Aspects of Indian Affairs from 1887 to 1957," *Annals of the American Academy of Political and Social Science* 311 (1957): 12–22; Janet A. Mc-Donnell, *The Dispossession of the American Indian* (Bloomington: Indiana University Press, 1991).

60. David Murray, *Modern Indians: Native Americans in the Twentieth Century* (England: British Association for American Studies, 1982), 12.

61. Virgil J. Vogel, *This Country Was Ours: A Documentary History of the American Indian* (New York: Harper and Row, 1972), 193.

62. Senate Committee on Indian Affairs, *Rulings of the U.S. Supreme Court as They Affect the Powers and Authorities of the Indian Tribal Governments: Hearing on the Concerns of Recent Decisions of the U.S. Supreme Court and the Future of Indian Tribal Governments in America*, 107th Cong., 2d sess., February 27, 2002, 45.

63. In *The Road*, Barsh and Henderson explain that the erosion of tribal sovereignty and the use of federal authority by the Supreme Court to determine federal Indian law cases began in the 1870s.

64. *United States v. McBratney*, 104 U.S. 621 (1881). See Harring, *Crow Dog's Case*, 54.

65. *Draper v. United States*, 164 U.S. 240 (1896). See Canby, *American Indian Law*, 131–32.

66. See also *Utah & Northern R. Co. v. Fisher*, 116 U.S. 28 (1885); and *Thomas v. Gay*, 169 U.S. 264 (1898).

67. *United States v. McBratney*, 624.

68. *United States v. Kagama*, 118 U.S. 375 (1886).

69. Harring, *Crow Dog's Case*, 142.

70. *United States v. Kagama,* 383–84. Samuel F. Miller was nominated by President Lincoln and sworn in as an associate justice in 1862. Oyez Project, s.v. "Samuel F. Miller."

71. Lone Wolf v. Hitchcock, 187 U.S. 553 (1903).

72. See Echo-Hawk, *In the Courts of the Conqueror.*

73. *Lone Wolf v. Hitchcock,* 564. Edward D. White was nominated by President Cleveland and sworn in as an associate justice in 1894. Oyez Project, s.v. "Edward D. White."

74. *Lone Wolf v. Hitchcock,* 566.

75. The Kansas Indians, 72 U.S. 737 (1867).

76. Ibid., 755–56.

77. Ibid., 757, 760.

78. The New York Indians, 72 U.S. 761 (1867).

79. Ibid., 770–71.

80. Ex parte Crow Dog, 109 U.S. 556 (1883). See Harring, *Crow Dog's Case.*

81. Talton v. Mayes, 163 U.S. 376 (1896).

82. Ibid., 384–85.

83. Morris v. Hitchcock, 194 U.S. 384 (1904).

84. Ibid., 393, 389. The opinion also read, "The Act of the Chickasaw Nation, approved by the Governor May 5, 1902, and by the President of the United States May 15, 1902, prescribing privilege or permit taxes, and the regulations of the Secretary of the Interior of June 3, 1902, governing the introduction by noncitizens of livestock in the Chickasaw Nation are valid, and not an exercise of arbitrary power, and they do not in any respect violate the Constitution of the United States" (384).

85. Vine Deloria Jr. and Clifford M. Lytle, *The Nations Within: The Past and Future of American Indian Sovereignty* (Austin: University of Texas Press, 1984).

86. John Howard Clinebell and Jim Thomson, "Sovereignty and Self-Determination: The Rights of Native Americans under International Law," *Buffalo Law Review* 27 (1978): 682.

87. In this period the Supreme Court decided Carpenter v. Shaw, 280 U.S. 363 (1930); United States v. Creek Nation, 295 U.S. 103 (1935); United States v. Shoshone Tribe of Indians, 304 U.S. 111 (1938); Tulee v. Washington, 315 U.S. 681 (1942); Seminole Nation v. United States, 316 U.S. 286 (1942); and Oklahoma Tax Commission v. United States, 319 U.S. 598 (1943).

88. Dalia Tsuk Mitchell, *Architect of Justice: Felix S. Cohen and the Founding of American Legal Pluralism* (Ithaca, N.Y.: Cornell University Press, 2007).

89. Frickey, "Common Law," 8.

90. Cohen, *Handbook,* 123.

91. Barsh and Henderson, *Road,* 113.

92. Cohen, *Handbook,* 123.

93. Brown v. Board of Education, 347 U.S. 483 (1954), 495; Plessy v. Ferguson, 163 U.S. 537 (1896).

94. Termination was characterized by three pieces of congressional legislation: House Concurrent Resolution 108 (1953), Public Law 280 (1953), and the Relocation Act of 1956.

95. Arthur V. Watkins, "Termination of Federal Supervision: The Removal of Restrictions over Indian Property and Person," *Annals of the American Academy of Political and Social Science* 311 (1957): 55.

96. Ruth Muskrat Bronson, "Ruth Muskrat Bronson Criticizes the Proposed Termination of Federal Trusteeship, 1955," in *Major Problems in American Indian History*, 2d ed., ed. Albert L. Hurtado and Peter Iverson (Boston: Wadsworth, 2001), 423.

97. Tee-Hit-Ton Indians v. United States, 348 U.S. 272 (1955).

98. However, the Tee-Hit-Ton Indians had a statutory cause of action for compensation under the Indian Claims Commission Act of 1946 for the taking of aboriginal lands.

99. Wilkinson, *American Indians*, 1.

Chapter 2

1. In *Road*, Barsh and Henderson view *Williams v. Lee* (1959) as one in a long line of cases from the early 1870s that relied on the use of federal authority to determine a federal Indian law case before the Supreme Court.

2. Dewi Ioan Ball, "Williams v. Lee (1959)—50 Years Later: A Reassessment of One of the Most Important Cases in the Modern-Era of Federal Indian Law," *Michigan State Law Review* 2010: 391–412.

3. Wilkins, *American Indian Sovereignty*, 376, defines tribal sovereignty as "the spiritual, moral, and dynamic cultural force within a given tribal community empowering the group toward political, economic, and, most importantly, cultural integrity; as well as maturity in the group's relationship with its own members, with other peoples and their governments, and with the environment."

4. "Bench Memo, No. 71-834-ASX, McClanahan, et al. v. Arizona State Tax Comm'n, Appeal from Arizona Court of Appeals, April 28, 1971; 14 Ariz. App. 452; 484 P.2d 221, Pet for review denied by Ariz Sup Ct on Sept 21, 1971," RIM, December 6 1972, 11, Box 156, Harry A. Blackmun Papers, Manuscript Division, Library of Congress, Washington, D.C. (hereafter Blackmun Papers).

5. "71-834—McClanahan v. State Tax Comm'n, of Arizona," W.O.D., Conference, December 15, 1972, 1, Box 1574, William O. Douglas Papers, Manuscript Division, Library of Congress, Washington, D.C. (hereafter Douglas Papers).

   Potter Stewart was nominated by President Eisenhower and sworn in as an associate justice in 1958. After serving in World War II, he entered private legal practice and local politics as a Republican in Cincinnati. In 1954 he was appointed to the U.S. Court of Appeals for the Sixth Circuit. During his time as a justice, Stewart was a centrist, voting with liberals on some issues and conservatives on others. Supreme Court of Ohio and the Ohio Judicial System, "Potter Stewart (Jan. 23, 1915-Dec. 7, 1985)," www.supremecourt.ohio.gov/MJC/places/pStewart.asp (accessed June 15, 2015).

6. Therefore, this analysis of one of the major post–World War II federal Indian law cases ties in with the dominant position taken by many scholars in Native American studies, specifically that the *Williams* opinion resulted in a positive outcome for Native America. See, Canby, *American Indian Law*; Frickey, "Common Law"; Getches, "Conquering the Cultural Frontier"; and Wilkinson, *American Indians*.

7. This process develops the interpretations of Canby, Frickey, Getches, Wilkinson, Barsh, and Henderson and builds on the interpretations of two noted scholars who have reassessed the positive interpretation of *Williams*. Although Wilkins, *American Indian Sovereignty*, 276, believes that Navajo sovereignty was reaffirmed by the *Williams* court, the language used in the opinion "departed from the *Worcester* ruling of

complete state exclusion from Indian country by holding that the states might be allowed to extend their jurisdiction into tribal trust land" of the reservation, unless it did not affect tribal government. Therefore, the uncertainty created by the Supreme Court, he argues, "dulled the emphatic *Worcester* holding" and along with *Warren Trading Post* and *McClanahan,* two other cases discussed later, weakened, and forever changed the relationship between the tribes and the States of the Union. Gould, "Consent Paradigm," 823–24, concurs with Wilkins's opinion that the Supreme Court relied on inherent tribal sovereignty but disagrees over the negative use of Supreme Court language. Gould argues that the circumstances involved in *Williams* weakened the broad language used by the Court to reaffirm the Indian sovereignty doctrine and concludes that if the reservation population had contained more nonmembers then the Supreme Court would not have relied on tribal sovereignty, and that the willingness of the Supreme Court to allow state authority onto the reservation fundamentally weakened tribal sovereignty. Wilkins and Gould suggest that in 1959 the Supreme Court began to move away from the sovereignty doctrine.

8. Many scholars argue that the change in the philosophy of the Supreme Court away from the sovereignty doctrine began during the 1970s and 1980s. There are diverse interpretations about the beginnings of the fundamental shift. See Senate Committee, *Rulings of the U.S. Supreme Court,* 40–41 (Robert T. Anderson), 45 (Willian C. Canby Jr.), 88 (Robert Yazzie); Jordan Burch, "How Much Diversity Is the United States Really Willing to Accept?" *Ohio Northern University Law Review* 20 (1994): 965; Deloria and Lytle, *American Indians,* 54; Gould, "Consent Paradigm," 895; Peter Maxfield, "Oliphant v. Suquamish Tribe: The Whole Is Greater than the Sum of the Parts," *Journal of Contemporary Law* 19 (1993): 396; Joseph William Singer, "Canons of Conquest: The Supreme Court's Attack on Tribal Sovereignty," *New England Law Review* 37 (2003), 649–50; Singer, "Sovereignty and Property," 3; Frank Pommersheim and John P. LaVelle, "Toward a Great Sioux Nation Judicial Support Center and Supreme Court," *Wicazo Sa Review* 17 (2002): 195; Judith V. Royster, "The Legacy of Allotment," *Arizona State Law Journal* 27 (1995): 44; Laurie Reynolds, "'Jurisdiction' in Federal Indian Law: Confusion, Contradiction, and Supreme Court Precedent," *New Mexico Law Review* 27 (1997): 359–86; Krakoff, "Undoing Indian Law"; David H. Getches, "Conquering the Cultural Frontier," 1592–95; Getches, "Beyond Indian Law: The Rehnquist Court's Pursuit of States' Rights, Color-Blind Justice and Mainstream Values," *Minnesota Law Review* 86 (2001): 267, 273–74; David J. Bloch, "Colonizing the Last Frontier," *American Indian Law Review* 29 (2004): 1; Robert N. Clinton, "The Dormant Indian Commerce Clause," *Connecticut Law Review* 27 (1995): 1057; Ralph W. Johnson and Berrie Martinis, "Chief Justice Rehnquist and the Indian Cases," *Public Land Law Review* 16 (1995): 1–25; and Krakoff, "Undoing Indian Law," 1205.

9. Duthu, "Thurgood Marshall Papers," uses the Marshall papers to examine the broad subject areas of taxation and criminal and civil jurisdiction case law from 1973 and argues that the workings of the Supreme Court were an aberration from the Indian sovereignty doctrine. In "Conquering the Cultural Frontier" Getches uses, in part, both the Thurgood Marshall papers and the William J. Brennan papers to provide insight into four key cases decided between 1978 and 1989 and observes that a 1990 memorandum from Justice Antonin Scalia to Justice William J. Brennan, according to which Scalia

was going to decide opinions on what he felt was best at the time, is proof that the Court was moving away from the sovereignty doctrine. See also Bethany Berger, "Williams v. Lee and the Debate over Indian Equality," *Michigan Law Review* 109 (2010): 1463–528; Berger uses limited information from these papers to discuss the *Williams* case.

10. The description of Supreme Court procedures in this section draws from Edward Lazarus, *Closed Chambers: The Rise, Fall and Future of the Modern Supreme Court* (New York: Penguin Books, 1999); Paul J. Wahlbeck, "Strategy and Constraints on Supreme Court Opinion Assignment," *University of Pensylvannia Law Review* 154 (2006): 1729–55; Supreme Court Opinion Writing Database, "The Opinion-Writing Process," http://supremecourtopinions.wustl.edu/ (accessed June 15, 2015); and David M. O'Brien, *Storm Center: The Supreme Court in American Politics*, 3rd ed. (New York: W. W. Norton, 1993).

11. Lazarus, *Closed Chambers*, 17–18.

12. Williams v. Lee, 358 U.S. 217 (1959), 217–18.

13. Frickey, "Common Law," 29.

14. "1957 Term No. 811, Williams v. Lee, No. 39, Cert to Supreme Court of Arizona," n.d., Box 1201, Douglas Papers.

15. "No. 39, 1958 Term, Williams v. Lee," DMC, 1, Box 188, Earl Warren Papers, Manuscript Division, Library of Congress, Washington, D.C. (hereafter Warren Papers). Earl Warren was nominated by President Eisenhower and sworn in as the fourteenth chief justice of the Supreme Court in 1953. Warren served as a Republican governor before his appointment to the Supreme Court. Although Eisenhower expected Warren to serve as a moderate conservative, instead he became a liberal, with a dedication to the principle of equality for over fifteen years. Oyez Project, s.v. "Earl Warren."

16. "No. 39, 1958 Term, Williams v. Lee," DMC, 2, Box 188, Warren Papers.

17. "Conference November 21, 1958, No. 39–Williams v. Lee," W.O.D., Box 1201, Douglas Papers. Charles Whittaker was sworn in as an associate justice in 1957 after being nominated by President Eisenhower. Whittaker, a Republican and conservative, previously served as a trial judge and became a judge at the Eighth Circuit Court of Appeals in 1956. Oyez Project, s.v. "Charles E. Whittaker."

18. "No. 39, 1958 Term," DMC, 2, Box 188, Warren Papers.

19. "Bench Memo, No. 39, 1958 Term, Williams v. Lee," MAF, 2, 3, Box 188, Warren Papers.

20. "No. 39, 1958 Term, Williams v. Lee," DMC, 2, Box 188, Warren Papers.

21. Williams v. Lee, 319 P.2d 998, 1001 (Ariz. 1958).

22. "No. 39, 1958 Term," DMC, 2–3, Box 188, Douglas Papers.

23. "1957 Term No. 811, Williams v. Lee, No. 39, Cert to Supreme Court of Arizona," n.d., Box 1201, Douglas Papers. William Orville Douglas was nominated as an associate justice by President Franklin Roosevelt and sworn in during 1939. Previously, Douglas, a liberal, had served as a law professor and on the Securities and Exchange Commission. He was nearly chosen as Roosevelt's running mate in the presidential election of 1944. An avid defender of individual rights with a distrust of government power, Douglas served for over thirty-six years, a record for continuous service on the Court. Oyez Project, s.v. "William O. Douglas."

24. "No. 39, 1958 Term," DMC, 2–3, Box 188, Douglas Papers.

25. "Bench Memo, No. 39, 1958 Term, Williams v. Lee," MAF, 5–6, Box 188, Warren Papers.

26. Ibid., 6–7. Public Law 280 involved the transfer of legal authority from the federal government to state governments. Initially, five states—California, Minnesota (except for the Red Lake Reservation), Nebraska, Oregon (except for the Warm Springs Reservation), and Wisconsin (except for the Menominee Reservation)—were granted extensive criminal and civil jurisdiction over tribal lands, and then Alaska, upon statehood, would also become the sixth state to have this authority. Other states were offered the opportunity of enacting Public Law 280, but tribal consent was required.

27. Ibid., 7–8.

28. William J. Brennan was sworn in as an associate justice in 1956 after being nominated by President Eisenhower. After completing a law degree at Harvard, he worked as a lawyer in New Jersey. Later he became a trial judge, and in 1952 he was promoted to the Supreme Court of New Jersey. In 1956, President Eisenhower wanted to appoint a Democrat to the Supreme Court to appear bipartisan for the 1956 presidential election, and in the end he settled on Brennan, a moderate. However, Brennan became the most liberal and influential justice on the modern Supreme Court, and Eisenhower later stated that the appointment was a mistake. Brennan served for over thirty-three years. Oyez Project, s.v. "William J. Brennan, Jr."; Melvin I. Urofsky, ed., *The Supreme Court Justices: A Biographical Dictionary* (New York: Garland, 1994).

29. "Conference November 21, 1958," W.O.D., Box 1201, Douglas Papers.

30. "Paul Williams and Lorena Williams, Husband and Wife, Petitioners vs. Hugh Lee, Doing Business as Ganado Trading Post," W.J.B., n.d., Box I:15, William J. Brennan Papers, Manuscript Division, Library of Congress, Washington, D.C. (hereafter Brennan Papers).

31. "Conference November 21, 1958," W.O.D., Box 1201, Douglas Papers; "Paul Williams and Lorena Williams, Husband and Wife, Petitioners vs. Hugh Lee, Doing Business as Ganado Trading Post," W.J.B., n.d., Box I:15, Brennan Papers.

32. "Conference November 21, 1958," W.O.D., Box 1201, Douglas Papers.

33. Hugo Lafayette Black was sworn in as an associate justice in 1937 after being nominated by President Franklin Roosevelt. Black was born and raised in Alabama and pursued a career in law after a year in medical school. After law school, he worked as a municipal court judge, a prosecuting attorney, and a private practitioner. During this time, he joined the Klu Klux Klan but soon rescinded his membership. In 1927 he was elected to the U.S. Senate as a Democrat and vigorously advocated the New Deal policies of President Roosevelt. Black, a southern progressive, was the first appointment of President Roosevelt to the Court and served for thirty-four years. He is now viewed as one of the most influential justices of the modern age; he interpreted the U.S. Constitution as literally as possible and was committed to judicial restraint. Oyez Project, s.v. "Hugo Lafayette Black"; Urofsky, *Supreme Court Justices*.

34. "Letter from Hugo Black to Murray Lincoln, June 14, 1965," Box 34, Hugo Lafayette Black Papers, Manuscript Division, Library of Congress, Washington, D.C. (hereafter Black Papers).

35. Felix Frankfurter was nominated as an associate justice by President Roosevelt and sworn in during 1939. He was born in Austria and raised in New York. After Harvard Law School, he worked as a private legal practitioner and entered government service

on more than one occasion. After ending his government service, Frankfurter accepted a position at Harvard Law School. As a member of the Supreme Court, he was an expert in constitutional law and advised President Roosevelt. Oyez Project, s.v. "Felix Frankfurter."

36. "Memorandum from Felix Frankfurter to Hugo Black, December 23, 1958," Box 338, Black Papers.

37. "Memorandum from Earl Warren to Hugo Black, January 5, 1959," Box 457, Warren Papers.

38. "Conference November 21, 1958," Box 1201, Douglas Papers.

39. "Draft to published opinion of Williams v. Lee," December 23, 1958, Box 457, Warren Papers. See also *Williams v. Lee*, 219–20.

40. "Draft (Re-circulated) of Williams v. Lee," January 10, 1959, Box I:19, Brennan Papers. See also *Williams v. Lee*, 220. This was the *Williams* infringement test used to determine whether state law was applicable over both tribal members and nonmembers on the reservation. If congressional legislation did not oust state law, then the question was whether state law infringed on the tribe. The infringement test was interpreted in two ways. First, it was read as a test that supported inherent tribal sovereignty: tribes had inherent sovereignty unless attributes of that sovereignty were revoked by an act of Congress; also, the tribes retained sovereignty on the reservation until it was proved that state action did not affect the tribe. Second, it was read as a test that supported the general presence of state law on the reservation until it was proved that state law infringed on the tribe.

41. Canby, *American Indian Law*, 243–44.

42. "Draft (Re-circulated) of Williams v. Lee," January 10, 1959, Box I:19, Brennan Papers. See also *Williams v. Lee*, 217–18.

43. Alex Tallchief Skibine, "Reconciling Federal and State Power inside Indian Reservations with the Right of Tribal Self-Government and the Process of Self-Determination," *Utah Law Review*, no. 4 (1995): 1148.

44. Frickey, "Common Law," 29, described this as a process "which could be dislodged only by agreement or statute, not by judicial decision."

45. "Draft (Re-circulated) of Williams v. Lee," January 10, 1959, Box I:19, Brennan Papers. See also *Williams v. Lee*, 223. Two principles arise from the summation of Justice Black. First, a nonmember conducting business with a tribal member on a reservation directly affected the ability of the tribe to govern and the ability of tribal government to function. Tribal government was sanctioned by three factors: tribes enjoyed inherent powers or sovereignty; tribes had authority from treaties; and pursuant to the Indian Reorganization Act of 1934 Congress explicitly recognized the sovereign powers of the tribes. Second, tribal government authority over the reservation existed whether a member or a nonmember was involved. This could be revoked only explicitly by Congress.

46. Canby, *American Indian Law*, 132, believes that the *Williams* case relied heavily on *Worcester* to prevent the application of state law on the reservation and in doing so held that concurrent jurisdiction interfered with tribal government.

47. Cohen, *Handbook of Federal Indian Law*, 123.

48. "Draft (Re-circulated) of Williams v. Lee," January 10, 1959, Box I:19, Brennan Papers.

See also *Williams v. Lee*, 222–23.

49. Allison M. Dussias, "Geographically-Based and Membership-Based Views of Indian Tribal Sovereignty: The Supreme Court's Changing Vision," *University of Pittsburgh Law Review* 55 (1993): 48.

50. Ball, "Williams v. Lee"; Dewi Ioan Ball, "The Silent Revolution: How the Key Attributes of Tribal Power Have Been Fundamentally Eroded by the United States Supreme Court from 1973" (Ph.D. dissertation, University of Wales, Swansea, 2007), 59.

51. "1957 Term No. 811, Williams v. Lee, No. 39, Cert to Supreme Court of Arizona," n.d., Box 1201, Douglas Papers.

52. "Paul Williams and Lorena Williams, Husband and Wife, Petitioners vs. Hugh Lee, Doing Business as Ganado Trading Post," W.J.B., n.d., Box I:15, Brennan Papers.

53. "Conference November 21," W.O.D., Box 1201, Douglas Papers.

54. "Bench Memo, No. 39, 1958 Term, Williams v. Lee," MAF, 2, Box 188, Warren Papers.

55. "1957 Term No. 811, Williams v. Lee, No. 39, Cert to Supreme Court of Arizona," n.d., Box 1201, Douglas Papers.

56. "Paul Williams and Lorena Williams, Husband and Wife, Petitioners vs. Hugh Lee, Doing Business as Ganado Trading Post," W.J.B., n.d., Box I:15, Brennan Papers; "Conference November 21," W.O.D., Box 1201, Douglas Papers.

57. "Bench Memo, No. 39, 1958 Term, Williams v. Lee," MAF, 2, Box 188, Warren Papers.

58. Ibid., 8, 4, 5.

59. Ibid., 8, 4, 3.

60. Kake Village v. Egan, 369 U.S. 60 (1962).

61. "Bench Memo, No. 326, 1959 Term, Metlakatla Indian Community v. Egan, Appeal from DC for the State of Alaska Timely, No. 327, 1959 Term, Organized Village of Kake v. Egan, Appeal from DC for the State of Alaska Timely," MHB, n.d., 1, 18, 12, Box 218, Warren Papers.

62. The cases cited included Langford v. Monteith, 102 U.S. 145 (1880); United States v. McBratney, 104 U.S. 621 (1881); Utah & Northern R. Co. v. Fisher, 116 U.S. 28 (1885); United States v. Kagama, 118 U.S. 375 (1886); Draper v. United States, 164 U.S. 240 (1896); and Thomas v. Gay, 169 U.S. 264 (1898). See Royster, "Legacy of Allotment."

63. *Kake v. Egan*, 72.

64. Charles F. Wilkinson, *American Indians*, 27, writes that *Kake* reinvigorated a general principle from three historic cases, termed the "*Kagama-McBratney-Lone Wolf*" line of cases, which supported the destruction of the tribes and undermined tribal sovereignty such that the tribes were viewed as "fading entities moving toward extinction." This general interpretation is supported by Blake A. Watson, "Thrust and Parry," 463.

65. *Kake v. Egan*, 73, 74.

66. Ibid., 62–64.

67. Ibid., 76.

68. Canby, *American Indian Law*, 133.

69. *Kake v. Egan*, 75.

70. Canby, *American Indian Law*, 133–34.

71. *Kake v. Egan*, 75, quoting New York ex rel. Ray v. Martin, 326 U.S. 496 (1946), 499.

72. Ibid., 74–75. The Court also cited *Thomas v. Gay*, in which the it upheld an Oklahoma territorial tax on cattle owned by nonmembers on lands leased to them by Native

Americans. Because the tax was on leased lands, it was considered to be indirect and too remote to affect the interests of the tribe.

73. Metlakatla Indians v. Egan, 369 U.S. 45 (1962). In contrast to *Kake v. Egan*, this case involved the question of state authority over tribal members on a reservation.

74. "Bench Memo, No. 2, 1961 Term, Metlakatla Indian Community v. Egan, Appeal from SC Alaska Timely, No. 3, 1961 Term, Organized Village of Kake v. Egan, Appeal from SC Alaska Timely," RGG, December 8, 1961, 11, 13, Box 218, Warren Papers.

75. "No. 2–Metlakatla Indian Community v. Egan, No. 3 Organized Village of Kake v. Egan, Conference December 15, 1961," W.O.D., 1, Box 1265, Douglas Papers.

76. Ibid.; "No. 2, Metlakatla Indian Community v. Egan," W.J.B., Box I:60, Brennan Papers.

77. "Bench Memo, No. 2, 1961 Term," RGG, 13, Box 218, Warren Papers.

78. Opinion of Felix Frankfurter circulated to the Court on February 6, 1962, 14, Box I:62, Brennan Papers. See the opinion of *Metlakatla Indians v. Egan*, 58–59. The statement made by Senator Gruening, March 6, 1962, was attached to a memorandum from Felix Frankfurter to the Court on March 12, 1962.

79. Watson, "Thrust and Parry," 466.

80. Warren Trading Post v. Tax Comm'n, 380 U.S. 685 (1965).

81. "No. 115, Warren Trading Post v. Arizona State Tax Commission," W.J.B., Box I:113, Brennan Papers.

82. "Warren Trading Post Co. v. Arizona State Tax Comm'n/64 Term No. 115, Appeal from Ariz Sup Ct, Memo of US in support of applnt.," JSC, July 24, 1964, Box 1332, Douglas Papers.

83. "Bench Memo, No. 115, 1964 Term, Warren Trading Post Co. v. Arizona State Tax Comm'n., Appeal from SC of Ariz.," DMF, March 2, 1965, 11, Box 263, Warren Papers.

84. "Warren Trading Post draft opinion, 1 April 1965," 6, Box I:122, Brennan Papers.

85. Wilkins, *American Indian Sovereignty*, 277.

86. "Bench Memo, No. 115, 1964 Term, Warren Trading Post Co," DMF, 7, 8, Box 263, Warren Papers.

87. "Memo to the Chief Justice, No. 115, 1964 Term, Warren Trading Post Co. v. Arizona State Tax Comm'n, Opinion of Black, J.," DMF, April 7, 1965, 2, Box 526, Warren Papers.

88. Warren Trading Post v. Tax Comm'n draft opinion, April 27, 1965, Box I:122, Brennan Papers.

89. *Warren Trading Post v. Tax Comm'n*, 690–91.

90. Ibid., 687.

91. Kennerly v. District Court of Montana, 400 U.S. 423 (1971).

92. Ibid., 426–27, quoting *Williams v. Lee*, 220.

93. Richard Nixon, *Public Papers of the Presidents of the United States: Richard Nixon, 1970* (Washington D.C.: Government Printing Office, 1971), 565–67.

94. Wilkinson, *American Indians*, 91.

95. DeCoteau v. District County Court, 420 U.S. 425 (1975).

96. McClanahan v. Arizona State Tax Comm'n, 411 U.S. 164 (1973).

97. Canby believed that *McClanahan* began the process, which changed the application of the sovereignty doctrine on the reservation to the presumption that state law "extended into Indian country unless a positive federal law or policy excluded it"; see Senate Committee, *Rulings of the U.S. Supreme Courts*, 45–46.

98. "No. 71-834—McClanahan v. State Tax Commission of Arizona, Argued: December 12, 1972," H.A.B, Box 156, Blackmun Papers. William Rehnquist was nominated by President Nixon and sworn in as an associate justice in 1972. After Stanford Law School, he completed a clerkship in the Supreme Court, practiced law, and eventually became a Republican Party official in Phoenix. Rehnquist, a staunch conservative who had been raised in a deeply conservative home, campaigned vociferously against liberal initiatives such as school integration. In 1969 he became assistant attorney general of the Office of Legal Counsel in the Department of Justice. As an associate justice, Rehnquist strongly advocated states' rights, and he often clashed with Justices Blackmun, Brennan, and Marshall. In time, his dissenting opinions formed strong conservative ideas. In 1986 he was appointed chief justice and thereafter began the ideological shift of the Court to a very conservative institution. Oyez Project, s.v. "William H. Rehnquist."

99. "No. 71-834 McClanahan v. Arizona, Conf. 12/15/72," Box 7, Lewis F. Powell Jr. Archives, Washington and Lee University School of Law, Lexington, Virginia (hereafter Powell Papers).

100. "71-834—McClanahan v. State Tax Comm'n, of Arizona," W.O.D., Conference, December 15, 1972, 1, Box 1574, Douglas Papers.

101. Thurgood Marshall was nominated by President Johnson and sworn in as the first black associate justice in 1967. Marshall, born in Baltimore, studied law at Howard University and many years later became head of the Legal Defense and Education Fund for the National Association for the Advancement of Colored People. In 1954 he was chief counsel in *Brown v. Board of Education,* one of the most famous cases in Supreme Court history. He also served on the U.S. Court of Appeals for the Second Circuit and as solicitor general. A liberal, Marshall was strongly committed to freedom and equality and applied these principles for over twenty-three years of service on the Court. Oyez Project, s.v. "Thurgood Marshall."

102. "Memorandum to the Conference from Thurgood Marshall, Re: No. 71-1263—Kahn v. Arizona State Tax Commission, March 28, 1973," Box 156, Blackmun Papers. The *Kahn* case referred to is Kahn v. Arizona State Tax Commission, 411 U.S. 941 (1973).

103. Duthu, "Thurgood Marshall Papers," 70.

104. "Bench Memo, No. 71-834-ASX, McClanahan," RIM, 4, Box 156, Blackmun Papers.

105. Ibid., 14.

106. "No. 71-834, McClanahan v. State Tax Commission of Arizona," W.J.B., n.d., 1, Box I:380, Brennan Papers. Warren E. Burger was nominated by President Nixon and sworn in as chief justice in 1969. After law school, Burger worked in private legal practice and engaged in politics with the Republican Party. Later on, he worked in the Department of Justice before being nominated to the U.S. Court of Appeals for the District of Columbia Circuit in 1956. As chief justice, Burger often sided with the conservative faction of the Court, but on the whole he was a pragmatist. Oyez Project, s.v. "Warren E. Burger."

107. "No. 71-834, McClanahan v. State Tax Commission of Arizona," W.J.B., n.d., 1, Box I:380, Brennan Papers. Byron White was sworn in as an associate justice in 1962 after being nominated by President Kennedy. White played professional football for the Pittsburgh Panthers (later Steelers) and the Detroit Lions. After gaining a Rhodes

Scholarship and completing a law degree at Yale, White clerked in the Supreme Court and then committed to private legal practice. Thereafter, he helped his close friend John Kennedy win the presidency and served as deputy attorney general from 1961. Although he was nominated by a Democratic president, White generally served for over thirty-one years as a conservative justice; the shift of the Supreme Court to a conservative majority under Rehnquist suited White's political ideas. Oyez Project, s.v. "Byron R. White"; Sheldon Goldman, *Picking Federal Judges: Lower Court Selection from Roosevelt through Reagan* (New Haven: Yale University Press, 1999).

108. "71-834—McClanahan v. State Tax Comm'n, of Arizona," W.O.D., Conference, December 15, 1972, 1, Box 1574, Douglas Papers. Harry A. Blackmun was nominated as an associate justice by President Nixon and was sworn in during 1970. When he was a child in Minnesota, one of Blackmun's earliest friends was eventual chief justice Warren Burger. Blackmun completed a law degree at Harvard and soon clerked for a federal appeals court judge in Minneapolis before becoming a private law practitioner. In 1959, President Eisenhower appointed Blackmun to the U.S. Court of Appeals for the Eighth Circuit. As a lifelong Republican, Blackmun was nominated to the Supreme Court as a conservative justice, and initially he aligned himself with fellow conservative Burger. However, over time Blackmun sided more and more with the liberals on the Court and, ironically, became isolated in an increasingly conservative Court during the 1980s and 1990s. Oyez Project, s.v. "Harry A. Blackmun."

109. "No-71-834-ASX, McClanahan, et al v. Arizona State Tax Comm'n appeal," JTR to Blackmun, February 11, 1972, 3, Box 156, Blackmun Papers.

110. "No. 71-834-ASX McClanahan, et al v. Arizona State Tax Comm'n appeal . . . ," JTR, May 1, 1972, 5, Box 156, Blackmun Papers.

111. "Bench Memo, No. 71-834-ASX, McClanahan, et al. v. Arizona State Tax Comm'n," RIM, 12, Box 156, Blackmun Papers.

112. The legal position of the justices contrasts with the interpretation offered by Wilkins, *American Indian Sovereignty*, 277, about the basis of the *McClanahan* opinion. Wilkins points out that "Arizona's tax law was excluded [from the reservation] because of the doctrine of preemption, not because of the Navajo Nation's inherent sovereignty."

113. "No. 71-834, CA—Ariz., Div. One, Rosalind McClanahan, Etc, Appellant v. State Tax Commission of Arizona," February 18, 1972, Box I:380, Brennan Papers.

114. "No. 71-834, McClanahan v. State Tax Commission of Arizona," W.J.B., n.d., 2, Box I:380, Brennan Papers.

115. Memorandum from Rehnquist to Marshall, "Re: No. 71-834—McClanahan v. State Tax Commission," February 23, 1973, Box I:291, Brennan Papers.

116. "No. 71-834 OT 1971, McClanahan v. Arizona State Tax Comm. Appeal from Arizona Ct. of App." JHW (n.d.), 1, Box 7, Powell Papers. Lewis F. Powell Jr. was nominated by President Nixon and sworn in as an associate justice in 1972. He attended Washington and Lee University and Harvard University before entering private legal practice. In 1964 he was elected president of the American Bar Association. Although a lifelong Democrat, Powell was nominated by Nixon because the president wanted a southern justice on the Court. Powell was a moderate before he joined the Supreme Court, and this moderation continued as an associate justice. He was cast in the middle of liberals and conservatives, and as the Court moved to the right his ideas and

principles obstructed a further conservative shift. "Retired Justice Lewis Powell Dies at 90," *Washington Post,* August 26, 1988.

117. "Bench Memo No 71-1031-CSX, Tonasket v. Wash., et al," RIM, December 9, 1972, 47, Box 158, Blackmun Papers.

118. "Bench Memo, No. 71-834-ASX, McClanahan," RIM, 11–12, Box 156, Blackmun Papers.

119. The *Kake* case was the first of the modern era to emasculate *Worcester* based on assimilation and allotment case law. The second case to do so was *McClanahan.* Again, the cases cited by the Supreme Court were those cited in *Kake v. Egan.* The *McClanahan* court said, "Similarly, notions of Indian sovereignty have been adjusted to take account of the State's legitimate interests in regulating the affairs of non-Indians. See, e.g., New York ex rel. Ray v. Martin, 326 U.S. 496 (1946); Draper v. United States, 164 U.S. 240 (1896); Utah & Northern R. Co. v. Fisher, 116 U.S. 28 (1885)." *McClanahan v. Arizona State Tax Comm'n,* 171.

120. "Draft opinion 1973 (n.d.)," Box 102, Thurgood Marshall Papers, Manuscript Division, Library of Congress, Washington, D.C. (hereafter Marshall Papers). See also *McClanahan v. Arizona State Tax Comm'n,* 171.

121. John Arai Mitchell argues that the *McClanahan* opinion severely weakened both *Williams* and *Worcester* by allowing state law onto the reservation, noting that it left them "in a state of flux, as it appeared to change the direction of precluding state authority within the reservation. Thus by focusing on whether federal law preempted the state action, the opinion [*McClanahan*] reduced the capacity of the tribal rights of self-government to preclude state authority." "A World without Tribes? Tribal Rights of Self-Government and the Enforcement of State Court Orders in Indian Country," *University of Chicago Law Review* 61 (1994): 711.

122. The quotation was followed by, "But if the crime was by or against an Indian, tribal jurisdiction or that expressly conferred on other courts by Congress has remained exclusive. . . . Essentially, absent governing Acts of Congress, the question has always been whether the state action infringed on the right of reservation Indians to make their own laws and be ruled by them." *McClanahan v. Arizona State Tax Comm'n,* 171–72, quoting *Williams v Lee,* 219–20.

123. "No. 71-834, McClanahan v. State Tax Comm'n of Arizona, 1st Draft, Justice Marshall, Feb. 7," RIM, February 8, 1973, Box 156, Blackmun Papers.

124. "Draft opinion 1973 (n.d.)," Box 102, Marshall Papers. See also *McClanahan v. Arizona State Tax Comm'n,* 172.

125. See Duthu, "Thurgood Marshall Papers," 68.

126. On the Red Power movement, see Ball and Porter, *Competing Voices;* Troy Johnson, Joane Nagel, and Duane Champagne, eds., *American Indian Activism: Alcatraz to the Longest Walk* (Urbana: University of Illinois Press, 1997); Paul Chaat Smith and Robert Allen Warrior, *Like a Hurricane: The Indian Movement from Alcatraz to Wounded Knee* (New York: New Press, 1996); Kenneth S. Stern, *Loud Hawk: The U.S. versus the American Indian Movement* (Norman: University of Oklahoma Press, 1994); and Robert A. Hecht, *The Occupation of Wounded Knee* (Charlotteville, N.Y.: SamHar Press, 1981).

127. "No. 71-738, Mescalero Apache Tribe v. Jones, 2/23/73," Fox, 2, Box 6, Powell Papers.

128. *Voices from Wounded Knee, 1973: In the Words of the Participants* (Rooseveltown, N.Y.: Akwesasne Notes, Mohawk Nation, 1974).

129. Deloria and Lytle, *American Indians*, 54.

130. "Bench Memo, No. 71-834-ASX, McClanahan, et al.," RIM, 12, Box 156, Blackmun Papers.

131. Quotation from "Justice for American Indians," *Monitor*, November 8, 1972, Box 592, Douglas Papers.

132. Quotation from "Injustice to the Red Man," In Our Opinion . . .—Editorial Comments, n.d. Box 592, Douglas Papers. Also contained in this box is a newspaper cutting by Florence Mouckley, "Tribes vs. 'Movement' Indians Dispute Best Way to Win Self-Government," *Christian Science Monitor*, May 25 or July 25, 1973.

133. Mescalero Apache Tribe v. Jones, 411 U.S. 145 (1973).

134. A state use tax taxes items brought in from another state, including personal property such as movable assets like cars and not money or investments.

135. "Bench Memo, No. 71-738, Mescalero Apache Tribe v. Jones, Cert to N.M. Ct of App (Hendley) Cert denied by N.M. Sup Ct on Oct 6, 1971," RIM, December 8, 1972, 32, Box 156, Blackmun Papers.

136. "No. 71-834, McClanahan v. State Tax Commission of Arizona," 1, Box I:380, Brennan Papers.

137. "Re: No. 71-834, McClanahan v. State Tax Comm'n of Arizona," memorandum from Byron White to Thurgood Marshall, February 21, 1973, Box 156, Blackmun Papers.

138. "Judge—, 71-738," lms to Marshall, n.d., Box 102, Marshall Papers.

139. "No. 71-738 Mescalero Apache Tribe v. Jones, Conf. 12/15/72," Box 6, Powell Papers.

140. Ibid.

141. *Mescalero Apache Tribe v. Jones*, 147–48.

142. Ibid., 148

143. Clinton, "Dormant," 1197.

144. Kathleen Corr, "A Doctrinal Traffic Jam: The Role of Federal Preemption Analysis in Conflicts between State and Tribal Vehicle Codes," *University of Colorado Law Review* 74 (2003): 723–24.

145. "Bench Memo, No. 71-834-ASX, McClanahan, et al.," RIM, 16, Box 156, Blackmun Papers.

146. Tonasket v. Washington, 411 U.S. 451 (1973).

147. "71-1031," H.A.B., n.d., 2, Box 158, Blackmun Papers.

148. "71-1031, 12–14–1972," H.A.B., December 14, 1972, Box 158, Blackmun Papers. John Paul Stevens was nominated as an associate justice by President Ford and was sworn in during 1975. Raised in Chicago, Stevens attended the University of Chicago and after World War II graduated from Northwestern University Law School. Soon after, he clerked at the Supreme Court and then worked at a law firm in Chicago. Stevens turned his attention to private legal practice and to teaching at Northwestern University and the University of Chicago law schools. In 1970, President Nixon appointed him to the U.S. Court of Appeals for the Seventh Circuit. As an associate justice for over thirty-four years, Stevens was a moderate with a liberal leaning. During the conservative shift of the Court he appeared more liberal and showed judicial restraint and moderation. Supreme Court of the United States, "Biographies of Current Justices of the Supreme Court," www.supremecourt.gov/about/biographies.aspx (hereafter Biographies of Current Justices), s.v. "John Paul Stevens"; Oyez Project, s.v. "John Paul Stevens."

149. "Bench Memo No. 71-1031-CSX, Tonasket v. Wash., et al," RIM, December 9, 1972, 44, Box 158, Blackmun Papers.
150. Ibid., 47, 50.
151. "No. 71-1031, Tonasket v. Washington, Appeal from Wash. SC: Rosellini, et al., 3/24/72," Fox, 4, Box 7, Powell Papers.
152. "No. 71-1031 Tonasket v. Washington, Argued 12/12/72," 2, Box 7, Powell Papers.
153. "Bench Memo No 71-1031-CSX, Tonasket v. Wash., et al," RIM, December 9, 1972, 46–50, Box 158, Blackmun Papers.
154. "71-1031," H.A.B., n.d., 3, Box 158, Blackmun Papers.
155. *Mescalero Apache Tribe v. Jones*, 148.

Chapter 3

1. Joseph Singer believes that the Supreme Court after 1973 did not diminish tribal authority over tribal members and points out that the Court "has not cut back much at all on the power of tribes over their own members. It is important to recall that this is perhaps the heart of tribal sovereignty; such power exists even when tribal members are on non-tribal land within reservation borders." Singer, letter to author, April 27, 2006.
2. For an in-depth and fascinating article about taxation, see Richard D. Pomp, "The Unfulfilled Promise of the Indian Commerce Clause and State Taxation," *Tax Lawyer* 63 (2011): 897–1222.
3. In contrast, Singer, "Canons of Conquest," 643, argues that the Supreme Court did not consider tribal authority over nonmembers to be limited or state authority to be inherent on the reservation, explaining that "this view about the relation between state and tribal power is inaccurate and misleading." Singer argues that federal power filled the void when tribes did not have authority over nonmembers, and in order for states to have power congressional legislation was required.
4. Philip P. Frickey, "Congressional Intent, Practical Reasoning, and the Dynamic Nature of Federal Indian Law," *California Law Review* 78 (1990): 1137–240; Frickey, "Common Law," 28. See also Gould, "Consent Paradigm," 810; Pevar, *Rights of Indians*, 129–35; and Wilkins, *American Indian Sovereignty*, 186–214. In 1973 the *McClanahan* court established what came to be known as the federal preemption doctrine, and in *Oliphant v. Suquamish Indian Tribe* (1978) the Court established what came to be known as the implicit divestiture doctrine. See generally Wilkinson, *American Indians*; and Deloria and Lytle, *American Indians, American Justice*.
5. United States v. Mazurie, 419 U.S. 544 (1975).
6. The analysis of the *Mazurie* case in this chapter supports and builds on the opinions of Gould and Deloria and Lytle. See Deloria and Lytle, *American Indians*, 55; Gould, "Consent Paradigm," 840; and Wilkinson, *American Indians*, 60.
7. "No 73-1018, United States v. Mazurie, Cert to CA 10," AG, November 6, 1974, 18, 17, Box 197, Blackmun Papers.
8. Buster v. Wright, 135 F. 947 (8th Cir. 1905).
9. "Preliminary Memo, Conf. Feb. 22, 1974, List 1, Sheet 2, No. 73-1018—United States v. Mazurie," Farr, February 12, 1974, 7, Box 197, Blackmun Papers. In Perrin v. United States, 232 U.S. 478 (1914), the Supreme Court ruled that congressional power prohibited the introduction of intoxicating liquors onto a reservation. This was done

to protect the "Indian wards of the Nation" (479). The Court ruled that the Yankton Sioux Tribe had ceded all unalloted lands to the United States in the 1894 agreement, and in Article 17 of the agreement it was made clear that no intoxicating liquors would be sold or given away on these lands. This was the basis of congressional power over the matter. The Supreme Court discussed the origins of this authority over the tribes: "The power of Congress to prohibit the introduction of intoxicating liquors into an Indian reservation, wheresoever situate, and to prohibit traffic in such liquors with tribal Indians, whether upon or off a reservation and whether within or without the limits of a state, does not admit of any doubt. It arises in part from the clause in the Constitution investing Congress with authority 'to regulate commerce with foreign nations, and among the several states, and with the Indian tribes,' and in part from the recognized relation of tribal Indians to the federal government" (482).

10. "No. 73-1018—United States v. Mazurie," H.A.B. November 10, 1974, 4, Box 197, Blackmun Papers.

11. Ibid.

12. "No. 73-1018, United States v. Mazurie," W.J.B., n.d., Box I:338, Brennan Papers.

13. Ibid. See "No. 73-1018, United States v. Mazurie, Conf. 1/15/74," Box 21, Powell Papers.

14. Moe v. Salish & Kootenai Tribes, 425 U.S. 463 (1976). See Michael Minnis, "Judicially-Suggested Harassment of Indian Tribes: The Potawatomis Revisit Moe and Colville," *American Indian Law Review* 16 (1991): 289–318.

15. "No. 74-1656, Moe v. Confederated Tribes 75-50—Confederated Tribes v. Moe," H.A.B., January 19, 1976, 3, 5, Box 225, Blackmun Papers.

16. Ibid., 5.

17. "Moe v. Confederated Salish and Kootenai Tribes, Nos. 74-1656 and 75-50, Re: Proposed draft by Justice Rehnquist," WHB, April 2, 1976, 2, Box 225, Blackmun Papers.

18. "No. 75-1656, Moe v. Confederated Salish and Kootenai Tribes, No. 75-50 Confederated Salish and Kootenai Tribes v. Moe, Appeal from three-judge district court (D. Montana)," Block, January 17, 1976, 2–3, Box 225, Blackmun Papers.

19. "No. 74-1656, Moe v. Confederated Tribes 75-50—Confederated Tribes v. Moe," H.A.B, 5, Box 225, Blackmun Papers.

20. "Moe v. Confederated Salish and Kootenai Tribes, Nos. 74-1656 and 75-50, Re: Proposed draft by Justice Rehnquist," WHB, April 2, 1976, 1, Box 225, Blackmun Papers.

21. *Moe v. Salish & Kootenai Tribes,* 482, 465.

22. "No. 75-1656, Moe v. Confederated Salish and Kootenai Tribes, No. 75-50 Confederated Salish and Kootenai Tribes v. Moe," Block, 10–11, Box 225, Blackmun Papers.

23. "No. 74-1656, Moe v. Confederated Tribes 75-50—Confederated Tribes v. Moe," H.A.B, 4, Box 225, Blackmun Papers.

24. Ibid., 3.

25. "No. 74-1656, 75-50, Moe v. Confederated Salish & Kootenai Tribes of Flathead Reservation," W.J.B., n.d., Box I:369, Brennan Papers; "No. 74-1656 Moe v. Confederated Salish and Kootenai Tribes of Flathead Reservation, No. 75-50 Confederated Salish and Kootenai Tribes of Flathead Reservation v. Moe," H.A.B., January 23, 1976, Box 225, Blackmun Papers.

26. "No. 74-1656, 75-50, Moe v. Confederated Salish & Kootenai Tribes of Flathead Reservation," W.J.B., n.d., Box I:369, Brennan Papers.

27. *Moe v. Salish & Kootenai Tribes*, 476.

28. Ibid., 480–81.

29. Bob Woodward and Scott Armstrong, *The Brethren: Inside the Supreme Court* (New York: Simon and Schuster, 1979), 412.

30. Oliphant v. Suquamish Indian Tribe, 435 U.S. 191 (1978).

31. Many scholars view *Oliphant* as the first case in which the Court moved away from the sovereignty doctrine; see, for example, Frickey, "Common Law," 34–35; and Russell Lawrence Barsh and James Youngblood Henderson, "Contrary Jurisprudence: Tribal Interests in Navigable Waterways before and after Montana v. United States," *Washington Law Review* 56 (1981): 628. For an invaluable critique of *Oliphant*, see Russell Lawrence Barsh and James Youngblood Henderson, "The Betrayal: Oliphant v. Suquamish Indian Tribe and the Hunting of the Snark," *Minnesota Law Review* 63 (1979): 609–40. See also Maxfield, "Oliphant v. Suquamish Tribe," 391–443; Robert J. Nordaus, G. Emlen Hall, and Anne Alise Rudio, "Revisiting Merrion v. Jicarilla Apache Tribe: Robert Nordhaus and Sovereign Indian Control over Natural Resources on Reservations." *Natural Resources Journal* 43 (2003): 260–61; and Steven Paul McSloy, "Back to the Future: Native American Sovereignty in the 21st Century," *New York University Review of Law and Social Change* 20 (1993): 217–302.

32. "76-5729, Suquamish," H.A.B., January 5, 1978, Box 270, Blackmun Papers.

33. Ibid.

34. "Preliminary Memo, Summer List, 9, Sheet 1, No. 76-1629, U.S. Wheeler," Campbell, August 8, 1977, 7, Box 268, Blackmun Papers.

35. "76-5729, Oliphant and Belgrade v. Suquamish Indian Tribe," Crane, January 3, 1978, Box 270, Blackmun Papers.

36. "No. 76-5729 Oliphant & Belgrade v. Suquamish Indian Tribe, To: Nancy, From: L.F.P., Jr., Date: January 3, 1978," 3, 4, Box 51, Powell Papers.

37. Ibid., 3.

38. Ibid., 1, 2.

39. "No. 76-5729, Oliphant v. Suquamish Indian Tribe," H.A.B., January 11, 1978, 1–2, Box 270, Blackmun Papers. The Parker reference is to Isaac C. Parker, judge of the U.S. Court for the Western District of Arkansas from 1875 to 1896, and his opinion in *Ex parte Kenyon*, 14 F. Cas. 353 (U.S.C.C., Ark., 1878). This opinion did not support tribal jurisdiction over non-Indians. Interestingly, the solicitor of the Department of the Interior released an opinion in 1970 that reaffirmed the ruling of Parker in *Ex parte Kenyon*, but this opinion of 1970 was withdrawn in 1974. Also, *Ex parte Kenyon* was not even a Supreme Court case and had never been considered for judgment in Washington, D.C. The final *Oliphant* opinion of Justice Rehnquist relied on these biased details to remove the inherent sovereignty of the tribes to prosecute nonmembers, ignoring treaties and case law that supported tribal control over territory and people as well as the fundamental principle that sovereignty existed with Native American tribes until taken away. See *Morris v. Hitchcock* (1904), 389.

40. Oral argument of Mark David Oliphant and Daniel B. Belgrade, Petitioners v. The Suquamish Indian Tribe, et al., Respondents, No. 76-5729, Monday, January 9, 1978, before the Supreme Court of the United States, 46–47.

41. "Memorandum to Mr. Justice Powell," From: Nancy, Re: Oliphant opinion, Feb. 27, 1978," 1, Box 51, Powell Papers.

42. Ibid., 1.

43. *Oliphant v. Suquamish Indian Tribe*, 191.

44. "No. 76-5729, Oliphant v. Suquamish Indian Tribe," H.A.B., January 11, 1978, 2, Box 270, Blackmun Papers.

45. "Re 76-1629—United States v. Wheeler, March 14, 1978," memorandum from Chief Justice Warren Burger to Justice Potter Stewart, Box 268, Blackmun Papers.

46. "Memorandum to the Conference, No. 76-5729, Oliphant v. Suquamish Indian Tribe," from Thurgood Marshall on March 3, 1978, Box 270, Blackmun Papers.

47. United States v. Wheeler, 435 U.S. 313 (1978).

48. "Re: No. 76-1629, United States v. Wheeler, Bench Memo, To: Mr. Justice Powell, From: Nancy Bregstein, Jan. 9, 1978," 10-11, Box 49, Powell Papers.

49. "Memorandum to the Conference, Re: No. 76-1629, United States v. Wheeler," from Thurgood Marshall, January 16, 1978, Box 268, Blackmun Papers. In addition, Justice Marshall was concerned about the relationship between the tribes and the United States: "What strikes me as peculiar about the relationship between the tribes and the federal government is the plenary nature of Congress' authority to act vis-à-vis the tribes. Unlike the states, whose sovereignty (and concomitant police power) is protected and recognized in the Constitution, the tribes continue to possess any criminal jurisdiction at all wholly at the sufferance of the federal government (absent limiting treaty language); and Congress has enacted numerous statutes arguably controlling the tribes' criminal jurisdiction, 18 U.S.C 1152, 1153, and the manner in which such jurisdiction is exercised, 25 U.S.C. 1301 et seq."

50. "No. 76-1629, United States v. Wheeler," H.A.B., January 13, 1978, 1, Box 268, Blackmun Papers.

51. *United States v. Wheeler*, 313, 328. See also Dussias, "Geographically-Based," 28.

52. "Re: No. 76-1629, United States v. Wheeler, Bench Memo, To: Mr. Justice Powell, From: Nancy Bregstein, Jan. 9, 1978," 3, 11, Box 49, Powell Papers.

53. "No. 76-1629 U.S. v. Wheeler, Conf. 1/13/78," 1, Box 49, Powell Papers.

54. "Re: No. 76-1629, United States v. Wheeler, Bench Memo, To: Mr. Justice Powell, From: Nancy Bregstein, Jan. 9, 1978," 3-4, Box 49, Powell Papers.

55. "No. 76-1629 U.S. v. Wheeler, Conf. 1/13/78," 3, Box 49, Powell Papers.

56. *United States v. Wheeler*, 326.

57. "Draft opinion, 1 March 1978." Box 452, Brennan Papers. See also *United States v. Wheeler*, 326.

58. Dussias, "Geographically-Based," 48.

59. Senate Committee, *Rulings of the U.S. Supreme Court*, 48. See also Dussias, "Geographically-Based," 17.

60. Johnson and Martinis, "Chief Justice Rehnquist"; Skibine, "Reconciling Federal and State Power."

61. Rey-Bear, "Flathead Water"; Maxfield, "Oliphant v. Suquamish Tribe," 440.

62. After *Oliphant* and *Wheeler* in 1978, the Supreme Court decided many more cases involving tribal criminal jurisdiction. In United States v. John, 437 U.S. 634 (1978), the Court held that federal criminal statutes for crimes in Indian country applied to lands reserved for the Mississippi Choctaws of Mississippi. In *Duro v. Reina* (1990), the Court ruled that tribes had no inherent criminal jurisdiction over Native Americans that were not a member of the tribe (see chapter 4). In Negonsott v. Samuels, 507 U.S. 99 (1993),

the Court decided that the State of Kansas had jurisdiction over all offenses committed by Native Americans on Native American reservations. In *United States v. Lara* (2004), the Court ruled that Congress had constitutional powers to lift restrictions placed on the tribes criminal jurisdiction over nonmember Native Americans (see chapter 4).

63. Washington v. Confederated Tribes, 447 U.S. 134 (1980).

64. "Re: No 78-630—Washington v. Confederated Tribes," memorandum from Blackmun to Brennan, December 14, 1979, Box 301, Blackmun Papers.

65. First Draft of Mr. Justice White, concurring in part and dissenting in part, January 21, 1980, 1–2, Box 301, Blackmun Papers.

66. *Colville*, 136.

67. Ibid., 156.

68. "78-630—State of Washington v. Confederated Tribes of the Colville Indian Reservation, Mr. Justice Stevens, dissenting in part," January 17, 1980, 2, Box 301, Blackmun Papers.

69. "Mr. Justice," memorandum from DTC to Blackmun, April 18, 1980, 2, Box 301, Blackmun Papers.

70. "First Draft of Mr. Justice Rehnquist, dissenting in part," January 16, 1980, 12, 1, Box 301, Blackmun Papers.

71. "Re: 78-630—State of Washington v. Confederated Tribes," memorandum from Rehnquist to Brennan, January 15, 1980, 1, Box 301, Blackmun Papers.

72. Johnson and Martinis, "Chief Justice Rehnquist," 21–22. See also Skibine, "Court's Use," 277.

73. "First Draft of Mr. Justice Rehnquist, dissenting in part," 1, January 16, 1980, Box 301, Blackmun Papers.

74. Ibid., 2, 4. See also *Colville*, 177, 179.

75. "First Draft of Mr. Justice Rehnquist, dissenting in part," January 16, 1980, 2, Box 301, Blackmun Papers.

76. "Re: 78-630—State of Washington v. Confederated Tribes," memorandum from Rehnquist to Brennan, January 15, 1980, 1, Box 301, Blackmun Papers.

77. "First Draft of Mr. Justice Rehnquist, dissenting in part," January 16, 1980, 2, 6, Box 301, Blackmun Papers.

78. "78-630 Washington v. Confederated Tribes," memorandum from Justice Powell to Justice Brennan, 1, Box 301, Blackmun Papers; "78-630 Washington v. Confederated Tribes," memorandum from Justice Powell to Justice Brennan, 1, Box 64, Powell Papers.

79. "78-630 Washington v. Confederate Tribes," memorandum from Powell to White, May 22, 1980, Box 301, Blackmun Papers; "78-630 Washington v. Confederate Tribes," memorandum from Powell to White, May 22, 1980, Box 64, Powell Papers .

80. "No. 78-630, Washington v. Confederated tribes of the Colville Indian Reservation," H.A.B., October 12, 1979, Box 301, Blackmun Papers.

81. "Washington v. Confederated Tribes, No. 78-630," DTC to Blackmun, October 4, 1979, Box 301, Blackmun Papers.

82. "Memo re Draft op (per WB) in Washington v. Confederated Tribes, No. 78-630," DTC to Blackmun, November 28, 1979, 1, Box 301, Blackmun Papers.

83. "78-630 Washington v. Colville Tribes, US, Others," H.A.B., October 4, 1979, 1, Box 301, Blackmun Papers.

84. Ibid.

85. "Memo re Draft op (per WB) in Washington v. Confederated Tribes, No. 78-630," DTC, 1, Box 301, Blackmun Papers.

86. "Questions, 78-630 Washington v. Confederated Tribes," H.A.B., October 5, 1979, Box 301, Blackmun Papers.

87. "Memo re Draft op (per WB) in Washington v. Confederated Tribes, No. 78-630," DTC, 2, Box 301, Blackmun Papers.

88. "Memo re Confederated Bands, 78-630 n.40," DTC to Blackmun, December 5, 1979, 1, Box 301, Blackmun Papers.

89. "Mr. Justice," memorandum from DTC to Blackmun, April 18, 1980, 2, Box 301, Blackmun Papers.

90. "78-630 Washington v. Confederated Tribes," memorandum from Justice Powell to Justice Brennan, 1, Box 301, Blackmun Papers; "78-630 Washington v. Confederated Tribes," memorandum from Justice Powell to Justice Brennan, 1, Box 64, Powell Papers.

91. "78-630 Washington v. Confederated Tribes," memorandum from Justice Powell to Justice Brennan, 2, Box 301, Blackmun Papers; "78-630 Washington v. Confederated Tribes," memorandum from Justice Powell to Justice Brennan, 2, Box 64, Powell Papers.

92. "Bench Memo, No. 78-630, Washington et al. v. Confederated Tribes at al.; Washington v. United States et al.," Crs to Marshall, September 16, 1979, 2, Box 239, Marshall Papers.

93. *Colville*, 156.

94. "Third Draft of Mr. Justice Brennan, opinion," December 18, 1979, 1–2, Box 301, Blackmun Papers.

95. Ibid., 14.

96. "Second Draft of Mr. Justice Brennan, opinion," December 5, 1979, 20, Box 301, Blackmun Papers.

97. "Re: No 78-630—Washington v. Confederated Tribes," memorandum from Marshall to Brennan, December 13, 1979, Box 301, Blackmun Papers.

98. "No. 78-630—State of Washington v. Confederated Tribes," memorandum from Brennan to all Justices, January 14, 1980, 1–2, Box 301, Blackmun Papers.

99. "No. 78-630—State of Washington v. Confederated Tribes," W.J.B., 1, Box 301, Blackmun Papers.

100. *Colville*, 166, 167, 172.

101. Ibid., 135–36.

102. *Oliphant v. Suquamish Indian Tribe*, 208.

103. *Colville*, 153.

104. Watson, "Thrust and Parry."

105. White Mountain Apache Tribe v. Bracker, 448 U.S. 136 (1980).

106. "Re: No. 78-1177—White Mountain Apache Tribe v. Bracker," memorandum from Thurgood Marshall to Byron White, March 28, 1980, 1, Box 304, Blackmun Papers.

107. "No. 78-1177 White Mountain Apache v. Bracker, Conf. 1/16/80," 3, Box 66, Powell Papers.

108. "78-1177, White Mountain Apache v. Bracker (Ariz)," H.A.B., January 13, 1980, Box 304, Blackmun Papers.

109. "Memo, re: White Mtn Apache Tribe v. Bracker, 78-1177; draft op from TM to: Blackmun, from: DTC," n.d., Box 304, Blackmun Papers.

110. "Re: No. 78-1177—White Mountain Apache Tribe v. Bracker," memorandum from Byron White to Thurgood Marshall, March 27, 1980, 2, Box 304, Blackmun Papers; "Re: No. 78-1177—White Mountain Apache Tribe v. Bracker," memorandum from Byron White to Thurgood Marshall, March 27, 1980, 2, Box 66, Powell Papers.

111. "Re: No. 78-1177—White Mountain Apache Tribe v. Bracker," memorandum from Thurgood Marshall to Byron White, 1, Box 304, Blackmun Papers; "Re: No. 78-1177—White Mountain Apache Tribe v. Bracker," memorandum from Thurgood Marshall to Byron White, 1, Box 66, Powell Papers. In Bryan v. Itasca County, 426 U.S. 373 (1976), Russell Bryan, an enrolled member of the Minnesota Chippewa Tribe, resided on land held in trust by the United States for the Chippewa Tribe on the Leech Lake Reservation in Minnesota. Itasca County, Minnesota, imposed a personal property tax on his mobile home. Bryan appealed and argued that the tax was contrary to federal law. The Supreme Court ruled that Public Law 280 did not grant states the authority to tax reservation Indians.

112. "Re: No. 78-1177—White Mountain Apache Tribe v. Bracker," memorandum from Byron White to Thurgood Marshall, 1, Box 304, Blackmun Papers.

113. "Re: No. 78-1177—White Mountain Apache Tribe v. Bracker," memorandum from Byron White to Thurgood Marshall, 1, Box 66, Powell Papers.

114. "Re: No. 78-1177—White Mountain Apache Tribe v. Bracker," memorandum from Thurgood Marshall to Byron White, 2, Box 304, Blackmun Papers; "Re: No. 78-1177—White Mountain Apache Tribe v. Bracker," memorandum from Thurgood Marshall to Byron White, 2, Box 66, Powell Papers.

115. *White Mountain Apache Tribe v. Bracker*, 142, 143.

116. Ibid., 143.

117. Ibid., 151. The Court cited *Warren Trading Post v. Tax Comm'n*, *Williams v. Lee*, and *Kennerly v. District Court of Montana*.

118. *White Mountain Apache Tribe v. Bracker*, 150–51.

119. Deloria and Lytle, *American Indians*, 206, note that after the *McClanahan* ruling the Supreme Court appeared to place tribal sovereignty "on a back shelf, hoping that it would be lost in the dust of time," but they also write that the *Bracker* case "was extremely important" because it validated the "role of tribal sovereignty" as a bona fide doctrine to prohibit state authority on the reservation. Although it is true that certain parts of the *Bracker* opinion did appear to reinvigorate tribal sovereignty by referring to *Williams*, these references by the majority opinion corresponded to the limited interpretation of *Williams* after 1973, which severely limited inherent tribal sovereignty. The majority opinion in *Bracker* relied almost exclusively on the use of congressional authority to bar state law.

120. *White Mountain Apache Tribe v. Bracker*, 142, 143.

121. "No. 78-1177, White Mountain Apache Tribe v. Bracker," W.J.B., n.d., Box I:494, Brennan Papers.

122. Central Machinery Co. v. Arizona Tax Comm'n, 448 U.S. 160 (1980).

123. "Memo to Blackmun from DTC, re: Central Mach. Co. v. Arizona State Tax Comm'n, No. 78-1604, draft opinion," n.d., Box 307, Blackmun Papers.

124. *Central Machinery Co. v. Arizona Tax Comm'n*, 166, quoting United States v. Price, 383 U.S. 787 (1966), 801.

125. "Bench Memo, No. 78-1604, Central Machinery. Co. v. Ariz. State Tax Comm'n," n.d., 4, Box 239, Marshall Papers.

126. "No. 78-1604, Central Machinery v. Arizona State, Conf. 1/16/80," 1, Box 67, Powell Papers.

127. "No. 78-1604, Central Machinery. Co. v. Ariz. State Tax Comm'n," H.A.B., n.d., 2, Box 307, Blackmun Papers.

128. Ibid.; "No. 78-1604, Central Machinery v. Arizona State Tax Commission," W.J.B., n.d., Box I:495, Brennan Papers.

129. "No. 78-1604, Central Machinery v. Arizona State, Conf. 1/16/80," 3, Box 67, Powell Papers. See "No. 78-1604, Central Machinery v. Arizona State Tax Commission," W.J.B., n.d., Box I:495, Brennan Papers.

130. *Central Machinery Co. v. Arizona Tax Comm'n*, 160.

131. "No. 78-1604, Central Machinery. Co. v. Ariz. State Tax Comm'n," H.A.B., 1, Box 307, Blackmun Papers.

132. *Central Machinery Co. v. Arizona Tax Comm'n*, 168.

133. Ibid., 172. Powell recognized the division between this case and *Moe v. Salish & Kootenai Tribes* and *Colville*. In *Central Machinery Co. v. Arizona Tax Comm'n* the majority worked from the presumption that state authority was precluded until Congress explicitly acted to sanction state authority, whereas the *Moe v. Salish & Kootenai Tribes* and *Colville* courts worked from the presumption that the states had power until Congress explicitly acted to reverse state authority over nonmembers on the reservation.

134. *Central Machinery Co. v. Arizona Tax Comm'n*, 169.

135. Ramah Navajo School Bd. v. Bureau of Revenue, 458 U.S. 832 (1982).

136. "Re: No 80-2162, Ramah Navajo School Board Inc. Lembke Construction Co., Inc., v. New Mexico Bureau of Revenue," CAR, April 27, 1982, 17, 19, Box 355, Blackmun Papers.

137. "No. 80-2162, Ramah Navajo School Bd., v. Bur., Conf., 4/30/82," 2, Box 88, Powell Papers.

138. "No. 80-2162, Ramah Navajo School Bd. v. N. Mex. Bur. of Rev. New," H.A.B., April 27, 1982, Box 355, Blackmun Papers.

139. "No. 80-2162, Ramah Navajo School Bd. v. Bureau of Revenue of New Mexico," H.A.B., April 30, 1982, 2, Box 355, Blackmun Papers. Sandra Day O'Connor was nominated by President Reagan and sworn in as the first female associate justice in 1981. She attended Stanford University Law School and served on the Stanford Law Review. In her class was future chief justice William H. Rehnquist. As a woman, O'Connor found it difficult to gain employment, but she served as deputy county attorney in San Mateo, California, and then as an attorney in the U.S Army in Germany, after which she returned to Arizona and opened her own law firm and became active in the Republican Party. In 1965 she became assistant state attorney general in Arizona and in 1969 she was appointed by the Arizona governor to occupy a vacant state senate seat. O'Connor was elected outright by voters in the state senate election of 1970 and won reelection in 1972. In the same year, she became the Republican majority leader in the state senate and the first woman in America to occupy such a position. In 1974,

O'Connor served as county judge in the Maricopa County Superior Court and in 1979 she was nominated to the Arizona Court of Appeals. As an associate justice in the Supreme Court, O'Connor sided with the conservatives but over time developed a more pragmatic and centrist role reflective of her natural conservatism. Biographies of Current Justices, s.v. "Sandra Day O'Connor"; Oyez Project, s.v. "Sandra Day O'Connor"; Sandra Day O'Connor Institute, "Sandra Day O'Connor," www.oconnorhouse.org/oconnor/biography.php (accessed June 15, 2015).

140. "No. 80-2162, Ramah Navajo School Bd. v. Bureau of Revenue of New Mexico," H.A.B., April 30, 1982, 1, Box 355, Blackmun Papers.

141. *Ramah Navajo School Bd. v. Bureau of Revenue*, 837. Federal preemption was based on a test, and the *Ramah* court explained that "pre-emption analysis in this area is not controlled by 'mechanical or absolute conceptions of state or tribal sovereignty'; it requires a particularized examination of the relevant state, federal, and tribal interests," 838, quoting *White Mountain Apache Tribe v. Bracker*, 145.

142. *Ramah Navajo School Bd. v. Bureau of Revenue*, 838.

143. Ibid., 843. This was also held to be the principle in a civil jurisdiction case, *New Mexico v. Mescalero Apache Tribe* (1983): "Our cases have rejected a narrow focus on congressional intent to pre-empt state law as the sole touchstone. They have also rejected the proposition that pre-emption requires 'an express congressional statement to that effect'" (334).

144. "No. 80-2162, Ramah Navajo School Bd., v. Bur., Conf., 4/30/82," 3, Box 88, Powell Papers.

145. *Ramah Navajo School Bd. v. Bureau of Revenue*, 847–48.

146. Ibid., 855, 848.

147. Merrion v. Jicarilla Apache Tribe, 455 U.S. 130 (1982). See Nordhaus, Hall, and Rudio, "Revisiting Merrion v. Jicarilla"; Bradley Scott Bridgewater, "Taxation: Merrion v. Jicarilla Apache Tribe: Wine or Vinegar for Oklahoma Tribes?" *Oklahoma Law Review* 37 (1984): 369–96; David Goldstein, "Indian Law: Indian Taxation of Non-Indian Mineral Lessees," *Tennessee Law Review* 50 (1983): 403–23; and David B. Wiles, "Taxation: Tribal Taxation, Secretarial Approval, and State Taxation—Merrion and Beyond," *American Indian Law Review* 10 (1983): 167–85.

148. "Amoco Production Co. and Merrion v. Jicarilla Apache Tribe, 80-11; 80-15, Argued 11/4/81," W.J.B., Box I:563, Brennan Papers.

149. "Memorandum to the Conference, No. 80-11—Merrion v. Jicarilla Apache Tribe, No. 80-15—Amoco Production Company v. Jicarilla Apache Tribe," memorandum from Harry A. Blackmun to the conference, June 17, 1981, Box 341, Blackmun Papers.

150. "80-11; 80-15—Amoco Production Company v. Jicarilla Apache Tribe; Merrion v. Jicarilla Apache Tribe, Memorandum of Justice Marshall," June 25, 1981, 1, 6, Box 341, Blackmun Papers.

151. "Draft opinion—Merrion v. Jicarilla Apache Tribe," January 14, 1982, Box 563, Brennan Papers. See also *Merrion v. Jicarilla Apache Tribe*, 159.

152. "Draft opinion—Merrion v. Jicarilla Apache Tribe," January 14, 1982, Box 563, Brennan Papers. See also *Merrion v. Jicarilla Apache Tribe*, 130; and Duthu, "Thurgood Marshall Papers," 83.

153. "Re: Nos. 80-11 & 80-15 Amoco Production Co. v. Jicarilla Apache Tribe; Merrion v.

Jicarilla Apache Tribe," memorandum from Rehnquist to Stevens, June 1, 1981, Box 341, Blackmun Papers.

154. "No. 80-11 & 15, Merrion & Amoco Production v. Jicarilla Apache Tribe," W.J.B., n.d., 2, Box I:554, Brennan Papers; "No. 80-11, Merrion v. Jicarilla Apache Tribe, No. 80-15, Amoco Production Company v. Jicarilla Apache Tribe," H.A.B., April 11, 1981, 2, Box 341, Blackmun Papers.

155. "No. 80-11 & 15, Merrion & Amoco Production v. Jicarilla Apache Tribe," W.J.B., n.d., 2, Box I:554, Brennan Papers.

156. "No. 80-11, Merrion v. Jicarilla Apache Tribe, No. 80-15, Amoco Production Company v. Jicarilla Apache Tribe," H.A.B., April 11, 1981, 2, Box 341, Blackmun Papers.

157. "Re: 80-11; 80-15—Merrion et al. v. Jicarilla Apache Tribe," memorandum from John Paul Stevens to Thurgood Marshall, December 1, 1981, Box 341, Blackmun Papers.

158. "No. 80-11 & 15, Merrion & Amoco Production v. Jicarilla Apache Tribe," W.J.B., n.d., 2, Box I:554, Brennan Papers.

159. Ibid.

160. *Merrion v. Jicarilla Apache* Tribe, 183–84.

161. Duthu, "Thurgood Marshall Papers," 81-88; Nordhaus, Hall, and Rudio, "Revisiting Merrion."

162. Kerr-McGee Corp. v. Navajo Tribe, 471 U.S. 195 (1985). In 1985, the Supreme Court also decided Montana v. Blackfeet Tribe, 471 U.S. 759 (1985). In this case it was ruled that the State of Montana was not allowed to tax the tribe's royalty interests from reservation lands leased under the Indian Mineral Leasing Act of 1938. And in California Board of Equalization v. Chemehuevi Tribe, 474 U.S. 9 (1985), the Court ruled that the State of California could require the tribe to collect state taxes for on-reservation cigarette sales to nonmembers.

163. "No. 84-68, Kerr-McGee v. Navajo Tribe," February 27, 1985, Box 426, Blackmun Papers.

164. "84-68 Kerr-McGee v. Navahos," February 23, 1985, Box 426, Blackmun Papers.

165. California v. Cabazon Band of Mission Indians, 480 U.S. 202 (1987).

166. "No 85-1708, California Riverside County . . . v. Cabazon . . . , Appeal from CA9 (Anderson, Farris, Nelson)," December 4, 1986, Brinkmann, 30, Box 475, Blackmun Papers.

167. "Mr Justice: Re: No. 85-1708, California v. Cabazon Band of Mission Indians," February 6, 1987, Beth B., 3, 2, Box 475, Blackmun Papers.

168. "Mr Justice: Re: No. 85-1708, *California v. Cabazon Band of Mission Indians*," February 12, 1987, Beth B., Box 475, Blackmun Papers.

169. Antonin Scalia was nominated by President Reagan and sworn in as an associate justice in 1986. Scalia attended Georgetown University and went on to Harvard Law School where he served as editor of the Harvard Law Review. Scalia taught law at the University of Virginia and then served as general counsel for the Office of Telecommunication Policy in the Nixon administration. Soon after, President Nixon nominated him to the Office of Legal Counsel in the Department of Justice. After the Watergate affair, Scalia worked at the American Enterprise Institute, a conservative think tank in Washington, D.C., Georgetown University Law Center, and the University of Chicago Law School. In 1982, President Reagan nominated him to the U.S. Court of Appeals for the District of Columbia Circuit. His actions as an associate justice on

the Supreme Court were strongly conservative with a philosophy of judicial restraint and a strict interpretation of the Constitution. Biographies of Current Justices, s.v. "Antonin Scalia"; Oyez Project, s.v. "Antonin Scalia."

170. Anthony Kennedy was nominated by President Reagan and sworn in as an associate justice in 1988. Born in California, Kennedy attended Stanford University and went on to Harvard Law School. After university, he worked as an associate in a law firm and in 1963 took over his father's legal practice. In time, Kennedy lobbied California politicians and helped Reagan as governor of California. In 1975, Kennedy was nominated to the U.S. Court of Appeals for the Ninth Circuit and became the voice of the Court's conservative minority. Kennedy was nominated to the Supreme Court after Senate opposition to Robert Bork, Reagan's first nomination, and the withdrawal of Douglas Ginsburg, Reagan's second nomination. Kennedy is a conservative justice, but during his tenure on the Supreme Court he has built coalitions with both conservatives and liberals and become part of the centrist bloc in the Court. Biographies of Current Justices," s.v. "Anthony M. Kennedy"; Oyez Project, s.v. "Anthony Kennedy."

171. Cotton Petroleum Corp. v. New Mexico, 490 U.S. 163 (1989).

172. Judith V. Royster, "Mineral Development in Indian Country: The Evolution of Tribal Control over Mineral Resources," *Tulsa Law Journal* 29 (1994): 541–637; Charley Carpenter, "Preempting Indian Preemption: Cotton Petroleum Corp. v. New Mexico," *Catholic University Law Review* 39 (1990): 639–71; Daniel Gluck, "A Tale of Two Taxes—Preemption on the Reservation: Cotton Petroleum Corp. v. Mexico," *Tax Lawyer* 43 (1990): 359–73; Kristina Bogardus, "Court Picks New Test in Cotton Petroleum," *Natural Resources Journal* 30 (1990): 919–28; Charles Breer, "Are State Severance Taxes Preempted When Imposed on Non-Indian Lessees Extracting Oil and Gas from Indian Reservations Land? Cotton Petroleum Corporation v. New Mexico," *Land and Water Law Review* 25 (1990): 435–45; Katherine B. Crawford, "State Authority to Tax Non-Indian Oil & Gas Production on Reservations: Cotton Petroleum Corp. v. New Mexico," *Utah Law Review* 1989 (1989): 495–519.

173. "87–1327, Cotton Petroleum Corp. v. New Mexico," H.A.B., February 12, 1988, Box 521, Blackmun Papers.

174. Ibid.

175. *Cotton Petroleum Corp. v. New Mexico*, 163.

176. The federal preemption test applied in *Cotton Petroleum Corp. v. New Mexico* was, as Marshall said in *White Mountain Apache Tribe v. Bracker*, "simply not the law" (151).

177. Alex Tallchief Skibine, "Reconciling Federal and State Power," 1152–56, argues that the principle adopted by Justice Marshall in *Bracker* gave way to the Rehnquist view or test articulated in *Colville*, which required an explicit congressional act to limit state power on the reservation. The Rehnquist view had been developing prior to *Colville* and further developed in the form of dissents through the 1980s.

178. The *Ramah* dissent explained that "the dominant trend of our cases is toward treating the scope of reservation immunity from nondiscriminatory state taxation as a question of pre-emption, ultimately dependent on congressional intent" (847–48) and that "there must be some affirmative indication that Congress did not intend the State to exercise . . . sovereign power" (855).

179. *Cotton Petroleum Corp. v. New Mexico*, 176.

180. Furthermore, the Court applied the rationale of *Moe*, where federal statutes did not automatically oust state authority over nonmembers on the reservation, rather than the rationale used in *Central Machinery*, where the existence and not the application of federal trader statutes ousted state law.

181. The *Ramah* dissent said, "The tradition of Indian sovereignty stands as an independent barrier to discriminatory taxes, and otherwise serves only as a guide to the ascertainment of the congressional will" (848).

182. *Cotton Petroleum Corp. v. New Mexico*, 189.

183. Oklahoma Tax Comm'n v. Potawatomi Tribe, 498 U.S. 505 (1991) (states tax nonmembers on the reservation); County of Yakima v. Yakima Nation, 502 U.S. 251 (1992) (states and local government had authority to impose real property taxes—ad valorem taxes—on fee lands alienated under the General Allotment Act of 1887 and owned by tribal members or the tribe. However, the county did not have authority to impose excise taxes on the sale of the same lands); Oklahoma Tax Commission v. Sac and Fox Nation, 508 U.S. 114 (1993) (states had no authority to tax tribal members earning income in Indian country—on tribal lands or alienated lands—or authority to impose a state vehicle excise tax and registration fees on tribal members); Department of Taxation and Finance of New York v. Milhelm Attea & Bros., Inc., 512 U.S. 61 (1994) (State of New York had authority to require the precollection of state taxes on cigarettes sold by tribal members to nonmembers. The wholesaler was therefore responsible for the precollection and payment of the tax); Oklahoma Tax Comm'n v. Chickasaw Nation, 515 U.S. 450 (1995) (state did not have authority to impose a fuel tax on fuel sold by the tribe on tribal trust lands. Also, tribal members working for the tribe but living outside the jurisdiction of the tribe were subject to a state income tax); Montana v. Crow Tribe, 523 U.S. 696 (1998) (tribes had no authority to sue the State of Montana to recover taxes paid by a nonmember company that operated a mining lease on the tribe's reservation); Cass County v. Leech Lake Band of Chippewa Indians, 524 U.S. 103 (1998) (state and local governments had authority to impose an ad valorem tax on reservation lands sold to nonmembers and later repurchased by the tribe); Arizona Dept. of Revenue v. Blaze Construction. Co., 526 U.S. 32 (1999) (states had authority to impose a tax on private company profits from contracts with the U.S. government); Chickasaw Nation v. United States, 534 U.S. 84 (2001) (tribes were not exempt from paying gaming taxes under Chapter 35 of the Indian Gaming Regulatory Act); City of Sherrill v. Oneida Indian Nation of New York, 544 U.S. 197 (2005) (local taxes applied to parcels of land originally within the historic Oneida Reservation sold to a nonmember in 1807 and repurchased by the Oneidas in 1997 and 1998. In addition, the Oneidas had no authority, arising from their ancient sovereignty, to regulate the parcels of land in question, because they had relinquished their authority long ago); Wagnon v. Prairie Band Potawatomi Nation, 546 U.S. 95 (2005) (State of Kansas had authority to apply a motor fuel tax to the receipt of fuel by off-reservation nonmember distributors who then delivered it to a tribally owned business on the reservation).

184. Montana v. United States, 450 U.S. 544 (1981).

185. "No. 79-1128, Montana v. United States," W.J.B., n.d., 1–2, Box I:524, Brennan Papers.

186. Ibid., 2.

187. No. 79-1128, Montana v. U.S., Conf. 12/5/80," 3, Box 75, Powell Papers.

188. "No. 79-1128, Montana v. United States," H.A.B., December 5, 1980, 1, Box 325, Blackmun Papers. See "No. 79-1128, Montana v. U.S., Conf. 12/5/80," Box 75, Powell Papers.

189. "No. 79-1128, Montana, et al., v. U.S.," from Dean to Blackmun, December 2, 1980, 13–15, Box 325, Blackmun Papers.

190. "No. 79-1128, Montana v. United States," W.J.B., n.d., 2, Box I:524, Brennan Papers.

191. "Bench Memorandum, To: Mr. Justice Powell, From: Peter Byrne, Date: December 2, 1980, Re: No. 79-1128, Montana v. United States," 11, 12, Box 75, Powell Papers.

192. "No. 79-1128, Montana v. United States," H.A.B., December 5, 1980, 2, 1, Box 325, Blackmun Papers.

193. "No. 79-1128, Montana v. United States," W.J.B., n.d., 2, Box I:524, Brennan Papers.

194. "No. 79-1128, Montana v. United States," H.A.B., December 5, 1980, 1, Box 325, Blackmun Papers.

195. "No. 79-1128, Montana v. United States, February 11, 1981, memorandum from Justice Powell to Justice Stewart," Box 75, Powell Papers. In light of Powell's concerns, the word "property" was taken out of the second draft. The first draft opinion read: "A tribe may also retain inherent power to exercise civil authority over the conduct of non-Indians on fee lands within its reservation when that conduct threatens or has some direct effect on the political integrity or the property or economic security of the tribe." "1st draft, No. 79-1128, State of Montana v. United States, 5 February, 1980," 20, Box 75, Powell Papers. The second draft opinion read: "A tribe may also retain inherent power to exercise civil authority over the conduct of non-Indians on fee lands within its reservation when that conduct threatens or has some direct effect on the political integrity, the economic security, or the health or welfare of the tribe." "2nd draft, No. 79-1128, State of Montana v. United States, 17 February, 1980," 20, Box 75, Powell Papers.

196. "No. 79-1128, Montana v. United States," H.A.B., December 5, 1980, 1, Box 325, Blackmun Papers. See "No. 79-1128, Montana v. U.S., Conf. 12/5/80," Box 75, Powell Papers.

197. Skibine, "Court's Use," 297, argues that this principle was transferred from the criminal to the civil context, pointing out that the Supreme Court's *Wheeler* opinion was crucial to the Montana court's formulation of its general rule.

198. "Draft opinion, 19 March 1981," Box 536, Brennan Papers. See *Montana v. United States*, 565; and Amy Crafts, "Nevada v. Hicks and Its Implication on American Indian Sovereignty," *Connecticut Law Review* 34 (2002): 1249–80.

199. "Draft opinion, 19 March 1981," Box 536, Brennan Papers. See *Montana v. United States*, 565–66.

200. The first exception held, in theory, that the tribes had inherent sovereignty despite the general rule claiming something to the contrary. In the second exception, if the tribes retained inherent sovereignty, then by default they ruled over lands without it having to be proved in the first instance.

201. The justices had neglected the acts of treaty making between Native American nations and the U.S. government, the opinion of Chief Justice Marshall in *Cherokee Nation*, and the opinion of Chief Justice John Marshall in *Worcester* as well as the concurring opinion of Justice McLean in the same case.

202. The tribe did not base any of its argument on the premise that regulating nonmember fishing and hunting on nonmember fee land harmed tribal government or had an adverse effect on the economy or health of the tribe. Skibine, "Court's Use," 298, explains that "Montana's 'general rule' was in fact not a general rule at all until the Court decided to make it so."

203. "Draft opinion, 19 March 1981," Box 536, Brennan Papers. See *Montana v. United States,* 564; McSloy, "Back to the Future;" and Laurie Reynolds, "Indian Hunting and Fishing Rights: The Role of Tribal Sovereignty and Preemption," *North Carolina Law Review* 62 (1984): 762.

204. "Draft opinion, 19 March 1981," Box 536, Brennan Papers. See *Montana v. United States,* 560.

205. "Draft opinion, 19 March 1981," Box 536, Brennan Papers. See *Montana v. United States,* 560, 557.

206. The General Allotment Act of 1887 broke up communally owned tribal reservation lands. Specified acres of land were allotted to tribal members, and the U.S. government sold the surplus lands to non-Indians. However, not all reservations were allotted and broken up.

207. "Draft opinion, 19 March 1981," Box 536, Brennan Papers. See *Montana v. United States,* 559.

208. In direct contrast to the interpretation of the *Montana* court, future Supreme Court cases extracted a general principle whereby any congressional act that affected the exclusive authority of the tribes over their lands could remove the tribal status of the lands. It did not matter whether the act was designed specifically to remove the tribal and trust status of the lands; if the act generally applied on the reservation, then it was considered to take away exclusive tribal control automatically.

209. Mescalero Apache Tribe v. State of New Mexico, 630 F.2d 724 (10th Cir. 1980).

210. "Memorandum to the Conference," memorandum from Potter Stewart, April 1, 1981, 1–2, Box 325, Blackmun Papers.

211. See Gould,"Consent Paradigm," 895.

212. New Mexico v. Mescalero Apache Tribe, 462 U.S. 324 (1983). See Stephen E. Woodbury, "New Mexico v. Mescalero Apache Tribe: When Can a State Concurrently Regulate Hunting and Fishing by Nonmembers on Reservation Land," *New Mexico Law Review* 14 (1983): 349–69.

213. "No. 82-331, New Mexico v. Mescalero Apache Tribe," April 22, 1983, 1, Box 384, Blackmun Papers.

214. Ibid.; "No. 82-331, New Mexico v. Mescalero Apache Tribe," n.d., 1, Box 590, Brennan Papers.

215. "82-331 N. Mex. v. Mescalero Apache," Blackmun, April 17, 1983, 2, Box 384, Blackmun Papers.

216. "No. 82-331, New Mexico v. Mescalero Apache Tribe," April 22, 1983, 2, Box 384, Blackmun Papers.

217. Ibid.

218. "New Mexico v. Mescalero Apache Tribe No. 82-331, Conference Memo," n.d., Box 619, Brennan Papers.

219. "82-331 N. Mex. v. Mescalero Apache," Blackmun, April 17, 1983, 1–2, Box 384, Blackmun Papers.

220. "New Mexico v. Mescalero Apache Tribe No. 82-331, Conference Memo," n.d., Box 619, Brennan Papers. A GVR is a procedure in which the Supreme Court summarily grants certiorari, vacates the decision below without finding error, and remands the case for further consideration by the lower court.

221. "Bench Memo: No. 82-331 New Mexico v. Mescalero Apache Tribe," April 18, 1983, 4, Box 306, Marshall Papers.

222. Justice Marshall wrote, "The exercise of state authority may also be barred by an independent barrier—inherent tribal sovereignty—if it 'unlawfully infringe[s] on the right of reservation Indians to make their own laws and be ruled by them." *White Mountain Apache Tribe v. Bracker*, 334, quoting *Williams v. Lee*.

223. "No. 82-331, New Mexico v. Mescalero Apache Tribe," n.d., 1, Box 590, Brennan Papers; "No. 82-331, New Mexico v. Mescalero Apache Tribe," April 22, 1983, 1, Box 384, Blackmun Papers.

224. "No. 82-331, New Mexico v. Mescalero Apache Tribe," April 22, 1983, 2, Box 384, Blackmun Papers; "No. 82-331, New Mexico v. Mescalero Apache, Conf. 4/22/83," 3, Box 101, Powell Papers.

225. "No. 82-331, New Mexico v. Mescalero Apache Tribe," n.d., 2, Box 590, Brennan Papers.

226. "No. 82-331, New Mexico v. Mescalero Apache Tribe," April 22, 1983, 2, Box 384, Blackmun Papers.

227. "No. 82-331, New Mexico v. Mescalero Apache Tribe, May 27, 1983," memorandum from Justice Lewis Powell to Justice Thurgood Marshall, Box 101, Powell Papers.

228. "Re: New Mexico v. Mescalero Apache Tribe, No. 82-331," memorandum from Justice Sandra Day O'Connor to Justice Thurgood Marshall, May 31, 1983, 1, Box 384, Blackmun Papers. In the *New Mexico v. Mescalero* opinion, Justice Marshall wrote, "Because of their sovereign status, tribes and their reservation lands are insulated in some respects by a 'historic immunity from state and local control,' Mescalero Apache Tribe v. Jones" (332). The language used by Marshall was virtually identical to the suggestions of Justice O'Connor.

229. "Re: New Mexico v. Mescalero Apache Tribe, No. 82-331," memorandum from Justice Sandra Day O'Connor to Justice Thurgood Marshall, May 31, 1983, 2, Box 384, Blackmun Papers. This concern was also raised by Justice Stevens in a memorandum to Justice Marshall on May 27, 1983.

230. Justice Marshall wrote in the final opinion, "Thus, when a tribe undertakes an enterprise under the authority of federal law, an assertion of state authority must be viewed against any interference with the successful accomplishment of the federal purpose" (336).

231. "Re: New Mexico v. Mescalero Apache Tribe, No. 82-331," memorandum from Justice Sandra Day O'Connor to Justice Thurgood Marshall, June 3, 1983, Box 384, Blackmun Papers.

232. *New Mexico v. Mescalero Apache Tribe*, 344.

233. Brendale v. Confederated Yakima Indian Nation, 492 U.S. 408 (1989). General discussions of this case are contained in Royster, "Legacy of Allotment," 50–57; Singer, "Sovereignty and Property"; Judith V. Royster, "Environmental Protection and Native American Rights: Controlling Land Use through Environmental Regulation," *Kansas Journal of Law and Public Policy* 1 (1991): 89–96; Thomas W. Clayton, "Brendale v. Yakima Nation: A Divided Supreme Court Cannot Agree over Who May Zone Nonmember

Fee Lands within the Reservation," *South Dakota Law Review* 36 (1991): 329–57; Craighton Goeppele, "Solutions for Uneasy Neighbors: Regulating the Reservation Environment after Brendale v. Confederated Tribes & Bands of Yakima Indian Nation," *Washington Law Review* 65 (1990): 417–36; and C. G. Hakansson, "Indian Land-Use Zoning Jurisdiction: An Argument in Favor of Tribal Jurisdiction over Non-member Fee Lands within Reservation Boundaries," *South Dakota Law Review* 73 (1997): 721–40.

234. "Bench Memorandum," T.M., January 10, 1989, 4, Box 453, Marshall Papers.

235. "(No. 87–1622) Brendale v. Confederated Tribes, Yakima, (No. 87–1697) Wilkinson v. Confederated Tribes, Yakima, (No. 87–1711) Yakima v. Confederated Tribes. Yakima," H.A.B., January 13, 1989, 1, Box 524, Blackmun Papers.

236. Ibid., 2.

237. See Duthu, "Thurgood Marshall Papers," 94.

238. "(No. 87–1622) Brendale v. Confederated Tribes, Yakima, (No. 87–1697) Wilkinson v. Confederated Tribes, Yakima, (No. 87–1711) Yakima v. Confederated Tribes. Yakima," H.A.B., January 13, 1989, 2, Box 524, Blackmun Papers.

239. "87–1622-Brendale v. Conf. Tribes," T.M., June 20, 1988, Box 552, Marshall Papers.

240. "Bench memorandum, Tuesday, January 10, 1989," 13, Box 453, Marshall Papers.

241. "Bench Memorandum," T.M., 5, Box 453, Marshall Papers.

242. "Mr. Justice: Re: Nos. 87–1622, 87–1697, 87–1711, Consolidated Indian Cases," from Eddie to Blackmun, May 30, 1989, 1, Box 524, Blackmun Papers.

243. "87–1622, 1697, 1711 Brendale v. Yakima Nation," H.A.B., January 8, 1989, 3, Box 524, Blackmun Papers.

244. "Nos 87–1622, 87–1697, 87–1711, Brendale v. Yakima Indian Nation, Wilkinson v. Yakima Indian Nation, County of Yakima v. Yakima Indian Nation, Cert to CA9 (Skopil, *Fletcher*, Poole)," Lazarus, January 7, 1989, 23, Box 524, Blackmun Papers.

245. Ibid., 25, 24.

246. "87–1622-Brendale v. Conf. Tribes," T.M., Box 552, Marshall Papers.

247. "Mr. Justice: Re: Nos. 87–1622, 87–1697, 87–1711, Confederated Tribes (consolidated cases)," from Eddie to Blackmun, June 5, 1989, 1, Box 524, Blackmun Papers.

248. Third draft dissent by Blackmun, January 6, 1989. Box 524, Blackmun Papers.

249. *Brendale v. Confederated Yakima Indian Nation*, 409–10.

250. South Dakota v. Bourland, 508 U.S. 679 (1993). General discussions are found in Frickey, "Common Law," 45–48; Veronica L. Bowen, "The Extent of Indian Regulatory Authority over Non-Indians: South Dakota v. Bourland," *Creighton Law Review* 27 (1994): 605–59; Robert Laurence, "The Unseemly Nature of Reservation Diminishment by Judicial, as Opposed to Legislative, Fiat and the Ironic Role of the Indian Civil Rights Act in Limiting Both," *North Dakota Law Review* 71 (1995): 393–413; and Skibine, "Court's Use."

251. "No. 91-2051, South Dakota v. Bourland," H.A.B., March 5, 1993, 2, Box 619, Blackmun Papers.

252. "Mr. Justice: Re: No. 91-2051, South Dakota v. Bourland," March 8, 1993, from Bill to Blackmun, Box 619, Blackmun Papers.

253. "No. 91-2051, South Dakota v. Bourland," H.A.B., 2, 1, Box 619, Blackmun Papers.

254. Ibid.

255. Ibid.

256. Ibid.

257. *South Dakota v. Bourland*, 691–93. See Todd Miller, "Easements on Tribal Sovereignty," *American Indian Law Review* 26 (2001): 112.

258. *South Dakota v. Bourland*, 692. As Frickey, "Common Law," 50–51, observes, the rulings of the Supreme Court determine that "congressional action should be broadly construed to immunize nonmembers from unilateral tribal regulation."

259. *South Dakota v. Bourland*, 697. Clarence Thomas was nominated by President George H. W. Bush and sworn in as an associate justice in 1991. Born and raised in Georgia, Thomas set out on a path to become a priest. He attended St. John Vianney Minor Seminary and then Immaculate Conception Seminary in Missouri but left the latter because of the severe racism he encountered. He graduated from Holy Cross and attended Yale Law School. After graduation, Thomas worked in the office of the state attorney general of Missouri and in 1977 he became a corporate lawyer. He returned to Missouri a few years later and worked as a legislative aide to Republican U.S. senator John Danforth. In 1980, Thomas accepted a post from President Reagan as the assistant secretary for civil rights in the Department of Education. Reagan promoted Thomas to head the Equal Employment Opportunity Commission. In 1990, Thomas was appointed by President Bush to the U.S. Court of Appeals for the District of Columbia Circuit. During his tenure as an associate justice, Thomas has been a staunch conservative. Biographies of Current Justices, s.v. "Clarence Thomas"; Oyez Project, s.v. "Clarence Thomas."

260. *South Dakota v. Bourland*, 694–95. Although Justice Thomas conceded that the tribe had "former rights," Congress had to act explicitly in order to grant rights to the tribe over nonmembers (693).

261. "No. 91-2051 S.D. v. Gregg Bourland, et al., Cert to CA8 (*Bowman*, Heanney [Sr], Bright [Sr])," from Bill to Blackmun, February 26, 1993, 22, Box 619, Blackmun Papers.

262. "Mr. Justice: Re: South Dakota v. Bourland, No. 91-2051," from Bill to Blackmun, June 10, 1993, Box 619, Blackmun Papers.

263. "91-2051, So. Dak. v. Bourland," H.A.B, March 1, 1993, Box 619, Blackmun Papers.

264. "Mr. Justice: Re: No. 91-2051, South Dakota v. Bourland," from Bill to Blackmun, March 8, 1993, Box 619, Blackmun Papers.

265. "No. 91-2051 S.D. v. Gregg Bourland, et al, Cert to CA8 (*Bowman*, Heanney [Sr], Bright [Sr])," from Bill to Blackmun, February 26, 1993, 23, Box 619, Blackmun Papers, quoting *Brendale v. Confederated Yakima Indian Nation*, 450.

266. *South Dakota v. Bourland*, 698–99, quoting *Colville*, 153–54. Blackmun argued that neither the state "nor the majority is able to identify any overriding federal interest that would justify the implicit divestiture of the Tribe's authority to regulate non-Indian hunting and fishing. In rejecting the Tribe's inherent sovereignty argument, the majority relies on the suggestion in Montana v. United States . . . that 'the "exercise of tribal power beyond what is necessary to protect tribal self-government or to control internal relations is inconsistent with the dependent status of the tribes, and so cannot survive without express congressional delegation." ' . . . I already have had occasion to explain that this passage in Montana is contrary to 150 years of Indian law jurisprudence, and is not supported by the cases on which it relied" (699).

267. "No. 91-2051 S.D. v. Gregg Bourland, et al, Cert to CA8 (*Bowman*, Heanney [Sr], Bright [Sr])," from Bill to Blackmun, February 26, 1993, 24, Box 619, Blackmun Papers.

268. "Mr. Justice: Re: South Dakota v. Bourland, No. 91-2051," Box 619, Blackmun Papers, quoting *United States v. Wheeler*, 323. The sovereignty doctrine was predominantly upheld by Brennan, Marshall, and Blackmun, but their retirement in 1990, 1991, and 1994, respectively, ultimately led to the erosion of that doctrine.

269. *Strate v. A-1 Contractors*, 520 U.S. 438 (1997). For a general overview of the legal history and decision, see Jamelle King, "Tribal Court General Civil Jurisdiction over Actions between Non-Indian Plaintiffs and Defendants: Strate v. A-1 Contractors," *American Indian Law Review* 22 (1997): 191–221; Wambdi Awanwicake Wastewin, "Strate v. A-1 Contractors: Intrusion into the Sovereign Domain of Native Nations," *North Dakota Law Review* 74 (1998): 711–736; and Skibine, "Court's Use."

270. *Strate v. A-1 Contractors*, 445, 453, quoting *Montana v. United States*, 565, 439. The *Strate v. A-1 Contractors* court deduced from *Montana v. United States* that the inherent jurisdiction of the tribal court did not exceed the government capacity of the tribe: "As to nonmembers . . . a tribe's adjudicative jurisdiction does not exceed its legislative jurisdiction. Absent congressional direction enlarging Tribal Court jurisdiction" (440). The lands in question were tribal trust lands before the federal right-of-way. It could be argued that the *Strate v. A-1 Contractors* opinion, based on the authority of state law on a state highway, applied the concession contained in footnote six of the *White Mountain Apache Tribe v. Bracker* opinion: "For purposes of this action petitioners have conceded Pinetop's liability for both motor carrier license and use fuel taxes attributable to travel on state highways within the reservation" (140). If the state taxed a state highway in *Bracker*, then it followed that the state had exclusive jurisdiction in *Strate v. A-1 Contractors*.

271. *Williams v. Lee*, 222.

272. Blackmun specifically cited *Colville*, *Merrion v. Jicarilla Apache Tribe*, National Farmers Union Ins. Cos. v. Crow Tribe, 471 U.S. 845 (1985), and Iowa Mutual Ins. Co. v. LaPlante, 480 U.S. 9 (1987) for the general proposition that tribes enjoy civil jurisdiction over nonmembers absent congressional action to the contrary.

273. The tribe relied on a statement from *National Farmers Union Ins. Cos. v. Crow Tribe* that purported to highlight tribal court jurisdiction over nonmembers in civil matters. The statement was highlighted by the *Strate v. A-1 Contractors* court: "'The existence and extent of a tribal court's jurisdiction will require a careful examination of tribal sovereignty, the extent to which that sovereignty has been altered, divested, or diminished, as well as a detailed study of relevant statutes, Executive Branch policy as embodied in treaties and elsewhere, and administrative or judicial decisions'" (449), quoting *National Farmers*, 855–56. However, the *Strate* court reconciled *National Farmers* with *Montana*. If there was no explicit legislation or treaty, the Court used the two *Montana* exceptions to determine the question of tribal inherent sovereignty.

The *Iowa Mutual Ins. Co. v. LaPlante* court said, "Civil jurisdiction over such activities presumptively lies in the tribal courts unless affirmatively limited by a specific treaty provision or federal statute" (18). The *Strate v. A-1 Contractors* court addressed the quotation like this: "The statement stands for nothing more than the unremarkable proposition that, where tribes possess authority to regulate the activities of nonmembers, '[c]ivil jurisdiction over [disputes arising out of] such activities presumptively lies in the tribal courts'" (453), quoting *Iowa Mutual*, 18. Although *Iowa Mutual* cited cases that relied on inherent sovereignty, these were reconciled within the framework of *Montana v. United States*.

274. Fredericks, "America's First Nations," 396.

275. Miller, "Easements," 112. Furthermore, "Following *Strate* the only tribal sovereign power that remained relatively intact was a tribe's ability to tax nonmembers within the boundaries of the reservation" (113), although this was fundamentally eroded in *Atkinson Trading Co., Inc. v. Shirley*, as we see below.

276. *Strate v. A-1 Contractors*, 440.

277. Although *Strate v. A-1 Contractors* involved a 6.59-mile road surrounded by trust lands, the Court ignored the rationale used in *Brendale v. Confederated Yakima Indian Nation* in which a tribe had authority over nonmember fee lands that were not only open to the public but also surrounded by trust lands. In *Strate v. A-1 Contractors*, the road constituted much less than the 1 percent of fee lands referred to in *Brendale v. Confederated Yakima Indian Nation*. See also King, "Tribal Court," 212.

278. Miller, "Easements," 122.

279. *Strate v. A-1 Contractors*, 459.

280. Krakoff, "Undoing Indian Law," 1262–63.

281. Atkinson Trading Co., v. Shirley, 532 U.S. 645 (2001). The tax case appears in this section, and not in the tax section, because it is important to show the influence that previous civil case law had on *Atkinson*. Cases that sanctioned inherent tribal sovereignty and the inherent right of the tribes to tax nonmembers include *Kerr-McGee v. Navajo Tribe*; *Merrion v. Jicarilla Apache Tribe*; *Washington v. Confederated Tribes (Colville)*; *Barta v. Oglala Sioux Tribe*, 259 F.2d 553 (8th Cir. 1958), cert. denied, 358 U.S. 932 (1959); *Iron Crow v. Oglala Sioux Tribe*, 231 F.2d 89 (CA8 1956) (tribes had inherent sovereignty until reversed by Congress); *Buster v. Wright*, 135 F. 947, 950 (CA8 1905), appeal dism'd, 203 U.S. 599 (1906) (Creek Nation's power to tax nonmembers "was one of the inherent and essential attributes of its original sovereignty," 950); and *Morris v. Hitchcock*, 194 U.S. 384 (1904).

For a general overview of the case, see Krakoff, "Undoing Indian Law"; Lavelle, "Implicit Divestiture Reconsidered"; and Matthew L. M. Fletcher, "In Pursuit of Tribal Economic Development as a Substitute for Reservation Tax Revenue," *North Dakota Law Review* 80 (2004): 759–807.

282. Although taxation fell within the broad area of civil jurisdiction, before *Atkinson* the Supreme Court separated civil and taxation case law into two distinct areas. Even though the *Montana* proposition was established in 1981, it was not applied in *Merrion v. Jicarilla Apache Tribe*, *Ramah Navajo School Bd. v. Bureau of Revenue*, *Kerr-McGee Corp. v. Navajo Tribe*, or *Cotton Petroleum Corp. v. New Mexico*.

283. *Atkinson Trading Co., Inc. v. Shirley*, 645.

284. Ibid., 650–52, 645.

285. Ibid., 654.

286. Nordhaus, Hall, and Rudio, "Revisiting Merrion," 283.

287. *Atkinson Trading Co., Inc. v. Shirley*, 657.

288. Ibid., 653.

289. Ibid., 653, quoting *Merrion v. Jicarilla Apache Tribe*, 137, quoting *Colville*, 152. However, the *Atkinson* court conceded that "there are undoubtedly parts of the *Merrion* opinion that suggest a broader scope for tribal taxing authority than the quoted language above. But *Merrion* involved a tax that only applied to activity occurring on the reservation" (653).

290. The *Merrion* court stated: "The Jicarilla Apache Tribe resides on a reservation in northwestern New Mexico. Established by Executive Order in 1887, the reservation contains 742,315 acres, all of which are held as tribal trust property. The 1887 Executive Order set aside public lands in the Territory of New Mexico for the use and occupation of the Jicarilla Apache Indians, and contained no special restrictions except for a provision protecting pre-existing rights of bona fide settlers" (133–34).

291. *Atkinson Trading Co., Inc. v. Shirley*, 657.

292. See Fletcher, "In Pursuit of Tribal Economic Development."

293. *Atkinson Trading Co., Inc. v. Shirley*, 652, quoting *Merrion v. Jicarilla Apache* Tribe, 137.

294. To limit the broad principle of *Merrion v. Jicarilla Apache Tribe*, the *Atkinson* court cited a passage from that case to support this point of view: "'[the tribe]' . . . has no authority over a nonmember until the nonmember enters tribal lands or conducts business with the tribe'" (653), quoting *Merrion v. Jicarilla Apache Tribe*, 566. But the *Atkinson* court misapplied the context of this statement. The *Merrion* opinion not only reaffirmed both the territorial sovereignty of the tribe over the reservation and the inherent sovereignty of the tribe to tax nonmembers on the reservation but explicitly rebuked the *Merrion* dissent and held that the power to exclude was a lesser power of territorial sovereignty: "We do not question that there is a significant territorial component to tribal power: a tribe has no authority over a nonmember until the nonmember enters tribal lands or conducts business with the tribe. However, we do not believe that this territorial component to Indian taxing power, which is discussed in these early cases, means that the tribal authority to tax derives solely from the tribe's power to exclude nonmembers from tribal lands" (142).

295. David Souter was nominated by President George H. W. Bush and sworn in as an associate justice in 1990. Souter attended Harvard University and Harvard Law School and after graduation worked at a law firm in New Hampshire. In 1968 he was appointed assistant attorney general in the criminal division of New Hampshire. In 1971 he was appointed assistant attorney general of New Hampshire and only a few years later became attorney general of New Hampshire. After two years he served as a trial judge in New Hampshire's trial courts. Soon thereafter he was appointed to the New Hampshire Supreme Court and in 1990 was appointed by President Bush to the U.S. Court of Appeals for the First Circuit. As an associate justice on the Supreme Court, Souter was a moderate and formed a moderate voting bloc with Justices O'Connor and Kennedy. He retired from the Supreme Court in 2009 after nearly nineteen years of service. Biographies of Current Justices, s.v. "David H. Souter."; Oyez Project, s.v. "David H. Souter."

296. *Atkinson Trading Co., Inc. v. Shirley*, 659–60, quoting *Montana v. United* States, 565.

297. Nevada v. Hicks, 533 U.S. 353 (2001). General discussions are found in Singer, "Canons of Conquest"; Melanie Reed, "Native American Sovereignty Meets a Bend in the Road: Difficulties in Nevada v. Hicks," *Brigham Young University Law Review* 2002 (2002): 137–74; Amy Crafts, "Nevada v. Hicks and Its Implication on American Indian

Sovereignty," *Connecticut Law Review* 34 (2002): 1249–80; Catherine Struve, "How Bad Law Made a Hard Case Easy: Nevada v. Hicks and the Subject Matter Jurisdiction of Tribal Courts," *University of Pennsylvania Journal of Constitutional Law* 5 (2003): 288–317; and Robert N. Clinton, "There Is No Federal Supremacy Clause for Indian Tribes," *Arizona State Law Journal* 34 (2002): 113–260.

298. *Nevada v. Hicks,* 358–59, quoting *Montana v. United States,* 565.

299. See Richard E. James, "Sanctuaries No More: The United States Supreme Court Deals Another Blow to Indian Tribal Court Jurisdiction," *Washburn Law Journal* 41 (2002): 347–64; and Stacy Leeds, "The More Things Stay the Same: Waiting on Indian Law's Brown v. Board of Education," *Tulsa Law Review* 38 (2002): 82.

300. Singer, "Canons of Conquest," 652.

301. *Nevada v. Hicks,* 359, quoting *Montana v. United States,* 564.

302. *Nevada v. Hicks,* 360–61, quoting *Montana v. United States,* 564, and *Williams v. Lee,* 220.

303. In contrast to the *Williams* broad interpretation of tribal internal relations, the language used by the *Hicks* court continued to limit the *Williams* test.

304. *Nevada v. Hicks,* 360, quoting *Montana v. United States,* 565.

305. Ibid., 391–96.

306. Ibid., 353, quoting *Montana v. United States,* 564.

307. Ibid., 360.

308. Ibid., 375, citing *Montana v. United States,* 565.

309. Canby, in Senate Committee, *Rulings of the U.S. Supreme Court,* 47, declared that the *Hicks* court "took the last step."

310. Although the Court applied the *Strate v. A-1 Contractors* rationale, the Ginsburg concurrence wanted limits on both *Strate v. A-1 Contractors* and the *Nevada v. Hicks* opinion.

311. *Nevada v. Hicks,* 357–58, 376–77, 364–65.

312. The *Hicks* court explicitly stated that if the concurring judgment of O'Connor was implemented "it . . . would, for the first time, hold a non-Indian subject to the jurisdiction of a tribal court" (374). This was patently not true. The case of *Williams v. Lee* explicitly held that a nonmember had to pursue a claim in tribal court, not in state court.

313. Ibid., 382.

314. Ibid., 361–62.

315. Ibid., 354. The Court qualified the authority of the state and said that states did not "exert the same degree of regulatory authority within a reservation as they do without" (362). Interests in the reservation had to be balanced between "the Tribes and the Federal Government, on the one hand, and those of the State, on the other." *Washington v. Confederated Tribes of Colville Reservation,* 156 (1980), 362.

316. *Nevada v. Hicks,* 365, quoting Brief for United States as *Amicus Curiae* 12–13, n. 7.

317. *Nevada v. Hicks,* 366, 364.

318. Ibid., 373.

319. Singer, "Canons of Conquest," 659, believes that in 2001 the ruling of the Supreme Court fundamentally destroyed the presumption of tribal sovereignty: "Loss of tribal sovereignty is not something that happened long ago; it was accomplished by the nine Justices of the United States Supreme Court in their 2001 ruling in Hicks."

320. Wagnon v. Prairie Band Potawatomi Nation, 546 U.S. 95 (2005).

321. U.S. Library of Congress, Congressional Research Service, *Wagnon v. Prairie Band Potawatomi Nation:* State Tax on Motor Fuels Distributed to Indian Tribal Retailers, by M. Maureen Murphy (Washington D.C.: Government Printing Office, 2005), 1–6.

322. Plains Commerce Bank v. Long Family Land and Cattle Co., 128 S. Ct. 2709 (2008). On the history of the case and the Supreme Court opinion, see Frank Pommersheim, "Plains Commerce Bank v. Long Family Land and Cattle Company, Inc.: An Introduction with Questions," *South Dakota Law Review* 54 (2009): 365–74.

323. John G. Roberts Jr. was nominated by President George W. Bush and sworn in as chief justice of the Supreme Court in 2005. Roberts attended Harvard University and was managing editor of *Harvard Law Review.* He clerked in the U.S. Court of Appeals for the Second Circuit and also in the Supreme Court, where he served William H. Rehnquist. In 1981, Roberts was hired as a special assistant to the U.S. attorney general and then as associate counsel to President Reagan. He also served as deputy solicitor general in Republican administrations. After the 1992 presidential election, Roberts moved to private practice. Many years later, President Bush nominated him to the U.S. Court of Appeals for the District of Columbia Circuit. As chief justice, Roberts has a conservative philosophy and is a moderate conservative on the Court. Judicial restraint and the application of precedent are important to him. Biographies of Current Justices, s.v. "John G. Roberts, Jr."; Oyez Project, s.v. "John G. Roberts, Jr."

324. Matthew L. M. Fletcher, "Tribal Consent," *Stanford Journal of Civil Rights and Civil Liberties* 8 (2012): 106. See also Tweedy, "Connecting the Dots."

325. Supreme Court of the United States, "13–1496 Dollar General Corp. v. Ms Band of Choctaw," www.supremecourt.gov/qp/13–01496qp.pdf (accessed August 25, 2015).

326. Native American Rights Fund, "In the Supreme Court of the Mississippi Band of Choctaw Indians: No. CV-02–05," http://sct.narf.org/documents/dollar_general_v_choctaw/miss_choctaw_supreme/mississippi-choctaw-supreme-court-opinion.pdf (accessed August 20, 2015).

327. Doe v. Dollar Gen. Corp., No. CV-02–05 (Miss. Choctaw Tribal Ct. July 28, 2005).

328. Doe v. Dollar Gen. Corp., Nos. CV-02–05, SC 2005–6 (Miss. Choctaw Sup. Ct. Feb. 8, 2008) (per curiam). See Native American Rights Fund, "In the Supreme Court of the Mississippi Band of Choctaw Indians: No. CV-02–05."

329. Dolgen Corp., Inc. v. Mississippi Band of Choctaw Indians, No. 4:08CV22, 2008 WL 5381906 (S.D. Miss. Dec. 19, 2008).

330. *Dolgencorp Inc. v. Mississippi Band of Choctaw Indians,* 846 F. Supp. 2d 650 (S.D. Miss. 2011).

331. *Dolgencorp, Inc. v. Miss. Band of Choctaw Indians,* 732 F.3d 409 (5th Cir. 2013), 9.

332. *Plains Commerce Bank,* 334–35.

333. On March 14, 2014, less than a year after its opinion, the U.S. Court of Appeals for the Fifth Circuit withdrew the original opinion and substituted it with another. The court affirmed the district court's judgment.

334. On February 13, 2016, Antonin Scalia, the most conservative justice on the Court, passed away. The *Dollar General* case is one of the biggest cases awaiting judgment in Indian country in many years, and only time will tell whether Scalia's death results in a more positive outcome for Native America in the final written opinion of the Court.

Chapter 4

1. Native American Rights Fund, "Tribal Supreme Court Project," www.narf.org/sct/supctproject.html (accessed September 15, 2013).

2. National Congress of American Indians (NCAI), "Tribal Sovereignty Protection Initiative, Summary of September 11th Tribal Leaders Forum: A Strategic Plan to Stop the Supreme Court's Erosion of Tribal Sovereignty," September 17, 2001, 1, 2, www.ncai.org/ncai/resource/documents/governance/Sept11Summary.pdf (accessed September 15, 2013).

3. Marcia Coyle, "Indians Try to Keep Cases Away from High Court," *National Law Journal*, March 30, 2010, www.law.com/jsp/article.jsp?id=1202447092378 (accessed September 15, 2013).

4. NCAI, "Tribal Sovereignty Protection Initiative," 1–3.

5. Susan Williams, "Memorandum, To: Legislative Options Sub-Committee Members, Re: Sovereignty Bill—Issues for Discussion, October 2, 2001," 1–2.

6. Ibid., 2.

7. "Indian Tribal Government and Economic Enhancement Act, Draft October 2, 2001," 3.

8. Ibid., 5.

9. Williams, "Memorandum, To: Legislative Options Sub-Committee Members," 4–5. In 1934, Nathan Margold was a solicitor at the Department of the Interior.

10. Ibid., 5.

11. Legislative Options Subcommittee Memorandum, "Tribal Sovereignty Protection Initiative—Drafting Subcommittee, Re: Discussion Draft of Legislation," October 16, 2001," 1.

12. Ibid.

13. Ibid., 2.

14. Ibid., 3–4.

15. Tom Schlosser, "A Viable Approach to Sovereignty Protection Legislation," e-mail to author, November 21, 2001.

16. Ibid.

17. Senate Committee, *Rulings of the U.S. Supreme Court*.

18. "Tribes Seek to Overturn Supreme Court," Indianz.com, February 27, 2002, www.indianz.com/News/show.asp?ID=law02/02272002–1 (accessed October 1, 2013).

19. NCAI, *2003 Annual Report* (Washington D.C.: National Congress of American Indians), 13.

20. NCAI, "Tribal Sovereignty Protection Initiative—Rapid City Flyer," May 2003.

21. Liz Hill, "Senators Announce Legislation to Protect 'American Indian Tribal Sovereignty,'" www.yvwiiusdinvnohii.net/News2003/0302/NCAI030225Legislation.htm (accessed September 15, 2013).

22. If the Supreme Court rules that a statute is in violation of the U.S. Constitution, then Congress has the option to amend the statute. See Matthew R. Christiansen and William N. Eskridge Jr., "Congressional Overrides of Supreme Court Statutory Interpretation Decisions, 1967–2011," *Texas Law Review* 92 (2014): 1317–541; Alex Glashausser, "A Return to Form for the Exceptions Clause," *Boston College Law Review* 51 (2010): 1383–450; J. Mitchell Pickerill, "The Supreme Court and Congress: What Happens

in Congress after the Court Strikes Down Legislation?" *Insights on Law and Society* Fall (2006): 10–27; and Abner J. Mikva and Jeff Bleich, "When Congress Overrules the Court," *California Law Review* 79 (1991): 729–50.

23. Ex parte Crow Dog, 109 U.S. 556 (1883).

24. Harring, *Crow Dog's Case.*

25. Kappler, *Indian Affairs,* Vol. 1, 32–33. Since the introduction of the act into law in 1885, it has since been amended by numerous other acts and can be found today, with amendments, at Cornell University Law School: Legal Information Institute, "§1153. Offenses Committed within Indian Country," www4.1aw.cornell.edu/uscode/18/1153.html (accessed July 29, 2008).

26. It may also be argued that Congress only responded to the decision of the Supreme Court and enacted legislation that provided jurisdictional authority that it had not previously granted.

27. Duro v. Reina, 495 U.S. 676 (1990).

28. *Duro v. Reina,* 677.

29. Public Law 102-137, 102d Cong., 1st sess. (October 28, 1991), the "Duro Fix."

30. Carrie E. Garrow and Sarah Deer, *Tribal Criminal Law and Procedure* (Lanham, Md.: AltaMira Press, 2004), 90.

31. United States v. Lara, 541 U.S. 193 (2004). See Tweedy, "Connecting the Dots"; and "Lara Case Called Most Important of Generation," January 21, 2004, Indianz.com, http://64.38.12.138/News/archives/003357.asp (accessed May 15, 2013).

32. *United States v. Lara,* 194.

33. See "Supreme Court Affirms Tribal Powers over All Indians," April 20, 2004, Indianz.com, http://64.38.12.138/News/2004/001422.asp (accessed May 15, 2013).

34. *United States v. Lara,* 193–94. Stephen G. Breyer was nominated by President William J. Clinton and sworn in as an associate justice in 1994. Breyer graduated from Stanford University in 1959 before earning a degree from Oxford University in 1961 and a law degree from Harvard Law School in 1964. He worked in the U.S. Department of Justice from 1965 to 1967 before embarking on an academic career at Harvard University from 1967 to 1994. During his time at Harvard, Breyer also served as a judge on the United States Court of Appeals for the First Circuit from 1980 to 1990 and its chief judge from 1990 to 1994. Breyer is part of the liberal wing of the Supreme Court. Biographies of Current Justices, s.v. "Stephen Breyer."

35. A bill to amend the Homeland Security Act of 2002 to include Indian tribes among the entities consulted with respect to activities carried out by the Secretary of Homeland Security, and for other purposes, 108th Cong., 1st sess., S. 578. The equivalent bill, H.R. 2242, was introduced in the House of Representatives on May 22, 2003.

36. *Congressional Record,* 108th Cong., 1st sess., 2003, 149, 37:3372.

37. Courtney A. Stouff, "Native Americans and Homeland Security: Failure of the Homeland Security Act to Recognize Tribal Sovereignty," *Penn State Law Review* 108 (2003): 375–94.

38. *Congressional Record,* 108th Cong., 1st sess., 2003, 149, 37:3372.

39. See Joyce Howard Price, "Indians Want Jurisdiction to Combat Terrorism Threat," *Washington Times,* January 26, 2004. In a working paper examining indigenous people in post-9/11 America, Sara Singleton argues that the United States should have

invested in building tribal capacities to respond to security threats: "There is solid evidence to indicate that heightened responsibility or sovereignty is a necessary condition of better performance and accountability on Indian reservations." "Not Our Borders: Indigenous People and the Struggle to Maintain Shared Lives and Cultures in post-9/11 North America," Working Paper 4, January 2009 (Bellingham: Border Policy Research Institute, Western Washington University), 16–17. Indeed, Singleton argues that from the turn of the century the preferred option of governments when dealing with problem issues had been to devolve authority, but with the issue of border policy the opposite was true, necessitating a "rigid, antiquated, top-down structure." This type of policy, she argues, was inefficient and detrimental to Native peoples, particularly those with "international borders abutting Indian reservations." This unfavorable policy, in her opinion, would "continue to pose a security threat" to Native peoples and their cultures.

40. *Congressional Record*, 108th Cong., 1st sess., 2003, 149, 37:3372.

41. Wilkinson, *American Indians*, 91.

42. DeCoteau v. District County Court, 420 U.S. 425 (1975).

43. Canby, *American Indian Law*, 113–14.

44. Senate Committee on Indian Affairs, *Tribal Government Amendments to the Homeland Security Act of 2002: S. 578 to Amend the Homeland Security Act of 2002 to Include Indian Tribes among the Entities Consulted with Respect to Activities Carried out by the Secretary of Homeland Security*, 108th Cong., 1st sess., July 30, 2003, 23, 24.

45. U.S. Library of Congress, Congressional Research Service, *Indian Tribal Government Amendments to the Homeland Security Act: S. 578 and Indian Tribal Sovereignty*, by M. Maureen Murphy (Washington, D.C.: Government Printing Office, 2003), 1, 5. Roman J. Duran, of the NAICJA, later criticized the same general presumption, arguing that "the assault of critics that feel there is no due process for criminal defendants in tribal courts is a fallacy. Again, a well-funded justice system will result in the excellence of such justice systems, affording individuals their rights and protections within those systems." Senate Committee on Indian Affairs, *Tribal Courts and the Administration of Justice in Indian Country: Senate Hearing 110–576*, 110th Cong., 2d sess., July 24, 2008, 8.

46. U.S. Library of Congress, Congressional Research Service, *Indian Tribal Government Amendments to the Homeland Security Act: S. 578 and Indian Tribal Sovereignty*, by M. Maureen Murphy, 5.

47. James Hawkins, e-mail to author, September 13, 2010.

48. Governors' Interstate Indian Council, "GIIC Resolution 2003_01, 54th Annual Conference, Walker, Minnesota, August 21, 2003," http://w1.paulbunyan.net/~giic/resolutions/2003_01.pdf (accessed November 3, 2012).

49. Letter from W. Ron Allen to author, September 14, 2010. However, Allen wrote, S. 578 ultimately "failed to pass because of the controversial Section 13."

50. Ibid. The assessment that the votes were not there has been supported by many who work within federal Indian Law. Lucy Simpson, a lawyer with the Indian Law Resource Center, believes that pro-sovereignty initiatives do not usually have much support in Congress for political reasons: "There are very few Congressional districts that have large Indian populations, so for the vast majority of Congressmen, Indian issues are not at the forefront." E-mail from Lucy Simpson to author, December 9,

2010. Professor Joseph Singer concurs with the reasoning that Congress has no political motivation to support tribal jurisdictional legislation: "In general, there is no political will in Congress to expand the power of tribes over non-Indians since this would likely be very politically controversial in the United States." E-mail from Joseph Singer to author, September 25, 2010.

51. E-mail from Kevin K. Washburn to author, August 26, 2010.

52. E-mail from Tom Schlosser to author, August 27, 2010.

53. Citizens Equal Rights Alliance, Press Release, "There's a Civil Rights Nightmare Waiting to Happen with Senator Inouye's S. 578 Amendment to the Homeland Security Bill," May 16, 2003, 1.

54. "Bill's Tribal Jurisdiction Provisions Contested," July 31, 2003, Indianz.com, http://64 .38.12.138/News/archives/000532.asp (accessed November 3, 2012).

55. *Duro v. Reina*, 707.

56. See, for example, Richard L. Warren, "The Potential Passage of Proposed Senate Bill 578 and Its Implications on Hicks v. Nevada and Twenty Years of Supreme Court Jurisprudence," *American Indian Law Review* 29 (2004): 383–402.

57. E-mail from David Wilkins to author, August 29, 2010.

58. See, for example, John Grisham, *The Innocent Man* (New York: Random House, 2006). For discussion of miscarriages of justice, see Mary L. Dudziak, "The Case of 'Death for a Dollar-Ninety-Five': Miscarriages of Justice and Constructions of American Identity," in *Making Sense of Miscarriages of Justice*, ed. Charles Ogletree and Austin Sarat (New York University Press, 2009); and Samuel R. Gross, "Lost Lives: Miscarriages of Justice in Capital Cases," *Law and Contemporary Problems* 61 (1998): 125–52.

59. Senate Committee, *Tribal Courts*, 38, see n. 792.

60. See Price, "Indians Want Jurisdiction."

61. William Norman Grigg, "America the Balkanized: American Indian Groups and Their Political Allies, Exploiting the Homeland Security Issue, Are Conducting a Quiet Power Grab," *New American* 19, no. 20 (2003).

62. Letter from W. Ron Allen to author, September 14, 2010.

63. Letter from Senator Maria Cantwell to author, May 14, 2004.

64. NCAI, *2004 Annual Report* (Washington, D.C.: National Congress of American Indians, 2004), 8.

65. NCAI, "Executive Director's Report to the NCAI Board—Memo, Re: Legislative Update, 1/15/2004," 3.

66. A bill to amend the Homeland Security Act of 2002 to include Indian tribes among the entities consulted with respect to activities carried out by the Secretary of Homeland Security, and for other purposes, 109th Cong., 1st sess., S. 477.

67. U.S. Library of Congress, Congressional Research Service, *Indian Tribal Government Amendments to the Homeland Security Act: S. 578 and Indian Tribal Sovereignty*, by M. Maureen Murphy (Washington, D.C.: Government Printing Office, 2005), 1.

68. Matthew L. M. Fletcher, "Resisting Federal Courts on Tribal Jurisdiction," *Colorado Law Review* 81 (2010): 990.

69. NCAI, "Tribal Sovereignty Protection Initiative Upcoming Meeting: Bismarck, N.D.," e-mail to author, May 26, 2005.

70. MacArthur v. San Juan County, 405 F.Supp.2d 1302 (D. Utah 2005), 1311–12.

71. Tribal Law and Order Act of 2010, Pub. L. No. 111–211, §202(a)(4), 124 Stat. 2261, 2263.

72. Senate Committee on Indian Affairs, *The Tribal Law and Order Act of 2009: Report 111–93*, 111th Cong., 1st sess., October 29, 2009.

73. Tribal Law and Order Act of 2010, Pub. L. No. 111–211, §202(a)(4), 124 Stat. 2261, 2262.

74. Ch. 341, §9, 23 Stat. 385 (codified as amended at 18 U.S.C. §1153 [2006]).

75. Pub. L. No. 90-284, §§201–203, 82 Stat. 77 (codified as amended at 25 U.S.C. §§1301–1303 (2006 & Supp. IV 2011]).

76. For an overview and insight into the complexity of criminal jurisdiction in Indian country, see U.S. Department of Justice, "689 Jurisdictional Summary," www.justice. gov/usao/eousa/foia_reading_room/usam/title9/crm00689.htm (accessed October 5, 2013). This page shows a chart from the U.S. attorneys' manual and summarizes which government has jurisdiction in various scenarios.

77. Senate Committee on Indian Affairs, *Law Enforcement in Indian Country: Senate Hearing 110–136*, 110th Cong., 1st sess., June 21, 2007, 63.

78. Doris M. Meissner, *Report of the Task Force on Indian Matters* (Washington, D.C.: Government Printing Office, October 1975), 77.

79. U.S. Department of Justice, "Report of the Executive Committee for Indian Country Law Enforcement Improvements: Final Report to the Attorney General and the Secretary of the Interior, October 31, 1997." This can be found at www.justice.gov/otj/ icredact.htm (accessed October 16, 2013).

80. Senate Committee, *Tribal Law and Order Act of 2009*, 2.

81. Senate Committee on Indian Affairs, *Examining S. 797, The Tribal Law and Order Act of 2009: Senate Hearing 111–214*, 111th Cong., 1st sess., June 25, 2009.

82. Senate Committee on Indian Affairs, *Examining Federal Declinations to Prosecute Crimes in Indian Country: Senate Hearing 110–683*, 110th Cong., 2d sess., September 18, 2008, 40.

83. Senate Committee, *Examining S. 797*, 5.

84. U.S. Senate Congressional Record, 111th Cong., 2d sess, June 23, 2010, S. 5366.

85. U.S. House of Representatives, Congressional Record—House, 111th Cong., 2d sess., July 21, 2010, H. 5863.

86. U.S. House of Representatives, Congressional Record—House, 111th Cong., 2d sess., July 21, 2010, H. 5864.

87. U.S. House of Representatives, "Final Vote Results for Roll Call 455," July 21, 2010, http://clerk.house.gov/evs/2010/r011455.xml (accessed October 21, 2013).

88. U.S. Senate Committee on Indian Affairs, "Concept Paper on Tribal Justice Systems," November 7, 2007, 11. For a copy, see www.indian.senate.gov/public/_files/Indian-crimeconceptpaper.pdf (accessed October 16, 2013).

89. Kevin K. Washburn e-mail to author, August 26, 2010.

90. Senate Committee on Indian Affairs, *Discussion Draft Legislation to Address Law and Order in Indian Country: Senate Hearing 110–432*, 110th Cong., 2d sess., June 19, 2008, 15. See also testimony by James S. Richardson Sr., president of the Federal Bar Association, who supported modification of the draft bill to extend tribal criminal jurisdiction to tribal courts over non-Indians in domestic and family violence.

91. Senate Committee on Indian Affairs, *Law and Order in Indian Country: Senate Hearing 110–408*, 110th Cong., 2d sess., March 17, 2008, 4.

92. Senate Committee on Indian Affairs, *Law Enforcement in Indian Country: Senate Hearing 110–136*, 110th Cong., 1st sess., June 21, 2007, 23.

93. Ibid., 35. On the jurisdiction table, see note 76 above.

94. Senate Committee, *Discussion Draft Legislation*, 33.

95. Senate Committee, *Law Enforcement in Indian Country*, 54. In addition, Washburn and Thomas B. Heffelfinger suggested that the committee examine the option of a partial *Oliphant* fix. Washburn argued that interested tribes should have criminal authority over non-Indians who committed misdemeanor crimes, violent crimes, and narcotics offenses. This was suggested as a pilot program. Heffelfinger argued for tribal criminal authority over non-Indians accused of domestic violence, child abuse, or drug dealing in Indian country.

96. Senate Committee, *Law and Order in Indian Country*, 66. See pages 9–13 of Enos's testimony for the numbers of Indians and non-Indians arrested by the Salt River police over many months.

97. Senate Committee, *Discussion Draft Legislation*, 65.

98. Senate Committee, *Examining S. 797*, 88.

99. Senate Committee, *Law and Order in Indian Country*, 3.

100. Ibid., 41.

101. Ibid., 42. Troy A. Eid, U.S. attorney from Colorado, argued that a congressional repeal of *Oliphant* based on these constitutional concerns would in the end "give non-Indians a far greater stake in the future of Indian country than would otherwise exist during our lifetimes. . . . Over time, that potential exposure of non-Indians to tribal courts and police departments, and federal and tribal policymakers' concern about such matters, [will] create an invaluable off-reservation constituency to support tribes in improving their criminal justice systems." Senate Committee, *Examining S. 797*, 48.

102. Senate Committee, *Law and Order in Indian Country*, 27. Humetewa reaffirmed her position: "If someone commits a crime here in the community, either tribal government will have jurisdiction, the state county attorney's office . . . can have jurisdiction dependent upon the particular circumstance of the crime, or if it falls into a major crime act violation, the U.S. Attorney's Office would address that prosecution, or if it's a non-Indian and it rises to a particular level of felony offense or even in some circumstances not, then the U.S. Attorney's Office would then look at it for potential felony crime jurisdiction" (27).

103. Senate Committee, *Law Enforcement in Indian Country*, 64–68.

104. Ibid., 70.

105. Despite the promises of federal money to support the Tribal Law and Order Act of 2010, there have been funding problems. In addition, there has been ambivalence about the effectiveness of the act itself. See generally Gideon M. Hart, "A Crisis in Indian Country: An Analysis of the Tribal Law and Order Act of 2010," *Regent University Law Review* 23 (2010): 139–85; Senate Committee on Indian Affairs, *Tribal Law and Order Act One Year Later: Have We Improved Public Safety and Justice throughout Indian Country?* 112th Cong., 1st sess., September 22, 2011; Samuel D. Cardick, "The Failure of the Tribal Law and Order Act of 2010 to End the Rape of American Indian Women," *Saint Louis University Public Law Review* 31 (2012): 539–78; Jasmine Owens,

"'Historic' in a Bad Way: How the Tribal Law and Order Act Continues the American Tradition of Providing Inadequate Protection to American Indian and Alaska Native Rape Victims," *Journal of Criminal Law and Criminology* 102 (2012): 497–524; and Seth J. Fortin, "The Two-Tiered Program of the Tribal Law and Order Act," *UCLA Law Review Discourse* 61 (2013): 88–109.

106. Kevin K. Washburn e-mail to author, August 26, 2010.

107. M. Brent Leonhard, "Closing a Gap in Indian County Justice: *Oliphant, Lara,* and DOJ's Proposed Fix," *Harvard Journal on Racial and Ethnic Justice* 28 (2012): 117–71; U.S. Department of Justice, Bureau of Justice Statistics, *American Indians and Crime,* by Lawrence A. Greenfeld and Steven K. Smith (Washington, D.C.: Government Printing Office, 1999); U.S. Department of Justice, Bureau of Justice Statistics, *A BJS Statistical Profile, 1992–2002: American Indians and Crime,* by Steven W. Parry (Washington, D.C.: Government Printing Office, 2004); Amnesty International, *Maze of Injustice: The Failure to Protect Indigenous Women from Sexual Violence in the USA* (New York: Amnesty International, 2007).

108. Senate Committee, *Examining S. 797,* 6.

109. Senate Committee on Indian Affairs, *Native Women: Protecting, Shielding, and, Safeguarding Our Sisters, Mothers and Daughters: Senate Hearing 112–311,* 112th Cong., 1st sess., July 14, 2011, 5–6.

110. "Obama Administration Record for American Indians and Alaska Natives," The White House, www.whitehouse.gov/sites/default/files/docs/american_indians_and _alaska_natives_community_record.pdf (accessed September 5, 2012).

111. U.S. Department of Justice, "Letter from Ronald Weich (Assistant Attorney General) to Joseph R. Biden," July 21, 2011, 2, 1, 4. This document can be found at www.justice. gov/tribal/docs/legislative-proposal-violence-against-native-women.pdf (accessed October 24, 2013).

112. Ibid., 7.

113. Ibid., 1.

114. Leonhard, "Closing a Gap," 164–65. In contrast, Tom Gede is concerned about the untested due process and equal protection rights of non-Indians in tribal court. He bases his analysis on a 2005 case involving the rights of a Native American before the tribal court of another tribe. Gede concludes that Congress had to decide whether the proposal was "warranted" because non-Indians would be subject to the "authority of an extraconstitutional sovereign to which they had not previously been subject" and to courts where the "customary guarantees of federal constitutional protections may be questioned." "Criminal Jurisdiction of Indian Tribes: Should Non-Indians Be Subject to Tribal Criminal Authority under VAWA?" *Engage* 12 (2012): 40–44.

115. U.S. Department of Justice, "Letter from Ronald Weich," 3.

116. U.S. Library of Congress, Congressional Research Service, *Tribal Criminal Jurisdiction over Non-Indians in the Violence Against Women Act (VAWA) Reauthorization and the SAVE Native Women Act,* by Jane M. Smith and Richard M. Thompson II (Washington, D.C.: Government Printing Office, 2012).

117. U.S. Senate, *Violence Against Women Reauthorization Act of 2011: Report 112–153,* 112th Cong., 2d sess., March 12, 2012, 32–33.

118. See Govtrack.us, "S. 1925 (112th): Violence Against Women Reauthorization Act of 2012 (On Passage of the Bill)," www.govtrack.us/congress/votes/112–2012/s87# (accessed October 15, 2013).

119. U.S. Senate, *Violence Against Women Reauthorization Act of 2011: Report 112–153*, 36–38. See Leonhard, "Closing a Gap," for analysis of Native American treaties that protected tribal authority over non-Indians.

120. *Oliphant v. Schlie*, 544 F.2d 1007 (9th Cir. 1976).

121. *Oliphant v. Suquamish Indian Tribe* (1978).

122. Leonhard, "Closing a Gap," 131. See Kappler, *Indian Affairs*, Vol. 2, for the Treaty with the Six Nations, Oct. 22, 1784, 7 Stat. 15.

123. U.S. Congress, "Congressional Record—House," 113th Cong., 1st sess., February 28, 2013, H. 738.

124. *Oliphant v. Suquamish Indian Tribe*, 197. See *United States v. Bailey*, F. Cas. 14,495 (C.C. Tenn.) (1834), holding that neither state nor federal authority could allow the prosecution of a non-Indian on a non-Indian crime within Indian country.

125. Kappler, *Indian Affairs*, Vol. 2, 12, for Treaty with the Choctaw, January 3, 1786, 7 Stat., 21.

126. Leonhard, "Closing a Gap."

127. In *Choctaw Nation v. Oklahoma*, 397 U.S. 620, 631 (1970), the Court stated, "Any doubtful expressions in treaties should be resolved in the Indians' favor," and in *Carpenter v. Shaw*, 280 U.S. 363, 367 (1930) it was held that "doubtful expressions are to be resolved in favor of [the Indians]."

128. Winters v. United States, 207 U.S. 564, 576–77 (1908).

129. U.S. Senate, *Violence Against Women Reauthorization Act of 2011: Report 112–153*, 48. For criticism of the Court's opinion and supporting evidence, see Richard B. Collins, "Implied Limitations on the Jurisdiction of Indian Tribes," *Washington Law Review* 54 (1979): 479–529; Maxfield, "Oliphant v. Suquamish Tribe"; Samuel E. Ennis, "Reaffirming Indian Tribal Court Criminal Jurisdiction over Non-Indians: An Argument for a Statutory Abrogation of Oliphant," *UCLA Law Review* 57 (2009): 553–605; Wilkins, *American Indian Sovereignty*; and Leonhard, "Closing a Gap."

130. See Bethany R. Berger, "Justice and the Outsider: Jurisdiction over Nonmembers in Tribal Legal Systems," *Arizona State Law Journal* 37 (2005):1047–125; and Kevin K. Washburn, "American Indians, Crime, and the Law," *Michigan Law Review* 104 (2006): 709–78.

131. U.S. Senate, *Violence Against Women Reauthorization Act of 2011: Report 112–153*, 38.

132. National Association of Criminal Defense Lawyers, "Coalition Letter to the Senate on the Violence Against Women Reauthorization Act of 2012 ('VAWA') (S. 1925)," April 23, 2012, www.nacdl.org/Advocacy.aspx?id=14904 (accessed October 3, 2013).

133. U.S. Senate, *S. 1925: An Act to reauthorize the Violence Against Women Act of 1994*. 112th Cong., 2d sess., April 26, 2012, 186–87; Kevin Washburn et al., n.d., "Letter from Law Professors: Constitutionality of Tribal Government Provisions in VAWA Reauthorization," April 21, 2012, 3–4, http://lawprofessors.typepad.com/files/vawa-letter-from-law-professors—-tribal-provisions.pdf (accessed October 5, 2013).

134. U.S. Senate, *Violence Against Women Reauthorization Act of 2011: Report 112–153*, 52.

135. Ibid.

136. *United States v. Lara*, 241.

137. U.S. Senate, *Violence Against Women Reauthorization Act of 2011: Report 112–153*, 38.

138. Leonhard, "Closing a Gap," 158.

139. *Worcester v. Georgia*, 560.

140. U.S. House of Representatives, *Violence Against Women Reauthorization Act of 2012: House Report 112–480 Part I*, 112th Cong., 2d sess., May 15, 2012. See Paul J. Larkin Jr. and Joseph Luppino-Esposito, "The Violence Against Women Act, Federal Criminal Jurisdiction, and Indian Tribal Courts," *BYU Journal of Public Law* 27 (2012): 6.

141. U.S. House of Representatives, *Violence Against Women Reauthorization Act of 2012: House Report 112–480 Part I*, 58.

142. Washburn et al., "Letter from Law Professors." See also Zachary S. Price, "Dividing Sovereignty in Tribal and Territorial Criminal Jurisdiction," *Columbia Law Review* 113 (2013): 657–732; Laura C. Sayler, "Back to Basics: Special Domestic Violence Jurisdiction in the Violence Against Women Reactivation Act of 2013 and the Expansion of Inherent Tribal Sovereignty," *Cardozo Law Review de novo* 1 (January 3, 2014): 1–34, http://ssrn.com/abstract=2233126; and Ennis, "Reaffirming Indian Tribal Court."

143. National Association of Criminal Defense Lawyers and National Association of Federal Defenders, "Advocacy Letter on H.R. 4970, the 'Violence Against Women Reauthorization Act of 2012,'" May 3, 2012, 15–16, www.nacdl.org/Advocacy.aspx?id=14904 (accessed October 15, 2013). For an interesting article about the application of tribal rights by tribal courts, see Rob Roy Smith, "Enhancing Tribal Sovereignty by Protecting Indian Civil Rights: A Win-Win for Indian Tribes and Tribal Members," *American Indian Law Journal* 1 (2012): 41–55. Smith argues that tribal courts should apply the Indian Civil Rights Act without exception in all cases to avoid negative publicity and judicial defeats in federal courts.

144. *United States v. Lara*, 212.

145. See Robert J. Miller, "American Indian Influence on the United States Constitution and Its Framers," *American Indian Law Review* 18 (1993): 133–60; and Leonhard, "Closing a Gap."

146. *Johnson v. McIntosh*, 21 U.S. 543 (1823), 593.

147. Generally, see *Johnson v. McIntosh* (1823) and *Worcester v. Georgia* (1832). These cases highlight the historical assumption regarding tribal criminal authority over non-Indians.

148. See Justice Brennan's dissenting opinion in *Duro v. Reina*: "The commission of a crime on the reservation is all the 'consent' that is necessary to allow the tribe to exercise criminal jurisdiction over the nonmember Indian" (707). Although Brennan was talking about a nontribal member, the rationale can be applied to non-Indians too.

149. U.S. House of Representatives, *Violence Against Women Reauthorization Act of 2012: House Report 112–480 Part I*, 58. The House relied on the CRS report on the bill, which stated that Congress might not have the authority to allow non-Indians to be subject to inherent tribal sovereignty.

150. U.S. Library of Congress, Congressional Research Service, *Tribal Criminal Jurisdiction over Non-Indians*, 7.

151. Ibid., 6.

152. U.S. House of Representatives, *Violence Against Women Reauthorization Act of 2012: House Report 112–480 Part I*, 245.

153. Ibid., 246.

154. "H.R. 4970 (112th): Violence Against Women Reauthorization Act of 2012 (On Passage of the Bill)," govtrack.us, www.govtrack.us/congress/votes/112-2012/h258 (accessed October 21, 2013).

155. Congressional Record, "Vol. 159, No. 22—Daily Edition," 113th Cong., 1st sess., February 12, 2013.

156. Sayler, "Back to Basics."

157. National Association of Criminal Defense Lawyers, "Coalition Letter to the Senate," 8.

158. U.S. Congress, "Congressional Record—House," 113th Cong., 1st sess., February 28, 2013, H. 738.

159. Ibid.

160. U.S. Congress, "Final Vote Results for Roll Call 55," http://clerk.house.gov/evs/2013/r011055.xml (accessed October 15, 2013).

161. When the legislation passed, the tribes that wanted to prosecute non-Indians for domestic violence crimes had to wait until March 7, 2015. However, under a pilot project, tribes could have prosecuted sooner if they applied to be a part of the project and showed that they could protect a defendant's right under federal law. Thereafter, the tribe had to wait for consent to proceed from the Department of Justice. See Department of Justice, "VAWA 2013 and Tribal Jurisdiction over Crimes of Domestic Violence," www.justice.gov/tribal/docs/vawa-2013-tribal-jurisdiction-overnon-indian-perpetrators-domesticviolence.pdf (accessed October 23, 2013).

162. U.S. Department of Justice, "Statement by Attorney General Eric Holder on the House Passage of the Reauthorization of the Violence Against Women Act: Thursday, February 28, 2013," www.justice.gov/opa/pr/2013/February/13-ag-253.html (accessed October 25, 2013).

163. After the passing of Justice Scalia in February 2016, it remains to be seen whether President Obama will be successful in appointing a justice and whether that justice will be supportive or dismissive of tribal rights.

164. Gede, "Criminal Jurisdiction"; National Association of Criminal Defense Lawyers, "Coalition Letter to the Senate." For an interesting argument about how to resolve these questions, see Price, "Dividing Sovereignty."

165. Ennis, "Reaffirming Indian Tribal Court"; Sayler, "Back to Basics."

166. Sayler, "Back to Basics."

167. Justice Kennedy in particular argued in *United States v. Lara* (2004) that tribal courts would require the consent of non-Indians to have any kind of criminal jurisdiction over them. If Kennedy cannot recognize inherent tribal sovereignty, then are there any other solutions to satisfy his consent theory? It has been well documented that in *Worcester v. Georgia* (1832) Chief Justice Marshall stated that a weaker sovereign did not surrender its sovereignty to govern to a more powerful ally. On the contrary, the more powerful ally protected but kept the sovereign powers of the weaker sovereign intact. Unfortunately, this relationship can give rise to problems. Over the course of federal Indian law, there has been fierce debate about the source of congressional power over Native American tribes. In *United States v. Kagama*

(1886), the Supreme Court declared that congressional authority, called plenary power, derived from Article I of the Constitution, whereby Congress has the power "to regulate commerce with foreign nations, and among the several states, and with the Indian tribes." If Article I is assumed to be the delegation of congressional authority over Native American issues, then surely the consent of non-Indians automatically transfers upon this power of Congress, regardless of congressional legislation or statement of intent. Nevertheless, we must not forget about the original concept of a stronger ally protecting a weaker sovereign. The authority of the weaker sovereign is undiminished within this relationship despite Supreme Court case law, termed common law, and federal statutes to the contrary. Interestingly, the Constitution, a set of rights, was agreed upon by a government and seen as applicable to individuals. However, these rights were purported to be "inalienable natural rights" that apply to Native Americans. See David Cole, "Are Foreign Nationals Entitled to the Same Constitutional Rights as Citizens?" *Thomas Jefferson Law Review* 25 (2003): 372. If the rights contained within the Constitution are natural rights merely enshrined in a document, then non-Indians are automatically protected under these rights within the sphere of an extraconstitutional body with inherent sovereignty.

168. For an in-depth discussion of the commerce clause, see Pomp, "Unfulfilled Promise."
169. See Tweedy, "Connecting the Dots"; and Valencia-Weber, "Supreme Court's Indian Law Decisions."

Chapter 5

1. See, for example, Skibine, "Court's Use"; Tweedy, "Connecting the Dots"; and Corntassel and Witmer, *Forced Federalism.*
2. Senate Committee, *Rulings of the U.S. Supreme Court,* 91.
3. NCAI, *Concept Paper, 2003 Legislative Proposal on Tribal Governance and Economic Enhancement 25 July 2002* (Washington D.C.: NCAI, 2002), 2; Joseph P. Kalt and Joseph William Singer, "Myths and Realities of Tribal Sovereignty: The Law and Economics of Indian Self-Rule," Harvard Project on American Indian Economic Development Joint Occasional Papers on Native Affairs 2004–03, 2004; Stephen P. McCleary, "A Proposed Solution to the Problem of State Jurisdiction to Tax on Indian Reservations," *Gonzaga Law Review* 26 (1991): 628; Senate Committee, *Rulings of the U.S. Supreme Court.*
4. Senate Committee, *Rulings of the U.S. Supreme Court,* 3–4, 9, 28–38, 51–54, 58; Senate Committee, *Tribal Government Amendments,* 33–36, 91–92.
5. Miller, "Easements," 114.
6. Merrion v. Jicarilla Apache Tribe, 455 U.S. 130 (1982).
7. Although White Mountain Apache Tribe v. Bracker, 448 U.S. 136 (1980), Central Machinery Co. v. Arizona Tax Comm'n, 448 U.S. 160 (1980), Ramah Navajo School Bd. v. Bureau of Revenue, 458 U.S. 832 (1982), and California v. Cabazon Band of Mission Indians, 480 U.S. 202 (1987) prevented concurrent tribal and state taxation of nonmember businesses on the reservation, after 1989 concurrent taxation was the norm.
8. Washington v. Confederated Tribes, 447 U.S. 134 (1980).

9. Ibid., 145

10. Ibid., 144–45.

11. Cotton Petroleum Corp. v. New Mexico, 490 U.S. 163 (1989).

12. Ibid., 170.

13. NCAI, *Concept Paper,* 2.

14. Ibid., 2.

15. Kalt and Singer, "Myths and Realities," 33.

16. Ibid., 32.

17. Senate Committee on Indian Affairs, *State and Federal Tax Policy: Building New Markets in Indian Country: Senate Hearing 112–619,* 112th Cong., 1st sess., December 8, 2011. The evidence presented in this hearing addressed the fundamental problems presented by state and local taxation of nonmember businesses on reservations along with their effect on tribes, tribal members, and nonmembers. See also McCleary, "Proposed Solution," 628.

18. *Cotton Petroleum Corp. v. New Mexico,* 208.

19. Atkinson Trading Co. v. Shirley, 532 U.S. 645 (2001).

20. Senate Committee, *Rulings of the U.S. Supreme Court,* 2–4, 9, 28–38, 51–54, 58; Senate Committee, *Tribal Government Amendments,* 33–36.

21. Senate Committee, *Tribal Courts,* 33.

22. NCAI, *Concept Paper,* 2.

23. Senate Committee, *Rulings of the U.S. Supreme Court,* 31.

24. Senate Committee, *Tribal Courts,* 35.

25. Senate Committee, *Rulings of the U.S. Supreme Court,* 31, 32.

26. Ibid., 91.

27. NCAI, *Concept Paper,* 2.

28. Senate Committee, *Rulings of the U.S. Supreme Court,* 3.

29. Senate Committee, *Tribal Government Amendments,* 35.

30. Senate Committee, *Rulings of the U.S. Supreme Court,* 92.

31. Ibid., 33.

32. Ibid., 31.

33. Pevar, *Rights of Indians,* 167. Civil jurisdiction includes family matters (marriage, divorce, child custody and adoptions), property matters (taxation, land use, inheritance), and the sales of goods and services.

34. Pommersheim, *Braid of Feathers.*

35. Babcock, "Civic-Republican Vision," 489–90.

36. Yvonne Mattson, "Civil Regulatory Jurisdiction over Fee Simple Tribal Lands: Why Congress Is Not Acting Trustworthy," *Seattle University Law Review* 27 (2004): 1064–65.

37. Montana v. United States, 450 U.S. 544 (1981); Brendale v. Confederated Yakima Indian Nation, 492 U.S. 408 (1989).

38. *Brendale v. Confederated Yakima Indian Nation,* 421.

39. Ibid., 460.

40. Senate Committee on Indian Affairs, *The Indian Reorganization Act—75 Years Later: Renewing Our Commitment to Restore Tribal Homelands and Promote Self-Determination,* 112th Cong., 1st sess., June 23, 2011, 70.

41. South Dakota v. Bourland, 508 U.S. 679 (1993); Strate v. A-1 Contractors, 520 U.S. 438 (1997).

42. Senate Committee, *Rulings of the U.S. Supreme Court*, 26.

43. Ibid., 35.

44. Nevada v. Hicks, 533 U.S. 353 (2001).

45. Senate Committee, *Rulings of the U.S. Supreme Court*, 27.

46. Ibid., 30.

47. Ibid., 53.

48. Senate Committee, *Indian Reorganization Act—75 Years Later*.

49. Kalt and Singer, "Myths and Realities," 4.

50. Senate Committee, *Rulings of the U.S. Supreme Court*, 35–36.

51. Ibid., 53.

52. But see Ronald Eagleye Johnny, "Nevada v. Hicks: No Threat to Most Nevada Tribes," *American Indian Law* 25 (2002): 381–85. Johnny does not consider *Nevada v. Hicks* to be of concern to his own tribe.

53. Senate Committee, *Rulings of the U.S. Supreme Court*, 30.

54. Babcock, "Civic-Republican Vision," 445.

55. Pevar, *Rights of Indians*, 142.

56. Oliphant v. Suquamish Indian Tribe, 435 U.S. 191 (1978).

57. U.S. Department of Justice, *American Indians and Crime*; U.S. Department of Justice, *BJS Statistical Profile*; NCAI, *Concept Paper*; Senate Committee, *Rulings of the U.S. Supreme Court*, 26–38, 92–95; Senate Committee, *Tribal Government Amendments*, 23, 37, 42–43, 50.

58. Generally, see Senate Committee, *Tribal Government Amendments*; Christopher B. Chaney, "The Effect of the United States Supreme Court's Decisions during the Last Quarter of the Nineteenth Century on Tribal Criminal Jurisdiction," *Brigham Young University Journal of Public Law* 14 (2000): 185–88; Robert Yazzie, "'Watch Your Six': An Indian Nation Judge's View of 25 Years of Indian Law, Where We Are and Where We Are Going," *American Indian Law Review* 23 (1999): 502–3; and NCAI, *Concept Paper*. See also the discussion of the Violence Against Women Reauthorization Act (2013) in chapter 4.

59. Chaney, "Effect," 174.

60. Senate Committee, *Tribal Government Amendments*, 23.

61. Chaney, "Effect," 180.

62. Geoffrey C. Heisey, "Oliphant and Tribal Criminal Jurisdiction over Non-Indians: Asserting Congress's Plenary Power to Restore Territorial Jurisdiction," *Indiana Law Journal* 73 (1998): 1055.

63. Senate Committee, *Law Enforcement in Indian Country*, 7.

64. Senate Committee, *Rulings of the U.S. Supreme Court*, 31.

65. Ibid., 44.

66. Senate Committee, *Tribal Government Amendments*, 186.

67. Senate Committee, *Tribal Law and Order Act One Year Later*, 57.

68. U.S. Department of Justice, *American Indians and Crime*, vi, 7.

69. U.S. Department of Justice, *BJS Statistical Profile*, 8–9.

70. Amnesty International, *Maze of Injustice*, 2.

71. Senate Committee, *Tribal Law and Order Act One Year Later*, 63.

72. Senate Committee, *Rulings of the U.S. Supreme Court*, 35

73. Ibid., 32.

74. Ibid., 92–95.
75. Senate Committee, *Tribal Government Amendments*, 50.
76. U.S. Department of Justice, *American Indians and Crime*, 30.
77. U.S. Department of Justice, *BJS Statistical Profile*, 19.
78. Larry Cunningham, "Deputization of Indian Prosecutors: Protecting Indian Interests in Federal Court," *Georgetown Law Journal* 88 (2000): 2198.
79. Senate Committee, *Examining Federal Declinations*, 4.
80. United States Government Accountability Office, "U.S. Department of Justice Declinations of Indian Country Criminal Matters," Report Number GAO-11–167R, December 13, 2010, 3.
81. Amnesty International, *Maze of Injustice*.
82. Senate Committee, *Tribal Government Amendments*, 209.
83. Senate Committee, *Law Enforcement in Indian Country*, 12–16.
84. Ibid., 32.
85. NCAI, *Concept Paper*, 2.
86. Senate Committee, *Native Women*, 54.
87. Senate Committee, *Tribal Government Amendments*, 186.
88. Senate Committee, *The Indian Reorganization Act—75 Years Later*, 74.
89. National Congress of the American Indian, *Concept Paper*, 2.
90. Senate Committee, *Law Enforcement in Indian Country*, 56.
91. NCAI, "Government to Government Models of Cooperation between States and Tribes," 2002, accessed via the Tribal Relations page of the NCAI website, www.ncai.org/policy-issues/tribal-governance/state-tribal-relations.
92. Senate Committee, *Tribal Courts*, 30.
93. Senate Committee, *Law Enforcement in Indian Country*.
94. Senate Committee, *Indian Reorganization Act—75 Years Later*, 72.
95. Senate Committee, *Tribal Government Amendments*, 23.
96. Chaney, "Effect," 186–87.
97. Yazzie, "Watch Your Six," 502–3.
98. Senate Committee, *Tribal Law and Order Act One Year Later*, 72.
99. Laurence, "Unseemly Nature," 413.

Chapter 6

1. Bruce E. Johansen and Willard Bill Sr., *Up from the Ashes: Nation-Building at Muckleshoot* (Auburn, Wash.: Muckleshoot Indian Tribe, 2014).
2. Wilkins, *American Indian Sovereignty*, 376; Clara Sue Kidwell and Alan Velie, *Native American Studies* (Lincoln: University of Nebraska Press, 2005), 75; Deloria and Lytle, *Nations Within*, 14.
3. Deloria in Bruce E. Johansen, *Encyclopedia of the American Indian Movement* (Santa Barbara, Calif.: Greenwood, 2013), 100–1.
4. Stephen Cornell and Joseph P. Kalt, "Sovereignty and Nation-Building: The Development Challenge in Indian Country Today," *American Indian Culture and Research Journal* 22 (1998): 188.
5. Lyons in Bruce Elliott Johansen, ed., *Enduring Legacies: Native American Treaties and Contemporary Controversies* (Westport, Conn.: Praeger, 2004), xiv.

6. Cornell and Kalt, "Sovereignty and Nation-Building," 187. Cornell and Kalt were writing about the 1990s and beyond in this quote, but the statement could also be applied to the situation of the tribes at the beginning of the 1970s.

7. After the successes of the Red Power movement, Vine Deloria Jr. hoped for the revival of Native America and believed that it would happen soon: "At present the visible poverty of Indian tribes veils the great potential of the Indian people from modern society. But in many ways the veil is lifting and brighter future is being seen. Night is giving way to day. The Indian will soon stand tall and strong once more." *Custer Died for Your Sins: An Indian Manifesto* (Norman: University of Oklahoma Press, 1988 [1969]), 241–42. Robert F. Berkhofer Jr. considered federal policy from the late 1960s and early 1970s as a catalyst for the revival of Native American rights: "[From] the Great Society of Lyndon B. Johnson and the New Federalism of Richard M. Nixon, Indian self-determination and political autonomy advanced. If Native Americans did not achieve as much home rule and freedom as their leaders sought under the slogan of tribal sovereignty, they escaped from the highly subordinated status of the classic reservation to gain official governments. . . . Although Native American factionalism continued, all sides of the political spectrum gained some voice, if not their will, in policy making." *The White Man's Indian: Images of the American Indian from Columbus to the Present* (New York: Vintage Books, 1979), 190.

8. Lyndon B. Johnson, *Public Papers of the Presidents of the United States: Lyndon B. Johnson, 1968–69*, Vol. 1 (Washington, D.C.: Government Printing Office, 1968), 336. See chapter 2 for background on the termination policy.

9. Nixon, *Public Papers*, 575, 566. See also Fredericks, "America's First Nations," 347–410.

10. Many writings in Native American history have addressed the resurgence of Native America, including these: Joanne Nagel, *American Indian Ethnic Renewal: Red Power and the Resurgence of Identity and Culture* (New York: Oxford University Press, 1997); Frederick E. Hoxie and Peter Iverson, eds., *Indians in American History: An Introduction*, 2nd ed. (Wheeling, Ill.: Harlan Davidson, 1998); Peter Iverson, *"We Are Still Here": American Indians in the Twentieth Century* (Wheeling, Ill.: Harlan Davidson, 1998); Charles Wilkinson, *Blood Struggle: The Rise of Modern Indian Nations* (New York: W. W. Norton, 2005); James S. Olson and Raymond Wilson, *Native Americans in the Twentieth Century* (Urbana: University of Illinois Press, 1984); Vine Deloria Jr., *Behind the Trail of Broken Treaties: An Indian Declaration of Independence* (Austin: University of Texas Press, 1985); and Sharon O'Brien, *American Indian Tribal Governments* (Norman: University of Oklahoma Press, 1989).

11. Olson and Wilson, *Native Americans*, 162.

12. Deloria and Lytle, *Nations Within*.

13. Duane Champagne, ed., *Chronology of North Native American History: From Pre-Columbian Times to the Present* (Detroit: Gale Research, 1994); Wilcomb Washburn, *The Indian in America* (New York: Harper and Row, 1975), 250; Stephen Cornell, *The Return of the Native: American Indian Political Resurgence* (New York: Oxford University Press, 1988), 4.

14. Cornell, *Return of the Native*, 187. See also Stephen Cornell and Joseph P. Kalt, "Reloading the Dice: Improving the Chances for Economic Development on American Indian Reservations," in *What Can Tribes Do? Strategies and Institutions in American*

Economic Development, ed. Stephen Cornell and Joseph P. Kalt, chap. 1 (Los Angeles: American Indian Studies Center, University of California, 1992), 12.

15. Cornell, *Return of the Native*, 6.

16. Wunder, *"Retained by the People,"* 176.

17. Laurence M. Hauptman and Jack Campisi, "Eastern Indian Communities Strive for Recognition," in *Major Problems in American Indian History*, 2nd ed., ed. Albert L. Hurtado and Peter Iverson (Boston: Wadsworth, 2001), 471.

18. Stephen Cornell and Joseph P. Kalt, "American Indian Self-Determination: The Political Economy of a Successful Policy," Harvard Project on American Indian Economic Development Joint Occasional Papers on Native Affairs, Working Paper No. 1, November 2010.

19. Ronald Reagan, "Statement on Indian Policy, January 24, 1983," Ronald Reagan Presidential Library, www.reagan.utexas.edu/archives/speeches/1983/12483b.htm (accessed September 15, 2005).

20. White House, President Barack Obama, "Executive Order—Establishing the White House Council on Native American Affairs," www.whitehouse.gov/the-press-office/2013/06/26/executive-order-establishing-white-house-council-native-american-affairs (accessed June 15, 2015).

21. Cornell, *Return of the Native*, 205.

22. Choctaw Nation v. Oklahoma, 397 U.S. 620 (1970).

23. Similarly, in Idaho v. United States, 533 U.S. 262 (2001) the Supreme Court ruled in favor of the Coeur d'Alene Tribe and held that pursuant to agreements between the tribe and the U.S. government the tribe had not lost title to the submerged lands of Lake Coeur d'Alene and the St. Joe River.

24. Menominee Tribe of Indians v. United States, 391 U.S. 404 (1968).

25. Ibid., 405–6.

26. Puyallup Tribe v. Department of Game, 391 U.S. 392 (1968).

27. Ibid., 392.

28. Department of Game v. Puyallup Tribe, 414 U.S. 44 (1973).

29. Puyallup Tribe, Inc. v. Department of Game, 433 U.S. 165 (1977).

30. In Washington v. Fishing Vessel Assn., 443 U.S. 658 (1979), the Supreme Court ruled that "the language of the treaties securing a 'right of taking fish . . . in common with all citizens of the Territory' was not intended merely to guarantee the Indians access to usual and accustomed fishing sites and an 'equal opportunity' for individual Indians, along with non-Indians, to try to catch fish, but instead secures to the Indian tribes a right to harvest a share of each run of anadromous fish that passes through tribal fishing areas" (659). Thus, treaty rights allowed tribes to fish, but there were limitations on access to fishing places.

31. Minnesota v. Mille Lacs Band of Chippewa Indians, 526 U.S. 172 (1999).

32. See, for example, Fisher v. District Court, 424 U.S. 382 (1976) (tribe had exclusive authority for the adoption of a reservation child who lived on the tribal reservation); Cappaert v. United States, 426 U.S. 128 (1976) (United States reserved water rights for Devil's Hole National Monument); Colorado River Water Conservation Dist. v. United States, 424 U.S. 800 (1976) (federal government reserved lands and also reserved the water rights for use on those lands); and Arizona v. California, 530 U.S. 392 (2000) (Quechan Tribe had the right to file a claim for increased water rights).

33. Jonathan B. Taylor and Joseph P. Kalt, "*Cabazon*, the Indian Gaming Regulatory Act, and the Socioeconomic Consequences of American Indian Governmental Gaming: A Ten-Year Review," Harvard Project on American Indian Economic Development, January 2005.

34. Eric Henson and Jonathan B. Taylor, "Native America at the New Millennium," Harvard Project on American Indian Economic Development, April 2002.

35. Ronald L. Trosper, "American Indian Poverty on Reservations, 1969–1989," in *Changing Numbers, Changing Needs: American Indian Demography and Public Health*, ed. Gary D. Sandefur, Ronald R. Rindfuss, and Barney Cohen, chap. 8 (Washington, D.C.: National Academy Press, 1996).

36. Stephen Cornell, Miriam Jorgenson, Joseph P. Kalt, and Katherine A. Spilde, "Seizing the Future: Why Some Native Nations Do and Others Don't," Harvard Project on American Indian Economic Development Joint Occasional Papers on Native Affairs 2005–01, 2005, 1.

37. Phillip Martin, "Phil[l]ip Discusses the Challenges of Economic Development, 1988," in *Major Problems in American Indian History*, 2nd ed., ed. Albert L. Hurtado and Peter Iverson (Boston: Wadsworth, 2001), 488.

38. Johansen and Bill, *Up from the Ashes*, 101–30 (Muckleshoot fishing rights). This protest had parallels to the U.S. civil rights movement in the South. Fishing rights activists marched with Martin Luther King Jr. during the 1960s.

39. United States v. Washington, 384 F. Supp. 312 (1974), 406. The following year, the Court of Appeals for the Ninth Circuit upheld the *Boldt* decision.

40. Washington v. Fishing Vessel Assn., 443 U.S. 658 (1979).

41. Johansen and Bill, *Up from the Ashes*, 147–200.

42. "Famed Treaty Rights Attorney Walter Echo-Hawk Visits MIT," *Muckleshoot Monthly* 13, no. 9 (November 2012), 1, www.muckleshoot.nsn.us/media/33179/november%20 2012%20low%20res.pdf (accessed August 23, 2015).

43. Cornell et al., "Seizing the Future," 2.

44. Confederated Salish and Kootenai Tribes Economic Development Office et al., "Confederated Salish and Kootenai Tribes Sustainable Economic Development Study: A Profile of the Flathead Reservation Economy and Tribal Member Job and Education Needs," Confederated Salish and Kootenai Tribes, September 2014, 18, www.cskt.org/ Final.CSKT.Sustainable.Economic.Development.Study.092514.pdf (accessed August 20, 2015)

45. Cornell and Kalt, "American Indian Self-Determination," 13.

46. Olson and Wilson, *Native Americans*, 181.

47. Mike McBride III, "Your Place or Mine? Commercial Transactions between Indian Tribes and Non-Indians in Oklahoma—New Rules for Tribal Sovereign Immunity," *Oklahoma Bar Journal* 67 (1996): 3183–256.

48. Kalt and Singer, "Myths and Realities," 2.

49. Manley A. Begay Jr., Stephen Cornell, Miriam Jorgensen, and Joseph P. Kalt, "Development, Governance, Culture: What Are They and What Do They Have to Do with Rebuilding Native Nations?" in *Rebuilding Native Nations: Strategies for Governance and Development*, ed. Miriam Jorgensen, chap. 2 (Tucson: University of Arizona Press, 2007).

50. Jason Kalish, "Do the States Have an Ace in the Hole or Should the Indians Call Their Bluff? Tribes Caught in the Power Struggle between the Federal Government and the States," *Arizona Law Review* 38 (1996): 1345–71; Nicholas Goldin, "Casting a New Light on Tribal Casino Gaming: Why Congress Should Curtail the Scope of High Stakes Indian Gaming," *Cornell Law Review* 84 (1999): 798–854.

51. Deloria and Lytle, *Nations Within*, 261.

52. California v. Cabazon Band of Mission Indians, 480 U.S. 202 (1987). See Connie K. Haslam, "Indian Sovereignty: Confusion Prevails—California v. Cabazon Band of Mission Indians, 107 S Ct. 1083 (1987)," *Washington Law Review* 63 (1988): 169–93; Kathleen M. O'Sullivan, "What Would John Marshall Say? Does the Federal Trust Responsibility Protect Tribal Gambling Revenue?" *Georgetown Law Journal* 84 (1995): 123–50; Naomi Mezey, "The Distribution of Wealth, Sovereignty, and Culture through Indian Gaming," *Stanford Law Review* 48 (1996): 711–37; and Stephanie A. Levin, "Betting on the Land: Indian Gambling and Sovereignty," *Stanford Law and Policy Review* 8 (1997): 125–35.

53. National Indian Gaming Commission, "Growth in Indian Gaming" data accessed via "Gross Gaming Revenue Reports," www.nigc.gov/commission/gaming-revenue-reports (accessed June 15, 2015).

54. National Indian Gaming Commission, "Gross Gaming Revenues" data accessed via "Gross Gaming Revenue Reports" www.nigc.gov/commission/gaming-revenue-reports (accessed August 21, 2015).

55. There are also tribes that have struggled to generate profits from their gaming enterprises.

56. Taylor and Kalt, "*Cabazon*," xi, i.

57. U.S. Bureau of the Census, *Preliminary Estimates of Business Ownership by Gender, Hispanic or Latino Origin, and Race: 2002* (Washington, D.C.: Bureau of the Census, 2005).

58. U.S. Bureau of the Census, *American Indian- and Alaska Native-Owned Firms: 2002* (Washington, D.C.: Bureau of the Census, 2006), 1.

59. U.S. Bureau of the Census, "2007 Survey of Business Owners Summaries of Findings," www.census.gov/econ/sbo/getsof.html?07aian (accessed December 25, 2012).

60. United States Census Bureau, "Statistics for All U.S. Firms by Sector, Gender, Ethnicity, and Race for the U.S. and States: 2012," http://factfinder.census.gov/faces/tableservices/jsf/pages/productview.xhtml?pid=SBO_2012_00CSA01&prodType=table (accessed August 25, 2015).

61. Kalt and Singer, "Myths and Realities," 1.

62. Taylor and Kalt, "*Cabazon*," xi.

Conclusion

1. "Bench Memo, No. 39, 1958 Term, Williams v. Lee," MAF, 4, 5, 8, Box 188, Warren Papers.

2. "1957 Term No. 811," Box 1201, Douglas Papers; "Paul Williams and Lorena Williams," Box I:15, Brennan Papers; "Conference November 21," Box 1201, Douglas Papers; "Bench Memo, No. 39, 1958 Term, Williams v. Lee," MAF, 2, Box 188, Warren Papers.

3. "Bench Memo, No. 326, 1959 Term, Metlakatla Indian," RGG, 13, and MHB, n.d., 1, Box 218, Warren Papers; "No. 2—Metlakatla Indian Community v. Egan, Conference

December 15, 1961," 1, Box 1265, Douglas Papers; "No. 2, Metlakatla Indian Community v. Egan," Box I:60, Brennan Papers.

4. "No. 115, Warren Trading Post v. Arizona State Tax Commission," Box I:113, Brennan Papers; "Warren Trading Post Co. v. Arizona State Tax Comm'n/64 Term No. 115," Box 1332, Douglas Papers; "Bench Memo, No. 115, 1964 Term, Warren Trading Post Co.," DMF 7, 11, Box 263, Warren Papers.

5. "Re: No. 71-1263—Kahn v. Arizona State Tax Commission," memorandum to the Conference from Thurgood Marshall, March 28, 1973, Box 156, Blackmun Papers; "Bench Memo No 71-1031-CSX, Tonasket v. Wash., et al," RIM, December 9, 1972, Box 158, Blackmun Papers.

6. "Bench Memo, No. 71-834-ASX, McClanahan, et al.," RIM, 4–5, Box 156, Blackmun Papers; "No. 71-834—McClanahan v. State Tax Commission of Arizona, Argued: December 12, 1972," Box 156, Blackmun Papers; "71-834—McClanahan v. State Tax Comm'n, of Arizona," Box 1574, Douglas Papers.

7. "Bench Memo, No. 71-834-ASX, McClanahan, et al. v. Arizona State Tax Comm'n," RIM, Box 156, Blackmun Papers.

8. "No. 73-1018, United States v. Mazurie, Cert to CA 10," AG, November 6, 1974, 17, 18, Box 197, Blackmun Papers; "No. 73-1018—United States v. Mazurie," H.A.B. November 10, 1974, 4, Box 197, Blackmun Papers; "No. 73-108, United States v. Mazurie," n.d., Box I:338, Brennan Papers; "No. 76-5729 Oliphant & Belgrade v. Suquamish Indian Tribe, To: Nancy, From: L.F.P., Jr., Date: January 3, 1978," 1–4, Box 51, Powell Papers; "Memorandum to Mr. Justice Powell," From: Nancy, Re: Oliphant opinion, Feb. 27, 1978," 1–4, Box 51, Powell Papers.

9. "No. 74-1656, Moe v. Confederated Tribes 75-50—Confederated Tribes v. Moe," 2–3, 5, Box 225, Blackmun Papers; "No. 75-1656, Moe v. Confederated Salish and Kootenai Tribes, No. 75-50 Confederated Salish and Kootenai Tribes v. Moe, Appeal from three-judge district court (D. Montana)," Block, January 17, 1976, 2, 11, Box 225, Blackmun Papers; "Moe v. Confederated Salish and Kootenai Tribes, Nos. 74-1656 and 75-50, Re: Proposed draft by Justice Rehnquist," WHB, April 2, 1976, 1–2, Box 225, Blackmun Papers.

10. "76-5729, Suquamish," January 5, 1978, Box 270, Blackmun Papers; "76-5729, Oliphant and Belgrade v. Suquamish Indian Tribe," 22–23, and Crane, January 3, 1978, 22, Box 270, Blackmun Papers; "Preliminary Memo, Summer List, 9, Sheet 1, No. 76-1629, U.S. Wheeler," Campbell, August 8, 1977, 7, Box 268, Blackmun Papers; "No. 76-5729, Oliphant v. Suquamish Indian Tribe," January 11, 1978, Box 270, Blackmun Papers; "Memorandum to the Conference, No. 76-5729, Oliphant v. Suquamish Indian Tribe," from Thurgood Marshall on March 3, 1978, Box 270, Blackmun Papers; "No. 76-5729 Oliphant & Belgrade v. Suquamish Indian Tribe, To: Nancy, From: L.F.P., Jr., Date: January 3, 1978," 1–4, Box 51, Powell Papers; "Memorandum to Mr. Justice Powell," From: Nancy, Re: Oliphant opinion, Feb. 27, 1978," 1–4, Box 51, Powell Papers.

11. In *New Mexico v. Mescalero Apache Tribe* (1983), the Supreme Court relied on the use of federal preemption to oust state law over nonmembers on the reservation. The Court did not use inherent tribal sovereignty; it was condemned to a footnote. This case was a positive result for Native America but it also built on the integrationist trend.

12. NCAI, *Concept Paper*, 2; Kalt and Singer, "Myths and Realities"; McCleary, "Proposed Solution," 628.

13. Senate Committee, *Rulings of the U.S. Supreme Court*, 3–4, 9, 28–38, 51–54, 58; Senate Committee, *Tribal Government Amendments*, 33–36.

14. Senate Committee, *Rulings of the U.S. Supreme Court*, 26–28, 30–33, 35–36, 53, 88–90, 93–95.

15. Senate Committee, *Tribal Government Amendments*, 23, 186; Senate Committee, *Rulings of the U.S. Supreme Court*, 31–32, 42, 44; Chaney, "Effect," 180.

16. U.S. Department of Justice, *American Indians and Crime*; U.S. Department of Justice, *BJS Statistical Profile*; NCAI, *Concept Paper*; Senate Committee, *Rulings of the U.S. Supreme Court*, 26–38, 92–95; Senate Committee, *Tribal Government Amendments*, 23, 37, 42–43, 50.

17. Senate Committee, *Tribal Government Amendments*, 23; Chaney, "Effect," 185–88; Yazzie, "Watch Your Six."

18. Letter from W. Ron Allen to author, September 14, 2010.

Bibliography

Manuscript Sources

Black, Hugo Lafayette, Papers. Manuscript Division, Library of Congress, Washington, D.C.

Blackmun, Harry A., Papers. Manuscript Division, Library of Congress, Washington, D.C.

Brennan, William J., Papers. Manuscript Division, Library of Congress, Washington, D.C.

Douglas, William O., Papers. Manuscript Division, Library of Congress, Washington, D.C.

Marshall, Thurgood, Papers. Manuscript Division, Library of Congress, Washington, D.C.

Powell, Jr., Lewis F. Papers. Lewis F. Powell Jr. Archives, Washington and Lee University School of Law, Lexington, Virginia

Warren, Earl, Papers. Manuscript Division, Library of Congress, Washington, D.C.

Legal Cases and U.S. Supreme Court Oral Arguments

Arizona v. California, 530 U.S. 392 (2000)

Arizona Dept. of Revenue v. Blaze Construction Co., 526 U.S. 32 (1999)

Atkinson Trading Co. v. Shirley, 532 U.S. 645 (2001)

Barta v. Oglala Sioux Tribe, 259 F.2d 553 (8th Cir. 1958), cert. denied, 358 U.S. 932 (1959)

Brendale v. Confederated Yakima Indian Nation, 492 U.S. 408 (1989)

Brown v. Board of Education, 347 U.S. 483 (1954)

Bryan v. Itasca County, 426 U.S. 373 (1976)

Buster v. Wright, 135 F. 947 (CA8 1905), appeal dism'd, 203 U.S. 599 (1906)

California v. Cabazon Band of Mission Indians, 480 U.S. 202 (1987)

California Board of Equalization v. Chemehuevi Tribe, 474 U.S. 9 (1985)

Cappaert v. United States, 426 U.S. 128 (1976)

Carpenter v. Shaw, 280 U.S. 363 (1930)

Cass County v. Leech Lake Band of Chippewa Indians, 524 U.S. 103 (1998)

Central Machinery Co. v. Arizona Tax Comm'n, 448 U.S. 160 (1980)

Cherokee Nation v. Georgia, 30 U.S. 1 (1831)

Chickasaw Nation v. United States, 534 U.S. 84 (2001)

Choctaw Nation v. Oklahoma, 397 U.S. 620 (1970)

City of Sherrill v. Oneida Indian Nation of New York, 544 U.S. 197 (2005)

Colorado River Water Conservation Dist. v. United States, 424 U.S. 800 (1976)

Cotton Petroleum Corp. v. New Mexico, 490 U.S. 163 (1989)

County of Yakima v. Yakima Nation, 502 U.S. 251 (1992)

DeCoteau v. District County Court, 420 U.S. 425 (1975)

Department of Game v. Puyallup Tribe, 414 U.S. 44 (1973)

Department of Taxation and Finance of New York v. Milhelm Attea & Bros., Inc., 512 U.S. 61 (1994)

Doe v. Dollar Gen. Corp., No. CV-02-05 (Miss. Choctaw Tribal Ct., July 28, 2005)

Doe v. Dollar Gen. Corp., Nos. CV-02-05, SC 2005–6 (Miss. Choctaw Sup. Ct., Feb. 8, 2008)

Dolgen Corp., Inc. v. Mississippi Band of Choctaw Indians, No. 4:08CV22, 2008 WL 5381906 (S.D. Miss., Dec. 19, 2008)

Dolgencorp Inc. v. Mississippi Band of Choctaw Indians, 846 F. Supp. 2d 650 (S.D. Miss. 2011)

Dolgencorp, Inc. v. Miss. Band of Choctaw Indians, 732 F.3d 409 (5th Cir. 2013)

Draper v. United States, 164 U.S. 240 (1896)

Duro v. Reina, 495 U.S. 676 (1990)

Ex parte Crow Dog, 109 U.S. 556 (1883)

Ex parte Kenyon, 14 F. Cas. 353 (U.S.C.C., Ark., 1878)

Fisher v. District Court, 424 U.S. 382 (1976)

Idaho v. United States, 533 U.S. 262 (2001)

Iowa Mutual Ins. Co. v. LaPlante, 480 U.S. 9 (1987)

Iron Crow v. Oglala Sioux Tribe, 231 F.2d 89 (CA8 1956)

Johnson v. McIntosh, 21 U.S. 543 (1823)

Kahn v. Arizona State Tax Commission, 411 U.S. 941 (1973)

Kake Village v. Egan, 369 U.S. 60 (1962)

The Kansas Indians, 72 U.S. 737 (1867)

Kennerly v. District Court of Montana, 400 U.S. 423 (1971)

Kerr-McGee Corp. v. Navajo Tribe, 471 U.S. 195 (1985)

Langford v. Monteith, 102 U.S. 145 (1880)

Lone Wolf v. Hitchcock, 187 U.S. 553 (1903)

MacArthur v. San Juan County, 405 F.Supp.2d 1302 (D. Utah 2005)

McClanahan v. Arizona State Tax Comm'n, 411 U.S. 164 (1973)

Menominee Tribe of Indians v. United States, 391 U.S. 404 (1968)

Merrion v. Jicarilla Apache Tribe, 455 U.S. 130 (1982)

Mescalero Apache Tribe v. Jones, 411 U.S. 145 (1973)

Mescalero Apache Tribe v. State of New Mexico, 630 F.2d 724 (10th Cir. 1980)

Metlakatla Indians v. Egan, 369 U.S. 45 (1962)

Minnesota v. Mille Lacs Band of Chippewa Indians, 526 U.S. 172 (1999)

Moe v. Salish & Kootenai Tribes, 425 U.S. 463 (1976)

Montana v. Blackfeet Tribe, 471 U.S. 759 (1985)

Montana v. Crow Tribe, 523 U.S. 696 (1998)

Montana v. United States, 450 U.S. 544 (1981)

Montana Catholic Missions v. Missoula County, 200 U.S. 118 (1906)

Morris v. Hitchcock, 194 U.S. 384 (1904)

National Farmers Union Ins. Cos. v. Crow Tribe, 471 U.S. 845 (1985)

Negonsott v. Samuels, 507 U.S. 99 (1993)

Nevada v. Hicks, 533 U.S. 353 (2001)

New Mexico v. Mescalero Apache Tribe, 462 U.S. 324 (1983)

New York ex rel. Ray v. Martin, 326 U.S. 496 (1946)

The New York Indians, 72 U.S. 761 (1867)

Oklahoma Tax Commission v. Chickasaw Nation, 515 U.S. 450 (1995)

Oklahoma Tax Commission v. Potawatomi Tribe, 498 U.S. 505 (1991)

Oklahoma Tax Commission v. Sac and Fox Nation, 508 U.S. 114 (1993)

Oklahoma Tax Commission v. United States, 319 U.S. 598 (1943)

Oliphant v. Schlie, 544 F.2d 1007 (9th Cir. 1976)

Oliphant v. Suquamish Indian Tribe, 435 U.S. 191 (1978)

Oral argument of Mark David Oliphant and Daniel B. Belgrade, Petitioners v. The Suquamish Indian Tribe et al., Respondents, No. 76–5729, Monday, January 9, 1978, before the Supreme Court of the United States

Perrin v. United States, 232 U.S. 478 (1914)

Plains Commerce Bank v. Long Family Land and Cattle Co., 128 S.Ct. 2709 (2008)

Plessy v. Ferguson, 163 U.S. 537 (1896)

Puyallup Tribe v. Department of Game, 391 U.S. 392 (1968)

Puyallup Tribe, Inc. v. Department of Game, 433 U.S. 165 (1977)

Ramah Navajo School Bd. v. Bureau of Revenue, 458 U.S. 832 (1982)

Seminole Nation v. United States, 316 U.S. 286 (1942)

South Dakota v. Bourland, 508 U.S. 679 (1993)

Strate v. A-1 Contractors, 520 U.S. 438 (1997)

Talton v. Mayes, 163 U.S. 376 (1896)

Tee-Hit-Ton Indians v. United States, 348 U.S. 272 (1955)

Thomas v. Gay, 169 U.S. 264 (1898)

Tonasket v. Washington, 411 U.S. 451 (1973)

Tulee v. Washington, 315 U.S. 681 (1942)

United States v. Bailey, 24 F. Cas. 937, No. 14,495 (C.C. Tenn.) (1834)

United States v. Creek Nation, 295 U.S. 103 (1935)

United States v. Forty-three Gallons of Whiskey, 93 U.S. 188 (1876)

United States v. John, 437 U.S. 634 (1978)

United States v. Kagama, 118 U.S. 375 (1886)

United States v. Lara, 541 U.S. 193 (2004)

United States v. Mazurie, 419 U.S. 544 (1975)

United States v. McBratney, 104 U.S. 621 (1881)

United States v. Rogers, 45 U.S. 567 (1846)

United States v. Shoshone Tribe of Indians, 304 U.S. 111 (1938)

United States v. Washington, 384 F. Supp. 312 (1974)

United States v. Wheeler, 435 U.S. 313 (1978)

Utah & Northern R. Co. v. Fisher, 116 U.S. 28 (1885)

Wagnon v. Prairie Band Potawatomi Nation, 546 U.S. 95 (2005)

Warren Trading Post v. Tax Comm'n, 380 U.S. 685 (1965)

Washington v. Confederated Tribes, 447 U.S. 134 (1980)

Washington v. Fishing Vessel Assn., 443 U.S. 658 (1979)

White Mountain Apache Tribe v. Bracker, 448 U.S. 136 (1980)

Williams v. Lee, 358 U.S. 217 (1959)

Winters v. United States, 207 U.S. 564 (1908)

Worcester v. Georgia, 31 U.S. 515 (1832)

Books and Articles

Alfred, Taiaiake. *Peace, Power, Righteousness: An Indigenous Manifesto.* Toronto: Oxford University Press, 1999.

Amnesty International, *Maze of Injustice: The Failure to Protect Indigenous Women from Sexual Violence in the USA* (New York: Amnesty International, 2007).

Babcock, Hope M. "A Civic-Republican Vision of 'Domestic Dependent Nations' in the Twenty-First Century: Tribal Sovereignty Re-envisioned, Reinvigorated, and Re-empowered." *Utah Law Review* 2005 (2005): 443–571.

Ball, Dewi Ioan. "The Silent Revolution: How the Key Attributes of Tribal Power Have Been Fundamentally Eroded by the United States Supreme Court from 1973." Ph.D. dissertation, University of Wales, Swansea, 2007.

———. "Williams v. Lee (1959)—50 Years Later: A Reassessment of One of the Most Important Cases in the Modern-Era of Federal Indian Law." *Michigan State Law Review* 2010 (2010): 391–412.

Ball, Dewi Ioan, and Joy Porter, eds. *Competing Voices from Native America.* Santa Barbara, Calif.: Greenwood Press, 2009.

Barsh, Russell Lawrence, and James Youngblood Henderson. "The Betrayal: Oliphant v. Suquamish Indian Tribe and the Hunting of the Snark." *Minnesota Law Review* 63 (1979): 609–40.

———. "Contrary Jurisprudence: Tribal Interests in Navigable Waterways before and after Montana v. United States." *Washington Law Review* 56 (1981): 627–85.

———. *The Road: Indian Tribes and Political Liberty.* Berkeley: University of California Press, 1980.

Begay Jr., Manley A., Stephen Cornell, Miriam Jorgensen, and Joseph P. Kalt. "Development, Governance, Culture: What Are They and What Do They Have to Do with Rebuilding Native Nations?" In *Rebuilding Native Nations: Strategies for Governance and Development,* edited by Miriam Jorgensen, chap. 2. Tucson: University of Arizona Press, 2007.

Berger, Bethany R. "Justice and the Outsider: Jurisdiction over Nonmembers in Tribal Legal Systems." *Arizona State Law Journal* 37 (2005): 1047–125.

———. "Williams v. Lee and the Debate over Indian Equality." *Michigan Law Review* 109 (2010): 1463–528.

Berkhofer Jr., Robert F. *The White Man's Indian: Images of the American Indian from Columbus to the Present.* New York: Vintage Books, 1979.

Bloch, David J. "Colonizing the Last Frontier." *American Indian Law Review* 29 (2004): 1–41.

Bogardus, Kristina. "Court Picks New Test in Cotton Petroleum." *Natural Resources Journal* 30 (1990): 919–28.

Bowen, Veronica L. "The Extent of Indian Regulatory Authority over Non-Indians: South Dakota v. Bourland." *Creighton Law Review* 27 (1994): 605–59.

Breer, Charles. "Are State Severance Taxes Pre-empted When Imposed on Non-Indian Lessees Extracting Oil and Gas from Indian Reservations Land? Cotton Petroleum Corporation v. New Mexico." *Land and Water Law Review* 25 (1990): 435–45.

Bridgewater, Bradley Scott. "Taxation: Merrion v. Jicarilla Apache Tribe: Wine or Vinegar for Oklahoma Tribes?" *Oklahoma Law Review* 37 (1984): 369–96.

Bronson, Ruth Muskrat. "Criticizes the Proposed Termination of Federal Trusteeship, 1955." In *Major Problems in American Indian History*, 2nd ed., edited by Albert L. Hurtado and Peter Iverson, 423–25. Boston: Wadsworth, 2001.

Burch, Jordan. "How Much Diversity Is the United States Really Willing to Accept?" *Ohio Northern University Law Review* 20 (1994): 957–79.

Burke, Joseph C. "The Cherokee Cases: A Study in Law, Politics, and Morality." *Stanford Law Review* 21 (1969): 500–31.

Canby Jr., William C. *American Indian Law in a Nutshell*. St. Paul, Minn.: West, 1998.

Cardick, Samuel D. "The Failure of the Tribal Law and Order Act of 2010 to End the Rape of American Indian Women." *Saint Louis University Public Law Review* 31 (2012): 539–78.

Carpenter, Charley. "Preempting Indian Preemption: Cotton Petroleum Corp. v. New Mexico." *Catholic University Law Review* 39 (1990): 639–71.

Champagne, Duane, ed. *Chronology of North Native American History: From Pre-Columbian Times to the Present*. Detroit: Gale Research, 1994.

Chaney, Christopher B. "The Effect of the United States Supreme Court's Decisions during the Last Quarter of the Nineteenth Century on Tribal Criminal Jurisdiction." *Brigham Young University Journal of Public Law* 14 (2000): 173–89.

Christiansen, Matthew R., and William N. Eskridge Jr. "Congressional Overrides of Supreme Court Statutory Interpretation Decisions, 1967–2011." *Texas Law Review* 92 (2014): 1317–541.

Clayton, Thomas W. "Brendale v. Yakima Nation: A Divided Supreme Court Cannot Agree over Who May Zone Nonmember Fee Lands within the Reservation." *South Dakota Law Review* 36 (1991): 329–57.

Clinebell, John Howard, and Jim Thomson. "Sovereignty and Self-Determination: The Rights of Native Americans under International Law." *Buffalo Law Review* 27 (1978): 669–714.

Clinton, Robert N. "The Dormant Indian Commerce Clause." *Connecticut Law Review* 27 (1995): 1055–249.

———. "State Power over Indian Reservations: A Critical Comment on Burger Court Decisions." *South Dakota Law Review* 26 (1981): 434–46.

———. "There Is No Federal Supremacy Clause for Indian Tribes." *Arizona State Law Journal* 34 (2002): 113–260.

Coffey, Wallace, and Rebecca Tsosie. "Rethinking the Tribal Sovereignty Doctrine: Cultural Sovereignty and the Collective Future of Indian Nations." *Stanford Law and Policy Review* 12 (2001): 191–210.

Cohen, Felix S. *Handbook of Federal Indian Law*. Washington, D.C.: Government Printing Office, 1941.

Cole, David. "Are Foreign Nationals Entitled to the Same Constitutional Rights as Citizens?" *Thomas Jefferson Law Review* 25 (2003): 367–88.

Collins, Richard B. "Implied Limitations on the Jurisdiction of Indian Tribes." *Washington Law Review* 54 (1979): 479–529.

Confederated Salish and Kootenai Tribes Economic Development Office, the University of Montana Bureau of Business and Economic Research, and the Sustainable Economic Development Project Partners. "Confederated Salish and Kootenai Tribes

Sustainable Economic Development Study: A Profile of the Flathead Reservation Economy and Tribal Member Job and Education Needs." Confederated Salish and Kootenai Tribes, September 2014.

Cornell, Stephen. *The Return of the Native: American Indian Political Resurgence.* New York: Oxford University Press, 1988.

Cornell, Stephen, Miriam Jorgenson, Joseph P. Kalt, and Katherine A. Spilde. "Seizing the Future: Why Some Native Nations Do and Others Don't." Harvard Project on American Indian Economic Development Joint Occasional Papers on Native Affairs 2005–01, 2005.

Cornell, Stephen, and Joseph P. Kalt. "American Indian Self-Determination: The Political Economy of a Successful Policy." Harvard Project on American Indian Economic Development Joint Occasional Papers on Native Affairs. Working Paper No. 1, November 2010.

———. "Reloading the Dice: Improving the Chances for Economic Development on American Indian Reservations." In *What Can Tribes Do? Strategies and Institutions in American Economic Development,* edited by Stephen Cornell and Joseph P. Kalt, chap. 1. Los Angeles: American Indian Studies Centre, University of California, 1992.

———. "Sovereignty and Nation-Building: The Development Challenge in Indian Country Today." *American Indian Culture and Research Journal* 22 (1998): 187–214.

Corntassel, Jeff, and Richard C. Witmer II. *Forced Federalism: Contemporary Challenges to Indigenous Nationhood.* Norman: University of Oklahoma Press, 2008.

Corr, Kathleen. "A Doctrinal Traffic Jam: The Role of Federal Preemption Analysis in Conflicts between State and Tribal Vehicle Codes." *University of Colorado Law Review* 74 (2003): 715–64.

Crafts, Amy. "Nevada v. Hicks and Its Implication on American Indian Sovereignty." *Connecticut Law Review* 34 (2002): 1249–80.

Crawford, Katherine B. "State Authority to Tax Non-Indian Oil & Gas Production on Reservations: Cotton Petroleum Corp. v. New Mexico." *Utah Law Review* 1989 (1989): 495–519.

Cunningham, Larry. "Deputization of Indian Prosecutors: Protecting Indian Interests in Federal Court." *Georgetown Law Journal* 88 (2000): 2187–210.

Debo, Angie. *A History of the Indians of the United States.* Norman: University of Oklahoma Press, 1970.

Deer, Ada. "Ada Deer Explains How Her People Overturned Termination, 1974." In *Major Problems in American Indian History,* 2nd ed., edited by Albert L. Hurtado and Peter Iverson, 457–60. Boston: Wadsworth, 2001.

Deloria Jr., Vine, ed. *American Indian Policy in the Twentieth Century.* Norman: University of Oklahoma Press, 1985.

———. *Behind the Trail of Broken Treaties: An Indian Declaration of Independence.* Austin: University of Texas Press, 1985.

———. *Custer Died for Your Sins: An Indian Manifesto.* Norman: University of Oklahoma Press, 1988 [1969].

Deloria Jr., Vine, and Clifford M. Lytle. *American Indians, American Justice.* Austin: University of Texas Press, 1983.

———. *The Nations Within: The Past and Future of American Indian Sovereignty.* Austin: University of Texas Press, 1984.

D'Errico, Peter. "American Indian Sovereignty: Now You See It, Now You Don't." Legal Studies Department, University of Massachusetts/Amherst, unpublished paper delivered as the inaugural lecture at the American Indian Civics Project, Humboldt State University, California, October 24, 1997.

Dudziak, Mary L. "The Case of 'Death for a Dollar-Ninety-Five': Miscarriages of Justice and Constructions of American Identity." In *Making Sense of Miscarriages of Justice*, edited by Charles Ogletree and Austin Sarat (New York University Press, 2009).

Dussias, Allison M. "Geographically-Based and Membership-Based Views of Indian Tribal Sovereignty: The Supreme Court's Changing Vision." *University of Pittsburgh Law Review* 55 (1993): 1–97.

Duthu, N. Bruce. "The Thurgood Marshall Papers and the Quest for a Principled Theory of Tribal Sovereignty: Fueling the Fires of Tribal/State Conflict." *Vermont Law Review* 21 (1996): 47–110.

Duthu, N. Bruce, and Dean B. Suagee. "Supreme Court Strikes Two More Blows against Tribal Self-Determination." *Natural Resources and Environment* 16 (2001): 118–22.

Echo-Hawk, Walter R. *In the Courts of the Conqueror: The 10 Worst Indian Law Cases Ever Decided*. Golden, Colo.: Fulcrum, 2010.

Endreson, Douglas B. L. "A Review of the 1990s and a Look at What's Ahead." *American Indian Law Review* 22 (1998): 611–22.

Ennis, Samuel E. "Reaffirming Indian Tribal Court Criminal Jurisdiction over Non-Indians: An Argument for a Statutory Abrogation of Oliphant." *UCLA Law Review* 57 (2009): 553–605.

Evans, Sterling, ed. *American Indians in American History, 1870–2001: A Companion Reader*. Westport, Conn.: Praeger, 2001.

Falkowski, James E. *Indian Law/Race Law: A Five-Hundred-Year History*. Praeger: New York, 1992.

Fixico, Donald L. *Termination and Relocation: Federal Indian Policy, 1945–1960*. Albuquerque: University of New Mexico Press, 1986.

Fletcher, Matthew L. M. "In Pursuit of Tribal Economic Development as a Substitute for Reservation Tax Revenue." *North Dakota Law Review* 80 (2004): 759–807.

———. "Resisting Federal Courts on Tribal Jurisdiction." *Colorado Law Review* 81 (2010): 973–1025.

———. "Tribal Consent." *Stanford Journal of Civil Rights and Civil Liberties* 8 (2012): 45–122.

Fortin, Seth J. "The Two-Tiered Program of the Tribal Law and Order Act." *UCLA Law Review Discourse* 61 (2013): 88–109.

Fouberg, Erin Hogan. *Tribal Territory, Sovereignty, and Governance: A Study of the Cheyenne River and Lake Traverse Indian Reservations*. New York: Garland, 2000.

Fredericks III, John. "America's First Nations: The Origins, History and Future of American Indian Sovereignty." *Journal of Law and Policy* 7 (1999): 347–410.

Frickey, Philip P. "Adjudication and Its Discontents: Coherence and Conciliation in Federal Indian Law." *Harvard Law Review* 110 (1997): 1754–84.

———. "A Common Law for Our Age of Colonialism: The Judicial Divestiture of Indian Tribal Authority over Nonmembers." *Yale Law Journal* 109 (1999): 1–85.

———. "Congressional Intent, Practical Reasoning, and the Dynamic Nature of Federal Indian Law." *California Law Review* 78 (1990): 1137–240.

Garrow, Carrie E., and Sarah Deer. *Tribal Criminal Law and Procedure.* Lanham, Md.: AltaMira Press, 2004.

Gede, Tom. "Criminal Jurisdiction of Indian Tribes: Should Non-Indians Be Subject to Tribal Criminal Authority under VAWA?" *Engage* 12 (2012): 40–44.

Getches, David H. "Beyond Indian Law: The Rehnquist Court's Pursuit of States' Rights, Color-Blind Justice and Mainstream Values." *Minnesota Law Review* 86 (2001): 267–362.

———. "Conquering the Cultural Frontier: The New Subjectivism of the Supreme Court in Indian Law." *California Law Review* 84 (1996): 1573–655.

Getches, David H., Charles F. Wilkinson, and Robert A. Williams Jr. *Federal Indian Law: Cases and Materials.* 3d ed. St. Paul, Minn.: West, 1993.

Gibson, Arrell Morgan. *The American Indian: Prehistory to Present.* Lexington, Mass.: D.C. Heath, 1980.

Glashausser, Alex. "A Return to Form for the Exceptions Clause." *Boston College Law Review* 51 (2010): 1383–450.

Gluck, Daniel. "A Tale of Two Taxes—Preemption on the Reservation: Cotton Petroleum Corp. v. Mexico." *Tax Lawyer* 43 (1990): 359–73.

Goeppele, Craighton. "Solutions for Uneasy Neighbors: Regulating the Reservation Environment after Brendale v. Confederated Tribes & Bands of Yakima Indian Nation." *Washington Law Review* 65 (1990): 417–36.

Goldin, Nicholas S. "Casting a New Light on Tribal Casino Gaming: Why Congress Should Curtail the Scope of High Stakes Indian Gaming." *Cornell Law Review* 84 (1999): 798–854.

Goldman, Sheldon. *Picking Federal Judges: Lower Court Selection from Roosevelt through Reagan.* New Haven: Yale University Press, 1999.

Goldstein, David. "Indian Law: Indian Taxation of Non-Indian Mineral Lessees." *Tennessee Law Review* 50 (1983): 403–23.

Gould, L. Scott. "The Consent Paradigm: Tribal Sovereignty at the Millennium." *Columbia Law Review* 96 (1996): 809–902.

Grigg, William Norman. "America the Balkanized: American Indian Groups and Their Political Allies, Exploiting the Homeland Security Issue, Are Conducting a Quiet Power Grab." *New American* 19, no. 20 (2003).

Grisham John, *The Innocent Man.* New York: Random House, 2006.

Gross, Samuel R. "Lost Lives: Miscarriages of Justice in Capital Cases." *Law and Contemporary Problems* 61 (1998): 125–52.

Haas, Theodore H. "The Legal Aspects of Indian Affairs from 1887 to 1957." *Annals of the American Academy of Political and Social Science* 311 (1957): 12–22.

Haddock, David D., and Thomas D. Hall. "The Impact of Making Rights Inalienable: Merrion v. Jicarilla Apache Tribe, Texaco, Inc. v. Short, Fidelity Federal Savings & Loan Ass'n v. De La Cuesta, and Ridgway v. Ridgway." *Supreme Court Economic Review* 2 (1983): 1–33.

Hagan, William T. *American Indians.* Chicago: University of Chicago Press, 1961.

———. *American Indians.* Rev. ed. Chicago: University of Chicago Press, 1979.

Hakansson, C. G. "Indian Land-Use Zoning Jurisdiction: An Argument in Favor of Tribal Jurisdiction over Non-member Fee Lands within Reservation Boundaries." *South Dakota Law Review* 73 (1997): 721–40.

Hanke, Lewis. "American Historians and the World Today: Responsibilities and Opportunities." *American Historical Review* 80 (1975): 1–20.

Harring, Sidney L. *Crow Dog's Case: American Indian Sovereignty, Tribal Law, and United States Law in the Nineteenth Century.* New York: Cambridge University Press, 1994.

Hart, Gideon M. "A Crisis in Indian Country: An Analysis of the Tribal Law and Order Act of 2010." *Regent University Law Review* 23 (2010): 139–85.

Haslam, Connie K. "Indian Sovereignty: Confusion Prevails—California v. Cabazon Band of Mission Indians, 107 S Ct. 1083 (1987)." *Washington Law Review* 63 (1988): 169–93.

Hauptman, Laurence M. *Tribes and Tribulations: Misconceptions about American Indians and Their Histories.* Albuquerque: University of New Mexico Press, 1995.

Hauptman, Laurence M., and Jack Campisi. "Eastern Indian Communities Strive for Recognition." In *Major Problems in American Indian History,* 2nd ed., edited by Albert L. Hurtado and Peter Iverson, 461–71. Boston: Wadsworth, 2001.

Hecht, Robert A. *The Occupation of Wounded Knee.* Charlotteville, N.Y.: SamHar Press, 1981.

Heisey, Geoffrey C. "Oliphant and Tribal Criminal Jurisdiction over Non-Indians: Asserting Congress's Plenary Power to Restore Territorial Jurisdiction." *Indiana Law Journal* 73 (1998): 1051–78.

Henson, Eric, and Johnathan B. Taylor. "Native America at the New Millennium." Harvard Project on American Indian Economic Development, April 2002.

Hertzberg, Hazel. *The Search for an American Indian Identity: Modern Pan-Indian Movements.* Syracuse, N.Y.: Syracuse University Press, 1971.

Hoxie, Frederick E., and Peter Iverson, eds. *Indians in American History: An Introduction.* 2nd ed. Wheeling, Ill.: Harlan Davidson, 1998.

Hurtado, Albert L., and Peter Iverson. "Continuing Challenges, Continuing Peoples, 1981–1999." In *Major Problems in American Indian History,* 2nd ed., ed. Albert L. Hurtado and Peter Iverson, chap. 15. Boston: Wadsworth, 2001.

———, eds. *Major Problems in American Indian History.* Lexington, Mass.: D.C. Heath, 1994.

Iverson, Peter. *"We Are Still Here": American Indians in the Twentieth Century.* Wheeling, Ill.: Harlan Davidson, 1998.

Jaimes, M. Annette, ed. *The State of Native America: Genocide, Colonization, and Resistance.* Boston: South End Press, 1992.

James, Richard E. "Sanctuaries No More: The United States Supreme Court Deals Another Blow to Indian Tribal Court Jurisdiction." *Washburn Law Journal* 41 (2002): 347–64.

Johansen, Bruce E. *Encyclopedia of the American Indian Movement.* Santa Barbara, Calif.: Greenwood, 2013.

———, ed. *Enduring Legacies: Native American Treaties and Contemporary Controversies.* Westport, Conn.: Praeger, 2004.

Johansen, Bruce E., and Willard Bill Sr. *Up from the Ashes: Nation-Building at Muckleshoot.* Auburn, Wash.: Muckleshoot Indian Tribe, 2014.

Johnny, Ronald Eagleye. "Nevada v. Hicks: No Threat to Most Nevada Tribes." *American Indian Law* 25 (2002): 381–85.

Johnson, Lyndon B. *Public Papers of the Presidents of the United States: Lyndon B. Johnson, 1968–69.* Vol. 1. Washington, D.C.: Government Printing Office, 1968.

Johnson, Ralph W., and Berrie Martinis. "Chief Justice Rehnquist and the Indian Cases." *Public Land Law Review* 16 (1995): 1–25.

Johnson, Troy R., ed. *Contemporary Native American Political Issues.* Walnut Creek, Calif.: AltaMira Press, 1999.

Johnson, Troy, Joane Nagel, and Duane Champagne, eds. *American Indian Activism: Alcatraz to the Longest Walk.* Urbana: University of Illinois Press, 1997.

Kalish, Jason. "Do the States Have an Ace in the Hole or Should the Indians Call Their Bluff? Tribes Caught in the Power Struggle between the Federal Government and the States." *Arizona Law Review* 38 (1996): 1345–71.

Kalt, Joseph P., and Joseph William Singer. "Myths and Realities of Tribal Sovereignty: The Law and Economics of Indian Self-Rule." Harvard Project on American Indian Economic Development Joint Occasional Papers on Native Affairs 2004–03, 2004.

Kappler, Charles J., ed. *Indian Affairs: Laws and Treaties,* Vol. 2. *Treaties.* Washington, D.C.: Government Printing Office, 1904.

Kidwell, Clara Sue, and Alan Velie. *Native American Studies.* Lincoln: University of Nebraska Press, 2005.

King, Jamelle. "Tribal Court General Civil Jurisdiction over Actions between Non-Indian Plaintiffs and Defendants: Strate v. A-1 Contractors." *American Indian Law Review* 22 (1997): 191–221.

Krakoff, Sarah. "Undoing Indian Law One Case at a Time: Judicial Minimalism and Tribal Sovereignty." *American University Law Review* 50 (2001): 1177–268.

Larkin Jr., Paul J., and Joseph Luppino-Esposito, "The Violence Against Women Act, Federal Criminal Jurisdiction, and Indian Tribal Courts." *BYU Journal of Public Law* 27 (2012): 1–39.

Laurence, Robert. "Symmetry and Asymmetry in Federal Indian Law." *Arizona Law Review* 42 (2000): 861–934.

———. "The Unseemly Nature of Reservation Diminishment by Judicial, as Opposed to Legislative, Fiat and the Ironic Role of the Indian Civil Rights Act in Limiting Both." *North Dakota Law Review* 71 (1995): 393–413.

Lavelle, J. P. "Implicit Divestiture Reconsidered: Outtakes from Cohen's Handbook Cutting Room Floor." *Connecticut Law Review* 38 (2006): 731–76.

Lazarus, Edward. *Closed Chambers: The Rise, Fall and Future of the Modern Supreme Court.* New York: Penguin Books, 1999.

Leeds, Stacy. "The More Things Stay the Same: Waiting on Indian Law's Brown v. Board of Education." *Tulsa Law Review* 38 (2002): 73–86.

Leonhard, M. Brent. "Closing a Gap in Indian County Justice: *Oliphant, Lara,* and DOJ's Proposed Fix." *Harvard Journal on Racial and Ethnic Justice* 28 (2012): 117–71.

Levin, Stephanie A. "Betting on the Land: Indian Gambling and Sovereignty." *Stanford Law and Policy Review* 8 (1997): 125–35.

Lopach, James J., Margery Hunter Brown, and Richmond L. Clow. *Tribal Government Today: Politics on Montana Indian Reservations.* Rev. ed. Boulder: University Press of Colorado, 1998.

Martin, Phillip. "Phil[l]ip Martin Discusses the Challenges of Economic Development, 1988." In *Major Problems in American Indian History*, 2d ed., edited by Albert L. Hurtado and Peter Iverson, 487–89. Boston: Wadsworth, 2001.

Mattson, Yvonne. "Civil Regulatory Jurisdiction over Fee Simple Tribal Lands: Why Congress Is Not Acting Trustworthy." *Seattle University Law Review* 27 (2004): 1063–106.

Maxfield, Peter C. "Oliphant v. Suquamish Tribe: The Whole Is Greater than the Sum of the Parts." *Journal of Contemporary Law* 19 (1993): 391–443.

McBride III, Mike. "Your Place or Mine? Commercial Transactions between Indian Tribes and Non-Indians in Oklahoma—New Rules for Tribal Sovereign Immunity." *Oklahoma Bar Journal* 67 (1996): 3183–256.

McCleary, Stephen P. "A Proposed Solution to the Problem of State Jurisdiction to Tax on Indian Reservations." *Gonzaga Law Review* 26 (1991): 627–59.

McDonnell, Janet A. *The Dispossession of the American Indian*. Bloomington: Indiana University Press, 1991.

McSloy, Steven Paul. "Back to the Future: Native American Sovereignty in the 21st Century." *New York University Review of Law and Social Change* 20 (1993): 217–302.

Meissner, Doris M. *Report of the Task Force on Indian Matters*. Washington, D.C.: Government Printing Office, October 1975.

Mezey, Naomi. "The Distribution of Wealth, Sovereignty, and Culture through Indian Gaming." *Stanford Law Review* 48 (1996): 711–37.

Mikva, Abner J., and Jeff Bleich. "When Congress Overrules the Court." *California Law Review* 79 (1991): 729–50.

Miller, Robert J. "American Indian Influence on the United States Constitution and Its Framers." *American Indian Law Review* 18 (1993): 133–60.

Miller, Todd. "Easements on Tribal Sovereignty." *American Indian Law Review* 26 (2001): 105–31.

Minnis, Michael. "Judicially-Suggested Harassment of Indian Tribes: The Potawatomis Revisit Moe and Colville." *American Indian Law Review* 16 (1991): 289–318.

Mitchell, Dalia Tsuk. *Architect of Justice: Felix S. Cohen and the Founding of American Legal Pluralism*. Ithaca, N.Y.: Cornell University Press, 2007.

Mitchell, John Arai. "A World without Tribes? Tribal Rights of Self-Government and the Enforcement of State Court Orders in Indian Country." *University of Chicago Law Review* 61 (1994): 707–32.

Morris, Glenn T. "International Law and Politics: Toward a Right to Self-Determination for Indigenous Peoples." In *The State of Native America: Genocide, Colonization, and Resistance*, edited by M. Annette Jaimes, chap. 2. Boston: South End Press, 1992.

Muckleshoot Monthly. "Famed Treaty Rights Attorney Walter Echo-Hawk Visits MIT," November 2012, 1.

Murray, David. *Modern Indians: Native Americans in the Twentieth Century*. England: British Association for American Studies, 1982.

Nagel, Joanne. *American Indian Ethnic Renewal: Red Power and the Resurgence of Identity and Culture*. New York: Oxford University Press, 1997.

National Congress of American Indians (NCAI). *Concept Paper, 2003 Legislative Proposal on Tribal Governance and Economic Enhancement 25 July 2002*. Washington, D.C.: National Congress of American Indians, 2002.

————. *2003 Annual Report*. Washington, D.C.: National Congress of American Indians, 2004.

Newton, Nell Jessup. "Federal Power over Indians: Its Sources, Scope, and Limitations." *University of Pennsylvania Law Review* 132 (1984): 195–288.

Nichols, Roger L. *The American Indian Past and Present*. 2d ed. New York: John Wiley and Sons, 1981.

Nixon, Richard. *Public Papers of the Presidents of the United States: Richard Nixon, 1970.* Washington, D.C.: Government Printing Office, 1971.

Nordaus, Robert J., G. Emlen Hall, and Anne Alise Rudio. "Revisiting Merrion v. Jicarilla Apache Tribe: Robert Nordhaus and Sovereign Indian Control over Natural Resources on Reservations." *Natural Resources Journal* 43 (2003): 223–84.

Norgren, Jill. *The Cherokee Cases: The Confrontation of Law and Politics*. New York: McGraw-Hill, 1996.

O'Brien, David M. *Storm Center: The Supreme Court in American Politics*. 3d ed. New York: W. W. Norton, 1993.

O'Brien, Sharon. *American Indian Tribal Governments*. Norman: University of Oklahoma Press, 1989.

Olson, James S., and Raymond Wilson. *Native Americans in the Twentieth Century*. Urbana: University of Illinois Press, 1984.

O'Sullivan, Kathleen M. "What Would John Marshall Say? Does the Federal Trust Responsibility Protect Tribal Gambling Revenue?" *Georgetown Law Journal* 84 (1995): 123–50.

Oswallt, Wendell H., and Sharlotte Neely. *This Land Was Theirs: A Study of North American Indians*. 5th ed. Mountain View, Calif.: Mayfield, 1996.

Owens, Jasmine. "'Historic' in a Bad Way: How the Tribal Law and Order Act Continues the American Tradition of Providing Inadequate Protection to American Indian and Alaska Native Rape Victims." *Journal of Criminal Law and Criminology* 102 (2012): 497–524.

Pevar, Stephen L. *The Rights of Indians and Tribes: The Authoritative ACLU Guide to Indian and Tribal Rights*. 3d ed. Carbondale: Southern Illinois University Press, 2002.

Pickerill, J. Mitchell. "The Supreme Court and Congress: What Happens in Congress after the Court Strikes Down Legislation?" *Insights on Law and Society* Fall (2006): 10–27.

Pommersheim, Frank. *Braid of Feathers: American Indian Law and Contemporary Tribal Life*. Berkeley: University of California Press, 1995.

————. "Coyote Paradox: Some Indian Law Reflections from the Edge of the Prairie." *Arizona State Law Journal* 31 (1999): 439–81.

————."Plains Commerce Bank v. Long Family Land and Cattle Company, Inc.: An Introduction with Questions." *South Dakota Law Review* 54 (2009): 365–74.

Pommersheim, Frank, and John P. LaVelle. "Toward a Great Sioux Nation Judicial Support Center and Supreme Court." *Wicazo Sa Review* 17 (2002): 183–232.

Pomp, Richard D. "The Unfulfilled Promise of the Indian Commerce Clause and State Taxation." *Tax Lawyer* 63 (2011): 897–1222.

Porter, Robert B. "The Meaning of Indigenous Nation Sovereignty." *Arizona State Law Journal* 34 (2002): 75–112.

Price, Joyce Howard. "Indians Want Jurisdiction to Combat Terrorism Threat." *Washington Times*, January 26, 2004.

Price, Monroe E. *Law and the American Indian: Readings, Notes, and Cases*. Indianapolis, Ind.: Bobbs-Merrill, 1973.

Price, Zachary S. "Dividing Sovereignty in Tribal and Territorial Criminal Jurisdiction." *Columbia Law Review* 113 (2013): 657–732.

Prucha, Francis Paul, ed. *Documents of United States Indian Policy*. 2nd ed. Lincoln: University of Nebraska Press, 1990.

Reed, Melanie. "Native American Sovereignty Meets a Bend in the Road: Difficulties in Nevada v. Hicks." *Brigham Young University Law Review* 2002 (2002): 137–74.

Rey-Bear, Daniel I. S. J. "The Flathead Water Quality Standards Dispute: Legal Bases for Tribal Regulatory Authority over Non-Indian Reservation Lands." *American Indian Law Review* 20 (1996): 151–224.

Reynolds, Laurie. "Indian Hunting and Fishing Rights: The Role of Tribal Sovereignty and Preemption." *North Carolina Law Review* 62 (1984): 743–93.

———. "'Jurisdiction' in Federal Indian Law: Confusion, Contradiction, and Supreme Court Precedent." *New Mexico Law Review* 27 (1997): 359–86.

Robertson, Lindsay G. *Conquest by Law: How the Discovery of America Dispossessed Indigenous Peoples of Their Lands*. New York: Oxford University Press, 2005.

Roosevelt, Theodore. *Compilation of the Messages and Papers of the Presidents, 1789–1902*. Vol. 11, edited by J. D. Richardson. Washington, D.C.: Government Printing Office, 1904.

Royster, Judith V. "Environmental Protection and Native American Rights: Controlling Land Use through Environmental Regulation." *Kansas Journal of Law and Public Policy* 1 (1991): 89–96.

———. "The Legacy of Allotment." *Arizona State Law Journal* 27 (1995): 1–78.

———. "Mineral Development in Indian Country: The Evolution of Tribal Control over Mineral Resources." *Tulsa Law Journal* 29 (1994): 541–637.

Sayler, Laura C. "Back to Basics: Special Domestic Violence Jurisdiction in the Violence Against Women Reactivation Act of 2013 and the Expansion of Inherent Tribal Sovereignty." *Cardozo Law Review de novo* 1 (January 3, 2014): 1–34.

Schneider, David, and Louis Furmanski. "The International Personality of Indigenous Peoples: An Account of North America." Paper presented at the annual meeting of the American Political Science Association, San Francisco, Calif., 1996.

Shattuck, Petra T., and Jill Norgren. *Partial Justice: Federal Indian Law in a Liberal Constitutional System*. Providence, R.I.: Berg, 1993.

Singer, Joseph William. "Canons of Conquest: The Supreme Court's Attack on Tribal Sovereignty." *New England Law Review* 37 (2003): 641–68.

———. "Sovereignty and Property." *Northwestern University Law Review* 86 (1991): 1–56.

Singleton, Sara. "Not Our Borders: Indigenous People and the Struggle to Maintain Shared Lives and Cultures in post-9/11 North America," Working Paper no. 4. Bellingham: Border Policy Research Institute, Western Washington University, January 2009.

Skibine, Alex Tallchief. "The Court's Use of the Implicit Divestiture Doctrine to Implement Its Imperfect Notion of Federalism in Indian Country." *Tulsa Law Journal* 36 (2000): 267–304.

————. "Reconciling Federal and State Power inside Indian Reservations with the Right of Tribal Self-Government and the Process of Self-Determination." *Utah Law Review*, no. 4 (1995): 1105–56.

Smith, Paul Chaat, and Robert Allen Warrior. *Like a Hurricane: The Indian Movement from Alcatraz to Wounded Knee*. New York: New Press, 1996.

Smith, Rob Roy. "Enhancing Tribal Sovereignty by Protecting Indian Civil Rights: A Win-Win for Indian Tribes and Tribal Members." *American Indian Law Journal* 1 (2012): 41–55.

Stern, Kenneth S. *Loud Hawk: The U.S. versus the American Indian Movement*. Norman: University of Oklahoma Press, 1994.

Stouff, Courtney A. "Native Americans and Homeland Security: Failure of the Homeland Security Act to Recognize Tribal Sovereignty." *Penn State Law Review* 108 (2003): 375–94.

Struve, Catherine. "How Bad Law Made a Hard Case Easy: Nevada v. Hicks and the Subject Matter Jurisdiction of Tribal Courts." *University of Pennsylvania Journal of Constitutional Law* 5 (2003): 288–317.

Taylor, Jonathan B., and Joseph P. Kalt. "*Cabazon*, the Indian Gaming Regulatory Act, and the Socioeconomic Consequences of American Indian Governmental Gaming: A Ten-Year Review." Harvard Project on American Indian Economic Development, January 2005.

Thornton, Russell. *American Indian Holocaust and Survival: A Population History since 1492*. Norman: University of Oklahoma Press, 1987.

Trosper, Ronald L. "American Indian Poverty on Reservations, 1969–1989." In *Changing Numbers, Changing Needs: American Indian Demography and Public Health*, edited by Gary D. Sandefur, Ronald R. Rindfuss, and Barney Cohen, chap. 8. Washington, D.C.: National Academy Press, 1996.

Tweedy, Ann E. "Connecting the Dots between the Constitution, the Marshall Trilogy, and United States v. Lara: Notes toward a Blueprint for the Next Legislative Restoration of Tribal Sovereignty." *University of Michigan Journal of Law Reform* 42 (2009): 651–717.

Urofsky, Melvin I., ed. *The Supreme Court Justices: A Biographical Dictionary*. New York: Garland, 1994.

U.S. Bureau of the Census. *American Indian- and Alaska Native-Owned Firms: 2002*. Prepared by the Company Statistics Division in cooperation with the Economic Census Branch, Bureau of the Census. Washington, D.C., 2006.

————. *Preliminary Estimates of Business Ownership by Gender, Hispanic or Latino Origin, and Race: 2002*. Prepared by Company Statistics Division in cooperation with the Economic Census Branch, Bureau of the Census. Washington, D.C., 2005.

————. *We the People: American Indians and Alaska Natives in the United States*. Census 2000 Special Reports. Prepared by Stella U. Ogunwole in cooperation with the Population Division, Bureau of the Census. Washington, D.C., 2006.

U.S. Department of Justice. Bureau of Justice Statistics. *American Indians and Crime*, By Lawrence A. Greenfeld and Steven K. Smith. Washington, D.C.: Government Printing Office, 1999.

————. *A BJS Statistical Profile, 1992–2002: American Indians and Crime*. By Steven W. Parry. Washington, D.C.: Government Printing Office, 2004.

U.S. Library of Congress. Congressional Research Service. *Indian Tribal Government Amendments to the Homeland Security Act: S. 578 and Indian Tribal Sovereignty*. By M. Maureen Murphy. Washington, D.C.: Government Printing Office, 2003.

————. *Indian Tribal Government Amendments to the Homeland Security Act: S. 578 and Indian Tribal Sovereignty*. By M. Maureen Murphy. Washington, D.C.: Government Printing Office, 2005.

————. *Tribal Criminal Jurisdiction over Non-Indians in the Violence Against Women Act (VAWA) Reauthorization and the SAVE Native Women Act*. By Jane M. Smith and Richard M. Thompson II. Washington, D.C.: Government Printing Office, 2012.

————. *Wagnon v. Prairie Band Potawatomi Nation: State Tax on Motor Fuels Distributed to Indian Tribal Retailers*. By M. Maureen Murphy. Washington, D.C.: Government Printing Office, 2005.

Valencia-Weber, Gloria. "The Supreme Court's Indian Law Decisions: Deviations from Constitutional Principles and the Crafting of Judicial Smallpox Blankets." *University of Pennsylvania Journal of Constitutional Law* 5 (2003): 405–82.

Vogel, Virgil J. *This Country Was Ours: A Documentary History of the American Indian*. New York: Harper and Row, 1972.

Voices from Wounded Knee, 1973: In the Words of the Participants. Rooseveltown, N.Y.: Akwesasne Notes, Mohawk Nation, 1974.

Wahlbeck, Paul J. "Strategy and Constraints on Supreme Court Opinion Assignment." *University of Pensylvannia Law Review* 154 (2006): 1729–55.

Warren, Richard L. "The Potential Passage of Proposed Senate Bill 578 and Its Implications on Hicks v. Nevada and Twenty Years of Supreme Court Jurisprudence." *American Indian Law Review* 29 (2004): 383–402.

Washburn, Kevin K. "American Indians, Crime, and the Law." *Michigan Law Review* 104 (2006): 709–78.

Washburn, Wilcomb. *The Indian in America*. New York: Harper and Row, 1975.

Wastewin, Wambdi Awanwicake. "Strate v. A-1 Contractors: Intrusion into the Sovereign Domain of Native Nations." *North Dakota Law Review* 74 (1998): 711–36.

Watkins, Arthur V. "Termination of Federal Supervision: The Removal of Restrictions over Indian Property and Person." *Annals of the American Academy of Political and Social Science* 311 (1957): 47–55.

Watson, Blake A. *Buying American from the Indians: Johnson v. McIntosh and the History of Native Land Rights* (Norman: University of Oklahoma Press, 2012).

————. "The Thrust and Parry of Federal Indian Law." *University of Dayton Law Review* 23 (1998): 437–514.

Wearne, Philip. *Return of the Indian: Conquest and Revival in the Americas*. London: Cassell, 1996.

Weeks, Philip, ed. *The American Indian Experience: A Profile, 1524 to the Present*. Wheeling, Ill.: Forum Press, 1988.

Wiles, David B. "Taxation: Tribal Taxation, Secretarial Approval, and State Taxation—Merrion and Beyond." *American Indian Law Review* 10 (1983): 167–85.

Wilkins, David E. *American Indian Sovereignty and the U.S. Supreme Court: The Masking of Justice.* Austin: University of Texas Press, 1997.

Wilkins, David E., and K. Tsianina Lomawaima. *Uneven Ground: American Indian Sovereignty and Federal Law.* Norman: University of Oklahoma Press, 2001.

Wilkinson, Charles F. *American Indians, Time, and the Law.* New Haven: Yale University Press, 1987.

———. *Blood Struggle: The Rise of Modern Indian Nations.* New York: W. W. Norton, 2005.

———. "Indian Tribes and the American Constitution." In *Indians in American History: An Introduction.* 2d ed., edited by Frederick E. Hoxie and Peter Iverson, chap. 5. Wheeling, Ill.: Harlan Davidson, 1998.

Williams, Robert A., Jr. "The Algebra of Federal Indian Law: The Hard Trail of Decolonizing and Americanizing the White Man's Indian Jurisprudence." *Wisconsin Law Review* 1986 (1986): 219–99.

———. *The American Indian in Western Legal Thought: The Discourse of Conquest.* New York: Oxford University Press, 1990.

———. *Like a Loaded Weapon: The Rehnquist Court, Indian Rights, and the Legal History of Racism in America.* Minneapolis: University of Minnesota Press, 2005.

Woodbury, Stephen E. "New Mexico v. Mescalero Apache Tribe: When Can a State Concurrently Regulate Hunting and Fishing by Nonmembers on Reservation Land." *New Mexico Law Review* 14 (1983): 349–69.

Woodward, Bob, and Scott Armstrong. *The Brethren: Inside the Supreme Court.* New York: Simon and Schuster, 1979.

Wunder, John R. *"Retained by the People": A History of American Indians and the Bill of Rights.* New York: Oxford University Press, 1994.

Yazzie, Robert. "'Watch Your Six': An Indian Nation Judge's View of 25 Years of Indian Law, Where We Are and Where We Are Going." *American Indian Law Review* 23 (1999): 497–503.

Congressional Documents

Congressional Record. 108th Cong., 1st sess., 2003. Vol. 149, pt 37.

———. Vol. 159, No. 22—Daily Edition. 113th Cong., 1st sess., February 12, 2013.

Senate Committee on Indian Affairs, *Discussion Draft Legislation to Address Law and Order in Indian Country: Senate Hearing 110–432,* 110th Cong., 2d sess., June 19, 2008.

———. *Examining Federal Declinations to Prosecute Crimes in Indian Country: Senate Hearing 110–683,* 110th Cong., 2d sess., September 18, 2008.

———. *Examining S. 797, The Tribal Law and Order Act of 2009: Senate Hearing 111–214,* 111th Cong., 1st sess., June 25, 2009.

———. *The Indian Reorganization Act—75 Years Later: Renewing Our Commitment to Restore Tribal Homelands and Promote Self-Determination,* 112th Cong., 1st sess., June 23, 2011.

———. *Law and Order in Indian Country: Senate Hearing 110–408,* 110th Cong., 2d sess., March 17, 2008.

———. *Law Enforcement in Indian Country,* 110th Cong., 1st sess., May 17, 2007.

———. *Law Enforcement in Indian Country: Senate Hearing 110–136,* 110th Cong., 1st sess., June 21, 2007.

———. *Native Women: Protecting, Shielding, and, Safeguarding Our Sisters, Mothers and Daughters: Senate Hearing 112–311,* 112th Cong., 1st sess., July 14, 2011.

———. *Rulings of the U.S. Supreme Court as They Affect the Powers and Authorities of the Indian Tribal Governments: Hearing on the Concerns of Recent Decisions of the U.S Supreme Court and the Future of Indian Tribal Governments in America.* 107th Cong., 2d sess., February 27, 2002.

———. *State and Federal Tax Policy: Building New Markets in Indian Country: Senate Hearing 112–619,* 112th Cong., 1st sess., December 8, 2011.

———. *Tribal Courts and the Administration of Justice in Indian Country,* 110th Cong., 2d sess., July 24, 2008.

———. *Tribal Government Amendments to the Homeland Security Act of 2002: S. 578 to Amend the Homeland Security Act of 2002 to Include Indian Tribes among the Entities Consulted with Respect to Activities Carried out by the Secretary of Homeland Security.* 108th Cong., 1st sess., July 30, 2003.

———. *The Tribal Law and Order Act of 2009: Report 111–93,* 111th Cong., 1st sess., October 29, 2009.

———. *Tribal Law and Order Act One Year Later: Have We Improved Public Safety and Justice throughout Indian Country?* 112th Cong., 1st sess., September 22, 2011.

U.S. Congress. Congressional Record—House." 113th Cong., 1st sess., February 28, 2013, H. 738.

U.S. House of Representatives. Congressional Record—House. 111th Cong., 2d sess, July 21, 2010, H. 5864.

———. *Violence Against Women Reauthorization Act of 2012: House Report 112–480 Part I.* 112th Cong., 2d sess., May 15, 2012.

U.S. Government Accountability Office. "U.S. Department of Justice Declinations of Indian Country Criminal Matters." Report Number GAO-11-167R, December 13, 2010.

U.S. Senate Congressional Record. 111th Cong., 2d sess, June 23, 2010, S. 5366.

U.S. Senate. *S. 1925: An Act to reauthorize the Violence Against Women Act of 1994.* 112th Cong., 2d sess., April 26, 2012.

———. *Violence Against Women Reauthorisation Act of 2011: Report 112–153.* 112th Cong., 2d sess., March 12, 2012.

Statutes

Appropriations Act of 1871. *U.S. Statutes at Large* 16 (1871): 544–71.

A bill to amend the Homeland Security Act of 2002 to include Indian tribes among the entities consulted with respect to activities carried out by the Secretary of Homeland Security, and for other purposes. 108th Cong., 1st sess., S. 578.

A bill to amend the Homeland Security Act of 2002 to include Indian tribes among the entities consulted with respect to activities carried out by the Secretary of Homeland Security, and for other purposes. 109th Cong., 1st sess., S. 477.

General Allotment Act. *U.S. Statutes at Large* 24 (1887): 388–91.

Public Law 102-137, 102d Cong., 1st sess., October 28, 1991.

Internet Resources

Bush Jr., George W. "Memorandum for the Heads of Executive Departments and Agencies, Government-to-Government Relationship with Tribal Governments." The White House. www.whitehouse.gov/news/releases/2004/09/20040923–4.html.

Governors' Interstate Indian Council. "GIIC Resolution 2003_01," 54th Annual Conference, Northern Lights Hotel and Events Center, Walker, Minn., August 21, 2003. http://w1.paulbunyan.net/~giic/resolutions/2003_01.pdf.

Govtrack.us. "H.R. 4970 (112th): Violence Against Women Reauthorization Act of 2012 (On Passage of the Bill)." www.govtrack.us/congress/votes/112–2012/h258.

———. "S. 1925 (112th): Violence Against Women Reauthorization Act of 2012 (On Passage of the Bill)." https://www.govtrack.us/congress/votes/112–2012/s87#.

Hill, Liz. "Senators Announce Legislation to Protect 'American Indian Tribal Sovereignty.'" NAIIP News Path, February 23, 2003. www.yvwiiusdinvnohii.net/News2003/0302/NCAI030225Legislation.htm.

Indianz.com. "Tribes Seek to Overturn Supreme Court." February 27, 2002. www.indianz.com/News/show.asp?ID=law02/02272002–1.

National Association of Criminal Defense Lawyers. "Coalition Letter to the Senate on the Violence Against Women Reauthorization Act of 2012 ('VAWA') (S. 1925)." April 23, 2012. www.nacdl.org/Advocacy.aspx?id=14904.

National Association of Criminal Defense Lawyers and National Association of Federal Defenders. "Advocacy Letter on H.R. 4970, the 'Violence Against Women Reauthorization Act of 2012.'" May 3, 2012. http://www.nacdl.org/Advocacy.aspx?id=14904.

National Congress of American Indians (NCAI). "Government to Government Models of Cooperation between States and Tribes," 2002. www.ncai.org/policy-issues/tribal-governance/state-tribal-relations.

———. "Tribal Sovereignty Protection Initiative, Summary of September 11th Tribal Leaders Forum: A Strategic Plan to Stop the Supreme Court's Erosion of Tribal Sovereignty." September 17, 2001. www.ncai.org/ncai/resource/documents/governance/Sept11Summary.pdf.

National Indian Gaming Commission. "Gross Gaming Revenue Reports." www.nigc.gov/commission/gaming-revenue-reports.

Native American Rights Fund. "In the Supreme Court of the Mississippi Band of Choctaw Indians: No. CV-02–05." August 20, 2015. http://sct.narf.org/documents/dollar_general_v_choctaw/miss_choctaw_supreme/mississippi-choctaw-supreme-court-opinion.pdf.

———. "Tribal Supreme Court Project." www.narf.org/sct/supctproject.html.

Oyez Project at IIT Chicago-Kent College of Law. June 15, 2015. www.oyez.org/courts/robt6.

Reagan, Ronald. "Statement on Indian Policy, January 24, 1983." Ronald Reagan Presidential Library. www.reagan.utexas.edu/archives/speeches/1983/12483b.htm.

Sandra Day O'Connor Institute. "Sandra Day O'Connor." June 15, 2015. www.oconnorhouse.org/oconnor/biography.php.

Supreme Court of Ohio and the Ohio Judicial System. "Potter Stewart (Jan. 23, 1915–Dec. 7, 1985)." June 15, 2015. www.supremecourt.ohio.gov/MJC/places/pStewart.asp.

Supreme Court of the United States. "Biographies of Current Justices of the Supreme Court." June 15, 2015. www.supremecourt.gov/about/biographies.aspx.

Supreme Court Opinion Writing Database. "The Opinion-Writing Process." June 15, 2015. http://supremecourtopinions.wustl.edu.

U.S. Bureau of the Census. "2007 Survey of Business Owners Summaries of Findings." www.census.gov/econ/sbo/getsof.html?07aian.

————. "Statistics for All U.S. Firms by Sector, Gender, Ethnicity, and Race for the U.S. and States: 2012." http://factfinder.census.gov/faces/tableservices/jsf/pages/product-view.xhtml?pid=SBO_2012_00CSA01&prodType=table.

U.S. Department of Justice. "Letter from Ronald Weich (Assistant Attorney General) to Joseph R. Biden." July 21, 2011. www.justice.gov/tribal/docs/legislative-proposal-vio-lence-against-native-women.pdf.

————. "Report of the Executive Committee for Indian Country Law Enforcement Improvements: Final Report to the Attorney General and the Secretary of the Interior." October 31, 1997. www.justice.gov/otj/icredact.htm.

————. "Statement by Attorney General Eric Holder on the House Passage of the Reauthorization of the Violence Against Women Act: Thursday, February 28, 2013." www.justice.gov/opa/pr/2013/February/13-ag-253.html.

Washburn, Kevin et. al. "Letter from Law Professors: Constitutionality of Tribal Government Provisions in VAWA Reauthorization." April 21, 2012. http://lawprofessors.typepad.com/files/vawa-letter-from-law-professors—-tribal-provisions.pdf.

Washington Post. "Retired Justice Lewis Powell Dies at 90." June 15, 2015. www.washingtonpost.com/wp-srv/national/longterm/supcourt/stories/powe11082698.htm.

White House, President Barack Obama. "Executive Order—Establishing the White House Council on Native American Affairs." June 15, 2015. www.whitehouse.gov/the-press-office/2013/06/26/executive-order-establishing-white-house-council-native-american-affairs.

————. "Obama Administration Record for American Indians and Alaska Natives." The White House. www.whitehouse.gov/sites/default/files/docs/american_indians_and_alaska_natives_community_record.pdf.

Index